E-Voting Case Law

A Comparative Analysis

Edited by

ARDITA DRIZA MAURER
Political Rights and New Voting Technologies Consultant, Switzerland

JORDI BARRAT
University of Catalonia/URV, Spain

Routledge
Taylor & Francis Group
LONDON AND NEW YORK

First published 2015 by Ashgate Publishing

Published 2016 by Routledge
2 Park Square, Milton Park, Abingdon, Oxon OX14 4RN
711 Third Avenue, New York, NY 10017, USA

First issued in paperback 2017

Routledge is an imprint of the Taylor & Francis Group, an informa business

British Library Cataloguing in Publication Data
A catalogue record for this book is available from the British Library

The Library of Congress has cataloged the printed edition as follows:
E-voting case law : a comparative analysis / by Ardita Driza Maurer and Jordi Barrat.
pages cm. -- (Election law, politics, and theory)
Includes bibliographical references and index.
ISBN 978-1-4724-4675-6 (hardback)
1. Electronic voting--Law and legislation. I. Driza Maurer, Ardita, author. II. Barrat, Jordi, editor.

K3293.E17 2015
342'.075--dc23

2015004771

ISBN 13: 978-1-138-09020-0 (pbk)
ISBN 13: 978-1-4724-4675-6 (hbk)

E-VOTING CASE LAW

If e-voting is the future, we need a path to it. There is no single route, however, with cost, reliability and the voting experience to be juggled. This collection draws together expert insights from across the globe, as a rich resource for those navigating the way.

Graeme Orr, University of Queensland, Australia, and author of *Ritual and Rhythm in Electoral Systems*

This is a significant contribution to the debates about electronic voting that are taking place in democracies across the world. Decision-makers seeking to balance key electoral principles – accessibility, security, trust, transparency, cost – must also understand the fundamental legal issues; and this book provides a fine overview.

Peter Wardle, The Electoral Commission, UK

In this very important book, the editors have put together a timely and highly needed discussion of legal decisions on the use of Information and Communication Technologies (ICT) in electoral matters. They have collected experiences from around the world, and deliver a systematic overview to the question of what requirements the judiciary puts forward to democratic innovations using ICT. This book has to be considered the upcoming standard reference for scholars and practitioners alike working or interested in the topic.

Robert Krimmer, Tallinn University of Technology, Estonia

In this book, renowned experts report important experiences of using electronic voting across different countries. The complexity of the matter is evidenced by the various reports of irregular occurrences that threaten basic constitutional principles involving electoral matters, such as transparency and security. The book contributes greatly to the subject of debate by revealing aspects usually omitted by governments and unknown by the media.

Luiz Fernando Martins Castro, Law and Informatics Commission of the Brazilian Bar Association (OAB/SP)

This significant and useful book provides a neutral and comprehensive analysis of e-voting case law worldwide. I highly recommend it as necessary reading for those willing to implement this type of technology.

Héctor T. Hernández, CPCIPC researcher, Córdoba, Argentina

Election Law, Politics, and Theory

Series Editor: David Schultz

Election Law, Politics, and Theory broadly examines election law at the national, subnational, and international or comparative levels. Titles in the series provide both empirical and theoretical analysis of topics and issues that affect voting, campaigns, and elections, and as such offer coverage of political as well as legal concerns and controversies. Useful for scholars, researchers, and practitioners in the field, volumes address such subjects as voting rights, reapportionment, ballot access, campaign finance reform, the courts and election regulation, and the role of actors including political parties and the media. The series' ultimate goal is to build scholarship in this key area by seeking to understand how elections function in an increasingly complex, technological, and global community, and the ways in which election law impacts outcomes, disputes, and eventually governance in particular nations and societies.

Other titles in this series

Ritual and Rhythm in Electoral Systems
A Comparative Legal Account
Graeme Orr
ISBN 978 1 4094 6076 3

Election Law and Democratic Theory
David Schultz
ISBN 978 0 7546 7543 3

Group Representation, Feminist Theory, and the Promise of Justice
Angela D. Ledford
ISBN 978 1 4094 1843 6

Political Parties and Elections
Legislating for Representative Democracy
Anika Gauja
ISBN 978 0 7546 7704 8

Contents

List of Laws

Legal instruments cited in the respective chapters.

Germany (Chapter 2)

Act on General and Representative Election Statistics in Elections to the German Bundestag and in the Election of Members of the European Parliament from the Federal Republic of Germany (*Wahlstatistikgesetz*) of 21 May 1999 (BGBl. 1999 I 1023)

Council of Europe, Recommendation Rec(2004)11 of the Committee of Ministers to member states, adopted by the Committee of Ministers on 30 September 2004 at the 898th meeting of the Ministers' Deputies on legal, operational and technical standards for e-voting

Federal Electoral Act (FEA) (*Bundeswahlgesetz*) as promulgated on 23 July 1993 (BGBl. 1993 I 1288, 1594), as last amended by Article 2 of the Act of 3 May 2013 (BGBl. 2013 I 1084)

Federal Voting Machine Ordinance (*Bundeswahlgeräteverordnung*) of 3 September 1975 (BGBl. 1975 I 2459), as last amended by Article 1 of the Ordinance of 20 April 1999 (BGBl. 1999 I 749).

German Constitution (*Grundgesetz*)

Guidelines for the Construction of Voting Machines (*Richtlinien für die Bauart von Wahlgeräten*)

Ordinance Amending the Federal Voting Machine Ordinance and the European Election Code (*Verordnung zur Änderung der Bundeswahlgeräteverordnung und der Europawahlordnung*) of 20 April 1999 (BGBl. 1999 I 749).

Ordinance on the Use of Vote Counting Devices in Elections to the German Bundestag (*Verordnung über die Verwendung von Stimmenzählgeräten bei Wahlen zum Deutschen Bundestag*) (BGBl. 1961 I 1618)

Austria (Chapter 3)

Act concerning the election of the Members of the European Parliament by direct universal suffrage (1976) OJ L 278/5, (2002) OJ L 283/1

Austrian Economic Chamber Act (*Bundesgesetz über die Kammern der gewerblichen Wirtschaft [Wirtschaftskammergesetz 1998 – WKG]*), Federal Law Gazette I 1998/103, last amendment Federal Law Gazette I 46/2014

Austrian State Treaty, Federal Law Gazette 152/1955
Charter of Fundamental Rights of the European Union
Council of Europe, Recommendation Rec(2004)11 of the Committee of Ministers to member states on legal, operational and technical standards for e-voting
Electoral Rules, Federal Law Gazette II 351/2008; new Electoral Rules were enacted in 2014 (Federal Law Gazette II 376/2014)
European Convention on Human Rights, Article 3 Protocol no. 1
Federal Constitutional Law
Students' Union Act (*Bundesgesetz über die Vertretung der Studierenden [Hochschülerinnen- und Hochschülerschaftsgesetz 1998 – HSG 1998]*), Federal Law Gazette I 1999/22, last amendment Federal Law Gazette I 2013/79. In 2014, the Students' Union Act 1998 was substituted by the Students' Union Act 2014, Federal Law Gazette I 45/2014
Treaty on European Union

Brazil (Chapter 4)

Brazilian Constitution of 1988
Federal Electoral Law n. 10.408, of 10 January 2002, Portuguese version http://www.planalto.gov.br/ccivil_03/Leis/2002/L10408.htm
Federal Electoral Law n. 10.704, of 1 October 2003, Portuguese version http://www.planalto.gov.br/ccivil_03/Leis/2003/L10.740.htm
Federal Law n. 12.034, of 29 September 2009 (VVPAT Act), Portuguese version http://www.planalto.gov.br/ccivil_03/_Ato2007-2010/2009/Lei/L12034.htm
Voluntary Voting System Guidelines, NIST/US-EAC, http://www.eac.gov/vvsg

India (Chapter 5)

Amendment to the Conduct of Elections Rules, Notification No. S.O. 230(E), dated 24 March 1992
Conduct of Elections Rules, 1961, Ministry of Law Notification No. S.O. 859, dated 15 April 1961, Gazette of India, Extraordinary, Part II, Section 3(ii), page 419
Constitution of India, 1950
ECI Guidelines, dated 3 May 2010, No. 51/8/6/2010-EMS, available at http://eci.nic.in/eci_main/CurrentElections/ECI_Instructions/ins310510.pdf
Notification No. S.O. 2470(E), dated 14 August 2013
Notification of the Election Commission, dated 13 May 1982
Press Note No. PN/ECI/41/2009, dated 8 August 2009, issued by the Election Commission of India
Representation of the People Act, 1950
Representation of the People Act, 1951

Representation of the People (Amendment) Act, 1988
Representation of the People (Amendment) Act, 2010

Estonia (Chapter 6)

Estonian Constitution, available at https://www.riigiteataja.ee/en/
Constitutional Review Court Procedure Act, available at https://www.riigiteataja.ee/en/eli/521012014004/consolide
Council of Europe, Guidelines on Certification of E-voting Systems, GGIS(2010)3, available at http://www.coe.int/t/dgap/democracy/activities/ggis/E-voting/E-voting%202010/Biennial_Nov_meeting/Guidelines_certification_EN.pdf
Council of Europe, Recommendation on Electronic Democracy, Rec(2009)1, available at https://wcd.coe.int/ViewDoc.jsp?id=1410627
Council of Europe, Recommendation Rec(2004)11 of the Committee of Ministers to member states on legal, operational, and technical standards for e-voting, available at https://wcd.coe.int/ViewDoc.jsp?id=778189
Council of Europe, Transparency of e-enabled elections, GGIS(2010)5, available at http://www.coe.int/t/dgap/democracy/activities/ggis/E-voting/E-voting%20 2010/Biennial_Nov_meeting/Guidelines_transparency_EN.pdf
Local Government Council Election Act, Draft nr. 607 SE in X *Riigikogu* proceedings, will be available at http://www.riigikogu.ee (direct link currently, 1 May 2015, unavailable, new direct links will be provided by 2016). See also drafts nr. 747 SE, 748 SE, 771 SE and 906 SE in IX *Riigikogu* proceedings
National Electoral Committee, Decree, 'The procedure for the organisation of electronic voting and the ascertaining of the results of electronic voting', available at https://www.riigiteataja.ee/akt/118032014016
OSCE/ODIHR, *Handbook for the Observation of New Voting Technologies*, available at http://www.osce.org/odihr/elections/104939?download=true
Riigikogu Election Act, available at https://www.riigiteataja.ee/en/eli/510032014001/consolide

France (Chapter 7)

Circulaire NOR: /A/08/00023/C, 1 February 2008, issued by the *Bureau des Elections et des Études Politiques / Ministère de l'Interieur*
Electoral Code: arts. L57-1 / L62 / L63 / L330-13 / R176-3 II
Règlement technique fixant les conditions d'agrément des machines à voter (Annexe à l'arrêté du 17 novembre 2003 / JORF 27 November 2003)

Argentina (Chapter 8)

Ushuaia

Carta Orgánica Municipal (art. 217), available at www.mininterior.gov.ar/municipios/pdf/co-ushuaia-tierra-fuego.pdf
Decreto 506/2003
Junta Electoral Municipal, Acta del 2/10/2003
Ordenanza Municipal n° 2578 (11/06/2003) Régimen electoral de la Ciudad de Ushuaia
Resolución n° 90/03 de fecha 23/9/2003 / Juzgado Electoral Provincial

San Antonio Oeste

Decreto local 3012/07 (Intendente San Antonio Oeste)
Decreto n° 1375/07 (Reglamento Voto Electrónico)
Decreto provincial 605/08 (Dina Huapi / Referendum)
Ley O n°4082/06 del sistema de voto electrónico (Provincia de Río Negro)

Pinamar

Decreto n° 2585/09 (convocatoria elecciones Pinamar)
Ley Electoral nº 5109 de la Provincia de Buenos Aires
Reglamento 1460/07 para la instrumentación del voto electrónico, available at http://www.gob.gba.gov.ar/legislacion/legislacion/07-1460.html
Resolución n° 930/11 (concejo deliberante Pinamar)

Marcos Suárez

Ordenanza n° 2157/10 (concejo deliberante Marcos Suárez), available at http://ves.cat/l_Ff

Las Higueras / La Falda

Código Electoral Provincial (Córdoba), available at http://www.justiciacordoba.gob.ar/jel/documentos/legislacion/L.9571.pdf
Córdoba, Tribunal Electoral Provincial ad Hoc, decretos de fecha 19/7/2011, 21/7/2011 y 4/8/2011, y Acta n° 3/11 (La Falda)
Decreto n° 1608/11, convocando a elección de autoridades municipales para el 26/6/2011
Decreto n° 1617/11 (municipio Las Higueras)
Resolución n° 31/10 de fecha 21/12/2010 (Juzgado Electoral Provincial) La Falda
Tribunal Electoral Provincial Ad-Hoc, Acuerdo n° 123, Serie 'C'

Finland (Chapter 9)

Election Act (714/1998), available at http://www.finlex.fi/fi/laki/kaannokset/1998/en19980714.pdf
Laki vaalilain muuttamisesta (880/2006), available at http://www.finlex.fi/fi/laki/alkup/2006/20060880

Mexico (Chapter 10)

ACU-69-11, 31 October 2011

Switzerland (Chapter 11)

Canton of Geneva Act on the Exercise of Political Rights of 15 October 1982 (LEDP; RSG A 5 05)
Federal Act of 17 December 1976 on Political Rights (SR 161.1; Federal Act on Political Rights)
Federal Act of 18 March 2005 on the Consultation Procedure (SR 172.061; VlG)
Federal Act of 12 June 2005 on the Federal Supreme Court (SR 173.110; Federal Supreme Court Act)
Federal Chancellery Ordinance of 13 December 2013 on Electronic Voting (SR 161.116)
Federal Constitution of the Swiss Confederation of 18 April 1999 (SR 101; BV)
Ordinance of 24 May 1978 on Political Rights (SR 161.11; Political Rights Ordinance)

USA (Chapter 12)

Americans with Disabilities Act of 1990, 42 U.S.C. § 12132
Cal. Elections Code § 19250
Help America Vote Act of 2002, 52 U.S.C. § 20901 et seq.
Military and Overseas Voter Empowerment Act of 2009, 52 U.S.C. § 20304 et seq.
Ohio Rev. Code § 3506.18
Pa. Const., Art. VII, § 1
Uniformed and Overseas Citizens Absentee Voting Act of 1986, 52 U.S.C. § 20301 et seq.
U.S. Const., Art. I, § 4
U.S. Const., Fourteenth Amendment
Voting Rights Act of 1965, 52 U.S.C. § 10301 et seq.

Australia (Chapter 13)

Absent Voters Electoral Act 1890 (S.A.)
Anti-Discrimination Act 1977 (N.S.W.)
Commonwealth Electoral Act 1918 (Clth)
Commonwealth Electoral Act 1922 (Clth)
Constitution Act 1975 (Vic.)
Constitution of Queensland 2001 (Qld)
Electoral Act 1889 (W.A.)
Electoral Act 1985 (S.A.)
Electoral Act 1992 (A.C.T.)
Electoral Act 2002 (Vic.)
Electoral Act 2004 (Tas.)
Electoral Amendment Regulations 2013 (New Zealand)
Electoral and Referendum Regulations 1940 (Clth)
Electoral Reform Amendment Act 2014 (Qld)
Imperial Acts Application Act 1980 (Vic.)
Local Government Amendment (Elections) Act 2011 (N.S.W.)
Local Government (Elections) Regulation 1998, r. 38 (5) and (8) and Schedule 8, Forms 4, 5 and 6
Local Government (General) Regulation 2005, r. 305 (5), (8) and Schedule 11, Forms 4, 5 and 6
Parliamentary Electorates and Elections Act 1912 (N.S.W.)
Referendum (Machinery Provisions) Act 1984 (Clth)
Statute of Westminster I 3 Edw. I c. 5 (1275)

Venezuela (Chapter 14)

Constitution of the Bolivarian Republic of Venezuela of 1999
Council of Europe, Recommendation Rec(2004)11 of the Committee of Ministers to member states on legal, operational and technical standards for e-voting, 30 September 2004
Electoral Law of 31 July 2009
Electoral Law of 19 November 2002 (*Ley Orgánica del Poder Electoral*)
General Rules of Law Process Election of 18 January 2013
Law of Suffrage and Political Participation (*Ley Orgánica del Sufragio y Participación Política*) of 1997
Organic Law of the Supreme Court of Justice of 19 May 2004
Rules on Procedure and Fingerprint Capture (*Normas sobre el Procedimiento de Captación de Huellas Dactilares y Garantía del Principio un Elector-Un Voto*), Gazette electoral number 207 of 12 August 2004
Rules Regulating the Referendum Process (*Normas para Regular los Procesos de Referendos Revocatorios de Mandatos de Cargos de Elección Popular*)

List of Cases

Cases cited in the respective chapters.

Germany (Chapter 2)

BVerfGE 123, 39 – Judgment of the Second Senate of 3 March 2009 on the basis of the oral hearing of 28 October 2008 in the combined cases 2 BvC 3/07 and 2 BvC 4/07. An official English translation is available at http://www.bundesverfassungsgericht.de/SharedDocs/Entscheidungen/EN/2009/03/cs20090303_2bvc000307en.html

BVerfGE 132, 39 – Judgement of the Second Senate of the Federal Constitutional Court of 4 July 2012 in the combined cases 2 BvC 1/11 and 2 BvC 2/11

Austria (Chapter 3)

Judgement of the German Constitutional Court of 3 March 2009, 2 BvC 3/07, 2 BvC 4/07

VfGH W I 2/2014 (22 August 2014)

VfSlg. 8590/1979

VfSlg. 10.412/1985

VfSlg. 12.023/1989

VfSlg. 14.440/1994

VfSlg. 17.951/2006

VfSlg. 19.592/2011 (13 December 2011)

Brazil (Chapter 4)

ADI n. 4543, available at http://redir.stf.jus.br/paginadorpub/paginador.jsp?docTP=TP&docID=941228

Decision of the Federal Constitutional Court of Germany of 3 March 2009, available at http://www.bundesverfassungsgericht.de/entscheidungen/cs20090303_2bvc000307.html

Decision of the Supreme Court of India of 8 October 2013, available at https://www.eff.org/document/dr-subramanian-swamy-vs-election-commission-india

India (Chapter 5)

A.C. Jose v. Sivan Pillai, (1984) 2 SCC 656
Annarao v. Amit, Election Petition No. 13 of 2009, decided by the High Court of Bombay at Aurangabad on 18 March 2013
Bhabhi v. Sheo Govind, (1976) 1 SCC 687
Dr. K. Laxman vs Nayini Narasimha Reddy decided by the Andhra Pradesh High Court on 18 January 2008
Dr. Madhavrao v. Ashok Chavan, Election Petition No. 11 of 2009, decided by the Bombay High Court on 18 October, 2012
Hari Vishnu Kamath v. Ahmad Ishaque, (1955) 1 SCR 1104
M. Narayana Rao v. G. Venkata Reddy, (1977) 1 SCC 771
Mahadeo v. Babu Udai Pratap Singh, (1966) 2 SCR 564
Manohar v Shankar, Election Petition No. 16 of 2009, decided by the High Court of Bombay at Aurangabad on 6 May 2011
Michael B. Fernandes v. C.K. Jaffer Sharief, AIR 2004 Kar 289
Order of the Supreme Court dated 22 February, 2013 passed in Writ Petition (Civil) No. 80 of 2013 (Nagendar Chindan v. Union of India)
Order of the Supreme Court dated 9 April 2013 passed in Special Leave Petition (Civil) No. 13735 of 2012 (Subramanian Swami v. Election Commission of India)
Order of the Supreme Court dated 2 May 2013 passed in Special Leave Petition (Civil) No. 13735 of 2012 (Subramanian Swami v. Election Commission of India)
Order of the Supreme Court dated 11 April 2014, Writ Petition (Civil) No. 265 of 2014 (Shamsheer VP v. Union of India)
Order of the Supreme Court dated 14 November, 2014 passed in Writ Petition (Civil) No. 80 of 2013 (Nagendar Chindan v. Union of India)
Order of the Supreme Court dated 12 January, 2015 passed in Writ Petition (Civil) No. 80 of 2013 (Nagendar Chindan v. Union of India)
Prof. Balraj Madhok v. Shashi Bhushan, (1972) 2 SCC 616
S. Baldev Singh v. Teja Singh Swatantar, (1975) 4 SCC 406
Sambhaji v. Bhaskarrao, Election Petition No. 1 of 2009, decided by the Bombay High Court at Aurangabad on 25 March 2011
Sanjay Pawar v Pankaj Chhagan Bhujbal, Election Petition No. 32 of 2009, decided by the High Court of Bombay on 7 August 2012
Sharad Madhavrao Patil v. Rohidas Chudaman Patil, 2008 (2) BomCR 883
Shashi Bhushan v. Prof. Balraj Madhok, (1972) 4 SCC 594
Shyam Sunder v. Satya Ketu, (1967) 1 SCR 752
Subramanian Swami v. Election Commission of India, (2013) 10 SCC 500
Subramaniam Swamy v. Election Commission of India, Judgment of the High Court of Delhi dated 17 January 2012 passed in Writ Petition (Civil) No. 11879 of 2009
Sushil Singh v. Prabhu Narain Yadav And Ors., AIR 2003 All 331

Estonia (Chapter 6)

Application of Tallinn City Council for constitutional review of the electronic voting provisions in the local government council election act. 20.09.2011, 3-4-1-16-11
Complaint of the Centre Party for invalidity of voting results in *Riigikogu* elections. 2011. 31.03.2011, 3-4-1-10-11
Complaint of the Centre Party for invalidity of voting results in *Riigikogu* elections 2011 (second complaint). 31.03.2011, 3-4-1-11-11
Complaint of an election coalition 'Jõhvi Noored' for invalidity of the voting results in municipal elections 2013. 19.11.2013, 3-4-1-57-13
Complaint of H.P for annulment of electronic votes cast in the *Riigikogu* elections 2011. 23.03.2011, 3-4-1-6-11
Complaint of P.P for annulment of electronic votes cast in the *Riigikogu* elections 2011. 21.03.2011, 3-4-1-4-11
Complaint of T.R for declaration of invalidity of the voting results of the *Riigikogu* elections 2011. 23.03.2011, 3-4-1-7-11
Constitutional Judgement 01.09.2005, 3-4-1-13-05
Petition of the President of the Republic to declare the Local Government Council Election Act Amendment Act, passed by the *Riigikogu* on 28 June 2005, unconstitutional

France (Chapter 7)

Decisions

Decision 2007-3415/3416/3417/3421
Decision 2007-3418/3450
Decision 2007-3449
Decision 2007-3606
Decision 2007-3742/3947
Decision 2007-3872
Decision 2012-4597/4626

Observations

[*Bilan General / Référendum des 28 et 29 mai 2005 sur la ratification du traité établissant une Constitution pour l'Europe*], (Paris, Conseil Constitutionnel 2005)
[Élection presidentielle 2007 / Bilan du premier tour] (Paris, Conseil Constitutionnel 2007a)
[Élection presidentielle 2007 / Bilan du second tour] (Paris, Conseil Constitutionnel 2007b)

Observations relatives aux élections législatives de juin 2007 (Paris, Conseil Constitutionnel 2008)
Observations sur l'élection présidentielle des 22 avril et 6 mai 2007, [2007] 134 *Journal Officiel de la République Française* 10247
Observations sur l'élection présidentielle des 22 avril et 6 mai 2012, 145 *Journal Officiel de la République Française* 10354

Argentina (Chapter 8)

Ushuaia

Resolución n° 97/03, la Junta Electoral Municipal

San Antonio Oeste

Sentencia n° 160/07 / Superior Tribunal de Justicia de la Provincia de Río Negro, available at http://ves.cat/l_Fc

Pinamar

Resoluciones de la Junta Electoral de la Provincia de Buenos Aires (22 and 26/3/2010)

Marcos Suárez

Auto 71/10 (Tribunal Superior de Justicia)
Resolución n° 3 (Junta Electoral Municipal / Marcos Suárez)

Las Higueras / La Falda

Auto n° 275/11 (Juzgado Electoral Provincial Córdoba)
Resolución 10/11 (Junta Electoral Municipal Las Higueras)

Finland (Chapter 9)

Helsinki Administrative Court, decisions 29 January 2009 Nos. 09/0052/2, 09/0053/2, 09/0054/2
Supreme Administrative Court, decision 2009:39 (9 April 2009 T. 899), available at http://www.finlex.fi/fi/oikeus/kho/vuosikirjat/2009/200900899, decision 9 April 2009 T. 900 and decision 9 April 2009 T. 901

Mexico (Chapter 10)

SUP-JRC-306/2011

Switzerland (Chapter 11)

Federal Supreme Court Decisions

1C_245/2009, François von Siebenthal (1 October 2009)
1C_257/2009, Chucri Canaan (1 October 2009)
1C_329/2011 and 1F_5/2012, Richard Hill (22 December 2011 and 19 April 2012)
1C_477/2012, 1C_563/2013 and 1C_136/2014, Richard Hill (27 March 2013, 29 August 2013 and 22 July 2014)
1P.29/2006, Messrs B. and S. (23 March 2006)

Geneva Court Decisions

ATA/153/2005, Mathias Schmocker (15 March 2005)
ATA/192/2005, Mathias Schmocker (5 April 2005)
ATA/807/2005, Messrs B. and S. (29 November 2005)
ATA/303/2011, Richard Hill (17 May 2011)
ATA/414/2011, Richard Hill (28 June 2011)
ATA/536/2011, Richard Hill (30 August 2011)
ATA/42/2012, Richard Hill (19 January 2012)
ATA/533/2012, Richard Hill (21 August 2012)
ATA/118/2014, Richard Hill (25 February 2014)

USA (Chapter 12)

American Association of People with Disabilities v. Harris, 647 F.3d 1093 (11th Cir. 2011)
American Association of People with Disabilities v. Shelley, 324 F.Supp.2d 1120 (C.D. Cal. 2004)
Anderson v. Celebrezze, 460 U.S. 780 (1983)
Andrade v. NAACP of Austin, 345 S.W.3d 1 (Tex. Sup. Ct. 2011)
Banfield v. Cortes, 922 A.2d 36 (Pa. Commw. Ct. 2007)
Black v. McGuffage, 209 F.Supp.2d 889 (N.D. Ill 2002)
Bryan v. Abramson, 2010 WL 7746073 (Virgin Is. Super. Ct. 2010)
Burdick v. Takushi, 504 U.S. 428 (1992)
Bush v. Gore, 531 U.S. 98 (2000)
California Council of the Blind v. County of Alameda, 985 F.Supp.2d 1229 (N.D. Cal 2013)

Chavez v. Brewer, 214 P.3d 397 (Ariz. Ct. App. 2009)
Common Cause v. Jones, 235 F.Supp.2d 1076 (C.D. Cal. 2002)
County of Nassau v. New York, 724 F. Supp. 2d 295 (E.D.N.Y. 2010)
Crawford v. Marion County Election Board, 553 U.S. 181 (2008)
Crowley v. Nevada, 678 F.3d 730 (9th Cir. 2012)
Favorito v. Handel, 684 S.E.2d 257 (Ga. Sup. Ct. 2009)
Gusciora v. Corzine, 2010 WL 444173 (N.J. Super. Ct. Law Div. 2010)
Kuznik v. Westmoreland County Board of Commissioners, 891 A.2d 728 (Pa. Sup. Ct. 2006)
Paralyzed Veterans of America v. McPherson, 2008 WL 4183981 (N.D. Cal. 2008)
Reynolds v. Sims, 377 U.S. 533 (2004).
Schade v. Maryland State Board of Elections, 382 Md. 522 (Md. Ct. App. 2004)
Southwest Voter Registration Education Project v. Shelley, 344 F.3d 882 (9th Cir. 2003)
Stewart v. Blackwell, 444 F.3d 843 (6th Cir. 2006)
Taylor v. Onorato, 428 F.Supp.2d 384 (W.D. Pa. 2006)
Texas Democratic Party v. Williams, 285 Fed.Appx. 194 (5th Cir. 2008)
Weber v. Shelley, 347 F.3d 1101 (9th Cir. 2003)
Wexler v. Anderson 452 F.3d 1226 (11th Cir. 2006)

Australia (Chapter 13)

Ashby v. White (1703) 2 Ld Raym 938; 92 ER 126
Attorney-General (Clth) (ex rel. McKinlay) v. Commonwealth (1975) 135 CLR 1
Australian Electoral Commission v. Johnston (2014) 251 CLR 463
Berrill's Petition (1976) 134 CLR 470
Bridge v. Bowen (1916) 21 CLR 582
Cameron v. Fysh (1904) 1 CLR 314
Fittler v. New South Wales Electoral Commission [2008] NSWADT 116
Get Up v. Electoral Commission (Clth) (2010) 189 FCR 165
Hudson v. Lee (1993) 177 CLR 627
Kean v. Kerby (1920) 27 CLR 449
King v. Jetstar Airways (2012) 286 ALR 149; (2013) 293 ALR 613
Langer v. Commonwealth (1996) 186 CLR 302
McGinty v. Western Australia (1996) 186 CLR 140
Mitchell v. Bailey (No. 2) (2008) 169 FCR 529
Rankin v. State Electoral Commissioner [2010] SAEOT 3
Roach v. Electoral Commissioner (Commonwealth) (2007) 233 CLR 162
Rowe v. Electoral Commissioner (Commonwealth) (2010) 243 CLR 1
Rudolphy v. Lightfoot (1999) 197 CLR 500
Sue v. Hill (1999) 199 CLR 462
Smith v. Australian Electoral Commission (2009) 175 FCR 523
Watkins v. Home Secretary [2006] 2 AC 395

Venezuela (Chapter 14)

Decision No. 163 of 18 December 2000
Mesa de la Unidad Democrática v CNE (2013) Constitutional Chamber TSJ
Militantes por la Libertad & Co. v CNE (2005) Electoral Chamber TSJ

Notes on Contributors

Jussi Aaltonen has been working in Finland as an election officer since 1994, starting in local administration and from 2005 onwards as Ministerial Advisor in the Ministry of Justice, which is the highest election authority in the Council of State in Finland. He is a member of the Working Group for Internet Voting set up by the Ministry of Justice in November 2013.

Rishab Bailey is an advocate based in New Delhi, India. He graduated from the National Law School of India University, Bangalore (2007) and began practice at Amarchand & Mangaldas & Suresh A Shroff & Co., Mumbai. Since 2010 he has worked with various human rights lawyers and NGOs in Delhi on issues connected to Internet governance, the protection of civil liberties, technology law and intellectual property. Notable amongst the organizations he has worked for are the Society for Knowledge Commons, Newsclick – an independent news website – and the Software Freedom Law Centre, India. Rishab is a consultant on law and policy to the global software company, ThoughtWorks.

Jordi Barrat is a senior lecturer in the Faculty of Law at the University of Catalonia/URV. He holds a PhD on constitutional law (León, Spain, 1997). His research is focused on electoral matters, namely e-voting issues. He is the director of EVOL2/eVoting Legal Lab (http://evol2.wordpress.com). He has been an international electoral observer and assistant in a number of countries (e.g. France, Norway, Belgium, Montenegro, Venezuela, Mexico, Honduras, Costa Rica) and has provided legal consultancy on electoral matters to various international institutions (e.g. Council of Europe, OSCE/ODIHR, IDEA, OAS, IFES).

Amílcar Brunazo Filho is an engineer at the Polytechnic School, University of Sao Paulo (1975) and founder and moderator of the Brazilian E-Voting Forum (1998), a platform focused on the reliability of electronic voting in Brazil which considers technical and legal issues of e-voting. In order to promote knowledge on the subject, he has travelled the country since 1999, serving as a panellist at several academic institutions, and also as a consultant for different Brazilian Political Parties. He has been a member of the Brazilian Independent Multidisciplinary Committee (CMind) since 2009, and has acted as an International Electoral Observer in Argentina (2011) and Ecuador (2014).

Ardita Driza Maurer is a jurist based in Switzerland. She specializes in political rights and new voting technologies and works as an independent consultant. Ardita was previously a member and director of the Swiss federal internet voting project at the Swiss Federal Chancellery. She currently provides legal expertise to ongoing work on the update of the Council of Europe Recommendation Rec(2004)11 on legal, operational and technical standards for e-voting.

Beat Kuoni works for the Swiss Federal Chancellery in Bern. He holds a degree in law from the University of Zurich and was a researcher at the Centre for Research on Direct Democracy (www.c2d.ch). His academic interests lie in the field of constitutional law, in particular in the area of political rights.

Ülle Madise is Legal Chancellor of the Republic of Estonia and Professor of Constitutional Law at the University of Tartu (Estonia). Her scholarly interests lie in the theory and practice of democratic institutions in the contemporary world.

Rubén Martínez Dalmau is Professor of Constitutional Law at the University of Valencia. He has been a researcher at the Jean Monnet European Polo, attached to the European Commission and directs 'Democracy +', an inter-university research group on constituent power and new constitutionalism. Martínez Dalmau's research focuses on democratic legitimacy and constituent power. He was an adviser to the Constituent National Assembly in Venezuela (1999), the Constituent Assembly of Bolivia (2006–2007) and the Constituent Assembly of Ecuador (2008) and participated in the drafting committees of the three constituent assemblies. He is the author of several articles and monographs, including 'Democracy, participation and electronic voting' (2007).

Melina Oswald is a legal clerk at the Austrian Constitutional Court. She studied law at the University of Vienna and at the London School of Economics and Political Science and worked as a research assistant in the Department of Constitutional and Administrative Law at the University of Vienna. In her doctoral thesis she specialized in immigration and asylum law and the right to private and family life. Her further research interests and professional expertise lie in the fields of constitutional law, Austrian and European human rights law, administrative law and higher education law.

José María Pérez Corti is a rapporteur of the State Court of Justice and has extensive experience of and a special interest in electoral processes, implementation of political reforms and legal matters of constitutional competence. Previously, he was a legal electoral official for more than 15 years (1995/2010). He has a distinguished and solid academic background and has had a significant university teaching career. He is currently recognized as an electoral and constitutional law expert, is widely published and is a distinguished advisor on the subjects.

Sebastian Seedorf is a senior legal advisor and the deputy head of the Interior Policy Division in the Federal Chancellery in Berlin, Germany. Before that, he worked for some years in the Electoral Law Division of the German Federal Ministry of the Interior with a focus on constitutional law matters in elections and comparative electoral law. Sebastian graduated from Dusseldorf University, earned a master's degree (LL.M.) from the University of Cape Town in South Africa and received a doctorate from Humboldt-University in Berlin. In 2007/2008 he was a senior researcher at the South African Institute for Advanced Constitutional, Public, Human Rights and International Law.

Rohit Sharma is an advocate practising independently before the Supreme Court of India. He graduated from the National Law School of India University, Bangalore (2006) and practised for one year before the Punjab and Haryana High Court before moving to the Supreme Court (2007). Sharma worked as an associate in the office of the Solicitor General of India (2007–2009) and in the office of the Attorney General for India (2009–2014). During his stint in the offices of the Solicitor General and the Attorney General, he appeared as the main assisting counsel in several matters of national importance covering issues of constitutional law, election law, and so on.

Augusto Tavares Rosa Marcacini is a lawyer in São Paulo, Brazil, specializing in IT, contracts and civil litigation. He is also Professor of Civil Procedure Law and of Law and Technology, a member of the Brazilian Independent Multidisciplinary Committee (CMind) since 2009, and a former Chairman of the Digital Society Commission of the Brazilian Bar Association, São Paulo Chapter (2004–2012). His main academic interests are access to justice and legal aid, judicial efficiency, e-justice, digital evidence, digital documents and signatures, cryptography and voting technology.

Greg Taylor is a senior lecturer in the Graduate School of Business and Law at R.M.I.T. University (the Royal Melbourne Institute of Technology) and an Honorary Professor of Marburg University, Germany. He has published widely in his areas of interest: legal history, comparative law and constitutional law. His work has been cited in the judgments of the Privy Council and the High Court of Australia, among others.

Daniel P. Tokaji is the Charles W. Ebersold and Florence Whitcomb Ebersold Professor of Constitutional Law at The Ohio State University, Moritz College of Law, and a Senior Fellow with Election Law @ Moritz. Professor Tokaji is an authority on election law and voting rights. He is a co-author of *Election Law: Cases and Materials* (5th ed. 2012), and *The New Soft Money: Outside Spending in Congressional Elections* (2014). He is also the author of *Election Law in a Nutshell* (2013) and numerous law review articles on voting rights, election administration and the role of the federal courts in American democracy. In addition to his scholarship, Professor Tokaji has litigated many civil rights and civil liberties cases, including cases on voting technology, voter registration, early voting, proof-of-citizenship requirements and freedom of speech.

Priit Vinkel is Chief of Staff of the Estonian National Electoral Committee and doctoral student at the Tallinn University of Technology. His scientific interests are electoral law, electoral systems and the improvement of electoral practice.

Foreword

Douglas W. Jones, The University of Iowa

When the Chartists demanded universal suffrage for the British people in 1839, they also proposed the use of voting machines. The advance in voting technology since that early proposal has been extraordinary. Today, various forms of electronic voting technology are routinely used in the casting or counting of votes in several of the world's largest democracies, and many more countries are using such technology on a smaller scale.

The technology used to count votes is rarely a major subject of public debate except after close elections. This was the case after the 2000 election in the United States, and after the elections of 2004 and 2013 in Venezuela, both of which are discussed here. The court cases following these and other elections are fascinating, but in many cases, the most telling lessons arise not from what the courts have decided, but from the evidence the courts ignored or overlooked.

The use of technology in elections is a fascinating example of the interaction between technology and public policy. How the law responds to advances in technology is worthy of study, and here, we see examples of a variety of responses. In most of the countries discussed here, technology has been the driving force, while the courts and legislatures have acted only in response to technological change. The chapters on Argentina and France are noteworthy illustrations, but most of the countries discussed here fit this pattern.

The legal landscape surrounding electronic voting is quite varied. In some countries, a uniform voting system is used nationwide. Brazil and India are noteworthy examples discussed here. In other places, there is considerable local autonomy, with a variety of different systems in use. Argentina, France, Switzerland and the United States are notable examples.

In the United States, mechanical voting machines were used to count the majority of the votes cast 90 years ago, and almost all of the votes cast today are counted electronically. The precedents set by the use of mechanical voting machines have also played a role in France and Germany. In contrast, Australia and Austria have been very conservative, making only limited and comparatively recent use of electronic voting.

In some countries, legal challenges to electronic voting have had a direct effect. The 2009 Constitutional Court decision in Germany is a leading example; it has had an international impact and is cited in several of the chapters included here. Elsewhere, the effect has been largely indirect. In Switzerland, for example, challenges that have failed in court have nonetheless spurred significant legislative responses.

The voting rights of expatriate citizens have been a significant factor behind the use of Internet voting in some jurisdictions. The chapters on Australia, France, Switzerland and the United States discuss this. The problems faced by disabled voters have also played a role. This has been a driving force behind the limited use of electronic voting in Australia, and has been the subject of several lawsuits in the United States.

A significant thread that permeates the discussions here is the relationship between government election authorities and voting system vendors. Electronic voting systems rely on commercial electronic and computer technology, and in most cases, entire electronic voting systems are the product of commercial vendors. In some cases, the vendors actually operate the voting system during elections. Do the transparency requirements for free and fair elections require that the contracts between election system vendors and the government be revealed? Can a free and fair election be held using mechanisms that are shielded from public scrutiny by trade secret laws? These questions have been answered differently in different countries.

Answers to these questions are emerging slowly, and at this point, there is no consensus. This book is certainly not the final word on the complex issues posed by electronic voting. It will take many more court decisions and legislative actions before we reach anything resembling a consensus on the issues raised here. It is to be hoped that this book will help inform that effort. Jurists, election administrators, those who challenge elections, and those who develop election technology can all learn something from the material presented here.

Foreword

Geo Taglioni, Swiss Federal Chancellery

Court Decisions Spur the Further Digitisation of the Democratic Process

Around the world, the digitisation of democratic procedures is steadily progressing, whether with the use of voting machines, or with the introduction of online voting systems. Political rights are being adapted to the new technologies of the twenty-first century. The needs of a society characterised by its increasing reliance on digital devices are being taken into account.

Thanks to the prudent use of new technologies, political participation will still be guaranteed even as lifestyles continue to change. The new technologies also make life easier for voters, for example by providing detailed instructions on navigating the complex election procedures, or by making it possible for people with disabilities to vote without help from others.

Public authorities, parliaments, politicians and academics are being called on to find solutions to a wide variety of challenges in this uncharted territory. They need to take an interdisciplinary approach.

Two factors make this process more difficult. First, it is not easy to compare exercising democratic rights with other processes that are largely digitised today. For example, the technologies used in e-banking cannot be applied wholesale to e-voting. New technical solutions must therefore be developed for this sensitive field. Secondly, political rights vary quite considerably from country to country. A solution developed for one particular country cannot simply be introduced in the same form in another country; country-specific solutions are required that take account of the different systems of political rights.

Thanks to the exchange of best practices at national and international levels, synergies can be exploited, duplication avoided and experiences shared.

The challenges of introducing digitised voting procedures arise in a variety of areas. Alongside the technical solutions, appropriate legal regulations must be established. The introduction of digital solutions in the field of political rights has in some cases been accompanied by drastic changes in existing legislation. In recent years, international and supranational organisations, such as the Council of Europe and the Organization for Security and Cooperation in Europe, have approved recommendations for implementing these projects. Countries that are attempting to digitise their democratic processes have enacted related legal principles. And this is precisely where the courts play a role.

The digitisation of voting procedures is an extremely sensitive issue, as it can affect trust in our democratic institutions. Opinions differ on the question of whether these developments in the digital sphere strengthen democracy or pose a threat to it.

The case law considers this contradiction and sheds light on the debate surrounding the adopted process of digitisation. It summarises the most important elements of this process and discusses the different sensitivities related to political rights. The process reveals the cultural and country-specific differences.

The analysis of the case law related to e-voting given here shows how court decisions have influenced the process of digitisation of voting procedures. On the basis of this case law analysis, definitions are being honed, serious problem areas identified and new approaches outlined.

Acknowledgements

The editors would like to thank the Swiss Federal Chancellery for their cooperation and critical input in preparing this publication.

The editors are indebted to Richard Hill, Geneva, for his contribution in reviewing the language of the book and his constructive remarks on substantive issues.

Special thanks go to the "Centro de Derechos Civiles y Políticos" (CEDEPOL) of the Autonomous University of Coahuila, Mexico, for their support.

This book is published with the support of the Swiss Federal Chancellery and of CEDEPOL.

CEDEPOL
CENTRO DE DERECHOS
CIVILES Y
POLÍTICOS

Chapter 1
E-Voting: What Do Judges Say?

Ardita Driza Maurer[1]

> Elections today are more honest than they were a century ago. Nonetheless, the battle is far from over, and we would be presumptuous to claim that we will ever achieve a perfect democracy.
>
> Douglas W. Jones and Barbara Simons, Broken Ballots, 2012

The adage 'there is no better way to learn about something than to write about it' proved particularly true with this book. When launching the idea of a publication on electronic voting (e-voting) case law we, the editors, were seeking to achieve mainly two things. First, to present an outline of the legislation that regulates e-voting in the countries considered and, second, to contribute to a better understanding of the significance of case law and its impact in shaping e-voting's future development. By placing e-voting and related case law into their respective contexts, however, the 16 authors featured in this book provide a broader, informative and easily accessible perspective on the historical, political and legal aspects of an otherwise very technical subject: the use of electronically backed solutions to cast a vote in political elections and referendums.

Why focus on case law? E-voting can be compared to the tip of an iceberg. It is the most visible part of a larger picture: the extensive use of computers and telecommunication networks in electoral procedures including voter registration, the administration of voter lists, vote tallying, etc. It also provides good evidence of the broader challenge faced by decision makers when 'traditional' processes such as referendums and elections start integrating high-tech and become dependent on it. Difficulties with regulating e-voting are symptomatic of electoral legislation that reacts only slowly to technical evolution. Several chapters in this book testify against the lack of legal provisions or their vagueness or inadequacy to regulate e-voting. Different reasons can explain this relative inertia, including 'good' ones, such as the stable character of electoral legislation, and 'bad' ones, such as the lack of cross-disciplinary knowledge needed to regulate domains at the crossroads of technology and law. As one might reasonably expect, national judges have been

1 The author wishes to thank Pierre Garrone of the Venice Commission, Richard Hill in Geneva, the co-editor of this book, Jordi Barrat, and Greg Taylor, R.M.I.T, Australia for their comments on a draft of this chapter. All arguments, conclusions and possible errors are the author's alone.

asked to intervene and to clarify the legal conditions that should govern the use of e-voting.

Case law has been pivotal in interpreting the meaning of broader electoral principles in an e-voting context. Judges have evaluated the constitutional conformity of e-voting-specific legislation as well as its implementation. Case law, especially of the highest courts, is an integral part of e-voting legislation and thus influences its future development. This publication is a first attempt to present in a structured way the contribution of judges in clarifying the conditions for the use of high-tech voting solutions.

Why adopt an international, comparative viewpoint? As e-voting raises new questions and challenges, claimants, defendants and judges seek references and naturally look at developments in other countries. Each country discussed in this book has some interesting e-voting case law; however, none has a relevant number of important decisions on e-voting to offer, on its own, enough insight. The different chapters mention the influence (or not) of international experiences with e-voting on the judicial opinions examined. We believe that comparing e-voting judicial decisions in different countries enriches our perspective. However, *comparaison n'est pas raison*,[2] so let us stress, electoral and political processes are country specific. Solutions adopted somewhere may not necessarily apply elsewhere, or may apply in a different way. Despite this, common trends are observed in several countries. The main contribution of this book would be to help identify them.

Outline of the Book

This publication is organized in three parts. Part I groups contributions that focus primarily on the application of broader, constitutional principles to e-voting. These include the principle of the public nature of elections (Germany), legal determination (Austria), the separation of powers and the impartiality of judges (Brazil), the transparency and verifiability of voting systems (India) and the principle of equality (Estonia).

Part II concentrates on e-voting regulations and their implementation. The following issues are highlighted: the suitability of the existing regulatory framework conceived for low-tech (mechanical) voting machines to regulate e-voting (France); provinces' extended regulatory powers and the discrepancies between provincial regulations of e-voting in a federal country (Argentina); issues of implementation such as the adequacy of voting instructions provided to the voter as well as the ergonomics of the voting platform (Finland); the relationship between parliamentary acts and statutory instruments, the role of political parties in ensuring the meaningful observation of e-voting, and the responsibility of individual voters (Mexico).

2 Comparisons are not decisive.

Part III turns to the role of politics in determining the development of e-voting. The common thread of the four chapters included here is that the introduction, use and development of e-voting are first a political matter, or even a broader, a societal one. The judges' explicit or implicit opinion seems to be that it is not up to the judiciary to define the contours of e-voting. When faced with e-voting related claims, the highest court (Switzerland) or lower ones (USA) have so far opted to refer issues of principle to the political branches of government. Elsewhere e-voting is restricted to a well delimitated subset of voters, such as the sight-impaired and overseas military personnel, and there is political consensus that it is necessary to wait before any widespread remote e-voting is introduced (Australia). Finally, as the last chapter in Part III shows (Venezuela), the technical merits and advantages of an e-voting solution cannot compensate for lack of political trust.

In Chapter 2 Sebastian Seedorf examines what is probably the best known and most referenced judicial decision on e-voting – Germany's Constitutional Court decision of March 2009 which declared unconstitutional the e-voting regulation and the use of e-voting machines in the parliamentary elections of September 2005. The Court derives a principle of 'the public nature of elections' from other constitutional principles and considers it a means to guarantee that the people, or the sovereign, trust that Parliament is elected according to the collective will of the voters. By applying this principle to e-voting, the Court reaches the conclusion that each voter must be able to comprehend the central steps in the elections and verify reliably that his or her vote has been recorded truthfully – without any special prior technical knowledge. This requirement, the contribution shows, has for the time being stopped any effort to introduce e-voting in Germany. It should be noted that both the principle of 'the public nature of elections' and the way it was applied to e-voting are, so far, specific to Germany.

Melina Oswald analyses in Chapter 3 the decision of the Constitutional Court of Austria of December 2011 which declared unconstitutional the administrative level regulation of e-voting for the Students' Union Elections of 2009. Unlike political elections, elections of self-administering bodies such as Unions are governed by 'ordinary' law and do not need a constitutional amendment. Despite this somewhat 'lower rank', the Court applied a strict interpretation of the principles of transparency and verifiability. Noting that there exists no principle of 'the public nature of elections' in the Austrian constitutional order, the Court still reached a conclusion similar to the German decision. The administrative regulation was declared unlawful because it was insufficiently detailed. Sufficient detail would mean, according to the Court, that the regulation allows the Electoral Commission, the body in charge of controlling elections and verifying results, to understand and control an e-voting system without outside help from computer specialists. The author demonstrates that the ruling has to be understood as a rejection of e-voting for the near future in all kinds of elections.

Chapter 4, by Amílcar Brunazo Filho and Augusto Tavares Rosa Marcacini, describes the failed attempts to introduce a Voter Verifiable Paper Audit Trail (VVPAT) requirement in Brazil. The authors show that the argument addressing the question of introducing the paper trail to audit the digital poll has swung back and forth like a pendulum in the last 20 years. The latest decision was adopted in November 2013 when Brazil's Supreme Court declared unconstitutional the law which introduced the VVPAT requirement. The authors criticize both the lack of technical understanding on the part of the Supreme Court judges – the decision being based on a manifest error of interpretation of the law – and their disproportionate reliance on the arguments of the Higher Electoral Court who opposed the VVPAT requirement. The authors argue that the extreme concentration of powers in the hands of members of a single entity, the Brazilian Higher Electoral Court (*TSE*), is problematic.

Chapter 5 brings us to India, where since 2004 the world's largest democratic elections have been conducted exclusively with electronic voting machines (EVMs). Rishab Bailey and Rohit Sharma discuss the issue of the vulnerability of EVMs to tampering or hacking as raised after the 2009 national elections. A Public Interest Petition requested the introduction of a paper trail along with EVMs as a necessary component of the legal requirement for free and fair elections. While the Delhi High Court refused to impose the requirement of a paper trail in the absence of concrete proof of the machines' vulnerability, the Supreme Court of India finally held in October 2013 that the paper trail is an indispensable requirement of free and fair elections. As the authors show, much of the credit for this position goes to the Election Commission which acted in an enlightened manner, admitting the challenges and proactively searching for solutions. The Election Commission took the decision to introduce paper trails before the Supreme Court decided that it was an indispensable requirement.

E- or rather i-voting judicial decisions in Estonia, a pioneer of internet voting, are discussed in Chapter 6 by Ülle Madise and Priit Vinkel. Case law includes two decisions on the constitutionality of e-voting legal acts and several others on more specific issues of a technical or operational nature. The Supreme Court has so far examined only the principle of equality, declaring that multiple voting – an option given to internet voters alone to cast several votes, only the last one being taken into account – is nevertheless constitutional as it offers an essential guarantee to the observance of free elections and secret voting. The authors point, however, to the existence of other potential constitutional issues related to i-voting which have so far not been dealt with by the courts and suggest possible answers. Additional principles, such as the security of online voting, are discussed in the cases related to specific implementations of i-voting. The authors highlight one of the main issues with internet voting: the difficulty or even impossibility of obtaining evidence, an issue which also arises in Switzerland (see Chapter 11).

Chapter 7 examines the role played by the *Conseil Constitutionnel* – France's equivalent of a Constitutional Court, in defining the legal requirements for e-voting machines and internet voting. Jordi Barrat shows that the *Conseil* deliberates on electoral issues with a triple profile. In addition to its role in judging disputes, it also advises the authorities on how to improve their work and it is consulted when new electoral legislation is introduced. The question arises whether this triple profile has somewhat blurred the message. The Conseil has at times situated the debate about e-voting on the field of voters' psychology rather than on the application of electoral principles. It has been more critical in its advisory role than when judging disputes. By establishing a line of continuity between mechanical voting machines and e-voting, the Conseil shows a lack of awareness of the technological leap. On the other hand, the executive branch responsible for e-voting has been responsive to the challenges of e-voting, both at the regulatory and implementation levels.

José María Pérez Corti, in Chapter 8, outlines the development of e-voting in Argentina, a federal state. This chapter discusses cases decided at the state level between 2003 and 2011. The author shows that legislation as it stands today is not fit for e-voting. Leaving e-voting regulatory powers to the electoral administration is problematic as it results in divergent solutions in different provinces. While federalism has had a positive impact in making sure that e-voting is introduced in a progressive way, the risk exists of splitting up the experiences and transforming the country into a laboratory for different solutions and models. Hence the importance of having some basic guidance in the federal law to harmonize states' regulations and solutions. Furthermore, the multiple roles assigned to electoral administration bodies may be responsible for inconsistent judgments.

The two judicial decisions of 2009 discussed in Chapter 9 by Jussi Aaltonen focus on problems that occurred during the only experience so far with internet voting terminals in selected polling stations in Finland in 2008. The judicial decisions consider issues of design of the voting interface, the usability of the system and the related information provided by the electoral administration to the voters. The courts found irregularities in all these elements. Given that such irregularity could have affected the result of the election the Supreme Administrative Court decided that the results of the e-voting channel could not be certified. New elections were ordered in the three e-voting municipalities and e-voting was discontinued. A recent proposal suggests the reintroduction of internet voting as a supplementary channel, however only in consultative municipal referenda.

In Chapter 10 Jordi Barrat discusses e-voting case law in Mexico, namely the decision of the Tribunal Electoral del Poder Judicial de la Federación, the court of last resort in electoral matters, on the implementation of internet voting for expatriates. The Court analysed the role of political parties during the implementation of electronic voting procedures and the hierarchical relationship between the Constitution, parliamentary acts and statutory regulations. The Court also addressed how to protect the secrecy of the ballot and the freedom of the voter when using internet voting in uncontrolled environments without, however, examining the multiple vote's potential – a remedy used to address such concerns in other internet voting countries such as Estonia and Norway. Internet voting was eventually used in the 2012 elections.

Chapter 11 on Switzerland, an early pioneer of internet voting, brings the e-voting debate to the political arena. Beat Kuoni explains that the Federal Supreme Court has dealt with e-voting in several cases, the latest decision dating from July 2014. The Court's position has been to look for evidence of specific irregularities and to dismiss general criticism. In the absence of such evidence, the Court has so far been supportive of e-voting solutions, stating that it is not its responsibility to go beyond the assessment of a specific vote, leaving it to the political system, informed by academia, to decide on the merits of e-voting. This position has probably been facilitated by the proactive role played by some key players. Recognizing the challenges raised in the appeals and aware of political pressure, federal authorities in charge of e-voting introduced new, detailed federal legislation on e-voting. Minimum requirements on issues such as verifiability and the transparency of e-voting came into force in January 2014. The author presents an interesting international comparison by pointing to the differences between the Swiss approach and the German and Austrian ones.

Daniel Tokaji's contribution in chapter 12 reviews e-voting related case law in the United States starting with the *Bush v. Gore* 2000 decision of the US Supreme Court, followed by other important lower court decisions on issues such as the replacement of punch card machines by newer (e-voting) technology, the need for a voter verifiable paper audit trail for electronic voting machines or the implementation of disability access requirements. Federal legislation, as well as state laws relevant to e-voting, are summarized and the chapter provides a clear overview of a complex legal system. The author shows that, although US courts have played – at least since 2000 – an active supervisory role in election administration matters in general, they have so far showed considerable restraint when it comes to voting technology. Faced with calls to accelerate the introduction of newer voting technology to replace older voting systems, or to offer access to the disabled, or with demands to prohibit it because of security concerns, US courts have mostly left the resolution of such questions to the political branches of government.

Greg Taylor discusses Australia's experience with e-voting in Chapter 13. The Australian federal jurisdiction and several states have introduced a number of electronically backed voting solutions such as voting machines, internet voting or e-mail voting. Fax and telephone voting are also used. Australia offers thus a wide range of solutions in a context of compulsory voting. With some exceptions, e-voting has been introduced on a limited scale, to satisfy the needs of specific groups of voters, mainly the disabled and voters living abroad or in remote areas. Despite being an early adopter of postal voting and despite the large use of electronically assisted counting, Australia has so far avoided an extension of e-voting. The author reports several possible reasons for this, among which the perceived advantage of the public performance of citizens' electoral duties and the lack of political will to introduce novelty in tried and tested democratic processes. Anti-discrimination case law may, however, create a push for more e-voting solutions.

Chapter 14, by Rubén Martínez Dalmau, deals with Venezuela, where e-voting was introduced to eradicate electoral fraud and improve transparency in elections and, according to the author, succeeded in doing so. Today the system is auditable thanks to the presence of the paper trail. However e-voting is implemented in a context of high political polarization. It is considered both a mark of transparency by some political factions and an element of suspicion by others. The author examines two major decisions, adopted in 2005 and 2013 by the Electoral Chamber and the Constitutional Chamber of the Supreme Court respectively. Faced with a claim that votes must be counted manually, the Court concludes that, by law, the count is automatic, with manual counting of the paper trail to be performed in well-defined circumstances. The Supreme Court's decisions have supported the constitutionality and transparency of e-voting. The presence of the paper trail has been instrumental in reaching these decisions. However, the author concludes, transparency alone is not sufficient to install trust. Even the most reliable and transparent technological tool is useless if citizens' perception points to the opposite direction, and this even if suspicion relies on unfounded fears.

E-Voting, the Law and Judges: An Attempt at a Comparative Approach

E-Voting Definition

What strikes one at first when considering e-voting experiences in the 14 countries studied are the multiple realities covered by the 'e-voting' label. This book holds to the same definition of e-voting as the Council of Europe 2004 'Recommendation Rec(2004)11 on legal, operational and technical standards for e-voting'.[3] The term refers to the use of electronic means in at least the casting of the vote covering e-voting both in controlled environments, typically the polling station, and in uncontrolled ones, such as the casting of a vote from home, on a personal device, uncontrolled by the electoral authorities and transmitted via the internet to the voting server. In most of the countries discussed, e-voting takes place in a controlled environment where direct recording electronic voting machines (DREs) are used. In others such as Estonia, Switzerland or Austria the term refers to internet voting from an uncontrolled environment. Elsewhere (e.g. in France, USA or Australia) both forms of e-voting are (or have recently been) in use. Internet voting from a controlled environment (polling station) has been introduced in only one of the countries discussed here: Finland.

In some places e-voting is *the* voting channel by which the whole electorate votes (Brazil, India, Venezuela). Elsewhere it may be just one of the channels proposed and may coexist with paper voting at the polling station, voting by mail, e-mail, phone, fax, etc. E-voting as a complementary channel may apply to the whole of the electorate or only to a specific group of voters, such as people

3 Council of Europe, Committee of Ministers, Council of Europe Recommendation Rec(2004)11 on legal, operational and technical standards for e-voting (Adopted by the Committee of Ministers on 30 September 2004 at the 898th meeting of the Ministers' Deputies), https://wcd.coe.int/ViewDoc.jsp?id=778189.

with certain disabilities or expatriates (e.g. internet voting is possible only for expatriates in France and in a majority of Swiss cantons that allow e-voting). It may be proposed throughout the country (Estonia) or only in some electoral districts. Half of the Swiss cantons propose internet voting and similar diversities are seen in other federal states such as Australia, Argentina and the United States. Local government has an important say on e-voting implementation, even in centralized states, as shown by France and Finland.

Alongside countries like Estonia that have generalized the use of e-voting and offer it on a regular basis, there are those where the status of e-voting is subject to an authorization from the government (or similar) to be issued for each specific use of e-voting (e.g. Switzerland or France). In all cases discussed in this book e-voting is used with binding effect and its results are official. In that sense e-voting is not experimental.

E-voting is currently in use in a majority of the countries studied. However the book also discusses recent judicial decisions which, by imposing stricter conditions on e-voting, have led to a *de facto* end of such activities (Germany, Austria) or where a specific use of e-voting was considered illegal and cancelled, thus discouraging its future use (Finland).

Another classification has emerged more recently: e-voting solutions of first and second generation. As explained in Chapter 4, on Brazil, first generation is often used to refer to solutions that are entirely dependent on specific voting system hardware and software. In that case the correctness of results depends entirely on the correctness of the voting system software. It is not possible for the voter (or in fact anybody) to verify the fate of a specific vote. Second generation indicates, by contrast, systems which offer the possibility of a control, which enables verifying that a specific vote was cast as intended and finally counted as intended quite separately and independently from the voting system hardware and software. In internet voting, however, such verifiability is based on cryptographic techniques, which – to the extent that they cannot be understood or verified by ordinary voters – may raise issues regarding public perceptions of trust.

There is so far no unique definition of first and second generation e-voting systems. In practice, however, e-voting machines equipped with a VVPAT and internet voting solutions that offer individual and universal verifiability are considered to be second generation systems. Second generation voting machines have been or are being introduced in countries such as Venezuela, India and several US states. Second generation internet voting systems are currently being introduced in Estonia and Switzerland after having been initially tested in Norway.[4] In addition to the lack of a clear definition of such systems, solutions introduced in different contexts vary.

4 The Norwegian internet voting project was discontinued in 2014. More on internet voting experiences conducted in 2011 and 2013 can be found at http://www.regjeringen.no/en/dep/kmd/prosjekter/e-vote-trial.html?id=597658.

The introduction of second generation systems has been motivated by an effort to ensure respect for the constitutional principle of transparency of elections in response to claims of insecurity in e-voting solutions. The aim is to enable voters to check if, and detect that, the vote has been changed due to malicious intervention such as malware, manipulated software or hardware, manipulation by voting officials, etc. In Venezuela the paper trail was introduced to satisfy requests made by opposition political parties. In Estonia, India and Switzerland verifiability was/is introduced in a context of political and scientific pressure on the initiative of the electoral authorities themselves and with confirmation from judges (India).

Finally, besides countries with a tradition of mechanical voting which gradually 'evolved' into e-voting (Germany, India, USA or France with respect to voting machines), there are others where e-voting was introduced 'from scratch' and accompanied much more radical changes such as the advent of a democratic regime (e.g. Brazil). Elsewhere e-voting is a new form of a remote (correspondence) voting channel (Australia, Estonia, Switzerland, Austria or France with respect to internet voting). These varied contexts have had an important impact on the development of e-voting. For example, in Switzerland internet voting was not subject to a discussion of issues of freedom and secrecy related to remote voting because of a pre-existing, generalized and very well accepted postal voting system used by almost 90 per cent of voters.

In addition to each country's specific electoral legislation and practice, the different types of e-voting described above need to be taken into account when comparing different judicial decisions on apparently similar issues.

E-Voting Legal Framework

The rule of law principle requires that decisions on the administration of elections must be based on laws. A cornerstone of electoral legislation is that it should be stable and not change frequently. But when elections rely on electronic solutions, frequent change is inevitable. Change is important for instance to ensure an adequate level of security over time. One obvious question then is: how does electoral legislation handle voting technology and how does it deal with the 'changing' aspect of e-voting?

A recent study[5] found that emerging international electoral standards on e-voting are struggling to catch up with the introduction of technology into the voting and counting process. The same can be said for national legislations on e-voting. Regulating e-voting has proven to be a challenging task, probably more challenging than, say, regulating e-banking, because of the requirements for anonymity and secrecy in voting. Broadly speaking, an e-voting legal framework consists of constitutional and legal principles, detailed regulations and soft

5 Barrat, J. and Goldsmith, B. (2012) *Compliance with International Standards: Norwegian E-vote Project*, http://www.regjeringen.no/upload/KRD/Prosjekter/e-valg/evaluering/Topic7_Assessment.pdf.

law such as the standards included in the Council of Europe Recommendation Rec(2004)11 on e-voting.

One main question is the conformity of lower-level e-voting-specific regulations with higher-level principles applicable to referendums and elections. Such principles are to be found in instruments like the Constitution and electoral law. Provisions of international binding law, such as Article 25 of the UN International Covenant on Civil and Political Rights[6] or Article 3 of Protocol 1 to the Convention for the Protection of Human Rights and Fundamental Freedoms,[7] are also part of the higher-level principles in countries that have ratified them. Higher-level principles are general, i.e. not e-voting-specific. The instruments that contain those principles are usually approved by the higher legislative bodies (the People and the Parliament).

For e-voting regulations to be useful and effective they must specify functional requirements (what the system must do) as well as performance requirements (levels of accuracy, speed, reliability, security etc.). They must also define how the systems can be tested and certified.[8] Defining such elements requires technical expertise. But, beyond the technical difficulties, the main challenge for the executive and its agencies when acting as e-voting rule-makers is a legal one: finding out what latitude they have. What do higher-level principles exactly cover? What does 'respect for the principles' imply?

The exact implications of principles like transparency are often not clear until the issue is raised and decided by the judge. In Germany the Constitutional Court enunciated the general principle of the public nature of elections and explained its significance in the e-voting context. In Germany, Austria and India the Courts gave a definition of transparency as applied to e-voting which the executive had not thought of or agreed with when initially introducing e-voting regulations – or even later, when presenting their arguments to the Court (Germany). Elsewhere detailed examination of the content of regulatory provisions and their compliance with constitutional principles was considered to be part of a political and academic debate best left to the government (Switzerland).

Experience shows that principles such as transparency, anonymity and security of voting methods (including prevention of vote buying) are questioned more strictly when dealing with bits (e-voting) than with paper (paper-based voting, including correspondence voting). In such discussions it often becomes clear that electoral legislation as it stands has several ambiguities and needs interpretation. It is not written in a sufficiently formal way to allow for an easy translation of

6 International Covenant on Civil and Political Rights. New York, 16 December 1966, https://treaties.un.org/Pages/ViewDetails.aspx?src=TREATY&mtdsg_no=IV-4&chapter=4&lang=en.

7 http://conventions.coe.int/treaty/en/treaties/html/009.htm.

8 Yard, M. (ed.) (2010) *Direct Democracy: Progress and Pitfalls of Election Technology*, IFES Election Technology Series, http://www.ifes.org/Content/Publications/Books/2010/Direct-Democracy-Progress-and-Pitfalls-of-Election-Technology.aspx.

legal prescriptions into operational rules for e-voting, much less to specify how to code the required software and procure the required hardware. It was certainly not written with automation in mind. Judicial review intervenes to clarify the meaning of principles and other provisions and thus plays a critical role, not just regarding the implementation and operation of e-voting, but also regarding public trust in e-voting.

The distribution of competences to regulate e-voting is an important aspect. Detailed regulation is usually left to the executive branch to allow for frequent updates that reflect the rapid changes in technology. This is, for example, the case in Mexico or in India where the government has introduced detailed provisions to regulate the way in which all aspects of elections are conducted, known as the Code of Elections Rules. However, as the Supreme Court of India found, the government and its agencies do not have full and unrestricted powers in the field of e-voting. They can regulate the conduct of elections only on a subsidiary basis with respect to legislation on the subject. In Mexico as well the Court recognized the broad regulatory competences of the electoral authority, stressing, however, the need for such regulations to respect the guiding principles of any electoral procedure, the main features being the right to vote and the ability to vote from abroad.

The inappropriateness of incorporating e-voting without a specific (federal) legal framework is discussed in Chapter 8, dedicated to Argentina. Provisions related to traditional paper voting are not always suitable for e-voting. For example, they are unable to ensure that e-voting mechanisms are transparent. In the absence of a federal e-voting specific regulation, provincial electoral management bodies have interpreted generic electoral provisions in different ways, ranging from absolute formalism to too broad judgments. This has resulted in a lack of coherence between instructions or judgments on e-voting in different provinces.

Clarity of provisions is an issue in Australia where state level e-voting regulation in New South Wales requires, for instance, procedures to be adopted by the Electoral Commission 'for the authentication of the eligible elector's vote'. It is unclear what this means, and the debates on the legislation as it passed through Parliament leave one no wiser, at least according to the author. There is potential for a challenge to the procedures.

Certain courts require that e-voting regulations be quite detailed. In Germany and Austria Constitutional Courts said that lower-level e-voting regulations must be sufficiently detailed and provide procedures that ensure a reliable control of the system (respectively by each voter or by a designated body) and subsequent judicial control. They quashed the insufficiently detailed administrative level e-voting regulations, finding them unlawful. Higher-level laws, containing broader principles applicable to e-voting, were, by contrast, considered to respect the constitutional principles in both cases. The Austrian judge even held that a stricter specification of the technical measures to be applied during the e-voting process in the (higher-level) law was not possible and could be problematic in light of the rapid development of technical standards.

The level of detail is an important aspect of an e-voting regulation. Detailed provisions are important to make sure that the implementation of technology complies with constitutional principles. The level of detail depends among others on the level of transparency required by the legislation or by politics. In Austria and Germany the Constitutional Courts required highly specific rules for a system that can be fully verified by people without technical knowledge. This appears difficult to achieve and no such rules have been introduced so far. In Estonia and Switzerland recent updates of e-voting regulations have introduced detailed rules on verifiability and on certification and audit procedures. However, auditing by experts chosen by democratic procedures is all that is necessary and there is no requirement that anyone without technical expertise should be able to verify the system itself. There are therefore no detailed rules on this aspect.

In Switzerland an additional layer of (lower-level) regulation was added to allow for more flexibility in updating regulations to technical developments. In addition to the Constitution and the law (approved by Parliament) as well as to the decree or ordinance (approved by the government) a third layer, in the form of a technical regulation, allows the Federal Chancellery – a governmental agency – to stipulate and frequently adapt technical requirements applicable to e-voting. However, this was not in direct reaction to case law. The introduction of verifiability in Estonia followed a similar path, with the introduction of more detailed regulation and the setting up of a dedicated agency – the electronic voting committee. In France, the *Conseil constitutionnel* proposed, in its advisory role and *de lege ferenda*, the introduction of more detailed provisions on e-voting.

An additional challenge illustrated by the Argentinean case is the *de facto* important role played by vendors during the hearings which are organized by the competent authorities to develop and complete the detailed e-voting regulations. Representatives and experts on the vendor side take in this case an active role in answering questions regarding not only the technical aspects of the system but also issues that determine legal and conceptual notions, which only the electoral organization or court should have the power to define. It is important therefore to have federal guidance on e-voting regulatory issues, the author concludes. More generally, it is important to distinguish between matters of public policy where the regulator has the upper hand and those related to the introduction of a specific voting technology and to make sure that the second respects the first.

Federal states experience yet another challenge: the appropriate level (federal or state) of e-voting regulation. In Switzerland, for example, cantons (states) have not made use of their important powers in the electoral field and e-voting regulation is mainly federal. Cantons have introduced 'lighter' regulations, often a copy-paste of federal provisions. Consequently, while Swiss federal rules on the organization of elections usually contain only a few minimum and common requirements, federal legislation on e-voting is much more detailed, exhaustive and voluminous. While, usually, most of the electoral details are decided at the cantonal level, resulting in a patchwork of cantonal legislations and practices, e-voting regulation is mainly federal and thus quite uniform throughout Switzerland (though the federal regulations do not apply directly to purely cantonal referendums and elections, which may thus be conducted, theoretically at least, under different rules).

An opposite trend is observed in two other federal countries – Argentina and the United States – where states enjoy an important degree of electoral autonomy as well. In Argentina federal regulation of e-voting is missing. Provinces have made use of their regulatory powers and as a result a patchwork of e-voting regulations prevails whose conformity with constitutional principles is now questioned. In the United States, state level legislation on e-voting is far more detailed and complete than the federal one. States have, for instance, introduced concepts such as verifiability, which is still missing at the federal level, and have their own rules on audits and recounts. Some make the paper record the official ballot in case of a recount. Whether such concepts need to be regulated uniformly throughout a federal country or may be regulated independently by each state remains open to debate and maybe case law. E-voting's conformity with constitutional principles might be more easily ensured throughout a federal country if detailed regulations are introduced at the higher (federal) level.

As the legislator and the judge face new questions in an e-voting context, they look for benchmarks. In addition to legislation and regulations applicable to e-voting, international soft law instruments are useful references and part of an e-voting regulatory framework in a broader sense. The Venice Commission's Code of Good Practice in Electoral Matters[9] and the Interpretative Declaration on the Stability of the Electoral Law[10] are helpful references when dealing with fundamental electoral principles and their interpretation. At a lower, regulatory level, the Council of Europe Recommendation Rec(2004)11 on legal, operational and technical standards for e-voting remains so far the unique international reference. Judges in countries as distant as Venezuela and Estonia have examined the Recommendation Rec(2004)11 when assessing e-voting specific rules and solutions. In Estonia the Supreme Court examined multiple voting's conformity with Rec(2004)11 provisions. Legislators have also looked at it when introducing e-voting regulations. The Recommendation is used as a legal benchmark by observers of e-voting. In the Finnish case, for instance, the information report on electronic voting in the Finnish municipal elections drawn up by the Council of Europe in 2008 (to which the appellants refer) considers e-voting from the perspective of the fundamental electoral principles identified by the Venice Commission and of the provisions of Recommendation Rec(2004)11.

---

9 Venice Commission, Code of Good Practice in Electoral Matters: Guidelines and Explanatory Report, adopted by the Venice Commission at its 51st and 52nd sessions (Venice, 5–6 July and 18–19 October 2002), CDL-AD(2002)023rev-e, http://www.venice.coe.int/webforms/documents/CDL-AD(2002)023rev.aspx.

10 Interpretative Declaration on the Stability of the Electoral Law, adopted by the Council for Democratic Elections at its 15th meeting (Venice, 15 December 2005) and the Venice Commission at its 65th plenary session (Venice, 16–17 December 2005), CDL-AD(2005)043-e, http://www.venice.coe.int/webforms/documents/CDL-AD(2005)043.aspx.

Adopted in 2004 by the Committee of Ministers, the Council of Europe Recommendation on e-voting timely responded to countries' need for guidance in the e-voting regulatory field and has accompanied them in a number of e-voting experiences during the past 10 years. It is, however, largely admitted that, due to rapid developments in this field, the Recommendation needs to be updated.[11] Judicial decisions will presumably be one useful source that will inform the updating work.

E-Voting Case Law: Discussion

E-voting and trust

Trust and mistrust have become buzzwords when discussing e-voting. Do they play a role in the judicial decisions discussed in this book and, if yes, how? Trust has several facets: the public trusts the election administration and the results of elections as reflecting the collective will; the public and the authorities trust technical expertise and technical solutions; the authorities trust that the voter will not abuse the system in the case of remote voting, and so on.

In several countries that employ e-voting the public has confidence in the election administration. Scholarly discourse in the past years, however, has emphasized the untrustworthy nature of electronic voting solutions – and this despite the best organizational efforts – unless certification, audits and, most importantly, verifiability are used to create trust. Switching from a logic of trust in well-administered voting channels to one of mistrust and related checks and controls has proven difficult for judges, especially as this implies having the necessary know-how to assess technical decisions taken by the electoral authorities. An additional cause of judicial restraint is the considerable flexibility enjoyed by most electoral authorities with the introduction of advanced voting technologies. Consequently, while judges have played an important role in supervising electoral authorities outside the context of e-voting (e.g. in the United States in particular since 2000, in Switzerland with respect especially to cantonal decisions[12]), they have been more reticent to second-guess the e-voting related decisions of electoral authorities. In other words, in the judicial context, 'trusting electoral authorities' may be considered a synonym for reticence to interfere with their extended competences and/or a lack of the knowledge required to do so.

As explained in the above section on the regulatory framework of e-voting, the challenge, also for judges, is to delimitate the authorities' manoeuvring room in introducing technology. Positions vary. In Brazil, the Court shows almost blind

---

11 Driza Maurer (2014) 'Ten Years Council of Europe Rec(2004)11: Lessons Learned and Outlook'. In: Krimmer, R., Volkamer, M., *Proceedings of Electronic Voting 2014 (EVOTE2014)*, TUT Press, Tallinn, pp. 111–17, http://www.e-voting.cc/wp-content/uploads/downloads/2014/10/evote2014_driza_maurer_p111-117.pdf.

12 Benedicte Tornay (2008) *La démocratie directe saisie par le juge: L'empreinte de la jurisprudence sur les droits populaires en Suisse*, Schultess.

trust in the arguments of the electoral authority – the Higher Electoral Court (TSE) thus accepting an argument based on a mistaken interpretation of the legal requirements. Electoral courts for their part, the chapter on Brazil argues, tend to overvalue the existing audit methods of e-voting (such as comparing the number of votes entered with the number of voters registered or the use of test voting) and this in spite of many negative scientific opinions on their adequacy. This 'chain of trust' results in decisions rejecting the introduction of verifiability methods that are becoming the norm in other countries.

Another facet is trust placed on the voter in the e-voting context. In Switzerland authorities and voters have high mutual trust. Family voting (that is, members of a family being forced to vote as the head of the family dictates) is not an issue in a country where almost 90 per cent of votes are sent by postal mail. As a result there is no perceived need to introduce special technical measures in the internet voting context alone. Switzerland has not introduced the multiple voting option as did, for example, Estonia where this tool is used to mitigate such potential abuses of the system. In Switzerland reference is made to existing penal provisions that condemn such abuses. However, the preventive effect of penal provisions in a context of internet voting from an uncontrolled location and device is questionable.

Eventually, and despite mutual trust or the multiple voting option, verifiability methods ended up imposing themselves (almost) everywhere, in addition to other checks. Trust remains, however, at the centre of the discussion. Verifiability is available in several configurations. With respect to DREs, while the German Court interpreted the principle of 'the public nature of elections' quite literally to mean imposing the possibility of people without technical knowledge verifying all steps in e-elections (potentially meaning manual recounts of VVPAT in all cases, making DREs useless), elsewhere (USA, Venezuela, India) the introduction of verifiability is limited to the introduction of a paper trail (VVPAT) accompanied with clear rules on the organization of selective, and preferably random, manual recounts. With respect to internet voting, the Austrian court required that each member of the electoral commission be able to verify all steps of the election, without technical assistance, which is considered impossible by today's standards. However, the author says, a careful reading of the decision may suggest that support of the electoral commission by technical experts would potentially be acceptable if such support was enshrined at the same normative level as the electoral principles. Elsewhere (Estonia, Switzerland) individual verifiability in internet voting is based on peer-reviewed and approved cryptographic solutions (which most people do not understand) while universal verifiability is delegated to democratically and transparently appointed (trusted) experts.

In New South Wales, Australia, where e-voting is allowed mainly for people abroad, the disabled or those in remote locations within the state, electoral administration intends to promote transparency and verifiability by requiring audits. However, legislation enables the computer programme to be kept secret and it also contains no specific requirement to act upon the defects in the system identified in the audits. The author argues that considerable trust is warranted in such a case given the high likelihood that the electoral authorities would act, and that politicians and the general public would demand action on defects that were drawn to their attention by that means (audits) or any other. Another proof of trust in electoral authorities in Australia is found in a Tasmanian innovation: email voting. It is not secret, but most voters are apparently not unduly concerned about the secrecy of their votes as far as the electoral officials are concerned. Furthermore there is no principle of the public nature of elections (meaning that all aspects of elections must be conducted openly in all respects, including the counting), nor full constitutional protection of the right to cast a valid vote. Although no general right exists for the citizens to be present or to have access to the computer programming, this should not cause alarm, according to the author, as a very strong democratic culture prevails in Australia, protected by a strong feeling for fairness in elections, egalitarianism, watchful media and a belief in democratic institutions.

In Venezuela the postulate that assumes that transparency and verifiability build trust is challenged because the particular climate of general political distrust prevents even the most transparent e-voting technology from inspiring trust. This example shows that existing political consent and a climate of trust are preconditions to introducing e-voting.

Trust and responsibility go hand in hand. In Estonia the Court has approved the Parliament's liberal approach to voting: the voters themselves decide whether to vote and which channel to use. It is the state's responsibility to provide voting options, keeping in mind that each alternative is just one of the possible ways of voting. With respect to e-voting responsibility lies with the voter to take care of the computer's security settings and, if necessary, to ask for technical support. Ultimately the voter can also vote in the traditional way in a polling station. On the other side responsibility lies with election organizers to adjust e-voting solutions to citizens' needs and to the evolving nature (and threats) of technical solutions. Despite such a trust-based approach, family voting (and other cases of coercion or vote buying) is considered an issue, which is why multiple voting is offered. The judge considered this in line with the principle of equality because of the specific risks of i-voting.

Interestingly in the Finnish case discussed in Chapter 9, the dissenting judge, who refused to cancel the e-voting result in the three municipalities, placed the responsibility on the voter's side. He argued that the instructions on the practical voting procedure in question had been clear and detailed enough. As proof of this he considered the fact that almost all the voters who used the electronic voting system completed the voting process correctly. A voter could have turned to a polling assistant if he or she had experienced any difficulties or uncertainties in completing the process. The voter had furthermore the option to choose between the new electronic voting system and traditional ballot voting.

The problem with evidence

Cases discussed in this book are mostly about overturning e-voting regulations and e-voting use in general and not about cancelling an e-vote because of alleged (let alone proven) specific irregularities. However, when faced with such claims, courts systematically look for evidence of irregularities and for the possible impact of irregularities on the final results. In the absence of such a link, courts decide not to cancel e-voting results. This reasoning is common to all countries and would apply also if there was evidence of irregularities but their impact considered negligible. Does the absence of irregularities prevent judges from further scrutinizing e-voting? Courts have adopted two kinds of positions.

The first kind of reaction is illustrated by the German and Estonian court decisions. The absence of evidence of concrete problems or of their impact on the results did not prevent the courts from going further and examining whether the detailed e-voting regulation and/or the decision to introduce e-voting conformed with higher legislation.

The second, and more widespread, kind of judicial reaction is illustrated by decisions in Switzerland and the United States and consists in rejecting claims related for instance to the security of the systems in the absence of proof of effective problems. What's more, courts did not examine whether the e-voting regulation or the decision on the specific use of e-voting conformed to superior law.

The Swiss Court opposed procedural arguments (the authorization to use e-voting did not infringe any procedural provisions) to substantive claims (checks on the correct functioning of the system, as foreseen in the regulation, were inadequate). To the appellant's claims that the system in question is designed in such a way that it is impossible to identify cases of manipulation, the Court replied that such complex technical evaluations are to be decided in the political and academic debate, the Court's review being limited to the specific vote. Another argument of the Swiss Court is that neither conventional voting methods, nor electronic voting can exclude irregularities entirely. In relation to internet voting, risk assessments play an important role. Its use is authorized by the Government, in the framework of its competences, based on such risk assessment.

In the United States, courts rejected claims related to the security of paperless DREs as no statistical evidence was produced showing that this type of equipment was more prone to error than DREs with VVPAT (this kind of evidence had been accepted previously in cases that required the replacement of punch-card technology by DREs). In France, the *Conseil* rejected several complaints due to the quantitative irrelevance of the possible outcomes.

However, as the chapter on Estonia shows, when it comes to e-voting or more particularly to internet voting, proof of irregularities may be impossible to obtain. Challengers who, for idealistic reasons, are tempted to organize an attack on the system to prove its alleged vulnerabilities will have to face claims under criminal law. The courts recognize the difficulty of obtaining evidence (so does, for example, the Swiss Court in its July 2014 decision) without, however, drawing consequences from that difficulty. When challengers sabotage their own vote and present it as evidence of the vulnerability of the system, courts have replied that manipulating one's own vote cannot be seen as proof of the overall lack of security of the internet voting system but as an invalid vote.

The chapter on Estonia points to an upcoming challenge. Following the introduction of vote verification methods, the handling of incidents has to be able to produce court-approved evidence. Obtaining sufficient evidence is, however, conceptually difficult due to the anonymity and secrecy of the vote. These two requirements often make it very difficult or even impossible to assess the accuracy of the presented claims. This problem does not only affect e-voting but also paper-ballot voting where it is possible to check the correct functioning of the overall system, however not the operation and 'destiny' of a single vote.

Courts have also examined the quality of evidence offered. Observing that procedures are followed closely, comparing the number of votes counted by the machine with the number of voters marked in the voters' registry by the polling staff, or the thorough technical examination of each voting machine type by the national metrology institute prior to an official approval, cannot be constitutionally sufficient proof of the correct functioning of an e-voting system, according to the German Court. The Swiss Court rejected a mere abstract or theoretical risk as not sufficient for a specific voting system to be declared invalid.

Judges' stance towards trust or evidence as discussed above is an indicator of the way the judiciary deals with complicated and new technical questions – such as those related to security – raised by e-voting.

Dealing with technical issues

In an e-voting context both legislators and judges face several new questions related to the use of new voting technologies or high-tech. They include:

- What does respect for fundamental principles mean in an e-voting context?
- How is it possible to make sure that an e-voting technical regulation complies with fundamental principles?
- How is it possible to make sure that fundamental principles and e-voting regulations are properly implemented in an e-voting technical solution?
- How is it possible to prove the contrary (meaning that technical solutions do not respect the regulation and/or fundamental principles) if such weaknesses have not led to irregularities in the outcome of the vote or if such irregularities are impossible to prove?

The case law examined in this book provides some elements of response. While no distinct jurisprudence is emerging regarding e-voting versus other forms of voting (the goal is the same for any voting channel: they should all respect fundamental principles and applicable legislation) it has become clear that the application of fundamental principles and generic requirements to high-tech voting solutions is not straightforward.

Evidence of problems and of their impact on the outcome of a vote (discussed above) is certainly a necessary precondition when considering the validation of the voting results. However, it seems to us odd to make it a precondition of the examination of all issues, including, for example, security issues. This mainly for two reasons. First, if there is a potential security flaw, say at the regulatory or at the implementation levels, the fact that no problem was evident on one specific voting occasion does not exclude possible problems in future implementations of e-voting. Second, in the e-voting case, the absence of proof of irregularities does not necessarily mean proof of absence of irregularities. Several courts have admitted that proof may be impossible to obtain.

Once the court decides to consider the detailed implementation of fundamental principles and generic requirements in the e-voting regulation or solution, it is faced with quite detailed technical questions, for example those related to security. Some courts have declared that both regulations and solutions should be formulated and built in such a way that each and every technical detail can be understood by and be verifiable by people without technical knowledge. As this seems impossible to achieve in the present state of knowledge, this reaction is assimilated to a *de facto* 'no' to e-voting. Other courts/legislators admit that security and other technical issues are tasks for experts. Thus they require the introduction of verifiability tools and increased transparency in procedures while accepting that the underlying technique can only be understood by experts.

Choosing between a strict interpretation of fundamental principles (which may bring certain forms of e-voting to a stop) or a less strict one (based on trade-offs) is linked not only to considerations of the overall electoral system and of the use of high-tech but also to the specific motivations behind the introduction of e-voting. For example, the existence (or not) of a broader vision on the introduction (or exclusion) of high-tech solutions to ensure an effective voting channel for, say, expatriates, the disabled, voters in remote areas, or to ensure the application of a broader governmental e-strategy, is certainly reflected in the case law as well. Courts adopt particular trade-offs, as the Mexican decision on the issue of secrecy shows.

Two additional points are worth noting. Firstly, the positions of both legislator and judges on technical issues, especially on security, do not reflect the partisan views of political parties. Often there is no clear unified position within a party, and those who have a strong opinion on such issues tend to push their views even against the party's advice. Indeed, more often, individual positions on e-voting technical questions mostly reflect personal knowledge and sensitivities. Clear political party positions on the security of an e-voting solution, where they exist, may be based more on political considerations (such as lack of trust and extreme political polarization in Venezuela) rather than on technical arguments. Secondly, no specific regional trends can be distinguished either. It certainly cannot be said that neighbour countries with similar democratic traditions, such as Austria, Germany and Switzerland, are heading in the same direction. In this case, a country's overall strategy on the introduction of new technologies and the specificities of its electoral system seem to be decisive (in the Swiss case such specificities include a system of direct democracy, the high number of voting events that take place each year, the generalization and success of postal voting, extended voting rights for the Swiss abroad). However, the structure of a country and the distribution of competences on electoral matters may be determinant, as shown by some similarities between the US and the Swiss (and to a certain extent the Argentinean and Australian) federal-based solutions.

Both legislators and judges need to develop a systematic approach to e-voting, and indeed more broadly to the use of technology in elections and referendums. Where to start? In the final chapter of this book – Chapter 15: 'Conclusions' – the editors present a few recommendations on how to handle the introduction of e-voting. The recommendations are as much lessons learned from personal experiences during the past 10 years as lessons drawn from experiences presented in the chapters of this book.

PART I
The Principles

Chapter 2

Germany: The Public Nature of Elections and its Consequences for E-Voting

Sebastian Seedorf

Introduction

Although voting machines had been legally in use in German elections for more than 40 years, only one court case on record dealt with their operation: the judgment of the Federal Constitutional Court (Bundesverfassungsgericht), Germany's highest court, of 3 March 2009.[1]

Since 1956, the Federal Electoral Act (FEA)[2] had allowed for the use of 'officially registered vote counting machines'[3] to replace the cumbersome manual counting of ballots by more efficient machine counts. In 1961, the Federal Ministry of the Interior, which is the government agency responsible for the regulation of election procedures, published the first statutory ordinance (decree, governmental regulation) on the use of machines with mechanical counting systems in federal elections.[4] From that time onwards mechanical voting machines were used in federal and state elections in which the voter either had to push a button for the different candidates and parties or to place an election token in an opening allotted to one of the candidates. However, the provisions of the federal ordinance which contained quite specific requirements for the construction of the voting machines proved to be a burden for the development of new types of voting machines.

---

1 Judgment of the Second Senate of 3 March 2009 on the basis of the oral hearing of 28 October 2008 in the combined cases 2 BvC 3/07 and 2 BvC 4/07. The judgment has been published in German in the Court's official records as BVerfGE 123, 39, in several German law journals and on the Court's website. An official English translation has been published on the Court's website: http://www.bundesverfassungsgericht.de/SharedDocs/Entscheidungen/EN/2009/03/cs20090303_2bvc000307en.html. The paragraphs of the judgment have been numbered and I cite the numbers from the English translation. Please note that the numbering deviates slightly from the numbering of the original German version.

2 *Bundeswahlgesetz* as promulgated on 23 July 1993 (BGBl. 1993 I 1288, 1594), as last amended by Article 2 of the Act of 3 May 2013 (BGBl. 2013 I 1084).

3 Section 35(3) FEA.

4 Ordinance on the Use of Vote Counting Devices in Elections to the German Bundestag (*Verordnung über die Verwendung von Stimmenzählgeräten bei Wahlen zum Deutschen Bundestag*) (BGBl. 1961 I 1618).

By the mid 1970s, politicians and officials felt that an open approach would be advantageous and decided to allow for the development of new, more sophisticated voting machines. But the exact nature and the direction of the technical developments was hard to predict. It was, therefore, regarded more appropriate not to specify any certain type of machine in the law.[5]

Consequently, the previous provision in the Electoral Act was replaced by a more detailed section 35a on 'vote casting with voting machines',[6] which introduced a two-fold regime: the Electoral Act stipulated only basic requirements while the same provision allowed the Federal Ministry of the Interior to decide and approve the specific technology and design and to regulate the procedure for the testing of voting machines. The Electoral Act itself contained neither a definition of a voting machine nor particular system requirements. Section 35 FEA stipulated that voting machines (when used instead of ballot papers and ballot boxes to facilitate the casting and counting of votes) must guarantee the secrecy of the ballot and that their design must be officially approved for individual elections or on a general basis. The Federal Ministry of the Interior was authorized to issue detailed provisions by means of an ordinance on the prerequisites for the design of voting machines. Those were defined as mechanically or electrically driven machines for the casting and counting of votes in elections and could be used in elections to the German Bundestag (the parliament) if their type was authorized and their use approved.[7]

However, despite the open legal regime, voting machines never really developed into a standard voting channel in Germany. As a government report explains, in the 1978 Bundestag election a mere 236 machines were used in Germany at that time.[8] This was due to the fact that the voting options on the machines were limited to a certain number of parties or candidates, so they could not be used in elections with more or party-independent candidates. Furthermore, the costs of purchase, storage, transport and maintenance of the machines were quite high,

5 Cf. the official memorandum of the new provision of Sec 35a Federal Electoral Act in Bundestags-Drucksache 7/2873 of 2 December 1974, page 40: 'Wegen der schwer überschaubaren weiteren Entwicklung der Wahlgeräte ist aus Zweckmäßigkeitsgründen eine besondere Ermächtigung zum Erlaß einer Wahlgeräteverordnung vorgesehen; sie ermöglicht eine einfachere Anpassung der in ihr enthaltenen Bestimmungen an neue technische Gegebenheiten'.

6 Section 35a in the Federal Electoral Act of 1975 is now section 35 (after the promulgation of the new version of the Federal Electoral Act on 1 September 1975 (BGBl. 1975 I 2325).

7 Section 1 of the Federal Voting Machine Ordinance (*Bundeswahlgeräteverordnung*) of 3 September 1975 (BGBl. 1975 I 2459), in the version of the Ordinance Amending the Federal Voting Machine Ordinance and the European Election Code (*Verordnung zur Änderung der Bundeswahlgeräteverordnung und der Europawahlordnung*) of 20 April 1999 (BGBl. 1999 I 749).

8 Report by the Federal Government to the Bundestag on the Use of Voting Machines in the Bundestag Election of 3 October 1976 (Bundestag-Drucksache 8/94).

so a lot of local municipalities (who decided as to whether voting machines were acquired) were reluctant to introduce voting machines, in particular when there were comparably little time gains in the counting of the ballots.[9]

In the 1990s electronic voting machines came on the market and in 1997 the Dutch manufacturer N.V. Nederlandsche Apparatenfabriek (NEDAP) approached the federal government to request approval for the use of one of its electronic vote casting devices. After some tests of the devices, both the Federal Electoral Act and the Federal Voting Machine Ordinance were amended to include computer-controlled voting machines.[10] The relevant provision thus reads.[11]

> Section 35 – Voting by Means of Voting Machines
> (1) Voting machines may be used instead of ballot papers and ballot boxes to facilitate the casting and counting of votes.
> (2) Voting machines as defined in subsection (1) above must guarantee the secrecy of the ballot. For use at elections to the German Bundestag, their design must be officially approved for individual elections or on a general basis. The Federal Ministry of the Interior shall decide on the approval of a voting machine on the application of the manufacturer. The permission of the Federal Ministry of the Interior must be obtained before an officially approved voting machine can be used. This permission may be given for individual elections or on a general basis.
> (3) The Federal Ministry of the Interior shall, by means of statutory ordinance not requiring the endorsement of the Bundesrat (Council of Constituent States), be authorized to issue detailed provisions on:
> 1. the prerequisites for the official approval of the design of voting machines as well as for the withdrawal and revocation of the approval,
> 2. the official approval procedure governing the design,
> 3. the procedure governing the examination of a voting machine for conformity with the officially approved design,
> 4. the public testing of a voting machine prior to its use,
> 5. the procedure governing the granting of official permission for the use of a voting machine as well as the withdrawal and the revocation of the permission,

9 Ibid.

10 Section 35(1) FEA originally allowed for the use of voting machines 'with separate counting devices'. These words were deleted with the Act on General and Representative Election Statistics in Elections to the German Bundestag and in the Election of Members of the European Parliament from the Federal Republic of Germany of 21 May 1999 (BGBl. 1999 I 1023) to allow for computer-controlled voting machines, which do not contain a 'separate' counting device but rather store and count the votes on the same storage medium that also stores the software of the voting machine.

11 I use the official translation of the Federal Electoral Act as provided by the Office of the Federal Returning Officer at: http://www.bundeswahlleiter.de/en/bundestagswahlen/downloads/rechtsgrundlagen/bundeswahlgesetz_engl.pdf.

6. the special points that have to be borne in mind in connection with the election as a result of the use of voting machines.
In the cases specified in numbers 1 and 3, the statutory ordinance shall be issued in agreement with the Federal Ministry of Economics and Technology.
(4) Section 33 subsection (1), first sentence, and subsection (2) shall apply as appropriate for the operation of a voting machine.

In the European Parliament Elections of 1999, electronic voting machines were used for the first time in Germany. In the Bundestag elections of 2002 and 2005 up to 1850 NEDAP voting machines of two different types were used.[12]

At the time, the use of electronic voting machines looked promising. Although they were still quite expensive (according to press reports at the time, a NEDAP voting machine had cost between 3,200 and 4,300 euros[13]), municipal electoral authorities were hopeful that the machines would help to save costs. Their use in federal, state and local elections did not only speed up the counting of the votes but required fewer poll workers. The costs for polling booths and the printing of ballot papers could be reduced. Volunteers were easier to motivate because the counting of the votes went much faster. Additionally, the use of voting machines would make it virtually impossible inadvertently to cast invalid votes. This was particularly true for local elections, which in many cases involve complex ballots, and include cumulative voting and voting for candidates from different party lists.

The Constitutional Court Case of 2009

The Court Proceedings

In the elections to the 16th German Bundestag on 18 September 2005, approximately 2 million voters had cast their votes on 1850 electronic voting machines (direct-recording electronic voting machines, DREs) of the NEDAP-types ESD1 and ESD2.[14]

After the elections, two voters lodged complaints against the use of voting machines in the elections. According to Article 41 of the German Constitution (Grundgesetz), an electoral complaint must first be lodged with the Bundestag, the German parliament, to start a formal 'scrutiny of elections' procedure. The Bundestag's decision was prepared by its own Election Scrutiny Committee (Wahlprüfungsausschuss). The plaintiffs argued that the deployment of computer-controlled voting machines had violated the principle of democracy, the principle

12 Cf. Bundestag-Drucksache 16/5194, p. 7.

13 Apparently, the City of Cologne had acquired 582 NEDAP voting machines for 1.9 million euros, the City of Dortmund 290 NEDAP voting machines for 1.3 million euros.

14 For a detailed description of the construction and operation of these machines, see Constitutional Court decision of 3 March 2009, at paragraphs 3–7.

of the rule of law, the principle of the public nature of elections and the principle of the official nature of elections. Furthermore, the voting machines were said not to be compatible with the Guidelines for the Construction of Voting Machines issued by the Ministry of the Interior.[15] The plaintiffs did not claim any manipulation or specific malfunction of any of the voting machines. The Bundestag rejected the complaints by a resolution of 14 December 2006 as being manifestly unfounded.[16]

The plaintiffs then appealed the Bundestag decision to the Constitutional Court. In the Court proceedings, the requirement that elections had to be held in public turned out to be the key point. The plaintiffs argued that the voting machines that had been used did not comply with this requirement. Because the cast votes were stored exclusively on an electronic storage medium and the votes were only counted electronically by the voting machine, there was no way to ascertain that the votes cast by the voters were inserted into the ballot box without a change, that the votes were not subsequently altered and that only the votes from the ballot box were counted at the end of the election.[17] Effective monitoring by the public and the polling staff was said to be impossible since a major part of the election act and the counting of the ballots took place only inside the voting machine.[18]

The Federal Ministry of the Interior and the Bundestag asked the Constitutional Court to dismiss the complaints. The Ministry argued that even with the use of voting machines, the election could still be monitored by the public. With regard to the casting of the ballot, the polling staff could ensure that only eligible voters were granted access to the voting machine. Since the machines were equipped with a control unit, the staff could also check that each voter had in fact voted and had only done so once – of course it was impossible for the polling staff to see for which party the voter had cast his or her vote.[19] With regard to the counting of the votes, not only could the public observe that the procedure for the automatic counting of the votes was followed closely, the polling staff (and any election observer) could also compare the number of votes counted by the machine with the number of voters marked in the voters' registry by the polling staff during election day to make sure that the device had registered and added all the votes cast.[20] Even though the votes cast were only stored on a computer chip,

---

15 According to Annex 1 to the Federal Voting Machine Ordinance these guidelines (*Richtlinien für die Bauart von Wahlgeräten*) regulate in particular the technical requirements to be made on the voting machines, and contain detailed stipulations for the identification, technical structure and functioning of the voting machines. Statements are made in this context on the display of the electoral choices, on operation and operability, on the ballot, on the storage of votes and on the creation of backups. The examination of the compliance of the voting machine with the above guidelines is a matter for the Physikalisch-Technische Bundesanstalt.

16 Bundestag-Drucksache 16/3600, appendices 1 and 2.

17 Constitutional Court decision of 3 March 2009, at paragraph 35.

18 Constitutional Court decision of 3 March 2009, at paragraph 35.

19 Constitutional Court decision of 3 March 2009, at paragraph 48.

20 Constitutional Court decision of 3 March 2009, at paragraph 49.

the so-called 'EPROMS', and indeed, the counting or tabulation of the individual votes could not be verified by the public, there were other safeguard measures in place to minimize the risk of a false result, in particular the thorough technical examination of each voting machine type by the national metrology institute providing scientific and technical services to the government (the Physikalisch-Technische Bundesanstalt) prior to an official approval.[21]

The government (and the Bundestag) also employed a more principled argument: the Constitution certainly did not require each distinct act, every little step and procedure of an election, to be subject to an individual check as this would 'overstretch' the constitutional principle of a public election.[22] Instead, as a typical consequence of the advance in technology, it could be expected that the voter would presume that the systems deployed were viable given that they had been examined and certified in a designated procedure prior to their deployment.[23]

The Constitutional Court invited other public institutions and private interest groups to file advisory opinions, among them the Chaos Computer Club, a well-known association of computer experts and hackers that does not hesitate to voice critical opinions. After an oral hearing on 28 October 2008 where expert witnesses gave evidence, the Court delivered its judgment on 3 March 2009. The ruling declared the Federal Ordinance on the Deployment of Voting Machines in Elections to the German Bundestag to be invalid as it did not ensure monitoring that complies with the constitutional principle of the public nature of elections. It further held that the use of the NEDAP voting machines in the elections of 2005 was against the Constitution and without a valid legal basis.

However, the Court did not declare the Bundestag election of 2005 to be invalid, because there was no indication that there had been any kind of malfunction of the voting machines or manipulation of the result. The official approval and use of voting machines, despite the inadequacy of the legal basis for the approval, did not per se mean that the election result was irregular. And even if it would be presumed that the use of the machines did change some of the votes (again, without there being any real indication that this had happened), by balancing the public interest in the rectification of an election fault and the public interest in a functioning parliament, the Court found that it was not constitutionally mandated to dissolve the Bundestag and to repeat the election.[24]

A remarkable aspect of the judgment is the complete absence of any reference to international legal instruments and a complete lack of international comparisons. The Court does not evaluate the German law, or the practical operation of the voting

21 Constitutional Court decision of 3 March 2009, at paragraph 49.

22 Constitutional Court decision of 3 March 2009, at paragraph 81.

23 Constitutional Court decision of 3 March 2009, at paragraphs 58–9; see also below 'The constitutional standard for e-voting' where this argument is discussed.

24 Cf. Constitutional Court decision of 3 March 2009, at paragraphs 160–64. The Court may also have been influenced by the fact that March 2009 was a mere six months prior to the next Bundestag election.

machines, against the Council of Europe's Recommendation on legal, operational and technical standards for e-voting.[25] It does mention the Dutch initiative 'We do not trust voting computers', but only because the Chaos Computer Club refers to the Dutch initiative and incorporates their findings in its own advisory opinion.[26]

The Constitutional Court's Reasoning

The Constitutional Court's judgment on the deployment and use of voting machines in the 2005 elections is divided into two main parts: firstly the constitutional standard of public elections and its consequences for the use of e-voting in general (section B.II of the judgment, paragraphs 105–37) and secondly the application of this constitutional standard to the relevant legal provisions, i.e. section 35 Federal Electoral Act and the Federal Ordinance (section B.III and B.IV of the judgment, paragraphs 138–54), and the use of the particular NEDAP voting machines (section B.V of the judgment, paragraphs 155–8).

The constitutional standard of public elections

The Court starts out with general remarks about the role of the public in elections and the importance of public scrutiny of the electoral process. The text of the Constitution, however, does not make any explicit reference to elections being public or having to comply with publicity requirements – it is just codified in section 31 of the Electoral Act that polling shall be public. Therefore, the Court deduces the concept of public elections from the constitutional principles of democracy, the republic and the rule of law, as these are mentioned in article 20 of the Constitution.[27]

Of particular importance here is the Court's understanding of the relation between democracy, trust and elections: 'The public nature of elections is [the] fundamental precondition for democratic political will-formation. It ensures the correctness and verifiability of the election events, and hence creates a major precondition for the well-founded trust of the citizen in the correct operation of the elections'.[28]

The Court here shows a somewhat functional understanding of the 'publicness' of an election. That an election is held in public is not an end in itself, but rather a means to ensure that trust and confidence can be built and sustained. It is that trust,

25 Rec(2004)11of the Committee of Ministers to member states, adopted by the Committee of Ministers on 30 September 2004 at the 898th meeting of the Ministers' Deputies.

26 Constitutional Court decision of 3 March 2009, at paragraph 84.

27 Constitutional Court decision of 3 March 2009, at paragraph 108.

28 Constitutional Court decision of 3 March 2009, at paragraph 107. To use 'the' instead of 'a' in my view better reflects the German original text.

the Court emphasizes, which enables a democracy to exist. Elections are crucial in that regard, because elections form the 'fundamental act of legitimisation'[29] of a government. To cast a vote in an election constitutes the major element of the transfer of public power from the people to the state bodies; it is the act in which a 'government of the people, by the people, for the people' is created. The Federal Constitutional Court here uses the phrase that casting a vote 'constitutes the basis for political integration'.[30] This refers to the idea that elections are not just a way to choose leaders and staff political institutions, but that elections offer a means and a moment to 'integrate' individual citizens to exercise public power collectively. In doing so, all individual citizens of a nation form a collective will. They create state unity and, ideally, experience a quasi-spiritual community. This so-called 'theory of integration' (Integrationslehre) has a long tradition in German political and constitutional thinking[31] and has featured prominently in several Constitutional Court decisions, in particular in those dealing with electoral law.[32]

Only an elected government can legitimately exercise power in a democracy. This legitimacy is based on the fact that the people know that the election with its specific outcome result is a genuine expression of their will. For the Court, an election without the trust of the electorate is insufficient. It is not enough that an election simply is free and fair and that a government has been democratically elected – the people must also be confident that this has been the case. The fact and the perception of the fact form the two sides of the same coin: compliance with the constitutional election principles (that is that an election has been free, fair, secret etc.) and confidence in compliance with them, constitute preconditions for a viable democracy.

The Court continues to emphasize that transparency and openness are essential conditions for the formation of such trust:

> The democratic legitimacy of the elections *demands* that the election events be controllable so that manipulation can be ruled out or corrected and unjustified suspicion can be refuted. This is *the only way* to facilitate the well-founded trust of the sovereign in the correct formation of the representative body. ... *Only* if the electorate can reliably convince itself of the lawfulness of the transfer act, if the elections are therefore implemented 'before the eyes of the public' is it *possible* to guarantee the trust of the sovereign in Parliament being composed

29 Constitutional Court decision of 3 March 2009, at paragraph 109.

30 Constitutional Court decision of 3 March 2009, at paragraph 109.

31 This theory was (probably) first elaborated on by Rudolf Smend in his book *Verfassung und Verfassungsrecht* of 1928. For an English account see the chapter on Smend in A. Jacobson and B. Schlink (eds), *Weimar: A Jurisprudence of Crisis* (Berkeley, CA, University of California Press, 2000).

32 See for example Judgement of the Second Senate of the Federal Constitutional Court of 4 July 2012 in the combined cases 2 BvC 1/11 and 2 BvC 2/11 (BVerfGE 132, 39) on the right to vote for Germans living out of the country.

> in a manner corresponding to the will of the voters that is necessary for the functioning of democracy and the democratic legitimacy of state decisions.[33]

For the Constitutional Court, individual citizens have no other tool at hand but the possibility of monitoring whether elections comply with the constitutional requirements. It is not sufficient that, of course, parliament and the government are already under a constitutional duty to ensure that the election procedure is designed constitutionally and is implemented properly, as this cannot impart the necessary legitimacy.[34] This also is demonstrated by the use of the word 'Grundvoraussetzung' (fundamental precondition, at paragraph 107 of the judgment), which is somewhat tautological and in a sense unnecessary as any (pre-)condition, even if it were not deemed 'fundamental', would have to be complied with. Only by transparency can the citizens ensure that their transfer of power has been accurate and does not suffer from a shortcoming. The democratic legitimacy of the elections requires that the election events be controllable so that manipulation can be ruled out or corrected and unjustified suspicion can be refuted.[35]

While in this first part of the judgment the Court makes it clear that 'controllability' is indeed a constitutional requirement of elections in general, the following paragraphs of the judgment become more detailed on the features and characteristics with which this public monitoring of elections has to comply. The principle of public elections gets transferred into a practical standard with which every electoral procedure, including e-voting, has to comply. The Court here answers the questions of what it practically means when 'the electorate' has to convince itself that an election has been lawful, who exactly has to be able to control the different steps in an election, and to what extent this control has to be possible.

On the first of these aspects the Court draws on the so-called 'principle of the republican state', a German Constitutional law term which encompasses ideas of democracy:

> In a republic , elections are a matter for the entire people and a joint concern of all citizens. Consequently, the monitoring of the election procedure must also be a matter for and a task of the citizen. Each citizen must be able to comprehend and verify the central steps in the elections reliably and without any special prior technical knowledge.[36]

On the second aspect (extent of the public control of elections) the Court employs an all-encompassing principle and states that all *essential* steps in the elections

---

33 Constitutional Court decision of 3 March 2009, at paragraph 109 (my emphasis, references omitted).

34 Constitutional Court decision of 3 March 2009, at paragraph 109.

35 Constitutional Court decision of 3 March 2009, at paragraph 109.

36 Constitutional Court decision of 3 March 2009, at paragraph 110.

have to be subject to public examination unless other constitutional interests justify an exception.[37] Particular significance attaches here to the monitoring of the casting of the ballot (the 'election act') and the counting and tabulation of results ('the ascertainment of the election result').[38] The voter has to 'reliably comprehend whether his or her vote is unfalsifiably recorded and included in the ascertainment of the election result, and how the total votes cast are assigned [to the different candidates/parties] and counted'.[39] The standard is, thus, both subjective and objective: every voter has to be able to convince himself or herself that his/her own ballot has been cast as intended and counted as cast. At the same time the entire system of tabulation of the results must be understandable to him or her. This does, however, not mean that every single act in the electoral management cycle, in the preparation and execution of an election, needs to be entirely public. Preparatory work by election officials does not need to be done under direct public scrutiny.[40] The Court thus employs a flexible standard with a presumption for public inspection in all electoral matters.

The constitutional standard for e-voting

Against this background, the Constitutional Court then develops a constitutional standard for the introduction and operation of e-voting (paragraphs 118–32 of the judgment) and the legislative frame (act of parliament, governmental regulation, administrative decision) in which this standard has to be implemented (paragraphs 133–7). In the judgment, the Court only had to deal with 'voting machines' (Wahlgeräte) as they were practically in use at the time and consequently only refers to those. But when its starts its reasoning on the constitutional standard of their deployment, it adds a qualifier, which effectively imposes that standard on all forms of e-voting as it now refers to 'voting machines which record the voters' votes in electronic form and determine the result of the election electronically'.[41] The Court itself may not have meant to place any particular significance on this formulation. It may have used it to indicate a distinction from purely mechanical voting devices. But since this kind of machine is nowhere in use anymore, the effect of the formulation is that all types of e-voting (including 'i-voting' on the internet) from the outset fall within the ambit of the Court's reasoning.

As a first consequence of its earlier reasoning on the public nature of elections, the Constitutional Court requires that when electronic voting machines are to be used it must be possible to check, reliably and without special expert knowledge, the essential steps in the casting of the vote and in the counting and tabulation of the results.[42] While this in itself is not surprising, but a rather consequent

37 Constitutional Court decision of 3 March 2009, at paragraph 112 (my emphasis).
38 Ibid.
39 Constitutional Court decision of 3 March 2009, at paragraph 113.
40 Constitutional Court decision of 3 March 2009, at paragraphs 113–14.
41 Constitutional Court decision of 3 March 2009, at paragraph 118.
42 Constitutional Court decision of 3 March 2009, at paragraph 119.

application of a defined legal standard, the court offers an additional argument to reinforce its claim. Here the court invokes the potentially greater risk e-voting poses to a manipulation of an election. E-voting is 'susceptib[le] to manipulation' and 'amenab[le] to error'.[43] Errors in the voting machine software are difficult to recognize from outside. 'Over and above this, such errors can affect not only one individual election computer, but all the devices used'.[44] In contrast to traditional vote-casting channels 'a major impact may in principle be achieved with relatively little effort by encroachments on electronically controlled voting machines'.[45] Manipulating just one voting machine can already change the votes of hundreds of voters; manipulations of the software running on an entire type of voting machine could affect even more votes. Because of this high degree of potential harm, which errors or manipulation could induce in elections, the Court concludes that special precautions need to be taken when employing e-voting in order to comply with the principle of the public nature of elections.[46]

It is therefore not enough that the voter should just trust the proper operation of an e-voting system. Instead, every voter must be able to verify – also without more detailed knowledge of computers – whether his or her vote has been 'recorded truthfully', i.e. that the vote has been cast as intended, stored and eventually counted as cast. In the view of the Court, it is not sufficient if the voter must rely on the functionality of the system without the possibility of personal inspection. Voting machines like the ones that had been used offer no practical proof of their truthful recording – usually the result is shown on a summary paper printout or an electronic display. With such limited evidence, voters and election officials can only examine whether the voting machine has processed as many votes as voters have been marked in the register by the polling staff, but it is 'not easily recognisable'[47] whether there have been programming errors in the software or deliberate election falsifications through manipulation of the software or of the voting machines.

In almost the same breath as its strict explanation of why e-voting with electronic storage of the vote cannot possibly be constitutional and why the degree of trust voters would have to have towards a machine cannot possibly be the basis for a credible election, the Court offers a *prima facie* way out. Just one paragraph later the judges point out that e-voting systems exist that print out a visible paper report of every single vote cast for the respective voter (in addition to electronic recording of the vote in the machine), 'which can be checked prior to the final ballot and are then collected to facilitate subsequent checking'.[48] However, as I

43 Constitutional Court decision of 3 March 2009, at paragraph 120.
44 Ibid.
45 Ibid.
46 Ibid.
47 Constitutional Court decision of 3 March 2009, at paragraph 122.
48 Constitutional Court decision of 3 March 2009, at paragraph 123.

will point out later, the e-voting systems the Court refers to here have their own problems to comply with the judgment.

As the simple comparison between the numbers of voters recorded in the polling station and the result delivered by the machine cannot be constitutionally sufficient proof of the correct functioning of an e-voting system, neither can the examination of sample devices in the context of a type approval procedure.

This is the second consequence the Court draws from its principle of a public nature of elections: When the Court emphasized that *each citizen* must be able to comprehend and verify the central steps in the elections reliably and without any special prior technical knowledge, it had to conclude that examinations and certifications of voting machines in a designated procedure prior to their deployment could not be sufficient. In recent years, some authors have claimed that mathematical calculations could be employed to show that there have been no manipulations to an e-voting system.[49] But in my view it would still be very doubtful whether the Constitutional Court would accept verifiability in electronic voting as adequate, even if it could be proved beyond any doubt according to the scientific standard of the day that the e-voting system has operated lawfully. For the average voter (without technical knowledge) all kinds of mathematical proofs remain a mystery.

It seems, too, that it would not be enough if the voting machines used in an election were to be tested officially ahead of an election with respect to their compliance with certain security requirements and their proper technical functioning. An election cannot be held to be under public scrutiny when only a simulation of the election is observed and supervised. Public trust in the electoral process is not built by a simulation of an election, but by public scrutiny of the election as such. Instead, it is necessary that everybody can verify an e-voting system when it is actually used in an election. All kinds of official testing neglect the personal experience of a voter understanding the voting procedure. Technical examinations and official approval procedures – whether they are done ahead of an election or during an election – can only be performed by interested specialists. By relying on such an evaluation, a crucial part of the election procedure is removed from the ordinary citizen. Consequently, even a comprehensive bundle of technical and organizational security measures (e.g. monitoring and safekeeping of the voting machines, comparability of the devices used with an officially checked sample at any time, criminal liability in respect of election falsifications and local organization of the elections) cannot compensate for a lack of controllability by the citizen of the essential steps in the election procedure.[50]

49 M. Henning, D. Demirel and M. Volkamer, 'Öffentlichkeit vs. Verifizierbarkeit – Inwieweit erfüllt mathematische Verifizierbarkeit den Grundsatz der Öffentlichkeit der Wahl', in *Transformation juristischer Sprachen, Tagungsband des 15. Internationalen Rechtsinformatik Symposiums (IRIS) 2012* (Vienna, OCG, 2012), pp. 213–20.

50 Constitutional Court decision of 3 March 2009, at paragraph 126.

The Court's evaluation of e-voting legislation

As regards the legislative frame in which e-voting would have to be implemented, the Constitutional Court employs a more lenient standard. The 'major requirements' for the implementation and use of e-voting would have to be regulated by an act of parliament, including the 'permissibility of the deployment of voting machines and the fundamental prerequisites for their deployment'.[51] This would most likely refer to decisions on the kind of e-voting system (i.e. DREs, scanners, internet voting), and decisions on whether there would have to be a back-up system in every polling station, etc. The more detailed preconditions for the approval of voting machines, as well as the procedures to be complied with, the details on the use of the voting machines in the elections and the guarantee of the principles of electoral law in the concrete deployment of voting machines, by contrast, do not require any detailed parliamentary regulation, but can be regulated by the government by means of an ordinance or a regulation.[52]

Based on all this background, the Court held that while the provision which generally created the possibility to cast a vote by way of e-voting (and granted the Federal Ministry of the Interior the authority to regulate all necessary details by way of an ordinance) passed constitutional scrutiny, the specific ordinance which provided for the implementation and use of voting machines was held to be unconstitutional. The Court held that the 'Federal Voting Machine Ordinance' did not ensure that only those voting machines could be approved (and used) which comply with the constitutional preconditions of the principle of the public nature of elections, previously laid out in the judgment:

> It particularly does not emerge from the Federal Voting Machine Ordinance that only voting machines may be deployed which enable the voter in casting his or her vote to ensure reliable monitoring of whether his or her vote is recorded in an unfalsified manner. The ordinance also does not make any concrete content and procedural requirements as to reliable subsequent monitoring of the ascertainment [read: tabulation] of the results.[53]

The machines actually used in the 2005 elections did not comply with the constitutional requirements either: none of the different types used provided effective monitoring of the casting of the ballot or the reliable verifiability of the election result. The votes were exclusively recorded on an electronic storage medium. Neither the voter nor the polling staff in the station, nor the citizens present in the polling station, were able to check whether the votes cast were recorded by the voting machines without falsification. Using the display on the control unit, the polling staff could only recognize whether the voting machines registered *a* ballot, but not whether the votes were recorded by the voting machines without changing

51 Constitutional Court decision of 3 March 2009, at paragraph 136.

52 Constitutional Court decision of 3 March 2009, at paragraph 137.

53 Constitutional Court decision of 3 March 2009, at paragraph 149 (my insertion).

the content in any way.[54] The counting and tabulation of the results by the voting machines also could not be verified by the public, since this was only done inside the machine. Nobody could verify whether the valid votes cast were correctly allotted to the candidates and parties. Everybody had to rely on a summary paper printout or an electronic display. A public examination was impossible.

This total defeat of the e-voting proponents (and the federal government) was only mitigated by the fact that the Court explicitly held that there would be no need to repeat the elections, not even in those constituencies which had used the voting machines, not the least because there were no indications that voting machines had worked incorrectly or might have been manipulated, and hence that the election result would have been different in the constituencies concerned without the deployment of the computer-controlled voting machines. In the eyes of the Court, the 'possible impact on the composition of the 16th German Bundestag can be regarded as marginal at most'.[55]

Consequences of the Judgment for E-voting

Since the judgment of the Constitutional Court, e-voting has no longer been in use in Germany, neither in the form of the traditional voting machines nor by other means. The judgment requires the government at least to issue a new federal ordinance on voting machines, since the previous one has been declared invalid. It would be necessary to add additional safeguards to the legal conditions required for voting machines so that indeed every voter is able to check the essential steps in the casting of the vote and in the determination of the results, reliably and without special expert knowledge, in order that the Court's condition be fulfilled.

This has not happened. The judgment was delivered in March 2009, and in September 2009 the next elections of the Bundestag were held. No voting machines were used in those elections. But in the years since 2009 no effort was made to rewrite the federal ordinance or to develop a new concept of circumstances under which voting machines could possibly be used again. The Bundestag election of 2013 was held in approximately 80,000 polling stations, in which traditional ballot papers were used, and an additional 10,000 polling districts for postal ballots. Not a single voting machine was used.

The Court's Suggestions for Improved Voting Machines

This total discontinuation of a technology which obviously offers some advantages (speed of vote counting, convenience for the voter, no unintended invalid ballots) may seem strange. Even more so when the parts of the judgment are considered in which the Constitutional Court seems to be inclined to be open to the deployment

54 Constitutional Court decision of 3 March 2009, at paragraph 157.

55 Constitutional Court decision of 3 March 2009, at paragraph 164.

of improved voting machines. In the judgment, the Court explicitly left the door open for electronic voting machines if the constitutionally required possibility of a reliable correctness check is ensured. The court even made quite specific suggestions in that regard:

> In particular, voting machines are conceivable in which the votes are recorded elsewhere in addition to electronic storage. This is for instance possible with electronic voting machines which print out a visible paper report of the vote cast for the respective voter, in addition to electronic recording of the vote, which can be checked prior to the final ballot and is then collected to facilitate subsequent checking.[56]

This 'voter-verifiable paper audit trail' ('VVPAT') seems to fulfil all the requirements put forward in the judgment. The voting machine does not only store and count the votes, but is equipped with a second, independent verification system, which every voter without computer knowledge can understand. With the paper slip at hand the voter can verify that his or her vote was cast as he or she had intended.

The Court went on to indicate particular technical solutions, such as the 'digital election pen' or a voting slip scanner.[57] The 'digital election pen' refers to a technology in which the voter uses a pen with a camera for the marking of a ballot which is printed on special, 'digital paper'. For the voter, the ballot paper looks like a traditional ballot paper, but it contains a microscopic dot pattern which uniquely identifies the position coordinates on the paper. The digital pen uses this pattern to read where the voter marks the ballot paper, and with it the candidate/party the voter has chosen, and uploads it to a computer. The voter still puts the marked ballot paper in the box. But the counting is done on the basis of the stored votes in the computer while the ballot papers are only used for the verification of the computer result.

A voting slip scanner records the information on a ballot paper subsequent to the actual voting. This can be done by using a normal ballot paper to cast the vote and putting it in the ballot box. After the vote is closed a scanner reads the ballot papers one after the other and automatically counts and tabulates the votes.

In Germany, none of these technologies have yet been introduced, because they all carry operational and legal risks which made the potential political costs of introducing the technology just too high. In fact, the Constitutional Court itself in the voting machines judgment set up criteria which make the introduction of e-voting systems with VVPAT highly cumbersome.

56 Constitutional Court decision of 3 March 2009, at paragraph 123.

57 Ibid.

Verification of the Result by Each Individual Voter

The Court made clear that it must be possible for the voter to check all the essential steps in the casting of the vote and in the determination of the results reliably and without special expert knowledge. When voting machines with a paper slip are introduced, the problem of verification seems to be solved, but it has only moved from the individual ballot to the counting/tabulation of all the votes cast using a single machine.

For the individual voter it is easy to compare the paper slip with his or her previously cast vote at the machine. But the counting and tabulation procedure is still done by the machine. The voter has to rely on the functionality of and trust in the correct working of the machine. Of course, the polling officials can compare all the paper slips with the result stored in the machine to verify that the votes were counted as cast. The Constitutional Court seems to have had this in mind when it stated that the voter must be able to verify whether his or her vote is recorded truthfully 'at least as a basis for a subsequent re-count, if the votes are initially counted with technical support'.[58]

But the Court seems to have paid little attention to the fact that this requirement of a personal possibility to inspect the machine's vote count renders it almost useless: a verification of the automatic counting by the machine is only possible with a subsequent manual counting. However, if the result of every machine would have to be counted manually again there is no point in using voting machines in the first place. Every machine count without manual recount means that again the machine has to be trusted, in other words that the voter (and everybody else) must rely on the functionality of the system. The Court's emphasis on the individual's possibility to perform personal verification leaves every machine count without manual recount open to a legal attack.

It seems highly unlikely that the Constitutional Court would accept a verification regime in which only in a number of randomly selected polling stations would the results of the voting machines be recounted manually. Firstly, the Court emphasized that *each citizen* must be able to comprehend and verify the central steps in the elections reliably and without any special prior technical knowledge.[59] Secondly, in its discussion of voting machines with a printed paper slip, the Court held that 'the result of the election can be reliably checked by the election authorities or by *interested citizens* without any special prior technical knowledge'.[60] This requirement of verification by each interested citizen seems to be fulfilled only if a manual recount has to be done whenever a single voter asks for it. It seems neither to be possible to require a voter to provide facts on which a suspicion of manipulation could be based nor to refer her to another polling station, in which the results of the voting machines are subjected to (randomly

58 Constitutional Court decision of 3 March 2009, at paragraph 121.

59 Constitutional Court decision of 3 March 2009, at paragraph 110 (my emphasis).

60 Constitutional Court decision of 3 March 2009, at paragraph 124 (my emphasis).

selected) verification recounts. In either case the voter would effectually be told to rely on the functionality of the system.

Furthermore, to lodge a complaint in the post-election 'election scrutiny procedure' (Wahlprüfungsverfahren), a citizen would have to show some piece of information which indicates that a manipulation or malfunction of a voting machine did happen. However, to show just that, a recount of the paper slips would be necessary, because this is the only way to determine discrepancies between the machine count and the manual count of the paper print outs.

The simple possibility that a manual recount could be requested by any voter for any voting machine implies a heavy burden on the election management body and makes the employment of voting machines highly unappealing. The requirement of a 'correctness control by the citizens' ('bürgerschaftliche Richtigkeitskontrolle')[61] whenever voting machines are employed has led the election authorities to refrain from the introduction of upgraded voting machines, including machines with VVPAT.

Secrecy of the Vote and Protection against Manipulations

Although the Constitutional Court placed the main accent on the verification of the counting and tabulation of the votes, the judgment also seems to apply the standard of monitoring elections and public control of them to a wider context:

> Only by the possibility of *monitoring whether the elections comply with the constitutional election principles* is it possible to ensure that the delegation of state power to the people's representation, which forms the first and most important part of the uninterrupted legitimisation chain of the people to the bodies and office-holders entrusted with state tasks, does not suffer from a shortcoming.[62]

Here the Court does not refer to the counting of the results only, but to the constitutional election principles which are stipulated in Article 38(1) of the German Constitution: 'Members of the German Bundestag shall be elected in general, direct, free, equal and secret elections'. This reference to the public monitoring of all other requirements of free and fair elections – of which secrecy is an essential one – leads to question whether e-voting could be employed in a way that makes the public control of the secrecy of the vote possible.

Individual control of the secrecy of the vote would imply that every voter could convince himself/herself that the entire technical process of the e-voting system employed does not allow any breaches of the secrecy of his/her vote and ensures the security of the election against any other kind of manipulation.

---

61 W. Schreiber, *Bundeswahlgesetz* (Köln, Carl Heymanns Verlag, 2013), § 35, at paragraph 2.

62 Constitutional Court decision of 3 March 2009, at paragraph 109.

Such a legal condition requires a certain design of voting machines with paper audit trails, which ensure that no connection could be established between the paper slip and the voter. With technologies like the digital pen it gets more complicated as the pen is usually returned to the polling staff after every vote cast by the voter and the information on the pen is transferred to a central computer unit. Thus, the system has to ensure in a convincing way for the voter that the secrecy of her vote has not been compromised in the process of such transfer. Hence, an election management body that would like to introduce e-voting in the light of this Court judgment would not only have to ensure the secrecy of information that has been stored electronically. It would also have to find a way to convince every individual voter without computer knowledge that he or she does not have to trust the secrecy of the e-voting system but that he or she can understand that the vote is secret. The election authority would, finally, have to include the time factor in its consideration: that is it has to make sure that the memory module in the e-voting system, which stored the information during the vote casting, could not somehow be hacked or reprogrammed while it is stored after an election (in Germany up to four years), with more sophisticated technology, to reveal the individual vote of a voter. To ensure the secrecy of the vote in any kind of e-voting system seems to be only possible with technical means and it is doubtful whether such means would be adequate to fulfil the requirement of public verification and monitoring by anybody 'without a more detailed knowledge of computers'. In its judgment of 3 March 2009, the German Constitutional Court did not explicitly rule on the standard of public monitoring or verification of the secrecy of the vote as this was not necessary for the case it had to decide. But the approach taken by the Court and the possible consequences outlined above show that the question of secrecy of the vote, and with it security of the system against manipulation, carry an enormous constitutional weight and involve high legal risks which would have to be considered thoroughly before the introduction of a new e-voting system in Germany.

Furthermore, the goal of protecting an electronically stored or transferred vote against manipulation or a breach of secrecy may lead an election authority to make great technical and organizational efforts with high costs, only to be constantly challenged by activist groups that would try to find ways to show that the system is still neither safe nor secret. This is what happened to the Dutch authorities when their original voting machines were subjected to critical scrutiny by an activist group which refuted one argument after the other which the authorities brought forward to 'prove' the security of their e-voting system. The experience of the Dutch authorities can well be applied to other jurisdictions: every effort by election authorities to make an e-voting system safe against manipulations and breaches of the secrecy of the vote may only be seen as an incentive for hackers, activist groups or critical individuals to show that the system can in fact be compromised and that manipulations and breaches of the secrecy of the vote are still possible, and to prove the government or election management body to be wrong. Every effort to further improve the security of the e-voting system may just create an even higher incentive or temptation to put more effort in to challenging the system. The election authority needs constantly to update, develop and improve its system for it not to be vulnerable to attacks. Hence, the election authority may be caught in a kind of 'security arms-race' where new layers of security need to be added all the time to keep the trust of the electorate. It may find itself in a situation where greater and greater monetary and human resources have to be devoted to create a constitutionally acceptable election environment. This is particularly important for the introduction of e-voting systems that include the casting of votes via the internet, such as the ones used or tested in Estonia, Norway or Switzerland.

It does not help to argue that the traditional voting channels such as ballot boxes or postal voting are not 100 per cent safe either. These traditional ways of casting a vote require only simple means to make them safe against almost (though not all) possible types of manipulations or breaches of secrecy, such as voting cabins or public counting of the ballots. Once a ballot box is opened, voters can be quite sure that their ballot papers cannot be traced back to them. The possibility of a breach of secrecy is higher with postal voting, but at least it is still limited to a few more or less random ballots. The scale of possible manipulations in the case of e-voting makes security considerations much more important and raises the constitutional standard.

Further Considerations

Besides these major burdens on elections authorities which would have to be dealt with before e-voting could be reintroduced in Germany, there are further considerations which need to be addressed.

An e-voting system with a voter-verifiable paper audit trail would require a regulation on how to deal with discrepancies between the machine count and an always possible manual recount. In my opinion there can be no doubt that the manual count of the paper print outs put in the ballot box would prevail, as only these are verifiable by the polling staff, interested voters and observers.

Another, related, problem is then how to deal with voters who, for whatever reason, do not put the paper printout in the ballot box. A single voter who does not put the paper into the box will automatically trigger a manual count, because otherwise it is impossible to determine in which way the foreseeable discrepancy between the machine count and the manual count will play out. Apparently, some available voting machines counter this problem by not handing out the paper to the voter, but by putting it automatically in an attached ballot box after the voter (and he or she alone) is able to see it for a couple of seconds behind a window within the machine.[63] With such a system, there will be no discrepancies between the number of votes cast with the machine and the number of paper slips in the ballot box. However, it is still necessary to introduce a procedure to deal with voters who

63 Apparently, this kind of voting machine is used in India.

claim that the vote on the slip that the machine has shown them under the window is not the one they had actually cast.

Conclusion

The judgment by the Constitutional Court in 2009 has effectively ended all initiatives on e-voting in Germany for the foreseeable future. The judges of the Constitutional Court may have thought that they merely outlawed a particularly crude and simple form of voting machines that do not fulfil minimum constitutional standards. They may have thought that they did not rule out improved ways of e-voting and that they even pointed to directions in which constitutionally viable e-voting systems may be developed. However, their principled and thoughtful decision is not easy to bring in line with the experimental and expert-driven reality of e-voting. The technological approach of information technology development in general, and e-vote systems in particular, is based on probabilities and algorithms rather than absolute principles: encryption codes work on the assumption that it would take so many years with the technology available *today* to break them. It is not possible to foresee when new technology may be available that could render a previously very good security system utterly useless.

Mathematicians may develop even more sophisticated and academically sound verification which really proves that no manipulation has occurred – any advance in technology seems to create an even greater distance between the few experts who really understand a technological system and the general population that can use the system, but could never comprehend its operation.

The German Constitutional Court decision of 2009 is a textbook case of a well-intended solution that in fact makes the problem insoluble. The Court gave an answer which effectively stopped any further development. In the interest of the best constitutional principles, it set a standard which no available and no conceivable e-voting system can completely fulfil.

But to dismiss the judgment of the Constitutional Court for its lack of technological thoughtfulness, or even vision, means overlooking the more significant philosophical and political core of the ruling: trust in public institutions by a society is such a fragile thing that sometimes a society needs to refrain from committing itself to certain developments to preserve it. If this means conducting things in an old-fashioned way, so be it. In terms of e-voting, every society has to find its own solution. But – and this is the important message we can draw from the German Court case – every advance may come with a price and every society has to decide if it is willing to pay it.

Bibliography and Further Reading

Maria Henning, Jurlind Budurushi and Melanie Volkamer, 'Elektronische Wahlen durch Stimmzettelbelege? Untersuchung möglicher Umsetzungen des Öffentlichkeitsgrundsatzes bei elektronischen Wahlen', in: *MultiMedia und Recht* (*MMR*), 2014, pp. 154–8.

Maria Henning, Denise Demirel and Melanie Volkamer, 'Öffentlichkeit vs. Verifizierbarkeit – Inwieweit erfüllt mathematische Verifizierbarkeit den Grundsatz der Öffentlichkeit der Wahl', in: *Transformation juristischer Sprachen, Tagungsband des 15. Internationalen Rechtsinformatik Symposiums (IRIS) 2012*, 2012, pp. 213–20.

Arthur Jacobson and Bernhard Schlink (eds), *Weimar: A Jurisprudence of Crisis*, Berkeley, CA: University of California Press, 2000.

Stephan Neumann, Anna Kahlert, Maria Henning, Philipp Richter, Hugo Jonker and Melanie Volkamer, 'Modeling the German Legal Latitude Principles', in: Maria A. Wimmer, Efthimios Tambouris and Ann Macintosh (eds), *Electronic Participation: Lecture Notes in Computer Science, 5th International Conference on eParticipation (ePart 2013)*, vol. 8075, Springer, September 2013, pp. 49–56.

Philipp Richter, *Wahlen im Internet rechtsgemäß gestalten*, Baden-Baden: Nomos, 2012.

Wolfgang Schreiber (ed.), *Bundeswahlgesetz*, 9th edition, Köln: Carl Heymanns Verlag, 2013.

Chapter 3
E-Voting in Austria: Legal Determination Matters

Melina Oswald[1]

Introduction

E-voting has had a rather brief history in Austria. The only elections in which e-voting has been applied in Austria so far were the elections of the National Students' Union in 2009. In 2001, the legislative basis of e-voting in the form of remote online voting was introduced for the elections of the representatives of students in the National Students' Union as well as for elections of the bodies of the Austrian Economic Chamber, both public-law associations representing their members' political interests. Then in 2008, e-voting was implemented in the Electoral Rules of the Students' Union.

The application of e-voting during the Students' Union's elections in 2009 was strongly criticised prior to its implementation. Furthermore the use of e-voting during the elections was unexpectedly low and in the aftermath several complaints were brought before the Constitutional Court. In 2011, the Constitutional Court ruled that the Electoral Rules of the Students' Union providing for e-voting were unlawful and quashed the respective regulation in the Electoral Rules, establishing strict requirements regarding the extent to which an e-voting system has to be specified by legal rules.

New Electoral Rules were only enacted in 2014. They do not provide for e-voting channels and with the legislative basis of e-voting for the elections of the students' representatives having been abolished, no signs point to a resumption of e-voting in elections for the Students' Union or elsewhere in the Austrian legal order. The establishment of e-voting for the election of students' representatives was intended to be a test phase with respect to elections of representative bodies of the state. Hence, the impacts of the ruling of the Constitutional Court declaring e-voting unlawful in this context reach far beyond the area of Students' Union elections.

In the following, first, the development of the implementation of e-voting for the elections of students' representatives will be briefly illustrated against the backdrop of the Austrian constitutional order. The second part of the chapter is dedicated to an analysis of the judgment of the Constitutional Court declaring

1 This chapter reflects only the author's personal views and opinions.

unlawful the e-voting system provided by the Electoral Rules of the Students' Union. Finally, the impact of this judgment beyond the elections of students' representatives will be assessed, concluding that the evolution of e-voting in Austria has – for the moment – come to an end.

E-voting in Austria

E-voting gained centre stage in the political agenda some 10 years ago when, influenced by respective developments at the EU level, the federal government enacted a strategy on the implementation of e-governance, and e-voting was discussed in the context of constitutional amendments of electoral law.[2] The only remote voting system provided for in the constitution is postal voting. Hence, there is no legal basis for e-voting with regard to those elections which are regulated in the constitution itself, i.e. the elections of the legislative bodies, the representative bodies at the municipal level, the Austrian members of the European Parliament and the President of the Republic of Austria. However, the implementation of e-voting in other areas led to a similar modification of the electoral principles as the implementation of postal voting in the constitution. In the following, I give a succinct overview of the relevant electoral principles and their evolution in the light of the implementation of postal voting through a constitutional amendment. Furthermore, I will present the legislative implementation of e-voting for the elections of self-administering bodies, e.g. the Students' Union, as well as the – so far single – application of e-voting for the elections of the representative bodies of the Students' Union in 2009.

Electoral Principles

The main features of the Austrian constitutional electoral system are the principle of proportional representation and the principles of equal, direct, personal, free and secret as well as universal suffrage.[3] These principles enshrined in the Austrian constitution are prescribed for the elections of the federal parliament, the parliaments of the states, the President of the Republic,[4] the Austrian members of the European Parliament and municipal representative bodies. In addition, Article

2 See Thomas M. Buchsbaum, 'Aktuelle Entwicklungen zu E-Voting in Europa' (2004) *Journal für Rechtspolitik*, 106; Klaus Poier, 'E-Voting – mehr als ein einmaliger Flop? Die Entscheidung des VfGH zur ÖH-Wahl 2009 und ihre Folgen für E-Voting in Österreich' in Gerhard Baumgartner (ed.), *Jahrbuch Öffentliches Recht 2013* (NWV 2013) 142.

3 Articles 23a, 26, 60, 95, 117 of the Federal Constitutional Law; Article 8 of the Austrian State Treaty, Federal Law Gazette 152/1955. For further details see Manfred Stelzer, *The Constitution of the Republic of Austria* (Hart 2011) 65 et seq.

4 Except for the principle of proportional representation.

3 of Protocol no. 1 of the European Convention on Human Rights[5] provides for the right to free elections of the legislature.[6] Furthermore, Article 39 paragraph 2 of the Charter of Fundamental Rights of the European Union provides that members of the European Parliament shall be elected by direct universal suffrage in a free and secret ballot.[7]

It has to be underlined that these constitutional prescriptions do not regulate the elections of bodies of the National Students' Union and the Austrian Economic Chamber, the only two institutions which have (or had)[8] a legislative basis for e-voting. The constitution prescribes that the organs of 'self-administering bodies', which include the National Students' Union and the Economic Chamber, are to be 'established according to democratic principles of [their] members'.[9] With regard to the National Students' Union, the Students' Union Act provides for biennial elections according to the principles of universal, equal, secret[10] and personal suffrage.[11] For the elections of the representative bodies of the Austrian Economic Chamber, the principles of universal, equal and secret suffrage and the principle of proportional representation are enshrined in the Austrian Economic Chamber Act.[12]

5 Which has constitutional status in Austria.

6 The interpretation of the principles according to Article 3 Protocol no. 1 may, however, differ from the electoral principles enshrined in the Federal Constitutional Law as in the interpretation of the former a comparative perspective in the light of the legal orders of the member states of the ECHR can play a role, see Christoph Grabenwarter, 'Briefwahl und E-Voting: Rechtsvergleichende Aspekte und europarechtliche Rahmenbedingungen' (2004) *Journal für Rechtspolitik*, 70.

7 See also Article 14 para. 3 TEU and Article 1 para. 3 of the Act concerning the election of the Members of the European Parliament by direct universal suffrage (1976) OJ L 278/5, (2002) OJ L 283/1.

8 N.B.: The legislative basis for e-voting was removed from the Students' Union Act in 2014, when the new Students' Union Act 2014 was enacted (Federal Law Gazette I 45/2014). Contrary to the Students' Union Act 1998, e-voting is no longer provided for Students' Union elections.

9 Article 120c para. 1 Federal Constitutional Law.

10 The principle of free vote is strongly connected with the principle of secrecy, see also Barbara Goby, 'E-Voting bei den ÖH-Wahlen 2009' in Sebastian Schmid, Veronika C. Tiefenthaler, Klaus Wallnöfer and Andreas W Wimmer (eds), *Auf dem Weg zum hypermodernen Rechtsstaat?* (Sramek 2011) 162.

11 Sec. 34 para. 1 of the Students' Union Act (*Bundesgesetz über die Vertretung der Studierenden [Hochschülerinnen- und Hochschülerschaftsgesetz 1998 – HSG 1998]*), Federal Law Gazette I 1999/22, last amendment Federal Law Gazette I79/2013. In 2014, the Students' Union Act 1998 was substituted by the Students' Union Act 2014, Federal Law Gazette I 45/2014, providing for the same principles.

12 Sec. 73 para. 1 of the Austrian Economic Chamber Act (*Bundesgesetz über die Kammern der gewerblichen Wirtschaft [Wirtschaftskammergesetz 1998 – WKG]*), Federal Law Gazette I 103/1998, last amendment Federal Law Gazette I 46/2014.

The Evolution of the Constitutional Electoral Principles

As has been mentioned, e-voting is not provided for the elections of the legislative bodies, the municipal representative bodies, the President of the Republic and the Austrian members of the European Parliament. In light of the constitutionally enshrined electoral principles, any form of remote e-voting for the elections of these bodies would have to be implemented by constitutional law. Any form of remote e-voting would at a minimum clash with the principles of secret, free and personal suffrage as they are understood in Austria. This becomes evident if the development of paper-based absentee voting in the Austrian constitution is considered.

In 1985, decades before the implementation of postal voting in the constitution, a law on municipal elections in the state of Lower Austria introduced paper-based remote voting by mail. The Constitutional Court quashed the provision as it was regarded as violating the principles of personal and secret suffrage.[13] In this judgment, the Constitutional Court clarified its understanding of the principles of free and secret vote as well as personal vote. This interpretation of the electoral principles is also significant for an assessment of the constitutionality of e-voting as far as the elections of legislative bodies, the municipal representative bodies, the President of the Republic and the Austrian members of the European Parliament are concerned.

According to the Court's interpretation, in light of free and secret suffrage the voter should not only be prevented from being influenced when casting her vote, but the voter must also be guaranteed not to fear any negative consequences from her choice. Furthermore, to be effective, the principle of secret vote, according to the Court, entails positive obligations of the part of the state, as it has to provide the features necessary for secret elections. The Court also stated that the principle of personal suffrage was to be understood as a requirement to be present personally at an election authority, i.e. either at a polling station or at any other state body entrusted with the tasks of the election authority, at the time the vote is cast. The purpose of the principle of personal vote was considered to be to prevent distortions of the voter's true will.

Postal voting, not yet constitutionally enshrined at this time, did not meet these conditions. In a system of postal voting, the duty of the legislator to guarantee the secrecy of the vote was considered to have been transferred to the individual voter.[14] A written statement from the voter confirming that the vote was taken personally

---

13 VfSlg. 10.412/1985.

14 Whether the principle of secret suffrage obliges the voter or merely protects her individual interests is not undisputed in scholarship (see Harald Eberhard, 'Die österreichische Wahlrechtsreform 2007' in Anna Gamper [ed.], *Entwicklungen des Wahlrechts am europäischen Fallbeispiel* [Springer 2010] 135 with further references). The constitutional amendment which introduced postal voting explicitly obliges the voter to affirm that the vote has been cast personally and unobserved (cf. Article 26 para. 6 Federal

and unobserved was not effective enough to guarantee the constitutional principle of the secrecy of the vote. Furthermore, casting a vote within the individual's private sphere was not compatible with the principle of personal vote. The Court acknowledged the necessity of providing alternative voting channels, e.g. for medical reasons, in order to implement the principle of universal voting. However, the Court deemed it indispensable that any such alternative included the attendance of a state representative at the time the vote was cast.[15]

As a consequence of the strict interpretation of the constitutional electoral principles by the Constitutional Court, remote voting had to be introduced by constitutional amendment. Hence, in 2007, the constitutional legislator amended the Federal Constitutional Law to provide for the possibility of paper-based postal voting under certain conditions.[16] Even if these conditions are not effectively controllable in practice, postal voting is theoretically only allowed if the reasons for its use are indicated by the voter (e.g. medical reasons, physical absence from the place of the voting authority or being abroad); further, the voter has to credibly identify herself and is obliged to affirm in writing that the vote has been cast personally and unobserved.[17]

This amounts to a modification and new understanding of the constitutional principles of personal, secret and free[18] suffrage, allowing postal elections under the conditions described.[19] In its ruling on an appeal brought before the Constitutional

Constitutional Law). Hence, the principle of secret suffrage is not at the free disposal of the voter (cf. again Eberhard, 135.).

15 Scholarship received this judgment critically as it was argued that, for example, the principle of personal suffrage only amounted to a prohibition of voting through representatives or legal entities; for further details see Christoph Grabenwarter and Beatrix Krauskopf, 'Entwicklungsstufen der Distanzwahl im Spannungsfeld des freien, geheimen und persönlichen Wahlrechts' in Anna Gamper (ed.), *Entwicklungen des Wahlrechts am europäischen Fallbeispiel* (Springer 2010) 156.

16 Articles 26 para. 6, 23a para. 4, 60 para. 1, 95 para. 4, 117 para. 2 Federal Constitutional Law. Before the implementation of postal voting, the use of so-called voting cards was enshrined for citizens living abroad (for an overview on the development of paper-based distance voting in Austria see Grabenwarter and Krauskopf [n 14] 166 et seq., see also Buchsbaum [n 2]).

17 The legislative implementation of postal voting in the procedural rules was criticised as not meeting these requirements adequately: Joachim Stern, 'Demokratie minus 2.0 – Die Distanzwahl ist verfassungsrechtlich höchst bedenklich' (2009) *juridikum*, 72.

18 The principle of free suffrage was explicitly formulated in the text of the Federal Constitutional Law only in 2007, Federal Law Gazette I 27/2007. Before this amendment, however, the principle was acknowledged by the Constitutional Court and enshrined in the Austrian State Treaty as well as the ECHR (see Grabenwarter and Krauskopf [n 14] 151–2). In its judgment on postal voting (VfSlg. 10.412/1985), the Constitutional Court treated the principle of free suffrage as being covered by the principle of secret suffrage.

19 Eberhard (n 13) 129; however, the principles of secret and personal suffrage were not abandoned by the introduction of postal voting, see Alexander Balthasar and Alexander Prosser, 'E-Voting in der "sonstigen Selbstverwaltung" – Anmerkgungen zum Beschluss

Court against the elections of the Austrian members of the European Parliament in 2014,[20] the Court reiterated that postal voting was constitutionally enshrined in the Austrian legal order and that this did neither violate the voting principles provided by legal acts of the European Union,[21] nor infringe the basic principle of democracy of the Austrian constitution.[22] As will be shown below, the modification of the constitutional electoral principles in order to introduce postal voting was transposed into the modification of the electoral principles for the elections of the bodies of the Students' Union by the implementation of e-voting in the Students' Union Act 1998.

As the constitutional amendments regarded postal voting in terms of paper-based remote voting and did not include e-voting,[23] the implementation of e-voting for the elections of the legislative bodies, the municipal representative bodies, the President of the Republic and the Austrian members of the European Parliament would have to be enshrined by another constitutional amendment.[24] As in the case of postal voting, the introduction of an e-voting system meeting similar security standards on the constitutional level would not amount to a 'total revision' of the constitution in the light of the democratic principle. In the course of the introduction of postal voting, the parliament requested the government further to advance arrangements for a future implementation of e-voting in Austria and thereby evaluate the respective experiences of other democratic states.[25] However, against the backdrop of the failed e-voting project at the level of elections of the

---

des VfGH vom 30. Juni 2011, B 1149, und zum Erkenntnis des VfGH vom 13. Dezember 2011, V 85–96' (2012) *Journal für Rechtspolitik*, 47 (pp. 55–6).

20 VfGH 22 August 2014, W I 2/2014.

21 The law of the European Union does, according to the Court, neither prescribe nor forbid the introduction of postal elections. Referring to the case law of the ECtHR regarding Article 3 Protocol No. 1 ECHR, the Court stated that since there was no common ground between the member states on the matter of postal voting, they had a wide margin of appreciation as to the regulation of voting procedures. The introduction of postal voting with sufficient safeguards as to the secrecy of vote and the personal use of the right to vote, aiming at a facilitation of the use of the right to vote for citizens, does, according to the Court, not deprive the voting principles of free and secret suffrage of their character and effectiveness.

22 Article 44 para. 3 of the Federal Constitution; for a 'total revision', i.e. a (constitutional) law infringing one of the basic principles of the constitution, a referendum is mandatory; see Stelzer (n 3) 32 et seq.

23 Cf. Grabenwarter and Krauskopf (n 14) 173.

24 See also Gabriele Kucsko-Stadlmayer, 'E-Voting und Europäischer Grundrechtsstandard' in Clemens Jabloner, Otto Lucius and Alfred Schramm (eds), *Theorie und Praxis des Wirtschaftsrechts. Festschrift für René Laurer* (Springer 2009) 94; Meinrad Handstanger, 'E-Voting und Wahlrecht' in Klaus Poier (ed.), *Demokratie im Umbruch: Perspektiven einer Wahlrechtsreform* (Böhlau 2009), 146.

25 Resolution 129 BlgNR 23. GP.

Students' Union, an establishment of e-voting through constitutional amendment is not likely in the near future.

The Legislative Implementation of E-voting

For the elections of the bodies of the Austrian Students' Union and the Austrian Economic Chamber the legislative implementation of e-voting was possible without a constitutional amendment as the above mentioned electoral principles relevant for these bodies are not enshrined in the constitution but provided by 'ordinary' law.[26] In 2001, voting by electronic means was enshrined in the respective laws.[27]

For the elections of students' representatives, e-voting was implemented through an administrative act. The Minister of Science and Research amended the Electoral Rules[28] in 2008,[29] introducing an e-voting system to be applied in addition to the traditional voting system. It was argued that especially in the area of students' representation an enhancement of the principle of universal vote was necessary as the mobility of students was ever increasing.[30] The implementation of e-voting for

26 As to the doctrine of the hierarchy of norms underlying Austrian constitutional law see Stelzer (n 3) 23 et seq.

27 Sec. 73 of the Economic Chamber Act and Sec. 34 para. 4 of the Students' Union Act 1998, Federal Law Gazette I 18/2001 and Federal Law Gazette I 29/2001. N.B: in 2014, a new Students' Union Act was enacted: Students' Union Act 2014, Federal Law Gazette I 45/2014. Contrary to the Students' Union Act 1998, e-voting is no longer provided for elections of the Students' Union. In the following, when reference is made to provisions of the Students' Union Act, the relevant provisions on e-voting in the prior Students' Union Act 1998 are addressed. As the elections of the representative bodies of the Students' Union are the only elections in which e-voting has been applied in Austria so far, the following discussion will focus on the legal bases for these elections.

28 The Electoral Rules have the legal form of an 'order', i.e. a general administrative act enacted by an administrative authority which has to have a legislative basis and be consistent with legislation and the constitution.

29 Federal Law Gazette II 351/2008. The software was developed by a private company according to a public procurement (see Gerda Marx, 'E-Voting bei den ÖH-Wahlen 2009' in Werner Hauser [ed.], *Jahrbuch Hochschulrecht 2010* [NWV 2010] 403–6). In 2014, new Electoral Rules were enacted (Federal Law Gazette II. 376/2014). They do not provide for e-voting, but for postal voting as a remote voting channel instead. In the following, when reference is made the Electoral Rules, the former Electoral rules, providing for e-voting, which were scrutinised by the Constitutional Court are addressed.

30 Goby (n 9) 170. With regard to the elections of the legislative bodies, the representative bodies of the municipalities, the President of the Republic, the Constitutional Court declared unconstitutional procedural rules that excluded citizens living abroad from the right to vote (VfSlg. 12.023/1989). These aspects, however, concerned the constitutionally enshrined electoral rules and, therefore, cannot be translated into the interpretation of universal suffrage along the lines of the Students' Union Act. In the context of the principle of universal suffrage, it must, furthermore, not be overlooked that

the elections of the bodies of the Students' Union, however, also encountered harsh critique by the student body and legal experts. It was, for example, criticised for being incompatible with constitutional standards of democratic decision making,[31] for violating data-protection law,[32] for not entailing sufficiently concrete safety and transparency measures,[33] and for using the Students' Union elections as a 'guinea pig' for the potential future implementation of e-voting at the constitutional level.[34]

The Austrian Students' Union Act 1998 specified the legal standards to be applied when e-voting would be introduced: the principles of universal, equal, secret and personal suffrage had to be adhered to, the system had to comply with the Data Protection Act, it had to meet certain standards regarding electronic signatures used during the process, and it had to guarantee that the electoral commission was able to fulfil its legal tasks.[35] The Act furthermore required any e-voting system to guarantee the secrecy of votes by using methods that would ensure tracing the votes back to the voter would be impossible; to provide for identification and authentication of the voter using only the data necessary for the election; to encrypt data and use electronic signatures in order to guarantee that votes would not be distorted; to provide for the possibility of changing the vote prior to casting it; to establish equivalence in the technical features with polling booths if e-voting were used as an in-person voting system; to legally oblige the voter to cast her vote unobserved, uninfluenced and personally; and to meet certain technical standards.[36]

The Application of E-voting at the Students' Union's Elections in 2009

At the elections of the representative bodies of the Austrian Students' Union in 2009, e-voting was – for the first and only time – applied in addition to the traditional voting procedure. Students had three options of casting their vote: in the traditional manner, in a polling booth during the election days; by making use of the newly established e-voting system via electronic terminals in the premises of the universities; or by casting their vote remotely via the internet.[37] The latter two options were accessible in advance, during the week preceding the start of the traditional voting period.[38]

---

even before the implementation of e-voting access to the elections of the Students' Union was rather broad in contrast to elections of state bodies, as elections were held on three subsequent weekdays on the premises of universities (Sec. 34 para. 2 Students' Union Act).

31 Stern (n 16).

32 Goby (n 9) 173–6.

33 Kucsko-Stadlmayer (n 23) 100–101.

34 Cf. Goby (n 9) 152–3.

35 Sec. 34 para. 4 Students' Union Act 1998.

36 Sec. 34 paras 5 and 6 Students' Union Act 1998.

37 Cf. Sec. 33 Electoral Rules.

38 Sec. 62 Electoral Rules.

The remote e-voting system consisted of an internet portal providing the users with information and linking them to the electronic booth. The Electoral Rules required the e-voting system to provide adequate state of the art measures in order to prevent associating the votes with the identity of the voter.[39] First, the voter had to identify herself with her 'citizen card', a chip card used for different e-government services.[40] The citizen card and a device necessary for its use were made available free of charge. The vote was cast via a web client.[41] Before the final vote was cast, the voter had to be given the chance to control her vote and, if necessary, to correct her entry.[42] After the vote was cast, the vote was encrypted and the voter had to affirm, using an electronic signature, that the vote had been cast personally, unobserved and uninfluenced. The vote was saved in its encrypted status until the end of the voting period. The electronic signatures were then removed and the votes mixed and subsequently decrypted and counted.[43]

The electoral commission used certain software that allowed it to start, interrupt or end the application of the e-voting system.[44] Members of the electoral commission as well as observers were allowed to inspect the source code of the web client.[45] Furthermore, the electoral commission was obliged to inform voters if their electronically cast vote had been cancelled as invalid, and to invite them to repeat the voting process by the traditional means.[46] The same procedure was applicable if less than three votes had been cast electronically for one eligible body.[47] The Electoral Rules also prescribed consideration of the standards set out in Rec(2004)11 of the Committee of Ministers to member states on legal, operational and technical standards for e-voting in the process of approval of the security standards of the e-voting system[48] as well as during the system's operation, especially by ensuring transparency of the process as well as secrecy of the vote.[49]

In application e-voting could not be considered a success: less than 2 per cent of the voters used the electronic channel,[50] the overall voter turnout, which had been

---

39 Sec. 64 para. 3 Electoral Rules.

40 Sec. 63 Electoral Rules.

41 Sec. 63 Electoral Rules.

42 Sec. 39 para. 5 Electoral Rules.

43 As to a detailed description of the e-voting procedure see Goby (n 9) 159–62.

44 Sec. 64 para. 4 Electoral Rules.

45 Sec. 62 para. 7 Electoral Rules.

46 Sec. 68 Electoral Rules.

47 Sec. 67 Electoral Rules. This was rightly criticised as not meeting the requirements of the principle of secret suffrage: Stern (n 16) 73.

48 Sec. 62 para. 3 Electoral Rules.

49 Sec. 65 para. 2 Electoral Rules.

50 This is remarkable especially if the characteristics of the concrete electorate – university students who represent a section of the society which is supposedly experienced with the use of the internet and does not fear the use of online technologies – are considered; in this regard see also Poier (n 2) 143. The reasons for this may be twofold: on the one hand, the practical need for remote voting systems as such may be lower than alleged, even for

extremely low in the same elections prior to the application of e-voting, sank from 28.7 per cent to 25.76 per cent, and the number of objections against the elections skyrocketed.[51] In the aftermath of the elections, several attempts were made to challenge the legal bases of e-voting (i.e. the legislative basis in the Students' Union Act 1998 as well as the implementation of e-voting in the Electoral Rules) in the Constitutional Court. Before the judgment at hand, the Court dismissed several complaints for formal reasons.

The Judgment of the Constitutional Court[52]

In its judgment of 13 December 2011 (VfSlg. 19.592/2011), the Constitutional Court finally ruled on the merits of the case. On the one hand, the Court approved the legislative implementation of e-voting in the Students' Union Act 1998 as consistent with constitutional requirements. On the other hand, it quashed the administrative Electoral Rules as unlawful, most notably because they did not sufficiently determine the e-voting procedure and its application. In this judgment the Court did not generally rule out the possibility of using e-voting in elections of bodies of self-administering associations. However, the requirements an e-voting system has to meet according to the Court would hardly be achievable in practice. Even though the judgment does not concern the application of e-voting at the constitutional level – which, as has been shown, would in any case need to be implemented by constitutional amendment – it can be regarded as generally having set the direction for future developments in the field of e-voting.

The Constitutionality of the Legislative Implementation of E-voting

The legislative basis for e-voting in the Students' Union Act 1998 was, according to the Court, not unconstitutional. The Court reiterated that the constitutionally enshrined electoral principles were not applicable in the present case. The specific electoral principles for the Students' Union were not enshrined in the constitution but in the Students' Union Act, thus, an act of ordinary law. Hence, the implementation of e-voting on the level of ordinary law was unproblematic

---

an electorate characterised by a high level of mobility and spontaneity (see Barbara Goby and Helmut Weichsel, 'Das E-Voting-Erkenntnis des VfGH: gesetzwidrige Ausgestaltung der ÖH-Wahlordnung' [2012] *Zeitschrift für Hochschulrecht*, 118 [p. 119]). On the other hand, the low use of e-voting during the elections of 2009 could have been caused by a lack of confidence among the voters in the newly established and highly discussed system. This latter aspect played an important role in the ruling of the Constitutional Court on the Electoral Rules for the Students' Union elections (see below).

51 See Goby and Weichsel (n 49) 122, with further references.

52 In the following, whenever reference is made to the judgment of the Constitutional Court, it refers to the Judgment of 13 December 2011, VfSlg. 19.592/2011.

as it merely constituted a further development of the voting principles.[53] As a consequence of the introduction of e-voting at the same normative level as the voting principles applicable for the elections of the Students' Union, the voting principles, especially the principles of personal and secret suffrage, were developed so as to include the general possibility of an e-voting system.

The only constitutional requirement for the elections of the bodies of the Students' Union was that the bodies be 'established according to democratic principles by the Students' Union's members'.[54] The Court clarified that these democratic principles were not to be equated with the constitutional electoral principles.[55] Contrary to the elections of the legislative bodies, the municipal representative bodies, the President of the Republic and the Austrian members of the European Parliament, the legislator, according to the Court, has a rather wide political margin regarding how to achieve democratic legitimacy in the bodies of self-administering associations. While the Court did not define this margin in general terms, it reiterated its prior case law on the elections of bodies of self-administering associations, according to which different deviations from the constitutional electoral principles were deemed to fall within the political margin of the legislator.[56] For example, postal voting prescribed for the elections of the bodies of the Agricultural Chamber had been deemed acceptable by the Constitutional Court long before the constitutional electoral principles were modified in this regard. In this case, very similarly to the reasoning on the legal basis of e-voting for the elections of the Students' Union in the present judgment, the Constitutional Court asserted that the introduction of postal voting by ordinary law could not violate voting principles which were enshrined on the same normative level, whereas the applicability of the constitutional electoral principles could not be deduced from the democratic principle of the constitution.[57]

According to the Court, sufficient legitimacy was achieved if the organs of self-administering bodies were elected autonomously by their members on a regular basis, thus allowing the members to influence their representatives in a democratic decision-making process. In light of the requirements for e-voting prescribed by the Students' Union Act 1998,[58] the Court had no doubt that these legal provisions set out the elections according to 'democratic principles'.

53 Similarly to the implementation of postal voting at the constitutional level, see *supra* 'The Evolution of the Constitutional Electoral Principles'.

54 See *supra* 'Electoral Principles'.

55 See also Kucsko-Stadlmayer (n 23) 99; Grabenwarter and Krauskopf (n 14) 173; Katharina Pabel and Michael Sonntag, 'E-Voting bei den ÖH-Wahlen gesetzwidrig' (2012) *Zeitschrift für Energie- und Technikrecht*, 175 (p. 179).

56 E.g. indirect elections and plurality votes (VfSlg. 17.951/2006) or the right to vote of legal entities (VfSlg. 14.440/1994).

57 VfSlg. 8590/1979.

58 See *supra* 'The Legislative Implementation of E-voting'.

On the subject of the verifiability of the electoral process, the Constitutional Court explicitly dissociated its reasoning from the judgment of the German Constitutional Court on voting machines. According to the German Court, the German constitution includes a principle of 'publicness' or public nature of elections.[59] The Austrian Court ruled that no such principle could be deduced from the constitutionally enshrined Austrian electoral principles. The German Constitutional Court derived the principle of the public nature of elections from the constitutional electoral principles in connection with the democratic and republican principles as well as the rule of law enshrined in the German Basic Law (Constitution). The German Court argued that adherence to the electoral principles and reliance on a voting system in that regard were necessary conditions for a functioning democracy. Hence, the democratic legitimacy of elections required a certain controllability of the electoral process.[60] Even though the same constitutional principles are enshrined in the Austrian constitution, for the Austrian Constitutional Court an explicit principle of the public nature of elections is not inherent in the Austrian constitutional order. Anyhow, in the case at hand the Court deduced similar arguments as to the necessary controllability and reliability of a voting system from the electoral principles (which, for the Students' Union, are enshrined in an act of ordinary law).[61] Hence, the Court followed a different doctrinal path to come to a similar outcome, i.e. that a voting system has to have a certain public controllability and verifiability: while the German Court derived the principle of the public nature of elections from the democratic and republican principles as well as the rule of law, and from this principle deduced a requirement of controllability and verifiability, the Austrian Court explicitly denied a constitutional principle of the public nature of elections, but interpreted the electoral principles (for the case at hand enshrined in an act of ordinary law) as requiring a voting system that could be verified and controlled by the voter and the public (mediated by the electoral commission).[62]

The Students' Union Act 1998 met this requirement. For, according to the relevant provisions, the Electoral Rules had to be designed so as to allow the electoral commission to fulfil all its legal duties, especially to monitor adherence to the electoral principles. According to the Court, the Electoral Rules had to be designed in compliance with these legal requirements, thus, rendering the e-voting system controllable, not just by the electoral commission, but also by the courts.

Furthermore, the Constitutional Court asserted that the respective legal provisions did not violate the Federal Act Concerning the Protection of Personal Data, as the powers of the electoral commission regarding personal data were

59 Judgment of the German Constitutional Court of 3 March 2009, 2 BvC 3/07, 2 BvC 4/07.

60 Ibid., para. 105 et seq.

61 See *infra* 'Verifiability and transparency'.

62 See *infra* 'Secret and personal vote: postal voting as a minimum standard' and 'Verifiability and transparency'.

sufficiently determined by law, and the law explicitly prescribed that the votes had to be anonymised before being submitted to the electoral commission.[63] According to the Court, the technical measures to be applied during the e-voting process could not be more strictly specified and if they were, they could even be problematic in light of the rapid development of technical standards.

The Unlawfulness of the Implementation of E-voting at the Administrative Level

Although the Constitutional Court did not generally rule out the introduction of e-voting, it came to the conclusion that the design of the e-voting system as provided by the Electoral Rules of the Students' Union implementing the respective provisions of the Students' Union Act 1998 was unlawful.

Interestingly, according to the Court, the Electoral Rules did not violate the voting principles established for the elections of students' representatives in the Students' Union Act, notably the principles of secret and personal suffrage. In this context, it is worth mentioning how the issue of early voting was addressed by the Court. The Court considered it unlawful that, according to the Electoral Rules, e-voting had to take place during the week before the traditional elections, because this contradicted a clear provision in the Students' Union Act 1998 which specified the exact election period without allowing any exceptions for the earlier operation of e-voting. Because of this clear breach of the Students' Union Act 1998, the Court did not have to discuss the issue of early voting with regard to a potentially lower level of information of the voter who decided to cast her vote via e-voting.[64] It has to be reiterated that, contrary to the constitutional electoral principles, free suffrage is not an explicit electoral principle for elections of the Students' Union according to the Students' Union Act. However, with regard to the constitutional requirement that the elections be designed along democratic principles,[65] the voting principles as a whole certainly intend to guarantee the free formation and expression of the voter's opinion. In its ruling on an appeal against the elections of the Austrian members of the European Parliament, the Court acknowledged early voting to be an inherent characteristic of postal voting as time for the delivery of ballots to the voter and from the voter to the voting commission had to be taken into consideration.[66] Arguably, however, the situation is rather different with (remote) e-voting as – certainly depending on the exact design of the e-voting system – the time frame for delivery is substantially shorter. Hence, the question of whether an e-voting system enabling early voting is compatible with the principle of free suffrage has not yet been answered.

---

63 For a different view according to which the legislative regulation was too indeterminate in this regard see Goby (n 9) 175–6; see also Marx (n 28) 397–8.

64 See Kucsko-Stadlmayer (n 23) 85; Goby (n 9) 163.

65 See *supra* 'Electoral Principles'.

66 VfGH 22 August 2014, W I 2/2014.

The main reason for the Court quashing the provisions on e-voting in the Electoral Rules was that they were too indeterminate.[67] The Court underlined that an electronic remote voting system created a tension between the principle of personal vote, which required identification of the voter, on the one hand, and the principle of secrecy of the vote on the other. Against this backdrop, the Electoral Rules had to detail sufficiently the technical system as well as the procedures to be applied so that a reliable control was possible.

Secret and personal vote: postal voting as a minimum standard

In order to assess whether the e-voting system met the electoral principles enshrined in the Students' Union Act,[68] it has to be kept in mind that the meaning of these principles had been modified by the introduction of e-voting. Just as the constitutional electoral principles had been modified by introducing postal voting via a constitutional amendment,[69] the principles enshrined in the Students' Union Act had been modified via an amendment of the Students' Union Act. The modification of electoral principles by the introduction of postal voting has to be considered rather similar to the modification of electoral principles by the introduction of remote e-voting through an amendment of the law at the same normative level, because both types of remote voting lead to similar risks with regard to the voting principles, especially the question of whether the vote is cast secretly, uninfluenced and personally.

As a consequence, according to the Constitutional Court, adherence to the electoral principles as modified by the establishment of postal voting constituted a certain minimum standard for the application of e-voting.[70] In other words, the Court stated that the electoral principles of the Students' Union Act, most notably the principles of secret and personal vote, were to be guaranteed at least to the extent that they were guaranteed when postal voting was applied.[71] Hence, for the

67 Here we can observe a certain contradiction to the Court's scrutiny of the legal provisions of the Students' Union Act 1998 in the light of the Act on Data Protection, as in the latter scrutiny it found that too high a legal specification of the technical measures to be applied could even be problematic in the light of the rapid development of technical standards; see *supra* 'The Constitutionality of the Legislative Implementation of E-voting'. In this regard see also Balthasar and Prosser (n 18) 76.

68 See *supra* 'Electoral Principles'.

69 See *supra* 'The Evolution of the Constitutional Electoral Principles'.

70 This has met with scepticism as the Students' Union Act 1998 did not provide postal voting for the elections of the Students' Union: Poier (n 2) 139; see also Pabel and Sonntag (n 54) 180.

71 As to the comparability of postal voting and e-voting regarding the necessary precautionary measures see also the Report of the Venice Commission on the Compatibility of Remote Voting and Electronic Voting with the Standards of the Council of Europe (2004), available at http://www.venice.coe.int/webforms/documents/CDL-AD%282004%29012.aspx. In this context it has to be considered that – of course depending on the concrete technical design of the system – e-voting could even meet higher security standards than

Court, the modification of the principles of secret and personal suffrage enshrined in the Students' Union Act 1998 by the implementation of e-voting was in principle equal to the modification of the same principles enshrined in the constitution by the introduction of postal voting.

However, the differences between postal voting and e-voting regarding the potential drawbacks of the systems, especially the higher vulnerability of an e-voting system to errors or manipulation due to its technical complexity, had, according to the Court, to be captured by creating particularly clear and specific procedural rules. Hence, e-voting did not generally violate the electoral principles in their modified form. The design of the voting procedure, however, mattered significantly.

Verifiability and transparency

In accordance with its prior case law on the state's positive obligations regarding adherence to the electoral principles,[72] the Court ascribed great importance to the transparency and verifiability of the e-voting system. Although, contrary to the German Constitutional Court, the Austrian Court did not acknowledge a principle of the public nature of elections in the context of the constitutional electoral principles,[73] it did, as will be shown subsequently, implicitly require of the design of the e-voting procedure a certain kind of 'publicness'.[74]

With regard to the legitimacy of election results, the role of the assigned electoral authorities guaranteeing the public's interest concerning the transparency, control and comprehensibility of the voting system is of utmost importance. During the election of students' representatives, the electoral commissions have several tasks, such as assessing the number of seats to be allocated to each organ, evaluating the nominations, overseeing the voting process, assessing the identity of the voter and the right to vote, deciding on the validity of a vote, analysing the results of the vote, allocating the seats to the candidates, announcing the results of the elections and deciding on objections against the election of some of the organs of the Students' Union.[75] Thus, the Constitutional Court required that the e-voting system employed in the election of the Students' Union be designed in such a way as to guarantee effective control of the procedure by the assigned authorities. Furthermore, subsequent control of the elections by the judiciary had to be possible.

According to the Constitutional Court, the e-voting system had to be reliably verifiable. Hence, it was necessary that the Electoral Rules regulated precisely how

---

postal voting, e.g. regarding the authentication of the voter or the submission of the vote: Balthasar and Prosser (n 18) 72 et seq.; see also Goby (n 9) 167.

72 See *supra* 'The Evolution of the Constitutional Electoral Principles'.

73 See *supra* 'The Constitutionality of the Legislative Implementation of E-voting'.

74 See also Balthasar and Prosser (n 18) 81–2.

75 Secs 39 and 45 Students' Union Act 1998, see also Secs 39 and 45 Students' Union Act 2014.

the electoral principles were concretely adhered to, as well as which procedures and technical systems were to be applied. Furthermore the methods and means by which the electoral commission could exercise control of the voting system, as well as the criteria to be considered thereby, had to be specified in the Electoral Rules.

The Constitutional Court asserted that the electoral commission had to be able to control the significant steps of the voting procedure and to assess the results without specific expert knowledge and without the help of experts.[76] Limiting the verification of the system to technical experts would certainly decrease the democratic standard of the elections.[77] In the systematic context of the Students' Union Act 1998 it was questionable whether this requirement had to be interpreted so strictly as to mean that the electoral commission should be able to control the e-voting system without any help at all: the Students' Union Act 1998 provided for technical support for the electoral commission in the form of a 'Confirmation Body' – a neutral, impartial and independent expert body along the lines of the Signature Law. Specifically, the Students' Union Act 1998 allocated a number of tasks to the Confirmation Body during the e-voting procedure, such as the certification of the technical components of the e-voting system with respect to relevant technical standards, supporting the electoral commission when the latter invalidated votes due to problems with the security or functionality of the system, and supporting the commission and the Minister of Science when dealing with complaints.[78] Since this Confirmation Body was provided for by the Students' Union Act (an act at the same normative level as the electoral principles applicable for the elections of the Students' Union), the requirement of verifiability had to be understood in the systematic context of the provisions of the same Act. Consequently, it would have to be considered lawful if the Electoral Rules also provided for support of the electoral commission by the Confirmation Body. From the Court's ruling it is not clear whether the Court considered this role of the Confirmation Body according to the Students' Union Act 1998. Since the newly established Students' Union Act 2014 offers no possibility for e-voting,[79] the function of the Confirmation Body in that regard has become obsolete as well. As to the general requirements for e-voting for Students' Union elections, it can be concluded that support of the electoral commission by technical experts would potentially ensure a sufficient standard of system verifiability, if this support were enshrined at the same normative level as the electoral principles. However, this would only be acceptable as long as the

76 This requirement has been met with scepticism by some: Poier (n 2) 154–5; Goby and Weichsel (n 49) 124; Pabel and Sonntag (n 54) 180; see also Balthasar and Prosser (n 18) 81.

77 See also Stern (n 16) 73. Furthermore, electoral procedures differ from other administrative procedures – where the support by experts is common – in the light of considerations on the rule of law (Poier [n 2] 154).

78 Sec. 34 para. 6, sec. 39 para. 5, sec. 44 para. 7, sec. 45 para. 8 Students' Union Act 1998.

79 See *infra* 'Outlook'.

dependence on technical experts would not lower the legitimacy of the elections in an extent that would counter the constitutional principle of democratic elections of the organs of self-administering bodies.[80]

In its decision to initiate the proceedings at hand, the Constitutional Court also announced that it would assess whether it was sufficient that the Electoral Rules only allowed the members of the electoral commissions and election observers to inspect the source code of the web client used in the e-voting system, or whether access should also be given to the public. In the proceedings before the Constitutional Court, the Minister of Science argued that it was not necessary to grant access to the wider public, because in a traditional voting system only the members of the electoral commission and the observers delegated by the parties are entitled to be present during the process of vote counting. In its final judgment, the Court did not mention this issue. It more generally required that the Electoral Rules set out the e-voting system such that its specifications are sufficient to allow the 'interested public' to verify the technical aspects of the voting procedure.[81]

Confidence of the individual voter

The Constitutional Court also touched upon the interests of the individual voter involved in the voting procedure asserting that, contrary to a traditional voting system, in an e-voting system adherence to the electoral principles could only be verified by voters having specific technical knowledge. Such knowledge could not be assumed for the vast majority of voters. From this, it can be concluded that the transparent verifiability of an e-voting system as elaborated above is not only necessary for the protection of public interests, but also the interest of the individual voter,[82] who needs to be assured that the voting principles are adhered to and that the vote is cast without distortions.

Outlook

As a consequence of the considerations set out above, the Constitutional Court quashed the provisions on e-voting in the Electoral Rules of the Students' Union. After the judgment of the Constitutional Court, the Electoral Rules were not amended until 2014.[83] The newly enacted Students' Union Act 2014,[84] containing the same electoral principles for the election of the Students' Union's bodies as the Students' Union Act 1998, removed the legal basis for e-voting for the Students'

80 See *supra* 'Electoral Principles'.

81 This again shows the similarity of the argument – although very different in doctrinal terms – with the principle of 'publicness' developed by the German Constitutional Court, see *supra* 'The Constitutionality of the Legislative Implementation of E-voting'.

82 See also Appendix I B.I. of Rec(2004)11.

83 Federal Law Gazette II 376/2014.

84 Federal Law Gazette I 45/2014.

Union and introduced postal elections as a remote voting channel instead. Accordingly, also the new Electoral Rules provide for postal voting as the only remote voting channel.

As has been pointed out above, the Court did not consider e-voting as a channel for elections that are not governed by the constitutional electoral principles[85] to be generally unlawful. The Court rather declared that the concrete design of the e-voting procedure at hand did not meet the necessary degree of specificity. According to the Constitutional Court, an e-voting system would have to be accompanied by highly specific rules of procedure. Importantly, the Court underlined that it is not sufficient that the system's verifiability and reliability merely be established by technical experts.

The high requirements determined for the e-voting system led to predictions that an e-voting system compatible with the conditions formulated by the Constitutional Court was not realisable in practice. In order to comply with the voting principles – whether enshrined in the constitution or in an act of ordinary law – a remote e-voting system will necessarily be of high technical complexity, because only a sophisticated technical system, using tools to identify the voter, encrypt and decrypt the votes and guarantee system security, will be able to comply with the voting principles, especially the principle of secret and personal suffrage.[86] It is highly questionable whether the particular tension between the necessary technical complexity of an e-voting system on the one hand, and the necessary transparency and controllability of the system on the other, can be overcome.[87] As long as technical standards do not develop enough for e-voting systems to fulfil both the requirements formulated by the Court – public verifiability of the system without lowering the legitimacy of the elections by creating dependency on technical experts, and compliance with the voting principles[88] – the ruling has to be understood as a rejection of e-voting for the near future.

Against this backdrop, it was argued that the Students' Union Act 1998 had to be interpreted in such a way that the introduction of an e-voting system must be possible in principle.[89] But in particular the requirement that an e-voting system

85 For these elections, an e-voting system would have to be introduced by constitutional amendment.

86 For a description of the e-voting procedure see *supra* 'The Application of E-voting at the Students' Union Elections in 2009'.

87 See Goby and Weichsel (n 49) 123.

88 Also before the judgment of the Constitutional Court, these considerations were seen to constitute a significant difference between e-voting and postal voting: Harald Eberhard, 'Demokratie und Wahlen' in Michael Holoubek, Andrea Martin and Stephan Schwarzer (eds), *Die Zukunft der Verfassung – Die Verfassung der Zukunft? Festschrift für Karl Korinek* (Springer 2010) 61–2. Of course, it can also be questioned whether the technical standards can ever be developed sufficiently to overcome this tension (see Eva Pentz, 'Richtungsweisend – nur wohin? Die Judikatur des VfGH zu E-Voting' [2012] *juridikum*, 6 [pp. 8–9]; Pabel and Sonntag [n 54] 184).

89 Poier (n 2) 152–5.

had to be verifiable and controllable in all its details without the help of experts would, according to this view, have to be rejected.[90] In this regard it must not be overlooked that the Students' Union Act 1998 only provided for e-voting as an additional voting channel which could only be introduced as long as the legal requirements, which were interpreted strictly by the Constitutional Court, were met. As long as these requirements could not be met, there was simply no room for an e-voting system to be introduced. Interpreting the legal requirements in such a way that an e-voting system had in any case to be realisable would undermine the strict legal safeguards as the latter would be limited by the factual technical possibilities.[91] In any case, with the enactment of the Students' Union Act 2014 resulting in the abolition of the legislative basis for e-voting in Students' Union elections, the question has become obsolete.

It has to be reiterated that the considerations of the Constitutional Court have implications beyond elections for the bodies of the Students' Union. As elections for the Students' Union were conceived as a test run for the application of e-voting at the constitutional level,[92] the constitutional establishment of e-voting for elections of the legislative bodies, municipal representation, the President of the Republic and the Austrian members of the European Parliament does not seem likely in the near future. Modification of the constitutionally enshrined electoral principles and the introduction of e-voting at the constitutional level would most probably encounter the same concerns as the introduction of e-voting in the Students' Union Act.

Finally, the ruling of the Constitutional Court is not to be understood as a rejection of any remote voting system. Of course, similar problematic tensions between adherence to the voting principles and the controllability and transparency of the system are inherent in any kind of remote voting system. By setting postal voting as a minimum standard for those elections not regulated by the constitutional voting principles, and not falling under the constitutional legal basis for postal voting, the Constitutional Court expressed a certain general openness towards remote voting procedures, which it confirmed recently in a judgment on an appeal against elections for the European Parliament.[93]

References

Alexander Balthasar and Alexander Prosser, 'E-Voting in der "sonstigen Selbstverwaltung" – Anmerkgungen zum Beschluss des VfGH vom 30. Juni 2011, B 1149, und zum Erkenntnis des VfGH vom 13. Dezember 2011, V 85–96' (2012) *Journal für Rechtspolitik*, 47.

90 Ibid., 155.

91 As to this question see also Balthasar and Prosser (n 18) 66 et seq.

92 See also Handstanger (n 23) 145 with further references.

93 See *supra*, 'The Evolution of the Constitutional Electoral Principles'.

Thomas M. Buchsbaum, 'Aktuelle Entwicklungen zu E-Voting in Europa' (2004) *Journal für Rechtspolitik*, 106.

Harald Eberhard, 'Die österreichische Wahlrechtsreform 2007' in Anna Gamper (ed.), *Entwicklungen des Wahlrechts am europäischen Fallbeispiel* (Springer 2010).

Harald Eberhard,, 'Demokratie und Wahlen' in Michael Holoubek, Andrea Martin and Stephan Schwarzer (eds), *Die Zukunft der Verfassung – Die Verfassung der Zukunft? Festschrift für Karl Korinek* (Springer 2010).

Barbara Goby, 'E-Voting bei den ÖH-Wahlen 2009' in Sebastian Schmid, Veronika C. Tiefenthaler, Klaus Wallnöfer and Andreas W Wimmer (eds), *Auf dem Weg zum hypermodernen Rechtsstaat?* (Sramek 2011).

Barbara Goby and Helmut Weichsel, 'Das E-Voting-Erkenntnis des VfGH: gesetzwidrige Ausgestaltung der ÖH-Wahlordnung' (2012) *Zeitschrift für Hochschulrecht*, 118.

Christoph Grabenwarter, 'Briefwahl und E-Voting: Rechtsvergleichende Aspekte und europarechtliche Rahmenbedingungen' (2004) *Journal für Rechtspolitik*, 70.

Christoph Grabenwarter and Beatrix Krauskopf, 'Entwicklungsstufen der Distanzwahl im Spannungsfeld des freien, geheimen und persönlichen Wahlrechts' in Anna Gamper (ed.), *Entwicklungen des Wahlrechts am europäischen Fallbeispiel* (Springer 2010).

Meinrad Handstanger, 'E-Voting und Wahlrecht' in Klaus Poier (ed.), *Demokratie im Umbruch: Perspektiven einer Wahlrechtsreform* (Böhlau 2009).

Gabriele Kucsko-Stadlmayer, 'E-Voting und Europäischer Grundrechtsstandard' in Clemens Jabloner, Otto Lucius and Alfred Schramm (eds), *Theorie und Praxis des Wirtschaftsrechts. Festschrift für René Laurer* (Springer 2009).

Gerda Marx, 'E-Voting bei den ÖH-Wahlen 2009' in Werner Hauser (ed.), *Jahrbuch Hochschulrecht 2010* (NWV 2010).

Katharina Pabel and Michael Sonntag, 'E-Voting bei den ÖH-Wahlen gesetzwidrig' (2012) *Zeitschrift für Energie- und Technikrecht*, 175.

Eva Pentz, 'Richtungsweisend – nur wohin? Die Judikatur des VfGH zu E-Voting' (2012) *juridikum*, 6.

Klaus Poier, 'E-Voting – mehr als ein einmaliger Flop? Die Entscheidung des VfGH zur ÖH-Wahl 2009 und ihre Folgen für E-Voting in Österreich' in Gerhard Baumgartner (ed.), *Jahrbuch Öffentliches Recht 2013* (NWV 2013).

Manfred Stelzer, *The Constitution of the Republic of Austria* (Hart 2011).

Joachim Stern, 'Demokratie minus 2.0 – Die Distanzwahl ist verfassungsrechtlich höchst bedenklich' (2009) *juridikum*, 72.

Chapter 4

Legal Aspects of E-Voting in Brazil

Amílcar Brunazo Filho and Augusto Tavares Rosa Marcacini

Introduction

Brazil started using electronic voting machines during its 1996 election. Since then, the utilization of voting machines has increased gradually; since 2000 every political election has been driven by electronic ballots, all over the country, from big cities like São Paulo and Rio de Janeiro, to small villages in the core of the tropical forest.

Although this could be considered a successful implementation of information technologies by a developing country, and in fact this initiative is seen as 'a big deal' by most Brazilians (thanks to massive propaganda[1] conducted by the electoral authorities), the way electronic electoral systems are used in Brazil is negative from the point of view of democratic standards and is not something of which to be proud.

This chapter presents an analysis of a recent decision taken in 2013 by the Brazilian Supreme Court on the implementation of paper audit trails in Brazilian voting systems.

1 Every two years, months before election day, electoral authorities undertake large campaigns, publishing advertisements on TV, radio and in newspapers. These campaigns are intended to inform voters on how and where to vote, but they are also used to spread positive views about the Brazilian electronic voting system. Some of the most recent ones can be seen online, at the Youtube channel of the Brazilian electoral authority: https://www.youtube.com/watch?v=vvxZK8E1BoM and https://www.youtube.com/watch?v=TskYGp6z9oE. The first was published for the 2010 elections, and states (in our translation): 'The whole world has always tried to build innovative machines. Scientists gathered to develop top-secret projects. Made endless tests. But they could never build a machine like this. A machine where people can choose the future. The Brazilian voting machine is cited as a security example all over the world. In the next election, give it more than your vote. Give it your confidence. Vote and help build the future of Brazil'. The second video is being used during the 2014 elections and presents numerous quotes about the voting machine. Some of them, in our English translation, state: 'it's secure, because since its implementation, there has been no fraud' (at 0:49 min) and 'the safety, transparency and speed of e-electoral process and our voting machine has attracted the curiosity and attention of many countries all over the world' (at 2:05).

Before commenting on this decision, the chapter briefly explains how political elections are organized in Brazil and how e-voting systems arose and were developed, including the relevant legal background.

Political Elections in Brazil: An Overview

Voting in Brazil is mandatory. According to article 14 of the Brazilian Constitution, every citizen between 18 and 70 years is obliged to vote; for citizens between 16 and 18 years, and above 70, voting is optional. For those who are obliged to vote, absence may be justified if the voter is not in his or her electoral district on the polling day; otherwise, they may be fined.

Elections take place every two years, alternating municipal elections with federal and state elections. For example, in 2010, elections were conducted to choose the President and State Governors and also legislative members, both at the federal and state levels. Elections for the executive and legislative branches took place on the same day. That is to say, at the same moment, voters are asked to express their preferences for the offices of President, Governor, Senator and Federal and State Representatives. Two years later, in 2012, it was time to vote for the municipal candidates, the Mayor and the Aldermen. For the positions in the executive branch, if no candidate achieves more than 50 per cent of the valid ballots, a second poll is held some weeks later, to choose between the two candidates that received the most votes. This applies to elections for the President and all Governors; for elections for Mayors, a second poll is conducted only in cities with more than 200 thousand voters. The first poll always takes place on the first Sunday of October, and the second poll, when needed, takes place on the last Sunday of that same month. For the Legislative Houses at the three levels (Federal, State and Municipal), candidates are chosen by a proportional system that takes into account the total votes obtained by each party, that is to say, the sum of votes received by each candidate of the same party and the votes given directly to the party itself (the voter has the option to vote for a candidate or just for a party). A proportional number of representatives that each party must have is calculated from the total votes received by each party – this is called the *electoral quotient*. The candidates having received the most votes in each party, up to the party's electoral quotient, are elected.

A specialized court within the judicial system is responsible for organizing and conducting elections, for developing rules and regulations for elections, and for acting as the judicial authority to resolve disputes. Before explaining this in more detail, we first outline the structure of the Brazilian judicial system.

The Brazilian judicial system is divided into five different kinds of courts and the Portuguese word *Justiça* is used to name each one of these structures: a) Labour Courts (*Justiça do Trabalho*), b) Electoral Courts (*Justiça Eleitoral*), c) Military Criminal Courts (*Justiça Penal Militar*), d) Federal Courts (*Justiça Federal*) and e) State Courts (*Justiça Estadual*). The first three are specialized in some kinds of lawsuits and are classified as Specialized Courts (*Justiças Especializadas*). In a few words, labour cases, cases concerning political elections, and military crimes fall under the jurisdiction of these three *Justiças*, respectively. Anything but these three kinds of cases is considered a common case, so it is presented before the Common Courts (*Justiça Comum*). The last two are Common Courts. *Justiça Federal* is organized by the Federal Union, while *Justiça Estadual* is organized by each Federate State. Thus there is one different *Justiça* in each State and another one for the Federal District.

For our subject, what matters is to know and understand the role of the Electoral Courts (*Justiça Eleitoral*) and the powers they hold. We first present a short explanation of the Electoral Courts' structure.

Unlike the other Brazilian courts, Brazilian Electoral Courts do not have a stable judiciary. Their bureaucracy is compounded of a fixed staff of public employees, but the judges are not fixed. Instead, each Electoral Court is formed mostly by judges of other judiciary courts, that are appointed to a position in the Electoral Court for a defined time.

At the top of Electoral Courts stands the Higher Electoral Court (*Tribunal Superior Eleitoral*), or *TSE*. This higher court is only inferior to the jurisdiction of the Brazilian Supreme Court (*Supremo Tribunal Federal*) or *STF*. According to the Brazilian Constitution of 1988, *TSE* is composed of at least seven judges (and there have only been seven since then), all of them are rotating members with a two-year mandate. Five of its magistrates are chosen among regular judges of the Brazilian Supreme Court (three members) and from the *Superior Tribunal de Justiça* (two members); the latter, which was not mentioned above, is a higher court situated above the two Common Courts (*Justiça Federal* and *Justiça Estadual*). The other two members of *TSE* are lawyers chosen by the Brazilian President from a six-name list approved by the Supreme Court.

Below *TSE* are 27 Regional Courts named *Tribunal Regional Eleitoral – TRE*, with jurisdiction over the 26 States and the Federal District. *TRE* judges also rotate. Five of them are judges of Federal and State Common Courts and two are lawyers named by the Brazilian President from a six-name list approved by the local State Court (*Tribunal de Justiça*).

As seen, this way of choosing electoral judges differs completely from what occurs in the rest of the Brazilian judicial system, where all members of all other courts, from the lower courts to the Supreme Court, are fixed magistrates, vested for life (or at least until they are 70-years-old, when, according to Brazilian law, all public employees must compulsorily retire).

Yet, this is not the most noticeable difference between Electoral Courts and the rest of the Brazilian judicial system.

Since the eighteenth century, inspired by the ideals of Montesquieu and by the French and American Revolutions, Western democracies have been based on the theory of division of powers, so that different organisms divide the political functions performed in the country, in a way that provides checks and balances among them. Brazil also follows this doctrine, so there is a legislative branch that creates the law, an executive branch that administrates the public services, and, of course, a judicial system empowered to resolve conflicts according to the law. Nevertheless, this division is not observed for what concerns political elections, since Electoral Courts concentrate the three separate functions in the hands of the same people (namely the judges of the Electoral Courts).[2]

Though there is an Electoral Code, a formal law approved by the legislative branch, *TSE* holds the power to rule on most of the minor details of an election, defining instructions for a myriad of subjects, from political parties' organization to allocating radio and TV time among them and their respective candidates, to the financial control and distribution of public funds to political parties. *TSE* also defines and controls the methods and procedures of the vote, including its organization and supervision. Further, the implementation of the entire voting process is also conducted by the Electoral Courts' staff: they provide all the facilities to collect and count the votes, and declare the final result.

Finally, Electoral Courts act as a proper judicial power, so their magistrates are the judges of all electoral processes. This not only means deciding conflicts between parties and candidates, but also includes the jurisdiction to decide the legality, accuracy or integrity of their own decisions regarding regulations and administration and management of the elections, including the validity of the final result they themselves have proclaimed.

This is how the Electoral Courts introduces themselves on their homepage:

> The Brazilian Electoral Justice is a specialized branch of the Judiciary Power, acting in three spheres: judicial, which highlights the competence to judge electoral matters; administrative, which is responsible for the organization and conduct of elections, referenda and plebiscites; and regulatory, that develops rules relating to the electoral process.[3]

2 A brief comparative report on electoral structures of different countries was written by two legal advisors of the Brazilian Senate. GUERZONI FILHO, Gilberto; SOARES, Paulo Henrique. *Funcionamento da Justiça Eleitoral em Alguns Países* (2000), http://www.brunazo.eng.br/voto-e/textos/SenadoEstudoSistemasEleitorais.odt.

3 Our translation. The original, in Portuguese, reads: 'A Justiça Eleitoral brasileira é um ramo especializado do Poder Judiciário, com atuação em três esferas: jurisdicional, em que se destaca a competência para julgar questões eleitorais; administrativa, na qual é responsável pela organização e realização de eleições, referendos e plebiscitos; e regulamentar, em que elabora normas referentes ao processo eleitoral', Electoral Courts homepage, http://www.justicaeleitoral.jus.br.

Electronic Voting in Brazil

First Experiences with Computerized Polls

The use of computerized devices in Brazilian elections began in 1982. Brazil was still a dictatorship at that time,[4] but democratic winds began increasingly to blow. This was the first time for years that State Governors would be chosen by popular suffrage.

In 1982 polls, e-counting systems were used in two States – Rio de Janeiro and Rio Grande do Sul – only to provide the final tallying. Paper ballots were manually counted in each Voting Precinct and the results for each candidate were registered in a document called *Ballot Box Bulletin* (*Boletim de Urna* or simply *BU*, in Portuguese). These *BUs* were then typed into an electronic system designed to add all votes and present the final result. At that time, this task was outsourced to private companies contracted by the Electoral Courts.

However, the immaturity of the computer system developed in the state of Rio de Janeiro generated a series of errors and sum inconsistencies during partial publication of the results. An important Brazilian newspaper – *Jornal do Brasil* – was doing its own counting and noted that void and blank votes decreased between the first and second partial results announced by the electoral authority. It was also noted that, while in official tallying the candidate supported by the military regime was leading, in the parallel counting the opposition candidate had more votes. This event became known as the *Proconsult Case*[5] – a reference to the name of the company whose systems failed – and the episode raised serious suspicions of fraud. The final tallying was then suspended and only continued after corrections had been made in the software and in other processes. Fortunately, at that time there were paper trails that allowed recounting and the mistakes were acknowledged by the Electoral Courts.

Also during the 1980s, in 1986, a national voters database was created, giving a unique voting number to each voter, in order to avoid the chances of double-voting.

---

4 Brazil's military dictatorship began in 1964, when army forces conducted a coup d'état, and ended in 1988, when a democratic Constitution was promulgated. During a great part of this period, there was no popular voting for President, State Governors or Mayors of capitals; for a period during that time, one third of the Senate was not directly elected. Absolute powers started to diminish during the 1980s, when people were progressively allowed to vote for these offices. Hence there were popular elections for Governors in 1982 and for Mayors of State capitals in 1985. The first presidential poll in almost three decades took place in 1989, after the 1988 Constitution was approved.

5 PORTO, Walter Costa. *A Mentirosa urna* (São Paulo: Ed. Martins Fontes, 2004), p. 219.

Using Voting Machines

When concentrated powers meet information technology
As mentioned above, Brazilian Electoral Courts concentrate in the hands of its few members all three political functions: regulatory, executive, judicial. Though it has been this way for decades, the recent implementation of electronic voting systems has brought this anomaly to the fore and with it considerations that it may be unbearable and harmful from the point of view of democratic political standards.

A noticeable phenomenon of the modern information society may be summarized in the expression 'code is law',[6] in which 'code' does not refer to the legislative acts (as in 'Civil Code') but to the raw software instructions. What the Brazilian experience clearly shows, then, is that when concentrated powers unite with the modern information technology (IT) apparatus the result is an almighty God of all voting processes, which is really what Brazilian Electoral Courts turned out to be.

Since the very introduction of Brazilian electronic voting systems, *TSE* has held the power to decide every technological detail, to choose which hardware and software must be used, and to determine the respective policies[7] with all their technical specifications. Since technology itself cannot be considered perfectly neutral because the use of technology is not separate from economic or political choices, the implementation of IT in Brazilian political elections can be seen a having placed additional power in the same hands in which excessive powers were already concentrated.

The pendulum movement
Without any public, open debate, electronic voting machines were first used in the 1996 elections. In all cities with more than 200 thousand voters, elections were carried out using Direct Recording Electronic voting machines (DRE). In Portuguese, this machine became known as *urna eletrônica* (electronic ballot box).

In the 2000 elections, about 400 thousand DRE voting machines were used across Brazil: it became the first country in the world to automate completely every step of its political polls, from the act of voting by all the voters to the final tallying and publication of the result.

---

6 'In real space we recognize how laws regulate – through constitutions, statutes, and other legal codes. In cyberspace we must understand how code regulates – how the software and hardware that make cyberspace what it is regulate cyberspace as it is. As William Mitchell puts it, this code is cyberspace's "law". Code is law' (LESSIG, Lawrence. *Code and Other Laws of Cyberspace* [New York: Basic Books, 1999], p. 6). What is said about cyberspace may also apply to major environments where IT is widely implemented and serves to manage human acts and/or behaviour, which certainly may include a country's whole electronic election infrastructure.

7 Such as the use of Open Source instead of proprietary software or other details like that.

As one can observe, the migration from paper ballots to digital ballots was done very quickly. After the partial use of electronic voting machines in just two elections (1996 and 1998), the next one was completely carried out with digital devices. This fast movement was efficient also in discouraging an open, public debate, especially when official propaganda largely presented the Brazilian voting system as a kind of technological proficiency, or as something of which Brazilian people should be very proud. It is common among critics of this voting system to say that propaganda about it forged such a national emotion among Brazilian people, that to point out its deficiencies could be compared to engaging in unpatriotic acts, like supporting Argentina's football team against Brazil in the final match of the World Cup. Even so, isolated critics[8] started to pop up here and there, but not in an organized way.

In 2001, a political scandal that occurred in the Federal Senate[9] drew public attention and shed some light on the national electronic voting systems. The Brazilian Senate used an electronic system to count senators' votes. Though in open polls (open ones comprise almost all polls taken in a legislative house) the electronic system couldn't do any potential harm, the scandal showed how the use of electronic voting systems to count *secret* ballots could cause severe trouble.

It was discovered that, due to security flaws, the secrecy of a specific secret poll taken the year before had been violated, and the Senate's Chairman been informed thoroughly on how each senator had voted. Apart from the political scandal itself, the publicly exposed fraud in the Senate's systems contributed to the initiation of a major debate about the national electronic voting system because it became clear that some of the flaws found in the Senate's system could also affect the general elections.

This debate led the legislative branch to approve a new Electoral Law, in January 2002,[10] that ordered the use of printers together with each voting machine, so that ballots could be printed and automatically deposited inside a ballot box, without any human contact with the printed ballot, thus creating a *paper trail*.[11]

---

8 Some examples of these initial criticisms may be seen in two articles published in 1999 and 2000 by two Brazilian Congressmen: REQUIÃO, Roberto. *A urna eletrônica e a legítima vontade popular* (August 2000), http://jus.com.br/artigos/1542/a-urna-eletronica-e-a-legitima-vontade-popular; BITTAR, Jacó. *Urna eletrônica: avanço ou retrocesso?* (May 1999) http://jus.com.br/artigos/1547/urna-eletronica-avanco-ou-retrocesso.

9 More detailed information on the scandal can be seen here (Portuguese version only): http://www.istoe.com.br/reportagens/36743_ENFORCADO.

10 It was the Federal Law n. 10.408, of 10 January 2002, Portuguese version: http://www.planalto.gov.br/ccivil_03/Leis/2002/L10408.htm.

11 As determined by article 59, § 4 of Federal Law n. 9.504, modified by Federal Law n. 10.408. Portuguese version http://www.planalto.gov.br/ccivil_03/Leis/2002/L10408.htm. In our translation: 'The voting machine must have a device that allows printing the ballot, its visual checking and automatic deposit, without hand contact, in a sealed ballot box, after being checked by the voter'.

The technical literature on electronic voting systems contains abundant criticism of elections that are completely conducted by electronic means,[12,13] all of it suggesting the use of some kind of physical audit trail that may be used as a counter-proof of the final result, by after-the-fact recounting if needed. We will therefore not explain here all the implications of an election solely conducted by the use of digital methods, nor the principles of how to audit the result using a physical trail.

The 2002 Electoral Law provided that the paper ballots of 3 per cent of the voting machines should be counted manually (that is, three out of every 100 machines would be randomly selected for auditing). However, much to the perplexity of anyone who has even a slight understanding of how to conduct an audit,[14] the ballot boxes to be counted would be selected *one day before* the election day. Of course, since the machines to be audited were known before the election day, everybody also knew which ones *would not be* audited. Even so this law could be considered, at the time, an important step forward in improving the security of Brazilian elections. At that time, one could expect that the next steps would correct the noted imperfection and more suitable means of auditing could be implemented thereafter. However, that was not what happened. Instead, since then rules on e-voting have swayed like a pendulum.

As there was not enough time to include printers in all voting machines – according to *TSE* – during the next elections, in October 2002, only a few districts employed the novelty of the paper trail. The experience, however, was considered negative (of course, by *TSE* members).[15]

The result was that the legislative power was convinced to change things back and new election rules were approved in October 2003,[16] abolishing the use of printed ballots – that had been used only once – or any other form of physical audit trail. As a kind of give-and-take, the paper trail was replaced by other ways of

---

12 MERCURI, Rebecca. *Electronic Vote Tabulation Checks and Balances*. Ph.D. dissertation, defended on 27 October 2000 at the School of Engineering and Applied Science of the University of Pennsylvania, Philadelphia, PA http://www.notablesoftware.com/Papers/thesdefabs.html.

13 RIVEST, R. et al. *A Modular Voting Architecture*. CalTech-MIT Voting Technology Project, USA (2001) http://people.csail.mit.edu/rivest/BruckJeffersonRivest-AModularVotingArchitecture.doc.

14 NORDEN, L.D. et al. *The Machinery of Democracy: Protecting Elections in an Electronic World* (New York: Brennan Center of Justice, NYU, 27 June 2006) http://www.brennancenter.org/sites/default/files/publications/Machinery_Democracy.pdf.

15 *TSE* has developed a video explaining why, on its own view, printed ballots are undesirable: it delays the voting process, there is low interest in recounting printing ballots, printers fails, there are high implementation costs and opportunities for fraud, https://www.youtube.com/watch?v=VKcJoMZHUmo.

16 Federal Law n. 10.704, of 1 October 2003, Portuguese version http://www.planalto.gov.br/ccivil_03/Leis/2003/L10.740.htm.

auditing the electronic voting devices, though they do not provide the same level of security or transparency.

First, for the first time external observers were allowed to examine (under very restrictive procedures) the software used in electronic voting machines and in tallying systems. All voting machines were also required to produce a recorded file named the Digital Ballots Register (*Registro Digital do Voto*). We will comment on these methods of auditing below.

By this time, academic studies on electronic voting systems started to point out the system's weaknesses and some of the conceptual difficulties it brought to the transparency of the political elections. DRE machines, as used in Brazil from the beginning until today, are computerized systems whose reliability depends completely on the faithfulness of the embedded software.

In 2000 Professor Rebecca Mercuri, of University of Pennsylvania, promoted the concept of the Voter-Verifiable Paper Audit Trail (VVPAT),[17] which was later extended to the Independent Voter-Verifiable Record (IVVR). Still in 2000, Bruce Schneier published notes about the incidents of that year's Florida elections, saying that more technology wouldn't solve those problems. He wrote:

> Certainly Florida's antiquated voting technology is partially to blame, but newer technology wouldn't magically make the problems go away. It could even make things worse, by adding more translation layers between the voters and the vote counters and preventing recounts.
>
> That's my primary concern about computer voting: There is no paper ballot to fall back on. Computerized voting machines, whether they have keyboard and screen or a touch screen ATM-like interface, could easily make things worse. You have to trust the computer to record the votes properly, tabulate the votes properly, and keep accurate records. You can't go back to the paper ballots and try to figure out what the voter wanted to do. And computers are fallible; some of the computer voting machines in this election failed mysteriously and irrecoverably.[18]

In 2006, a paper written by Rivest and Wack introduced the terminology software-independent and software-dependent voting systems 'to describe whether or not the correctness of election results depends in an essential way on the correctness of voting system software'. They finally state that 'the ability to prove the correctness of software diminishes rapidly as the software becomes more complex. It would

17 MERCURI, Rebecca. *Electronic Vote Tabulation Checks and Balances*. Ph.D. dissertation, defended on 27 October 2000 at the School of Engineering and Applied Science of the University of Pennsylvania, Philadelphia, PA, http://www.notablesoftware.com/Papers/thesdefabs.html.

18 SCHNEIER, Bruce. *Voting and Technology*, https://www.schneier.com/crypto-gram-0012.html#1.

effectively be impossible to adequately test future (and current) voting systems for flaws and introduced fraud, and thus these systems would always remain suspect in their ability to provide secure and accurate elections'.[19]

In Brazil, what can be seen as the first organized movement demanding more transparency in its electronic voting machines emerged in academia. In 2003 eight Professors of Engineering and Computer Science from some of the most prestigious Brazilian universities published a manifesto (which became known as *The Professors' Manifesto*) expressing their concerns on the reliability of the Brazilian electronic voting system.[20]

Though the knowledge regarding voting machines' weaknesses and limitations are somewhat well known in higher academic circles, this is still a very hermetic subject for the average citizen. Even so, in 2009 the thesis on the necessity of using some kind of *physical trail* to audit the electronic voting machines achieved the support of Brazilian congressmen and a new law was approved, swinging the pendulum back again. In spite of the strong opposition expressed by electoral authorities when the bill was still in discussion in Parliament,[21] their arguments were rejected by Brazilian congressmen and a new VVPAT Act was approved. This became article 5 of the Federal Law n. 12.034[22] of 29 September 2009.

According to the VVPAT Act, from 2014 on, voting machines would be required to print the ballots to permit later audits. Then, after publication of the final result, the paper ballots of 2 per cent of voting machines would be manually counted, in a public session conducted by Electoral Courts, and compared to the numbers provided by the computerized system. Fixing a five-year term in which to implement the printing system also seemed wise, as it would give the electoral authorities time to adapt all devices and the whole voting system. It seemed, finally, that the software-independent voting machine concept had been adopted in Brazil.

Opposition to this VVPAT Act, however, continued to thrive. In the next legislature, in 2010, a new bill was proposed to revoke the use of printed ballots. This time, however, the arguments were thoroughly rejected by Brazilian House of Representatives that considered purely electronic counting to be unconstitutional because it did not comply with the Publicity Principle.[23]

---

19 RIVEST, R.R.; WACK, J.P. *On the Notion of 'Software Independence' in Voting Systems* (USA: National Institute of Standards and Technology [NIST], 28 July 2006), http://people.csail.mit.edu/rivest/pubs/RW06.pdf.

20 DEL PICCHIA, Walter, et al. *Manifesto dos Professores* (September 2003) available in Portuguese,http://www.votoseguro.com/alertaprofessores/.

21 BRAZIL. Federal Senate. *Minutes of the 29th Meeting of CCJC* (2009), http://www.brunazo.eng.br/voto-e/arquivos/SenadoCCJata-20-8-09.pdf.

22 Available in Portuguese: http://www.planalto.gov.br/ccivil_03/_Ato2007-2010/2009/Lei/L12034.htm.

23 http://migre.me/jrpqT.

Since then, electoral authorities have waged a vigorous campaign against the VVPAT Act. A video[24] was even produced, reproducing the same (and inaccurate) arguments previously rejected by the House of Representatives the year before. This video was officially exhibited during the 51st Meeting of the Council of Presidents of Electoral Courts[25] that, then, decided to present a request to the General Attorney.[26]

As a consequence, on 18 January 2011, the General Attorney filed a claim[27] in the Brazilian Supreme Court, arguing that the print audit method established in the VVPAT Act was unconstitutional; the claim reproduced exactly the words found in the request received from the electoral authorities. In November 2013, this claim was upheld unanimously by the judges of that Court. We analyse this decision in the sections below.

The authorized audit methods

Before analysing this Brazilian Supreme Court decision, we present some comments on the auditing methods hitherto accepted and utilized by Electoral Courts. As we briefly mentioned above, respected experts in the electronic security field say that there is no better way to audit electronic polls than by using some kind of physical trace as an audit trail. Elections in Brazil have provided vivid proof of the truth of that assertion.

The attempt to examine fully all software used by Electoral Courts proved to be a very difficult, or even impossible endeavour. Part of the difficulty originated from the auditing limits established by *TSE*, which made examiners' actions a mere formality, restricting the possibility of actually finding something. In a few words, the software codes were not made public. Only authorized institutions (all political parties, plus the Public Ministry and the Brazilian Bar Association) could appoint inspectors, and they were not permitted to take the software source code to their offices. Examination of all code had to be done (visually) at computers working in a controlled access room at the *TSE* headquarters. And the observers were obliged to sign a non-disclosure agreement[28] to gain access to the documents and source code. Furthermore, the comprehensive examination of software code (the full code is spread among dozens of thousands of text files), with the purpose of detecting

24 http://www.votoseguro.com/videos/ADI4543-videoTSE.mp4.

25 BRAZIL. Council of Presidents of Electoral Courts. *Minutes of the 51st Meeting* (2010), http://www.votoseguro.org/arquivos/ADI4543-Council-Presidents.pdf.

26 http://redir.stf.jus.br/paginadorpub/paginador.jsp?docTP=TP&docID=941230.

27 ADI n. 4543, http://redir.stf.jus.br/paginadorpub/paginador.jsp?docTP=TP&docID=941228.

28 The NDA says the observer is obliged to keep secret everything he or she will access or come to know during the audit proceeding. The full text of this NDA is included in a report published by the Brazilian Computing Society: GRAAF, Jeroen van de; CUSTODIO, Ricardo Felipe. *Tecnologia Eleitoral e a Urna Eletronica*, Relatorio SBC (2002), http://www.sbc.org.br/index.php?option=com_jdownloads&Itemid=195&task=finish&cid=107&catid=77.

and avoiding any security breach, is a very slow and difficult task that cannot be done by anyone: it requires a high level of specialized professional knowledge.

As Rivest and Wack note:

> Finding all errors in a large system is generally held to be impossible in general or else highly demanding and extremely expensive. Our ability to develop complex software vastly exceeds our ability to prove its correctness or test it satisfactorily within reasonable fiscal constraints (extensive testing of a voting system's software would certainly be cost-prohibitive). A voting system for which the integrity of the election results depends on the correctness of its software will always be somewhat suspect and require routine checks of its software, even after extensive (and expensive) federal testing and certification.[29]

Even if those obstacles could be overcome, the major problem in auditing voting machines would be to trust that the software that runs inside them on the polling day is the same as that which was previously examined (even if it had been fully examined). The use of digital signatures didn't make things better. Using digital signatures only means that examiners will use their private key to sign the executable files. This was done in a very formal ceremony that took place at *TSE* some weeks before the election. An officer executes some commands and the text files with code are compiled into executable files. There seems to be no way to confirm that the text files used in the compilation are the same as those that were previously reviewed. It is something that happens inside the silicon chips and the storage devices belonging to the Electoral Courts.

Though this may not be the opinion of Brazil's electoral officers, attempts to examine the software code simply confirmed Rebecca Mercuri's opinion:

> Electronic balloting and tabulation makes the tasks performed by poll workers, challengers, and election officials purely procedural, and removes any opportunity to perform bipartisan checks. Any computerized election process is thus entrusted to the small group of individuals who program, construct and maintain the machines.[30]

Furthermore, the so-called *Registro Digital do Voto* was simply a useless way of auditing nothing, that only added more problems to the system as it proved to be an open flaw that enabled breaking the secrecy of individual votes. The *Registro* is a kind of database table in which the complete ballot of each voter is recorded as a single line. Each line records the options selected by an individual voter. In

29 RIVEST, R. et al. *A Modular Voting Architecture* (USA: CalTech-MIT Voting Technology Project, 2001), http://people.csail.mit.edu/rivest/BruckJefferson Rivest-AModularVotingArchitecture.doc.

30 MERCURI, Rebecca. *Rebecca Mercuri's Statement on Electronic Voting* (2007[2001]), http://www.notablesoftware.com/RMstatement.html.

order to protect the secrecy of the vote, the sequence of records is randomized during the elections. However, as computers can only produce pseudo-random functions, someone could easily break the randomization by reverse engineering. Indeed, it was broken by Professor Diego Aranha during one of the restricted audit sessions conducted by *TSE*.[31] Even if a better way of randomizing the records were employed (and it is impossible to confirm that the creators of the software did not leave any kind of backdoor to reverse it) the ultimate question remains: what can such a register prove? It is provided by the same software that counts the votes. Since the counting routines may be compromised, the attacker could easily compromise this register itself!

In conclusion, the experience of all kinds of auditing methods proposed by the Brazilian Electoral Courts demonstrated that none of them is able to provide complete confidence in digital voting systems. The real scenario confirms Mercuri's, Schneiers' and Rivest's theories. As will be seen in the following sections, Electoral Courts tend to overvalue these audit methods in spite of the negative scientific opinions of them.

Another auditing procedure used by Electoral Courts since 2002 is referred to as parallel voting (*votação paralela*). This consists of randomly selecting two, three or four[32] voting machines in each State a day before the election, when all machines are ready to be used in their respective voting districts. Each of these machines is taken from its place, substituted by another one to be used in the election, and then submitted to this supposed test. Tests consist in the public casting of some votes during the election day, starting and finishing at the same time as the real poll. Then, at the end of the day, the results presented by the digital votes are checked with the votes that were publicly cast on these selected machines. Besides the use of a minimal number of machines, compared to the hundreds of thousands of devices used all over the country (0.03 per cent of all voting machines), this method cannot detect sophisticated internal attacks.[33]

A brief report on the current world scene

In Brazil, DRE machines are known as first generation voting machines, while the systems that follow the software-independent concept are considered to belong to the second generation of devices. First generation voting machines have been abandoned by several countries that had previously tried them. Some countries

31 ARANHA, D.F. et al. *Software Vulnerabilities in the Brazilian Voting Machine. In Design, Development, and Use of Secure Electronic Voting Systems* (USA: IGI Global, 2014), https://sites.google.com/site/dfaranha/pubs/aranha-karam-miranda-scarel-12-book.

32 The number is defined by *TSE*, according to the total number of voting machines of each State.

33 REZENDE, Pedro A. D.; BRUNAZO FILHO, Amílcar. *Security Measures for Brazil's e-Vote Act Two: Parallel Testing* (2003), http://www.cic.unb.br/docentes/pedro/trabs/Brazilvote2.htm.

replaced them with second generation machines, while others simply returned to paper ballots.

In 2004 Venezuela became the first country to adopt a second generation electronic voting system for all districts.[34] In 2007 *Voluntary Voting System Guidelines* were published in the United States, recommending the use of software-independent systems and excluding pure DRE machines.[35] In 2008 DRE machines were also abandoned in the Netherlands. In 2009 the Federal Constitutional Court of Germany declared that DRE machines are unconstitutional because they do not comply with the principle of the public nature of elections, since ordinary voters have no way to verify how their digital vote was processed.[36] In 2013 the Supreme Court of India mandated the implementation of VVPAT in DRE machines starting with the general elections of 2014.[37] Second generation voting machines have also been used in Russia, Belgium, Argentina, Mexico and Ecuador.

Though Brazil was the first country fully to implement digital voting in its political elections, it is the only one to use pure DRE, software dependent, voting machines comprehensively.

The Court Case: The Declaration of Unconstitutionality of the VVPAT Act

An Overview

As noted above, Brazil has been using electronic voting machines since 1996 and the methods used to audit the digital poll have swung back and forth like a pendulum. The use of physical trails as auditing methods, though recommended by renowned specialists in computer security, has been strongly opposed by Electoral Courts, especially *TSE* members.

The first attempt to introduce printed ballots as an audit trail lasted less than one election, as the law was immediately changed to ban this method.

When another law again mandated the use of paper ballots, another unexpected action was taken by the Brazilian electoral authorities: the law was challenged as unconstitutional before the Brazilian Supreme Court. More surprising, though, was the Supreme Court's decision, which held that a method of auditing digital

34 Since 2004, DRE machines with VVPAT have been in use in Venezuela. The printed register is inserted into ordinary ballot boxes by the voter and the paper ballots of 54 per cent of voting machines are counted manually to check the integrity of the final results.

35 *Voluntary Voting System Guidelines*, v. 2007 (USA: NIST/US-EAC, 2007), Introduction 2.4, http://www.eac.gov/vvsg.

36 Original decision of the Federal Constitutional Court of Germany of 3 March 2009, available at: http://www.bundesverfassungsgericht.de/entscheidungen/cs20090303_2bvc000307.html.

37 Original decision of the Supreme Court of India of 8 October 2013, available at: https://www.eff.org/document/dr-subramanian-swamy-vs-election-commission-india.

voting systems that has been advocated by several scholars around the world was unconstitutional.

Control of Constitutionality in Brazil

Before considering the details of this judicial case, it is worth seeing how the control of constitutionality is provided in Brazil. As in most countries, the Constitution is the highest set of rules and overrides all other laws. None of them can conflict with constitutional provisions. When an unconstitutional law is approved by Parliament and made enforceable, it may still be declared unconstitutional by the courts.

There are two ways in which a law may be declared to be unconstitutional by the judicial system. One way, referred to as *direct control*, is initiated by an action filed before the Brazilian Supreme Court. This action is known as a Direct Action of Unconstitutionality (Ação Direta de Inconstitucionalidade) or *ADI*. The other way is to argue the unconstitutionality before any court, when the issue is relevant to the judgment of a particular lawsuit. This is known as *indirect control*. While the decision given by indirect control only applies to that single case, direct control provides a definitive decision about constitutionality that must be followed by the whole country. A law declared unconstitutional by the Supreme Court when deciding a direct action is eliminated completely from the legal system.

Any person can allege the unconstitutionality of a law in any common lawsuit (indirect control), but only certain entities may propose an *ADI* before the Supreme Court, as stated in article 103 of the Brazilian Constitution.[38]

ADI n. 4543

On 18 January 2011 an *ADI* was filed before the Brazilian Supreme Court by the chief of the Federal Public Ministry.[39] The action requested the declaration of unconstitutionality of the VVPAT Act, which mandated the use of printed ballots as audit trails. The arguments, however, were unsustainable. The plaintiff argued that the printing system would violate the voter's secrecy.

One of the argued points derived from a clear misunderstanding of the second paragraph of article 5 of the VVPAT Act, which states:

---

38 Article 103. The direct action of unconstitutionality and the declaratory action of constitutionality may be proposed by: I – the Republic's President; II – the Bureau of Federal Senate; III – the Bureau House of Representatives; IV – the Bureau of the State House of Representatives or the Federal District House of Representatives; V – the State or Federal District Governor; VI – the Republic's General Attorney; VII – the Federal Counsel of Brazilian Bar Association; VIII – a political party represented in Parliament; IX – a nationwide union confederation or class entity.

39 The Public Ministry (*Ministério Público*) is a State organ that mainly exerts accusatory functions in criminal proceedings. Its chief is the Procurador Geral da República (Republic's General Attorney), who is allowed to propose an ADI (see note 38).

> Following confirmation of the vote by the voter, the voting machine will print a unique identification number of the ballot associated with its own digital signature.[40]

The plaintiff, however, argued that the voter would have to sign the electronic ballot with his or her own digital signature and thus his or her identity could be linked to it. It must be noted that there is no neutral pronoun in Portuguese, so the original expression used in article 5 could mean both 'his' or 'its' digital signature. We translated it above as 'its own digital signature' as it seems obvious that the signer is the voting machine. Voters do not even have digital signatures to use in such circumstances and the voting machines have no external connection to smart cards whatsoever, nor was such a thing established in the VVPAT Act. Thus, to think that voters should sign their own votes seems nonsense.

Having committed this basic inaccuracy, the plaintiff concentrates its efforts on stating how secret polls are essential to democracy and are protected by the Brazilian Constitution. But this, of course, is not the main point. It is just an obvious statement that no one would dare to deny. But, if the signature is that of the machine, there is no harm to the voter's secrecy.

The other plea presented in this ADI by the General Attorney pointed out that the rule prescribed in the fifth paragraph of the same article 5 would allow a voter to vote more than once. This is our translation of that article:

> Identification of the voter by his biometry or by typing his name or voter's number is permitted, given that the identification machine has no connection with the voting machine.[41]

Anyone knowing the risks of using electronic voting machines would understand that this rule is intended to protect the secrecy of the voter. Once the voter's name – or number or other identification data – is inserted in an electronic identification device, it is almost impossible to be sure that no communication takes place between the identification device and the voting device. So this paragraph mandated that the identification and voting machines must be two (or more) separate machines.

Once again, the plaintiff proved to know very little about computing or voting machine security: the plaintiff stated that if the devices were not connected, *nothing* could prevent the voter from voting twice (or more) when he or she is inside the voting booth, face to face with the voting machine.

---

40 In Portuguese: 'Após a confirmação final do voto pelo eleitor, a urna eletrônica imprimirá um número único de identificação do voto associado à sua própria assinatura digital'.

41 In Portuguese: 'É permitido o uso de identificação do eleitor por sua biometria ou pela digitação do seu nome ou número de eleitor, desde que a máquina de identificar não tenha nenhuma conexão com a urna eletrônica'.

It is well known that several countries (Belgium, Russia, India, USA, Canada, Mexico, Venezuela, Peru, Ecuador, Argentina)[42] employ electronic voting machines with this kind of electronic identification and auditing methods that do not compromise voters secrecy or allow the voter to vote more than once. It depends only on how the digital system is built, and that has nothing to do with the Constitution!

These were the only two reasons presented by the plaintiff to support the unconstitutionality of the VVPAT Act. The action also requested interim suspension of the law until final judgment.

As in other ADIs, the President, the Senate and the House of Representatives were asked to provide their opinions on the case. The House of Representatives only gave some information on the legislative proceedings regarding the law, stating they were regular and lawful, without presenting any criticism of the plaintiff's allegations. The Senate's and President's answers, on the other hand, supported the dismissal of the ADI. The Senate's defence pointed out that it seems to be obvious that it was not the voter who would digitally sign the ballots, but the voting machine.

A Political Party – PDT (*Partido Democrático Trabalhista*) – also asked to participate in the action as *amicus curiae*, a request that was accepted. This party expressed its opinion to the effect that there was no unconstitutionality in the VVPAT Act, supporting its statements with four technical reports signed by four full professors[43] from some of Brazil's most prestigious universities. It also pointed out that VVPAT is commonly accepted by foreign courts in the countries where it has been introduced.

So, it was with profound astonishment that we all witnessed the Brazilian Supreme Court's first decision, accepting the plaintiff's arguments and ordering a provisional suspension of the law's enforcement on 9 October 2011. The suspension was unanimously approved by all nine judges who took part in the court session.

It is worth mentioning that not only did the judges fully accept the two factual mistakes presented by the plaintiff, they also expressed their deep confidence in the Brazilian voting machines and the audit methods employed by the electoral authorities. The rapporteur, Judge Carmen Lúcia, firmly stated that 'the security, efficiency, impartiality and ethics of the electronic voting system, as adopted in Brazil, is not only respected and praised all over the world, as having had its invulnerability tested, but also as having proven to be technically and legally

42 BRUNAZO FILHO, Amílcar. *Modelos e Gerações dos equipamentos de votação eletrônica* (2014), http://www.brunazo.eng.br/voto-e/textos/modelosUE.htm.

43 Clovis Torres Fernandes, Instituto Tecnológico de Aeronáutica (ITA); Jorge Stolfi, Universidade Estadual de Campinas (UNICAMP); Michael Stanton, Universidade Federal Fluminense (UFF); Walter Del Picchia, Escola Politécnica da Universidade de São Paulo (POLI-USP).

sound'.[44] After simply transcribing, without further analysis, seven items previously written by the IT Secretary of *TSE*, the same judge concluded that the printing system would be a 'vulnerability item' that could compromise a 'model system of efficiency of voting proceedings'. Maybe unaware that no digital system is fail-proof, she also stated that 'since 1996, Electoral Courts create and implement, with continuous improvements, a strict security system, in parallel with computerization processes, that ensure total inviolability and transparency of electronic voting'.[45]

Judge Dias Toffoli declared that 'when the system that works in Brazil is shown to foreign scholars, to the foreign Courts, in fact we always receive, all of us, the highest praise and compliments'.[46] Considering that the objective of the VVPAT Act was to avoid machines counting a vote for another candidate, instead of the one the voter effectively chose, the judge expressed his confidence that 'during the elections, this is done by a much safer method – with ample public supervision – in a far less expensive and much more practical way, that is by parallel voting'.[47,48]

Judge Ricardo Lewandowsky also stated that the Brazilian voting system is 'a paradigm to the whole world' and that 'attaching an electromechanical printer to the voting machines would, in my view, be the same as putting a steam compass in a jet plane'.[49] He also presented in his judgment the future improvements that *TSE* is developing: the biometric control of voters and tracking voting machines while in transit to the voting places using GPS devices.

Judge Ayres Britto claimed that he became worried when the VVPAT Act was proposed in the Parliament, because he was the President of *TSE* at the time and appointed a committee to study the new propositions. He expressly referred to the printing ballots system as a 'regression'.

---

44 In Portuguese: 'a segurança, eficiência, impessoalidade e moralidade do sistema de votação eletrônica, tal como adotado no Brasil, é não apenas acatado e elogiado em todos os cantos do planeta, como testado em sua invulnerabilidade e comprovado em sua higidez sistêmica e jurídica'. The term 'impessolidade' (literally 'absence of personality') means, in this context, the quality of something that is institutional, that does not depend on who is leading it, that should work fine no matter who controls it. We have translated it as 'impartiality'.

45 In Portuguese: 'Desde 1996, a Justiça Eleitoral elabora e implanta, com aperfeiçoamento continuado, rigoroso sistema de segurança, paralelamente ao processo de informatização, que garante total inviolabilidade e transparência da votação eletrônica'.

46 In Portuguese: 'quando se coloca aos estudiosos estrangeiros, aos tribunais estrangeiros, o sistema que funciona no Brasil, realmente sempre recebemos, todos nós, os mais altos elogios e cumprimentos'.

47 In Portuguese: 'No momento da votação, isso é feito por esse meio muito mais seguro – com a participação de ampla fiscalização da sociedade -, de uma maneira muito menos onerosa e muito mais prática, que é a votação paralela'.

48 Parallel voting is explained above in the section 'The authorized audit methods'.

49 In Portuguese: 'Acoplar uma impressora eletromecânica às urnas eletrônicas equivaleria, a meu ver, dotar o avião a jato de uma bússola a vapor'.

Judge Gilmar Mendes, despite pointing out that the German Senate had ordered the use of printed ballots to audit electronic polls, believed that the Brazilian voting system 'already widely permits these verifications'.

Based on these reasons, the Brazilian Supreme Court decided to suspend the VVPAT Act on 9 October 2011. Then, on 6 November 2013, the Court gave its final decision, finding the law unconstitutional. The complete decision had not yet been published at the time this chapter was written (July 2014), but its motives, verbally presented by the judges during the court session, do not differ from the ones presented in the previous provisional decision.

A Critical View of the Decision

There are two important aspects to consider here. First, it's clear that information technology and especially computer security is not an easy subject, most people are not able to understand it fully, nor can they establish adequate comparisons between the world of atoms and the world of bits. Lawyers and judges, even the more highly educated ones, are no exception.

Digital devices have become common in many scenarios of modern life and it is not a simple task for the average citizen to understand what a computer can provide securely, what level of security it is able to ensure, and what it cannot do.

Two decades ago, Carl Sagan warned us about the risks of a technology-dependent society where almost nobody is able to understand the technology:

> We've arranged a global civilization in which most crucial elements – transportation, communications, and all other industries; agriculture, medicine, education, entertainment, protecting the environment; and even the key democratic institution of voting – profoundly depend on science and technology. We have also arranged things so that almost no one understands science and technology. This is a prescription for disaster. We might get away with it for a while, but sooner or later this combustible mixture of ignorance and power is going to blow up in our faces.[50]

The reasons presented by the Brazilian Supreme Court judges are based on a belief that the Brazilian voting system is at a *state-of-the-art* level of security, while this cannot be confirmed by any professional with solid knowledge of digital security.

On the other hand, it is plainly noticeable how *TSE*'s technical advice influenced the judges. All of the Supreme Court Judges are, were or will be *TSE* judges. The same criticism presented above, regarding the concentration (or lack of separation) of power, is pertinent here with regard to the *TSE*'s powers to rule, execute and judge the elections. When the Supreme Court judges anything that involves *TSE* decisions or polices, it seems to be very difficult for it to maintain an impartial

---

50 SAGAN, Carl. *The Demon-Haunted World: Science as a Candle in the Dark* (Kindle e-book) position 551.

position. When deciding this *ADI*, the judges openly praised the electronic systems adopted by *TSE*, and expressed their concerns about any 'unauthorized' changes, that is, changes that that did not come with the approval of *TSE*'s IT department.

These two aspects are responsible for a judicial decision that is full of technical mistakes, that leads Brazil down a path with voting machines that is the opposite of that being taken internationally. Furthermore, regarding the second aspect, it is doubtful that this decision has been taken under due process of law as it cannot be said that the judges were impartial. The Brazilian Constitution guarantees the due process of law in article 5, LIV, which states: 'nobody will be deprived of his liberty or his property without the due process of law'. Once the Brazilian Constitution establishes several other principles on civil and criminal process, the due process of law is considered a complementary clause.[51] The impartiality of the judges is a central point in this issue, since no due process can be guaranteed by a judge that is not independent, that has any interest in the case or that is somehow involved in it.[52]

Conclusions

The pendulum has swung again. Once more, *TSE* policies were successful in banishing any proposal to audit Brazilian voting machines that does not originate from its technical department. This has been caused by a model in which *TSE* has concentrated powers, which, as usual, leads to authoritarianism and corporatism, the final consequence of which is that Brazil – though it has been using electronic voting machines for almost two decades – is still using first generation devices, that do not comply with the principle of the public nature of elections nor with the software-independence principle.

Once unconstitutional – as happened here – the law is considered void, so the printed paper trail it ordered is no longer mandatory. It is not clear whether the Court would also consider unconstitutional any other law that might establish some kind of physical trail in the future, since what was considered unconstitutional was not the printing system itself, but the method defined in the law, which, in the Court's view, would violate voter secrecy.

---

51 DINAMARCO, Cândido Rangel. *Instituições de Direito Processual Civil*, v. I (São Paulo: Malheiros, 2001), p. 243.

52 To preserve judicial independence, the Brazilian Constitution imposes some prohibitions on all judges: they can't, for instance, carry any other office or job, except as a teacher (that rule intends to avoid personal involvement with several kinds of interests: economical, political, professional), nor may they take part in any partisan political activity (article 95). *TSE* members, however, are entitled to decide cases in which their own rules and instructions (such as numerous technical details of the e-voting system) may be criticized by the litigants.

To transform its voting devices to second generation standards, Brazil should make them Independent Verification Systems, with the records of votes cast handled according to the following protocol, as stated in *Voluntary Voting System Guidelines*.[53]

> At least two cast vote records of the voter's selections are produced and one of the records is then stored in a manner that it cannot be modified by the voting system. For example, the voting system creates a record of the voter's selections and then copies it to unalterable storage media.
>
> The voter must be able to verify that both cast vote records are correct and match before leaving the polling place, e.g., verify his or her selections on the voting machine summary screen and also verify the second record on the unalterable storage media.
>
> The verification processes for the two cast vote records must be independent of each other, and at least one of the records must be verified directly by the voter.
>
> The contents of the two cast vote records also can be checked later for consistency through the use of unique identifiers that allow the records to be linked.

In our opinion, the decision does not prevent another law, with different words – that explicitly avoid any misunderstandings about the voters' secrecy – from being approved in the future by the Brazilian Congress to introduce VVPAT, in accordance with the cited guidelines.

As quoted above, the motives given by the Supreme Court judges apparently expose some degree of unfamiliarity with electronic systems, computer security and even the decisions of other courts or authorities around the world regarding similar issues. If the Court were aware of what the VVPAT model means in terms of security, a different decision could be surely expected. However, during the years since e-voting was introduced in Brazil, it has been observed that different Court members have expressed their complete confidence in whatever *TSE* technical staff says or does, suggesting that the main issue here seems to be less the technological knowledge (or lack of it) than the extreme concentration of powers in the hands of members of a single entity, the Brazilian Electoral Higher Court (*TSE*).

---

53 *Voluntary Voting System Guidelines*, v. 2009 (USA: NIST/US-EAC, May 2009) Volume 1, Section 7.8, http://www.eac.gov/assets/1/AssetManager/VVSG_Version_1-1_Volume_1_-_20090527.pdf.

References

ARANHA, D.F. et al. *Software Vulnerabilities in the Brazilian Voting Machine. In Design, Development, and Use of Secure Electronic Voting Systems* (USA: IGI Global, 2014), https://sites.google.com/site/dfaranha/pubs/aranha-karam-miranda-scarel-12-book.

BITTAR, Jacó. *Urna eletrônica: avanço ou retrocesso?* (May 1999), http://jus.com.br/artigos/1547/urna-eletronica-avanco-ou-retrocesso.

BRAZIL. Council of Presidents of Electoral Courts. *Minutes of the 51st Meeting* (2010), http://www.votoseguro.org/arquivos/ADI4543-Council-Presidents.pdf.

BRAZIL. Federal Senate. *Minutes of the 29th Meeting of CCJC* (2009), http://www.brunazo.eng.br/voto-e/arquivos/SenadoCCJata-20–8-09.pdf.

BRAZIL. Supremo Tribunal Federal. *ADI n. 4543*, http://www.stf.jus.br/portal/processo/verProcessoAndamento.asp?incidente=4019347.

BRUNAZO FILHO, Amílcar. *Modelos e Gerações dos equipamentos de votação eletrônica* (2014), http://www.brunazo.eng.br/voto-e/textos/modelosUE.htm.

BRUNAZO FILHO, Amílcar; CORTIZ, Maria Aparecida. *Fraudes e defesas no voto eletrônico* (São Paulo: All Print, 2006).

CUNHA, Sérgio Sérvulo da, et al. *Relatório sobre o Sistema Brasileiro de Votação Eletrônica* (São Paulo, 2010), http://www.brunazo.eng.br/voto-e/textos/RelatorioCMind.pdf.

DEL PICCHIA, Walter, et al. *Manifesto dos Professores* (September 2003), http://www.votoseguro.com/alertaprofessores/.

DINAMARCO, Cândido Rangel. *Instituições de Direito Processual Civil*, v. I. (São Paulo: Malheiros, 2001).

GRAAF, Jeroen van de; CUSTODIO, Ricardo Felipe. *Tecnologia Eleitoral e a Urna Eletronica*, Relatorio SBC (2002), http://www.sbc.org.br/index.php?option=com_jdownloads&Itemid=195&task=finish&cid=107&catid=77.

GUERZONI FILHO, Gilberto; SOARES, Paulo Henrique. *Funcionamento da Justiça Eleitoral em Alguns Países* (2000), http://www.brunazo.eng.br/voto-e/textos/SenadoEstudoSistemasEleitorais.odt.

LESSIG, Lawrence. *Code and Other Laws of Cyberspace* (New York: Basic Books, 1999).

MERCURI, Rebecca. *Electronic Vote Tabulation Checks and Balances*. Ph.D. dissertation, defended on 27 October 2000 at the School of Engineering and Applied Science of the University of Pennsylvania, Philadelphia, PA.

——. *Rebecca Mercuri's Statement on Electronic Voting* (2007[2001]), http://www.notablesoftware.com/RMstatement.html.

NORDEN, L.D. et al. *The Machinery of Democracy: Protecting Elections in an Electronic World* (New York: Brennan Center of Justice, NYU, 27 June 2006), http://www.brennancenter.org/sites/default/files/publications/Machinery_Democracy.pdf.

PORTO, Walter Costa. *A Mentirosa urna* (São Paulo: Ed. Martins Fontes, 2004).

REQUIÃO, Roberto. *A urna eletrônica e a legítima vontade popular* (August 2000), http://jus.com.br/artigos/1542/a-urna-eletronica-e-a-legitima-vontade-popular.

REZENDE, P.A.D. *Electronic Elections: A Balancing Act*, Department of Computer Science University of Brasília, http://www.cic.unb.br/~rezende/trabs/Brazil_election.html.

REZENDE, P.A.D.; BRUNAZO FILHO, Amílcar. *Security Measures for Brazil's e-Vote Act Two: Parallel Testing* (2003), http://www.cic.unb.br/docentes/pedro/trabs/Brazilvote2.htm.

RIVEST, R. et al. *A Modular Voting Architecture* (USA: CalTech-MIT Voting Technology Project, 2001), http://people.csail.mit.edu/rivest/BruckJeffersonRivest-AModularVotingArchitecture.doc

RIVEST, R.R.; WACK, J.P. *On the Notion of 'Software Independence' in Voting Systems* (USA: National Institute of Standards and Technology [NIST], 28 July 2006), http://people.csail.mit.edu/rivest/pubs/RW06.pdf.

SAGAN, Carl. *The Demon-Haunted World: Science as a Candle in the Dark* (New York: Ballantine Books, 1996).

SCHNEIER, Bruce. *Applied Cryptography* (2nd edition, New York: John Wiley & Sons, 1996).

——. *Designing Voting Machines to Minimize Coercion*, https://www.schneier.com/crypto-gram-0707.html#8.

——. *Internet Voting vs. Large-Value e-Commerce*, https://www.schneier.com/crypto-gram-0102.html#10.

——. *Voting and Technology*, https://www.schneier.com/crypto-gram-0012.html#1.

Voluntary Voting System Guidelines, v. 2007 (USA: NIST/US-EAC, 2007) Introduction 2.4, http://www.eac.gov/vvsg.

Voluntary Voting System Guidelines, v. 2009 (USA: NIST/US-EAC, May 2009) Volume 1, Section 7.8, http://www.eac.gov/assets/1/AssetManager/VVSG_Version_1-1_Volume_1_-_20090527.pdf.

Chapter 5

E-Voting Case Law in India

Rishab Bailey and Rohit Sharma

Introduction

The idea of "democracy"—literally meaning rule of the people—is today the bedrock of most political systems across the world. The concept itself however has remained far from immutable despite the near universal acceptance of its merits (at least in principle).[1] In recent times, events following the financial crisis of 2007–08 in "developed" countries, the numerous rebellions and uprisings in the Middle East following the Arab Spring of 2011, and the failure of popular revolutions in Africa to establish sustainable democratic systems, question the immutability and application of the idea.[2]

India's democracy, the world's largest, faces fewer doubts. India's record of smooth transition of power after national or provincial elections is proof of its democracy's strength and stability. This is incredible, since skeptics had thought it highly improbable that India could sustain democratic institutions, owing to the sheer number and diversity of its people.[3]

A key reason behind this successful experiment with a political system that was completely new to the subcontinent as recently as 100 years ago is the conduct of free and fair elections, a task entrusted to the Election Commission by the Constitution of India.[4] Conduct of national elections in India is a Herculean task in every sense of the word.[5] The recent elections to the Lok Sabha (the Lower

1 In 1941, there were only 11 democracies in the world, whereas by 2000, around 120 countries representing 63 percent of the world total had some form of democratic political system in place. "What's gone wrong with democracy," *The Economist*, March 1–7, 2014.

2 See generally "What's gone wrong with democracy," *The Economist*, March 1–7, 2014.

3 See generally Ramachandra Guha, *Unnatural Nation, India After Gandhi: The History of the World's Largest Democracy*, Pan Books, 2008.

4 Article 324 (1) of the Constitution of India provides that "The superintendence, direction and control of the preparation of the electoral rolls for, and the conduct of, all elections to Parliament and to the Legislature of every State and of elections to the offices of President and Vice-President held under this Constitution shall be vested in a Commission (referred to in this Constitution as the Election Commission)."

5 The task force for conducting a countrywide general election consists of nearly 5 million polling personnel and civil police forces. Cited from Election Commission of India website, "About ECI," http://eci.nic.in/eci_main1/the_setup.aspx, visited on July 5, 2014.

House of Parliament) held in early 2014 had more than 834 million registered electors[6] spread across 29 States and 7 Union Territories, voting for more than 8,200 candidates from 460 political parties.[7]

The Election Commission of India rightly receives immense credit for the successful conduct of elections of this magnitude.[8] Behind the mammoth exercise lies a web of rules and regulations that constitute the legal framework for the conduct of free and fair elections. The legal framework has transformed over the last six decades in response to the opportunities and challenges presented by evolving technology. Technological advances have allowed for safer and more efficient ways for casting and counting votes, and have also provided opportunities for enfranchising traditionally disenfranchised sections such as Non-Residents Indians (NRIs), etc.

This chapter studies the evolution of the legal framework governing use of electronic voting in India's elections through a study of case law laid down by the Supreme Court and the High Courts in India. The reader will observe that Courts of Law have played an important role in evolution of the legal framework governing conduct of elections, since parties to Election disputes regularly question the merits and demerits of technological changes brought about by the Government or the Election Commission. In conclusion, the authors look at the challenges that lie ahead in achieving the objective of free and fair elections through the use of technology.

The Legal Framework

As already noted above, the Constitution of India entrusts the task of conducting elections to the Election Commission of India. The Constitution also empowers Parliament to make law with respect to all matters relating to the conduct of elections, including the preparation of electoral rolls and other matters necessary for securing the "due" constitution of the concerned legislature.[9]

Parliament has primarily enacted two laws in pursuance of this power. The Representation of the People Act, 1950[10] provides for allocation of seats in the

---

6 From the Press Information Bureau, Election Commission of India Release, "464 political parties participated in General Elections 2014," May 21, 2014, http://pib.nic.in/elections2014/eleRelease.aspx?opt=1.

7 Seven national parties, 34 state parties and 322 unrecognized parties. From the Press Information Bureau, Election Commission of India Release, "464 political parties participated in General Elections 2014," May 21, 2014, http://pib.nic.in/elections2014/eleRelease.aspx?opt=1.

8 For instance see the Hon'ble President of India's address to Parliament, June 9, 2014, http://pmindia.nic.in/details54.php, visited on June 29, 2014.

9 Article 327 of the Constitution of India.

10 Hereinafter referred to as *the 1950 Act*.

lower House of Parliament and the provincial legislatures, the determination of constituencies for the purposes of elections to the legislatures, and the qualifications of voters and preparation of electoral rolls. Until recently, a person had to be ordinarily resident in a constituency to be registered as a voter.[11] With effect from 10th February, 2011, a new Section 20A was introduced in the 1950 Act to enable citizens of India who have not acquired the citizenship of any other country to be registered as voters without the requirement of ordinarily residing in a constituency in India.[12] However, the right to be enrolled as a voter carries little meaning when the person concerned is unable to travel to India to actually cast his vote during elections. This may change, thanks to calls from several quarters for enabling Non-Resident Indians (NRIs) to vote through online and other means. However, introduction of alternative means of casting votes is not exactly straightforward, and will require tinkering with established rules for casting votes. As this chapter shows, new means for casting votes cannot simply be introduced by experimenting with new technology, but require careful formulation and amendment of existing rules and procedures.

The detailed provisions for conduct of elections and other matters are contained in the Representation of the People Act, 1951.[13] Part V of *the 1951 Act* contains provisions relating to the conduct of elections, in which Chapter IV relates to the Poll. Interestingly, with regard to prescribing the manner of voting at polls, Parliament has delegated the task to the Government of India, which prescribes the manner of voting through Rules made after consultation with the Election Commission.[14] These Rules are placed before each House of Parliament for any modifications.[15] The Government of India has made detailed provisions to regulate the manner in which all aspects of elections are conducted, known as the Conduct of Elections Rules, 1961.[16]

---

11 Section 19 of the 1950 Act.

12 Section 20A, inserted vide the Representation of the People (Amendment) Act, 2010, provides that every citizen of India, whose name is not included in the electoral roll, who has not acquired the citizenship of any other country and who is absenting from his place of ordinary residence in India owing to his employment, education or otherwise, whether temporarily or otherwise, is entitled to have his name registered in the electoral roll in the constituency in which his place of residence as mentioned in his passport is located.

13 Hereinafter referred to as *the 1951 Act*.

14 Section 59 of *the 1951 Act* provides "At every election where a poll is taken votes shall be given by ballot in such manner as may be prescribed ...." The term "prescribed" is defined in Section 2(g) of *the 1951 Act* as "prescribed by rules made under this Act." Rule making power under the Act is conferred by Section 169(1) upon the Central Government, subject to prior consultation with the Election Commission.

15 Section 169(3) of *the 1951 Act*.

16 Published vide Ministry of Law Notification No. S.O. 859, dated April 15, 1961. See Gazette of India, Extraordinary, Part II, Section 3(ii), page 419 [hereinafter referred to as *the Rules*].

The Rules lay down voting in person as the norm,[17] subject to exceptions of voting by postal ballot or through proxy.[18] Voting by postal ballot is permitted[19] for members of the Armed Forces who have not opted to vote by proxy (known as service voters),[20] persons holding high offices like the President of India, Governors of States, Cabinet Ministers, etc.,[21] voters on election duty,[22] electors subjected to preventive detention,[23] and persons notified by the Election Commission.[24] Voting through proxy is permitted only for members of the Armed Forces who have opted to vote through proxy (known as classified service voters).[25] *The 1951 Act* permits the Central Government to allow voting by postal ballot for members of the armed police force of a State serving outside the State, or employees of the Government of India posted outside India,[26] but this has not yet been done.

Difficulties Faced with the Use of Ballot Papers in Elections

The Rules originally contemplated voting only through the use of ballot papers.[27] However, the use of ballot papers presented several problems that led to a variety

---

17 Rule 16 reads "*Save as hereinafter provided, all electors voting at an election shall do so in person at the polling station provided for them under Section 25 or, as the case may be, at the place of polling fixed under Section 29.*"

18 Part III of *the Rules* contains the detailed procedure to be followed for voting by post, while the procedure for voting through proxy is contained in Part IIIB.

19 The voter can choose to vote in person instead of by post.

20 Section 60(a) of *the 1951 Act* read with Section 20(8)(a) of *the 1950 Act* read with Rules 18(a)(ii) and 17(a) of *the Rules*.

21 Rules 18(a)(i) and 17(b) of *the Rules* read with Section 20(4) of *the 1950 Act*. Notification No. S.O. 959, dated April 18, 1960 has declared the following offices as covered by Section 20(4): (1) the President of India; (2) the Vice-President of India; (3) the Governors of States; (4) the Cabinet Ministers of the Union or of any State; (5) the Deputy Chairman and Members of the Planning Commission; (6) the Ministers of State of the Union or of any State; (7) the Deputy Ministers of the Union or of any State; (8) the Speaker of the House of the People or of any State Legislative Assembly; (9) the Chairman of any State Legislative Council; (10) the Lieutenant Governor of Union Territories; (11) the Deputy Speaker of the House of the People or of any State Legislative Assembly; (12) the Deputy Chairman of the Council of States or of any State Legislative Council; and (13) the Parliamentary Secretaries of the Union or of any State.

22 Rules 18(a)(iii) and 17(c) of *the Rules*.

23 Section 60(d) of *the 1951 Act* read with Rule 18(a)(iv) of *the Rules*.

24 Section 60(c) of *the 1951 Act* read with Rule 27B of *the Rules*.

25 Section 60(a) of *the 1951 Act* read with Section 20(8)(a) of *the 1950 Act* read with Rule 27M of *the Rules*.

26 Section 60(b)(i) of *the 1951 Act* read with Section 20(8)(c) and (d) of *the 1950 Act*.

27 Rule 30 of *the Rules*.

of election disputes[28] in Courts, such as the issuance of wrong ballot papers,[29] mistakes in printing a candidate's name on the ballot paper,[30] the use of Roman instead of Arabic numerals,[31] ballot papers not bearing a mark at the prescribed place,[32] etc.

Ballot papers have also been at the center of very serious and far-reaching allegations, such as in the case of *Shashi Bhushan* v. *Prof. Balraj Madhok*.[33] This case was brought before the Supreme Court by the successful candidates from South Delhi and Delhi-Sadar constituencies in the national elections held in 1971, against an order passed by the Delhi High Court permitting inspection of ballot papers at the insistence of the unsuccessful candidates. The allegation of the unsuccessful candidates was that the ruling Congress party (to which the successful candidates

---

28 The Supreme Court of India is the apex court in the country. Election disputes are originally filed in an Election Tribunal or in the High Court of a State. There would be numerous examples of elections disputes stemming from problems with ballot papers in these regional courts. However, this chapter only refers to election disputes that reached the Supreme Court by way of appeal.

29 In *Hari Vishnu Kamath* v. *Ahmad Ishaque*, (1955) 1 SCR 1104, the Polling Officer had issued ballot papers meant for State Legislative Assembly elections containing a brown bar, instead of papers meant for Parliamentary elections with a green bar. The Election Commission condoned the mistake since the mistake was brought to its notice before the counting of votes had taken place. But the Supreme Court struck down the entire election on the basis that use of ballot papers that were not prescribed for national elections violated Rule 28 of *the Rules*.

30 In *Mahadeo* v. *Babu Udai Pratap Singh*, (1966) 2 SCR 564, the name of a candidate was printed as "Udai Bhan Pratap Singh" in the ballot papers, even though his actual name as per electoral rolls was "Udai Pratap Singh." The Supreme Court rejected the candidate's plea that this mistake rendered the election (in which he was unsuccessful) void, mainly because the symbol chosen by the candidate was correctly shown in the ballot papers and therefore there was no confusion regarding the candidate's identity due to the mistake in printing his name in the ballot papers. It was also held by the Court that Rule 56(2)(g), which prescribed the form and design of ballot papers, was not infringed in this case because Rule 56(2)(g) did not govern mistakes in contents of the ballot papers.

31 In *Shyam Sunder* v. *Satya Ketu*, (1967) 1 SCR 752, the unsuccessful candidate in an election to the U.P. Legislative Council had sought rejection of votes where the voters had indicated first preference for a candidate by using Roman numeral "I" in the ballot papers, instead of the Arabic "1." The Supreme Court rejected the argument by holding that even though Rule 73(2)(a), which provides that a ballot paper on which the figure 1 is not marked shall be invalid, contained the figure 1 in the form of an Arabic numeral, but that did not mean that the rule intended that the figure 1 on the ballot paper can only be marked in the Arabic form and in no other.

32 In *M. Narayana Rao* v. *G. Venkata Reddy*, (1977) 1 SCC 771, the Supreme Court rejected as invalid ballot papers on which voters had indicated their preference for a candidate on the back of the ballot paper instead of at the prescribed place on the front of the paper, holding that this amounted to the ballot paper containing no mark at all.

33 (1972) 4 SCC 594.

belonged) had rigged the election in collusion with the Election Commission. The manner of rigging alleged was that the ballot papers had been chemically treated and the symbol of Congress candidates in the ballot papers mechanically stamped using invisible ink. It was further alleged that due to the chemical treatment of ballot papers, the mark put at the time of polling disappeared after a few days and the stamping mechanically placed earlier emerged. Though the Supreme Court commented on the absurdity of the allegations, it nevertheless allowed inspection of a few samples of ballot papers, mainly because the allegations were being made in several places in the country with some persistence and the Court felt that in these circumstances it would damage the democratic fabric of society if these rumors were allowed to persist. Eventually, however, inspection of samples revealed that the theory of the mechanical treatment of ballot papers was absolutely unfounded.[34]

Petitions for inspection of ballot papers were filed in Courts with such frequency that the Supreme Court had to chide the election authorities to respond sensitively to demands for re-counting votes in close contests in order to reduce the feeling of injustice at the initial stage itself.[35] The Court, around this time, also crystallized the principles on which the Courts must decide requests for the inspection of ballot papers.[36]

Teething Troubles with the Introduction of Electronic Voting Machines

The problems associated with the use of ballot papers led to the Election Commission experimenting with Electronic Voting Machines in the late 1970s and early 1980s. However, initial attempts to introduce Electronic Voting Machines ran into legal trouble. In the case of *A.C. Jose* v. *Sivan Pillai*,[37] the election to Parur Assembly Constituency in the Kerala Legislative Assembly was called into question on the grounds that votes had been cast by means of electronic machines,[38] which had been permitted by the Election Commission through a Notification dated May 13, 1982.

The case brought the nature of the powers of the Election Commission under the Constitution to the fore.[39] With respect to the Notification permitting use of

34 The Supreme Court's decision after inspection of the ballot papers is reported as *Prof. Balraj Madhok* v. *Shashi Bhushan*, (1972) 2 SCC 616.

35 *S. Baldev Singh* v. *Teja Singh Swatantar*, (1975) 4 SCC 406.

36 *Bhabhi* v. *Sheo Govind*, (1976) 1 SCC 687.

37 (1984) 2 SCC 656.

38 19,182 votes out of 30,450 were cast by means of electronic machines.

39 It was argued on behalf of the successful candidate and the Election Commission that by virtue of Article 324 of the Constitution, the Election Commission enjoyed plenary powers in matters of superintendence, direction and control of elections, and consequently, its directions would prevail even over any Act of Parliament or Rules framed thereunder. The Supreme Court rejected the theory of plenary powers propounded on behalf of the Commission, and held that the Election Commission could pass any orders or directions

electronic voting machines, the Court found that the notification ran contrary to Section 59 of *the 1951 Act* and *the Rules*, which only permitted voting by use of ballot papers. The Court referred to Section 61 of the 1951 Act and observed that Parliament intended the use of only ballot papers for casting of votes (with "ballot" being understood in its narrower and more traditional sense to exclude voting using machines).[40] Adopting a rather strict interpretation of the provision, and in the absence of any specific mandate for the use of electronic machines in the statute, the Court declared the use of Electronic Voting Machines unlawful, and directed a re-poll in the polling stations where these machines had been used.

Interestingly, however, when the advantages of Electronic Voting Machines over ballot papers were brought to the attention of the Court, the Court left it to the Legislature and the Government to give necessary legal sanction to Electronic Voting Machines.

Statutory Amendments to Authorize the Use of Electronic Voting Machines

Faced with the Supreme Court's judgment in the *A.C. Jose* case, Parliament had to step in to enable the Election Commission to use Electronic Voting Machines at elections. The Representation of People (Amendment) Act, 1988[41] introduced Section 61A into *the 1951 Act* thereby permitting use of voting machines for polling,[42] and made a consequential amendment in Section 58 to include, as a

---

in relation to the conduct of elections only when there was no Parliamentary legislation or rules on the subject. But where there is an Act of Parliament or rules made thereunder, the Commission cannot override the same.

40 There are no reasons given by the Court for arriving at this interpretation. Section 61 of *the 1951 Act* prescribes the special procedure for preventing personation of electors. It *inter alia* enables the making of rules for marking of the thumb or any other finger with indelible ink of every elector who applies for a ballot paper for the purpose of voting. Though Section 61 does not expressly exclude the use of Electronic Voting Machines for the casting of votes, the Supreme Court appears to have been persuaded by the reference only to ballot papers to hold that Section 61 militates against the use of Electronic Voting Machines.

41 Act 1 of 1989.

42 Section 61A reads: "61A.Voting machines of elections.- Notwithstanding anything contained in this Act or the machines, in such manner as may be prescribed, may be adopted in rules made thereunder, the giving and recording of votes by voting such constituency or constituencies as the Election Commission may, having regard to the circumstances of each case, specify. Explanation.- For the purpose of this section, 'voting machine' means any machine or apparatus whether operated electronically or otherwise used for giving or recording of votes and any reference to a ballot box or ballot paper in this Act or the rules made thereunder shall, save as otherwise provided, by construed as including a reference to such voting machine wherever such voting machine is used at any election."

circumstance justifying directions for fresh elections, the development of a mechanical failure in a voting machine.

Thereafter, *the Rules* were amended[43] and Chapter II titled "Voting by Electronic Voting Machines" was introduced into Part IV of *the Rules*. Rule 49A prescribes that every electronic voting machine shall have a control unit and a balloting unit and shall be of such design as may be approved by the Election Commission. *The Rules* prescribe in detail how the voting machine is to be prepared,[44] the details that have to be recorded before permitting an elector to vote,[45] the manner in which votes are to be cast through voting machines,[46] the procedure for sealing the voting machine after the poll[47] and transmission of the voting machine to the returning officer.[48]

The Acceptance of EVMs by the Judiciary

Since the initial use of Electronic Voting Machines (EVMs) had presented the unsuccessful candidate with a convenient legal escape, the use of machines in the national elections held in 1999 also became the subject matter of a few election petitions. In *Michael B. Fernandes* v. *C.K. Jaffer Sharief*,[49] an unsuccessful candidate in elections to Yelahanka Parliamentary constituency in Karnataka challenged the constitutionality of Section 61A of *the 1951 Act* and cited inherent defects in Electronic Voting Machines as the basis for setting aside the election. The High Court of Karnataka relied on the evidence of scientists who had designed the EVMs and gave its stamp of approval to EVMs citing efficiencies such as cost reduction and the purported imperviousness of EVMs to tampering and rigging.

The Court noted that developments in technology ensured that the defects in EVMs (as referred to by the Supreme Court in the *A.C. Jose* v. *Sivan Pillai case*[50]) were no longer of relevance as all these defects had been corrected in the newer version of the machine. Balancing the probabilities of malpractice caused by the use of EVMs (which in the Court's opinion was zero) with the benefits gained by using electronic voting (such as cost reductions, time saved, reduction of certain

43 Amended vide Notification No. S.O. 230(E) dated March 24, 1992.

44 Rules 49B and 49E.

45 Rule 49L.

46 Rule 49M.

47 Rule 49T.

48 Rule 49V.

49 AIR 2004 Kar 289.

50 In this case, the Court was appraised of various drawbacks in the EVM system which centered around the absence of any means to adequately identify certain types of invalid votes such as when a vote was cast after closing time, where votes were cast by the same person in more than one constituency or in different booths in the same constituency, where a dead person was impersonated and a vote cast, etc.

types of malpractice found in the traditional system of voting), the Court found the challenge against the use of EVMs untenable.

After the judiciary's stamp of approval, the Election Commission placed its full weight behind the country-wide adoption of EVMs, with the result that voting by ballot paper was completely phased out in the national elections of 2004.

While there have been continued challenges to the use of EVMs from time to time, with most of these petitions alleging fraud or technical problems with the use or handling of the EVMs, in almost all cases,[51] Courts have rejected the contentions outright based on the reasoning cited in the cases mentioned previously, and more commonly because petitioners have usually failed to provide any material particulars (or substantial fact based evidence) of how the EVMs have been misused or tampered with.[52]

The Introduction of a Paper-Trail System to EVMs

After the national elections in 2009, the issue of the vulnerability of EVMs to tampering or hacking was raised in various quarters, and a Public Interest Petition was also filed in the Delhi High Court[53] seeking directions to the Election Commission to introduce a system of "paper-trail" along with EVMs, so that immediately upon voting, a receipt is delivered to the voter indicating that name of the candidate in favor of which his or her vote has been registered. A paper trail would also ensure an alternative method of recounting—rather than merely relying on the electronic record. It was contended that a "paper-trail" was a necessary component of the legal requirement of free and fair elections.

---

51 See for instance (a) *Sambhaji* v. *Bhaskarrao*, Election Petition No. 1 of 2009, decided by the Bombay High Court at Aurangabad on March 25, 2011, (b) *Sanjay Pawar* v. *Pankaj Chhagan Bhujbal*, Election Petition No. 32 of 2009, decided by the High Court of Bombay on August 7, 2012, (c) *Annarao* v. *Amit*, Election Petition No. 13 of 2009, decided by the High Court of Bombay at Aurangabad on March 18, 2013, (d) *Manohar v Shankar*, Election Petition No. 16 of 2009, decided by the High Court of Bombay at Aurangabad on May 6, 2011 (e) *Sharad Madhavrao Patil* v. *Rohidas Chudaman Patil*, 2008 (2) BomCR 883, and (f) *Dr. Madhavrao* v. *Ashok Chavan*, Election Petition No. 11 of 2009, decided by the Bombay High Court on October 18, 2012. In all these cases it was alleged that EVMs were tampered with but no material particulars were provided and as a result the election petitions were dismissed at the preliminary stage itself.

52 An exception is the case of *Sushil Singh* v. *Prabhu Narain Yadav And Ors*, AIR 2003 All 331, where the EVM used for the election showed one candidate as having won the first three times a re-check was conducted, but showed another candidate as having won the election when counting was reconducted for the fourth time. Hearing a plea for return/rejection of the Petition, the Court found enough merit in the allegations to order trial.

53 *Dr. Subramanian Swamy* v. *Election Commission of India*, Writ Petition (Civil) No. 11879 of 2009.

The Election Commission, encouraged by the Judiciary's observations regarding the infallibility of its machines, took the rather incredible stand that there was absolutely no possibility of tampering with or rigging its EVMs.

This is despite serious concerns being raised about the vulnerability of EVMs to fraudulent practices,[54] including by a group of international security researchers who have released a study demonstrating certain simple ways[55] in which Indian EVMs can be attacked and election results skewed.[56] This study highlights the problems with relying only on a machine based system to record votes—in particular given that the micro controllers of the EVMs use proprietary, pre-programmed software manufactured outside the country (that therefore cannot be read or verified). Rather bizarrely, one of the engineers who carried out these tests was arrested by the Maharashtra police for purportedly illegally acquiring the EVM he used to demonstrate his claims![57]

In order to buttress its claims regarding the invulnerability of the EVMs to tampering, in August 2009, the Commission invited people to demonstrate the vulnerability of any one of a hundred EVMs randomly selected by it from 10

---

54 An interesting instance is that of the Election Petition of *Dr. K. Laxman* v. *Nayini Narasimha Reddy* decided by the Andhra Pradesh High Court on January 18, 2008, In this case, the Petitioner received zero votes and therefore contested the validity of the result contending that the EVMs had been rigged and that it was impossible for him to have not received any votes (he even had witnesses deposed who claimed to have voted for him). The Petitioner's witness, a technical expert from Electronics Corporation of India Ltd. (one of the manufacturers of the EVMs) deposed that (contrary to the claims of the Election Commission), the micro-chips or micro controllers for the EVMs were in fact manufactured in the US where certain data was also fed into the micro controllers. While also admitting that there was no way of checking whether a vote had been correctly recorded by the EVMs he denied all suggestions that any manipulation of the software on the EVMs was possible so as to tamper with the data recorded by it. The Court, however, held against the Petitioner on facts stating that he had failed to prove the election had been materially affected by any improper counting of votes. Press Release "India's Electronic Voting Machines Proven Insecure," April 28, 2010, http://www.indiaevm.org/press.html.

55 One attack involves replacing a small part of the machine with a look-alike component that can be silently instructed to steal a percentage of the votes in favor of a chosen candidate. These instructions can be sent wirelessly from a mobile phone. Another attack uses a pocket-sized device to change the votes stored in the EVM between the election and the public counting session (which in India can be weeks later).

56 Hari K Prasad, J Alex Halderman, Rop Gonngrijp, "India's EVMs are vulnerable to fraud: Security analysis of India's Electronic Voting Machines," http://www.indiaevm.org/paper.html. The Press Release by this group of experts titled "India's Electronic Voting Machines proven insecure," April 28, 2010, http://www.indiaevm.org/press.html.

57 Sreejiraj Eluvangal, "EC defends arrest of engineer who exposed EVM flaws," *DNA*, August 26, 2010, http://www.dnaindia.com/mumbai/report-ec-defends-arrest-of-engineer-who-exposed-evm-flaws-1428821, Times News Network, "EVM controversy takes a political turn," *The Times of India*, August 26, 2010, http://timesofindia.indiatimes.com/india/EVM-controversy-takes-a-political-turn/articleshow/6438841.cms.

states, and released a Press Note highlighting the salient features of EVMs and reiterating its stand that EVMs used by the Commission were completely fool-proof.[58] Given that no one was able to demonstrate adequately the vulnerability of EVMs on this occasion, the Commission has taken no further steps to secure EVMs other than the (previous) issuance of guidelines on the storage, movement, and physical verification of EVMs (in order *inter alia*, to prevent theft of the machines from the places of storage).[59]

The Delhi High Court, while rightly observing that the vulnerability of EVMs to fraud could not be ruled out, refused to direct the introduction of a system of "paper-trail" in the absence of concrete proof of the machines' vulnerability and in the absence of any statutory provision requiring the same.[60] The Court repeatedly noted the various benefits of the electronic voting system used by the Commission (such as transparency and the ease of conducting elections), and pointed out that introducing a paper trail would carry certain risks if not properly planned and implemented (such as misuse, malpractice and even the possibility that the secrecy of the ballot may be compromised). The Court, while noting the need for greater transparency and trust in the electoral system, essentially called for the Commission to carry out further consultation with all relevant stakeholders in order to examine issues surrounding the challenges to conducting elections using EVMs (such as security concerns).

When the matter was appealed before the Supreme Court, the Election Commission informed the Court that it was in a position to adopt the Voter-Verifiable Paper Audit Trail (VVPAT) system into its Electronic Voting Machines.[61] Thereafter, pursuant to directions of the Supreme Court, the Election Commission filed an affidavit informing the Court that it had approved the design of VVPAT and also indicating the other steps that it would follow to implement this system.[62] Vide a Notification dated August 14, 2013, *the 1961 Rules* were amended to provide for the use of printers for a paper trail along with the Electronic Voting Machines.[63]

Finally, in its judgment dated October 8, 2013,[64] the Supreme Court held that the "paper trail" is an indispensable requirement of free and fair elections and that the confidence of voters in the system could only be achieved through transparency which necessitated the need to introduce an accurate and verifiable

58 Press Note No. PN/ECI/41/2009 dated August 8, 2009, issued by the Election Commission of India.

59 ECI Guidelines dated May 3, 2010, No. 51/8/6/2010-EMS, http://eci.nic.in/eci_main/CurrentElections/ECI_Instructions/ins310510.pdf.

60 *Subramaniam Swamy* v. *Election Commission of India*, Judgment dated January 17, 2012 passed in Writ Petition (Civil) No. 11879 of 2009.

61 Order dated April 9, 2013 passed in Special Leave Petition (Civil) No. 13735 of 2012.

62 Order dated May 2, 2013 passed in Special Leave Petition (Civil) No. 13735 of 2012.

63 Notification No. S.O. 2470(E) dated August 14, 2013.

64 *Subramanian Swami* v. *Election Commission of India*, (2013) 10 SCC 500.

system of voting. However, in the same breath, the Court paradoxically allowed the Election Commission to introduce the VVPAT system in a phased manner.

In the 2014 national elections, EVMs with the VVPAT system were used in eight constituencies in eight different states.

Introduction of Alternative Methods of Voting for Non-Resident Indians (NRIs)

As noted above, the right conferred by Section 20A of the 1950 Act has remained meaningless for NRIs who find it impossible to leave their country of residence to cast their votes at elections. This has led to calls for conferring the right to vote on NRIs through online or other alternative means, and the issue has received some attention in both the local and international press. Three petitions have also been filed in the Supreme Court of India seeking directions to the Election Commission to permit NRIs to vote through online or other facilities.[65] The Supreme Court had called upon the Election Commission and the Government of India to file their responses to these petitions.[66]

The Election Commission, after carrying out consultations with all major political parties in India, has opined that while measures such as personal voting at diplomatic stations and Internet voting are not presently feasible, certain measures such as the use of proxy voting and e-postal ballots (where a ballot paper is sent electronically to the non resident voter, filled in and returned by post to the election authorities) could be utilized.[67] Interestingly, the Election Commission rejects the use of Internet based voting primarily because present technology cannot adequately deal with the various security concerns raised in this context. The Report of the Election Commission has been taken on record by the Supreme Court of India, but the Court is yet to finally decide the matter.[68]

The Union of India has stated in the Supreme Court that it agrees with the recommendations of the Election Commission in this regard (i.e. to extend voting

---

65 See for instance, *Nagendar Chindan* v. *Union of India*, Writ Petition (Civil) No. 80 of 2013, *Naresh Kumar Hanchate* v. *Union of India*, Writ Petition (Civil) No. 1010 of 2013 and *Dr Shamsheer VP* v. *Union of India*, Writ Petition (Civil) No. 265 of 2014, all filed before the Supreme Court of India.

66 See order dated February 22, 2013 passed by the Supreme Court in Writ Petition (Civil) No. 80 of 2013, available at http://courtnic.nic.in/supremecourt/temp/80201332222013p.txt, visited on 18th May, 2015.

67 See Report of Committee for Exploring Feasibility of Alternative Options for Voting by Overseas Electors, Constituted by the Election Commission of India, October 2014, available at http://eci.nic.in/eci_main1/current/NRI%20Voting_Final%20draft23012015.pdf, visited on May 3, 2015.

68 See the order dated 14th November, 2014 passed by the Supreme Court in Writ Petition (Civil) No. 80 of 2013, available at http://courtnic.nic.in/supremecourt/casestatus_new/querycheck_page2.asp, visited on 18th May, 2015.

rights to non residents through the aforementioned methods) and accordingly has sought time to carry out the necessary amendments to the Representation of the People Act, 1951.[69] However, the issue is unlikely to be resolved soon, with the Rajya Sabha, the Upper House of Parliament, recently voting on a calling of attention notice brought by the opposition (which has a majority in this House) stating that implementing e-voting for non residents (through proxy voting or e-postal ballots) was too risky, and further questioning the government on why it was in a rush to ensure voting rights for non residents but not for domestically displaced or migrant people.[70]

While both the Government and Election Commission have rejected the possibility of voting rights either through EVMs or the Internet to be extended to non residents, it should be noted that the first Internet voting initiative in India was carried out during the Municipal Corporation Elections held in April 2011 in Gandhinagar, Gujarat, and a committee constituted by the Election Commission is studying the model to explore its wider implementation.[71]

Conclusion

The use of technology has gone a long way to strengthen Indian democracy. Electronic Voting Machines have permitted results of elections conducted for over a month to be declared on the day of commencement of counting. There have been no established claims of improper recording of votes. The costs and man-hours saved are enormous, and introduction of the VVPAT system is a welcome addition to assuage any fears of rigging or hacking of machines, although it re-introduces the problems associated with the use of paper in elections of this magnitude.

However, the increased use of technology does not mean that election malpractice is an issue of the past. India continues to face numerous hurdles in its democratic process—ranging from instances of booth capturing involving physical assault and intimidation to more insidious issues such as communal polarization, use of undeclared funds by political parties, and so on. In addition, there is the

69 See the Order of the Supreme Court dated January 12, 2015, in Nagender Chindam v. Union of India, Writ Petition No. 80 of 2013, available at http://courtnic.nic.in/supremecourt/casestatus_new/querycheck_page2.asp, visited on 18th May, 2015.

70 Abantika Ghosh, "Opposition to Government: When Migrants Cant Vote, Why the Rush to Let NRIs?", The Indian Express, April 29, 2015, available at http://indianexpress.com/article/india/india-others/opposition-to-govt-when-migrants-cant-vote-why-the-rush-to-let-nris/, visited on May 3, 2015, and Times News Network, "E-Voting for NRIs too risky, say Rajya Sabha members", The Times of India, April 29, 2015, available at http://timesofindia.indiatimes.com/india/E-voting-for-NRIs-too-risky-say-Rajya-Sabha-members/articleshow/47090020.cms, visited on May 3, 2015.

71 Ritika Chopra, "Election Commission of India may opt for Gujarat online model for NRI voting," June 29, 2014, http://articles.economictimes.indiatimes.com/2014-07-29/news/52186810_1_election-commission-nris-voting-rights, visited on August 31, 2014.

issue of low voter turnouts in India (where it is not compulsory to vote)—which it is believed, by some, could be changed by putting in place more convenient systems of voting (for instance the use of online voting).

While there is much to commend in the manner of conduct of elections in India, it is vital that the Election Commission continues to function in an independent and enlightened manner, including by ensuring the use of best practices from around the world. For instance, the acceptance of electronic voting and the development of technology, particularly the Internet, has led to calls for the use of online voting to be recognized in law, but the Election Commission has rejected the possibility for the time being citing security concerns. Further, while the issue of voting rights for Indians resident abroad has received tremendous attention in the local and international press, a similar level of interest is absent when it comes to the case of migrant workers within India. The Election Commission and the Government have cited practical difficulties in enabling distance voting for this large section of India's labour workforce, which traditionally represents one of the most disenfranchised groups in India.[72]

With a by and large supportive judiciary, the Election Commission has essentially been given a free hand in working within the previously mentioned statutes and regulations to ensure the conduct of free and fair polling in India. Successive governments too, have generally been supportive of measures adopted by the Election Commission to improve election processes in India. It is therefore incumbent on the Election Commission to take a considered and dispassionate view on critical issues such as the continued introduction of technical measures to aid India's election processes, given the importance of ensuring that *all* Indian citizens are permitted to take part in the democratic process.

References

Articles

Abantika Ghosh, "Opposition to Government: When Migrants Cant Vote, Why the Rush to Let NRIs?", The Indian Express, April 29, 2015, available at http://indianexpress.com/article/india/india-others/opposition-to-govt-when-migrants-cant-vote-why-the-rush-to-let-nris/, visited on May 3, 2015.

72 See Dhananjay Mahapatra, "NRIs Can Vote, Not Migrant Labourers: Centre and EC", The Times of India, April 14, 2015, available at http://timesofindia.indiatimes.com/india/NRIs-can-vote-not-migrant-labourers-Centre-and-EC/articleshow/46914718.cms, visited on May 3, 2015 and "The Big Picture, E Voting for NRIs and Migrant Labour: Pros and Cons", Insights on India, April 30, 2015, available at http://www.insightsonindia.com/2015/04/30/the-big-picture-e-voting-for-nris-and-migrant-labour-pros-and-cons/, visited on May 3, 2015.

Ritika Chopra, "Election Commission of India may opt for Gujarat online model for NRI voting," June 29, 2014, http://articles.economictimes.indiatimes.com/2014-07-29/news/52186810_1_election-commission-nris-voting-rights, visited on August 31, 2014.

Dhananjay Mahapatra, "NRIs Can Vote, Not Migrant Labourers: Centre and EC", The Times of India, April 14, 2015, available at http://timesofindia.indiatimes.com/india/NRIs-can-vote-not-migrant-labourers-Centre-and-EC/articleshow/46914718.cms, visited on May 3, 2015.

"The Big Picture, E Voting for NRIs and Migrant Labour: Pros and Cons", Insights on India, April 30, 2015, available at http://www.insightsonindia.com/2015/04/30/the-big-picture-e-voting-for-nris-and-migrant-labour-pros-and-cons/, visited on May 3, 2015.

Election Commission of India, "About ECI," http://eci.nic.in/eci_main1/the_setup.aspx, visited on July 5, 2014.

Sreejiraj Eluvangal, "EC defends arrest of engineer who exposed EVM flaws," *DNA*, August 26, 2010, http://www.dnaindia.com/mumbai/report-ec-defends-arrest-of-engineer-who-exposed-evm-flaws-1428821.

Express News Service, "SC: NRIs voting via Internet may open Pandora's Box," *The Indian Express*, April 12, 2014, http://indianexpress.com/article/india/india-others/sc-nris-voting-via-internet-may-open-pandoras-box/, visited on July 13, 2014.

The Hon'ble President of India's address to Parliament, June 9, 2014, http://pmindia.nic.in/details54.php, visited on June 29, 2014.

Hari K Prasad, J Alex Halderman, Rop Gonngrijp, Press Release, "India's Electronic Voting Machines proven insecure," April 28, 2010, http://www.indiaevm.org/press.html.

——, "India's EVMs are vulnerable to fraud: Security analysis of India's Electronic Voting Machines," http://www.indiaevm.org/paper.html.

The Press Information Bureau, Election Commission of India Release, "464 political parties participated in General Elections 2014," May 21, 2014, http://pib.nic.in/elections2014/eleRelease.aspx?opt=1.

Press Trust of India, "Election Commission exploring voting through Internet for NRIs," *The Indian Express*, April 7, 2014, http://indianexpress.com/article/india/politics/election-commission-exploring-voting-through-internet-for-nris/, visited on July 13, 2014.

Times News Network, "EVM controversy takes a political turn," *The Times of India*, August 26, 2010, http://timesofindia.indiatimes.com/india/EVM-controversy-takes-a-political-turn/articleshow/6438841.cms.

Times News Network, "E-Voting for NRIs too risky, say Rajya Sabha members", The Times of India, April 29, 2015, available at http://timesofindia.indiatimes.com/india/E-voting-for-NRIs-too-risky-say-Rajya-Sabha-members/articleshow/47090020.cms, visited on May 3, 2015.

"What's gone wrong with democracy," *The Economist*, March 1–7, 2014.

Books

Ramachandra Guha, *Unnatural Nation, India After Gandhi: The History of the World's Largest Democracy*, Pan Books, 2008.

Reports

Report of Committee for Exploring Feasibility of Alternative Options for Voting by Overseas Electors, Constituted by the Election Commission of India, October 2014, available at http://eci.nic.in/eci_main1/current/NRI%20Voting_Final%20draft23012015.pdf, visited on May 3, 2015.

Chapter 6

A Judicial Approach to Internet Voting in Estonia

Ülle Madise and Priit Vinkel

Introduction

Estonia is a small nation in Northern Europe, a Member of the European Union and NATO and has one of the most advanced e-governments in the world. It is the only country where all adult inhabitants are obliged to possess electronic identity and where countrywide remote I-voting[1] with binding results in all elections and referendums has been allowed since 2005. The share of online voters has risen to 24.3 per cent in the 2011 *Riigikogu* (Estonian Parliament) elections and 30.5 per cent in the 2015 *Riigikogu* elections. The compulsory e-ID as a universal access key to public and private e-services is a critical success factor for I-voting, advanced e-Health[2] solutions, digital signature, electronic tax board etc.

Using the Internet for public services raises several constitutional and cyber security problems. Neither abandoning e-services nor simply denying threats is a proper solution. Netizens[3] require the redesigning and rethinking of many institutions, concepts and principles to protect values of democracy in the Internet era. Indeed, using new technologies is just a means, not an end. Thus the benefit should outweigh the cost and risks; and judicial control over the executive,

1 The Estonian concept of remote I-voting does not limit the environment of the voter, so, contrary to the concept of electronic voting used in many countries (kiosk voting, voting machines etc.), I-voting is not offered in polling stations. However, many public and private establishments like banks or libraries offer internet access to the public during elections.

2 Estonian e-Health comprises four systems: an electronic health record, digital registration, digital prescriptions and a digital image.

3 The term 'netizen' was coined by Michael Hauben in 1992 while studying at Columbia University. See also Michael Hauben and Ronda Hauben, Netizens: On the History and Impact of Usenet and the Internet (Los Alamitos, CA: IEEE Computer Society Press, 1997). As pointed out by several thinkers like James Fishkin, there is a need for some new approaches and tools to improve decision-making and participation. See e.g. The Centre for Deliberative Democracy website http://cdd.stanford.edu/ (accessed 1 August 2014). For opposing statements see Hubertus Buchstein 'Online Democracy, Is it Viable? Is it Desirable? I-voting and Normative Democratic Theory' in Norbert Kersting and Harald Baldersheim (eds), *Electronic Voting and Democracy: A Comparative Analysis* (Basingstoke: Macmillan 2004).

including electoral administration in the case of Internet Voting, must be real and possible.

The chapter starts with brief overview of Estonian electoral law, and the electoral system, administration and experience. Some light is then shed on the technical solution chosen as well as the testing, auditing and verification of the system. This serves as an introduction to the discussion of court procedure and judgements in cases related to the Internet voting scheme.

Electoral Law, System and Administration

Electoral Law

According to the Estonian Constitution[4] members of the *Riigikogu*, as well as local government councils and European Parliament, shall be elected in free, general, equal and direct elections, and voting shall be secret. There is no special regulation for I-voting in the constitution. The legal framework for I-voting is given in electoral law. The provisions are almost the same in all legal acts regulating voting procedures, whereas the most detailed provision is stipulated in the Riigikogu Election Act.[5] In addition, the National Electoral Committee adopts a decree[6] on the detailed provisions concerning the organization of I-voting. After the first adoption processes in 2002 and 2005, the I-voting regulation was furthermore enhanced in 2012 when a special committee of the parliament worked out regulations containing the formation of the electronic voting committee, adding detailed procedural provisions to the law etc.

Furthermore, different Council of Europe guidelines and the OSCE/ODIHR observing and assessing reports on e-voting (including I-voting)[7] have served

---

4 Translations of Estonian legal acts can be found at https://www.riigiteataja.ee/en/. The updated official versions of all legal acts are available at the State Gazette, www.riigiteataja.ee (in Estonian).

5 See Chapter 7, 'Electronic Voting', https://www.riigiteataja.ee/en/eli/ee/510032014001/consolide/current.

6 It is named 'the procedure for the organisation of electronic voting and the ascertaining of the results of electronic voting', it can be found here: https://www.riigiteataja.ee/akt/118032014016 (in Estonian).

7 Council of Europe recommendation on legal, operational, and technical standards for e-voting, Rec(2004)11, available at https://wcd.coe.int/ViewDoc.jsp?id=778189; Recommendation on Electronic Democracy, Rec(2009)1, available at https://wcd.coe.int/ViewDoc.jsp?id=1410627; Guidelines on Certification of E-voting Systems, GGIS(2010)3, available at http://www.coe.int/t/dgap/democracy/activities/ggis/E-voting/E-voting%202010/Biennial_Nov_meeting/Guidelines_certification_EN.pdf; and Transparency of e-enabled elections, GGIS(2010)5, http://www.coe.int/t/dgap/democracy/activities/ggis/E-voting/E-voting%202010/Biennial_Nov_meeting/Guidelines_transparency_EN.pdf. OSCE/ODIHR, *Handbook for the Observation of New Voting Technologies*, available at

as examples and sources of best practice in developing the Estonian solutions and regulations.

Although not a part of legal norms' hierarchy, the recommendation[8] issued by the Council of Europe has been referred to by the Supreme Court of Estonia.[9]

Electoral System

The Estonian parliament consists of 101 members who are elected in 12 electoral districts comprising five to 14 mandates each. The voter chooses a party-list candidate or an independent candidate. The electoral results are determined based on both election district results and national list results by a proportional electoral system. The number of parties in the parliament had fallen to four by 2011, but got back to six in 2015. The proportional system is used at local and European Parliament elections as well.

As Estonia is a small country with around 1 million eligible voters, many of those residing temporarily or permanently abroad,[10] the number of voting channels has been high in Estonia throughout the years. Every vote counts and every voter should have the possibility to vote in the most convenient way. Beside the traditional Election Day voting, there are several additional voting channels ranging from embassy and postal voting for voters permanently residing abroad and voting on ships flying the Estonian flag, to different channels of voting outside the voting district of residence and home voting for those voters unable to visit the polling place.[11] In this large mix of channels, I-voting is just one additional possibility for the voter.

---

http://www.osce.org/odihr/elections/104939?download=true. The OSCE/ODIHR Election Assessment Mission has observed Internet voting in Estonia (parliamentary elections 2011) http://www.osce.org/odihr/77557, in Norway (municipal election 2011) http://www.osce.org/odihr/88577, and in Switzerland (Federal elections 2011) http://www.osce.org/odihr/87417, all accessed 1 August 2014.

8 The Estonian Supreme Court case 3-4-1-13-05 [2005] (http://www.nc.ee/?id=381 in English).

9 See p. 17 of the judgement: 'Although the Recommendation of the Council of Europe is not a legally binding document, it summarises the understanding of the democratic states of Europe of the conformity of electronic voting with the election principles inherent to democratic states, and it is thus an appropriate tool for interpreting the Constitution'.

10 For the latest data see Ene-Margit Tiit 'Estonian Census 2011' [2013] *Papers on Anthropology*, 22, 234.

11 The complete list of voting channels in the 2015 *Riigikogu* elections will be: voting on Election Day, home voting on Election Day, voting abroad (by mail or in embassies, by temporal or permanent abroad residents), voting on ships, Internet voting, advance voting in special locations (penitentiaries, nursing homes, hospitals etc.), advance voting in all polling stations, advance voting in special polling stations (voters outside residence), advance voting in county centres.

In Estonia, voting is not compulsory and there is no required minimum turnout. The overall turnout rates are quite standard in Eastern European terms; in parliamentary elections the turnout ranges from 57 to 68 per cent.[12]

Electoral Administration

The National Electoral Committee (NEC) manages electoral administration in Estonia. This seven-member politically independent body consists of high public officials. Other electoral committees are built up hierarchically starting from voting district (polling place) committees and ranging to municipal and county committees. In 2012 the parliament decided that a new electoral committee – electronic voting committee – would be established for the technical administration of I-voting. All committees are subordinated to the NEC which organizes training for electoral officials and resolves electoral complaints in the first instance. The rulings of the NEC can be contested directly in the Supreme Court.

The Estonian I-voting Solution

For I-voting, the voter needs an Internet connected computer (Windows, Linux and iOS are supported) and any type of e-ID (either ID-card, electronic-ID or mobile-ID).[13]

All Major Principles of Traditional Voting are Followed

The Estonian concept seeks to follow all the principal steps of traditional voting in order to maintain the connection with traditional elections and to make the concept more understandable for the voter. This includes basic electoral principles such as freedom, universality, uniformity and secrecy (anonymity) of the vote. In addition, and in order to include familiar values from traditional elections, a 'virtual double envelope' scheme is used. This means, similar to paper voting, the Internet vote is encrypted in the voter's computer (put in a blank envelope) and marked with the voter's data using a digital signature (put in a larger envelope with the voter's data on it).[14]

---

12 A detailed overview of Estonian elections can be found in Alo Heinsalu, Arne Koitmäe, Mihkel Pilving and Priit Vinkel, 'Elections in Estonia 1992–2011' [2012] National Electoral Committee and National Library, http://issuu.com/vabariigi_valimiskomisjon/docs/elections_in_estonia_1992-2011_eng/1, accessed 1 August 2014.

13 See also: Priit Vinkel, 'I-voting in Estonia' in Peeter Laud (ed.), *Lecture Notes in Computer Science: NordSec 2011, Tallinn, Estonia 26–28 October 2011* (Berlin: Springer, 2012).

14 See also: Sven Heiberg, Peeter Laud and Jan Villemson, 'The Application of I-voting for Estonian Parliamentary Elections of 2011' in Aggelos Kiyaias and Helger Lipmaa (eds), *E-voting and Identity* (Dordrecht: Springer, 2012).

Virtual Voting Booth[15]

In order to prevent coercion and possible breaking of the freedom and secrecy of voting, it is possible to change (replace) the I-vote an unlimited number of times during advance polling days. Only the last vote is counted. Another option is to go to the polling place and submit a paper vote during advance voting. In this case the paper ballot is counted. In this way the so-called virtual voting booth is created. A voter who has experienced undue influence while voting via the Internet can make her or his independent electoral choice.

I-voting Is Held for a Seven-Day Period

The voting period starts 10 days before Election Day at 9 a.m. and is closed four days before Election Day at 6 p.m. Voting is possible throughout the whole period, i.e. 24 hours a day for seven days.

Digital Voter's Register

The Estonian Population Register is used for obtaining the voter lists. The same lists are used as printed lists in polling places and electronically on the Internet. The correct, timely and efficient compiling of these lists allows for the easy introduction of remote voting.

Voter Identification with Electronic-ID

The Estonian ID card and the Mobile-ID solutions offer a secure, proven and sophisticated means for identification of the voter in the electronic environment. The e-ID solution is used throughout the private and governmental sector to identify the person and for digital signing.[16]

Verifiable Vote

Since 2013, a system that allows the voter to get information regarding whether the vote was cast as intended and accepted by the central system as cast has been implemented, it being legally binding from the 2015 parliamentary elections. Secondary channels, like smart phones are used in that matter.[17]

---

15 Also 'voter's right to replace the I-vote'.

16 More can be found in: Ülle Madise and Epp Maaten, 'I-voting in Estonia' in David Rios Insua and Simon French (eds), *E-Democracy: A Group Decision and Negotiation Perspective* (Dordrecht: Springer, 2010) and Ülle Madise and Priit Vinkel, 'Constitutionality of Remote I-voting: The Estonian Perspective' [2011] *Juridica International*, 18.

17 See a short description of the verification scheme at http://www.vvk.ee/public/Verification_of_I-Votes.pdf, accessed 1 August 2014.

I-Voting Experience 2005–2015

Estonia-wide remote I-voting with binding results was used for the first time in municipal elections 2005.[18] Since 2005 this way of voting has been used in eight elections, the 2015 *Riigikogu* elections being the most recent (see Table 6.1). But, as already emphasized, I-voting is one of many voting channels and will not replace the traditional paper based solutions in the foreseeable future.

Table 6.1 I-voting statistics for 2005–2015

	2005 ME	2007 PE	2009 EPE	2009 ME	2011 PE	2013 ME	2014 EPE	2015 PE
Number of I-votes	9,681	31,064	59,579	106,786	145,230	136,853	105,170	181,084
Repeated I-votes	364	789	910	2,373	4,384	3,045	2,019	4,593
Number of I-voters	9,317	30,275	58,669	104,413	140,846	133,808	103,151	176,491
I-votes cancelled by paper ballot	30	32	55	100	82	146	46	162
I-votes counted	9,287	30,243	58,614	104,313	140,764	133,662	103,105	176,329
Total number of votes cast	502,504	555,463	399,181	662,813	580,264	630,050	329,766	577,910
I-votes out of all votes cast	1.9%	5.5%	14.7%	15.8%	24.3%	21.2%	31.3%	30.5%
I-votes among total advance votes	7.2%	17.6%	45.4%	44.0%	56.4%	50.5%	59.2%	59.6%
I-votes cast abroad (no. of countries)	n.a.	2% (51)	3% (66)	2.8% (82)	3.9% (105)	4.2% (105)	4.7% (98)	5.7% (116)

Note: ME – municipal government elections; PE – parliamentary elections; EPE – European Parliament elections

Source: National Electoral Committee.

18 Political and legal debates are analysed in: Wolfgang Drechsler and Ülle Madise, 'Electronic Voting in Estonia' in Norbert Kersting and Harald Baldersheim (eds), *Electronic Voting and Democracy: A Comparative Analysis* (Basingstoke: Macmillan, 2004).

One of the declared aims of launching online voting in Estonia was to increase voter turnout, which perhaps could be described more realistically as broadening access possibilities and stopping the decrease in participation. Scholars point out on the positive side that I-voting also could and should better accommodate the needs of disabled voters.[19]

The actual impact of Internet voting on the turnout does not lend itself to objective analysis.[20] One can determine the variations of turnout in different election years (comparing equivalent types of elections) and attempt to clarify the causes underpinning variations with the aid of sociological studies. Perhaps the most important question is what proportion of the electorate would not have participated in the voting had the Internet voting opportunity not been provided. There does not exist a way of obtaining empirical evidence. We must, therefore, come to terms with unverifiable claims made by the voters themselves. The only exception is the case where Internet voting provides the only possibility for the elector to vote and he or she takes advantage of this possibility. For example, the local government council elections in Estonia do not provide the possibility of voting abroad by postal ballot or at a diplomatic representation. Nonetheless, it is possible to vote over the Internet when abroad.[21]

Trechsel and Vassil concluded, in the report prepared for the Council of Europe following the experience of Internet voting, that education and income, as well as place of residence, are not important factors in the choice of Internet voting over other voting channels.[22] Moreover, Trechsel and Vassil have drawn some interesting conclusions in the 2011 report, where they state that the ICT variables (computing knowledge and frequency of Internet usage) which were important predictors of Internet voting usage in 2005 and 2007 have disappeared since the 2009 elections.[23]

---

19 See, e.g.: Mieke Loncke and Jos Dumortier, 'Online Voting: A Legal Perspective' [2004] *International Review of Law, Computers and Technology*, (18)1.

20 See e.g.: Kristjan Vassil and Till Weber, 'A Bottleneck Model of E-voting: Why Technology Fails to Boost Turnout' [2011] *New Media and Society*, 13(8).

21 Ülle Madise and Epp Maaten, 'I-voting in Estonia' in David Rios Insua and Simon French (eds), *E-Democracy: A Group Decision and Negotiation Perspective* (Dordrecht: Springer, 2010).

22 Alexander Trechsel, *Internet Voting in the March 2007 Parliamentary Elections in Estonia: Report for the Council of Europe, 2007*, available at http://www.vvk.ee/public/dok/CoE_and_NEC_Report_EVoting_2007.pdf, accessed 1 August 2014.

23 Alexander Trechsel and Kristjan Vassil, *Internet Voting in Estonia: A Comparative Analysis of Five Elections since 2005* (Council of Europe and European University Institute, 2011), available at http://www.vvk.ee/public/dok/Internet_Voting_Report_20052011_Final.pdf, accessed 1 August 2014.

An Overview of the Estonian Judicial and Constitutional Review System

Pursuant to the Constitution, the highest court in Estonia, the Supreme Court, is also the court of constitutional review. Besides Administrative, Criminal and Civil Chambers, there is also a Constitutional Review Chamber. This Chamber consists of nine judges elected by the Supreme Court for five years. Members of the Chamber shall not be elected for longer than two terms of office. The Chief Justice of the Supreme Court shall be the chairman and presiding judge of the Chamber and at least one member from the Civil, Criminal and Administrative Chambers of the Supreme Court shall belong to the Chamber. Usually constitutional review cases are decided by a panel of five justices, in exceptional cases *en banc*.[24]

The organization of constitutional review in Estonia differs from the system of separate Constitutional Courts established in most European countries. However, the Estonian model has some significant advantages compared to other European countries. Besides diminishing expenses, the system ensures the uniformity of judicial practice and excludes possible conflicts between the highest instances of the administrative and general court system and the constitutional court in the interpretation of law and the Constitution. The Estonian system also decreases the possibility of constitutional review becoming politicized: the instance of constitutional review belongs to the highest court of the state judicial system, the members thereof being appointed from among the justices by the highest court itself.

The most important function of the Constitutional Review Chamber is to check that the laws adopted by the parliament are in compliance with the norms and principles established by the Constitution.

Pursuant to the Constitution, the Supreme Court has the right to declare any legal act invalid that is in conflict with the provisions or essence of the Constitution.[25]

Election complaints, in their essence administrative cases, have been given a special regulation in the electoral acts. All such complaints are discussed in the first two instances, in county and national electoral committees respectively. The procedure is swift, the complaint has to be filed within three days and the committee has five working days to reach a verdict. The third instance is the Constitutional Chamber of the Supreme Court where a swift course is also paved, with only seven working days provided for the court to reach a verdict.

24 All 19 judges sitting.

25 General constitutional review can be initiated by the President of the State, the Chancellor of Justice, a local government council (in specific matters) and the courts. Specific review of a provision could also be achieved through the election complaints procedure.

The Judicial Approach to I-voting

Types of Cases in I-voting Issues

The cases on the matter of I-voting can be divided into three broad categories: general constitutional review; complaints against electoral administration; and criminal offences. In Estonia the court procedure is different for each of these categories.

General constitutional review
The question of the constitutionality of legal acts (in this case electoral acts) and single provisions concerning the general concept of I-voting is the subject of the regular constitutional review procedure as described above. The most prominent case in this category is the discussion about the principle of uniformity and secrecy in the case of I-voting.[26] The President of the Republic issued a petition to the Supreme Court in order to declare the component of multiple voting unconstitutional.

In addition to this process, one direct complaint to the Supreme Court was issued by Tallinn City Council, again on the premise of the infringement of the principle of uniform municipal elections.[27] Both cases are discussed further below.

Complaints against electoral administration
Specific issues concerning the technical or operational functioning and preparation of I-voting are raised through the procedure of complaints against the electoral administration (elaborated in the previous section) during or after the electoral procedures in given elections. Until 2012, the Estonian National Electoral Committee was the *de iure* organizer of I-voting, therefore the complaints were issued directly to the Supreme Court. However, since the introduction of the Electronic Voting Committee, a specialists' committee formed by the National Electoral Committee, all disputes are settled in the first instance by the NEC, and after that it is possible to file a complaint with the Supreme Court.

After the 2011 parliamentary elections, five cases of this type were initiated, and after the 2013 municipal elections, one more: a complaint of P.P. for annulment of all Internet votes based on security issues in the system,[28] a complaint of a candidate, H.P. for annulment of all Internet votes because of a technical glitch

26 The Estonian Supreme Court case 3-4-1-13-05 [2005] (http://www.nc.ee/?id=381 in English).

27 The Estonian Supreme Court case 3-4-1-16-11 [2011] (http://www.nc.ee/?id=11&tekst=RK/3-4-1-16-11 in Estonian).

28 The Estonian Supreme Court case 3-4-1-4-11 [2011] (http://www.nc.ee/?id=1243 in English).

involving too large font sizes and a non-transparent Windows taskbar,[29] a complaint of T.R for annulment of all given votes, based on security issues in the system that was used,[30] two complaints of the Centre Party to annul election results because of shortcomings in I-voting,[31] and in 2013 a complaint of an election coalition against I-voting and other basics of the electoral system in general.[32] After the 2015 Riigikogu elections, one specific I-voting related complaint was issued, by V.K for annulment of all given votes because of a changed Election Day procedure, but as the complaint did not affect the subjective rights of the complainant, the case was dismissed.[33]

Criminal offences

Cases of selling or buying Internet votes, violence against or influence of an I-voter, cyber-attacks against the I-voting system, misuse of another person's e-ID in electoral matters and similar are not processed by the electoral administration and fall under the jurisdiction of the police; thus they are taken to standard criminal court. By 2014, no criminal cases tied specifically to I-voting have been discussed in court.

A Constitutional Review of I-voting[34]

The most important case in this category concentrated on the equality aspect of I-voting. The court did not evaluate all aspects of I-voting and has thus left the door open for further constitutional disputes.

In 2005, just a few months before the planned first launch of online voting, the President of the Republic refused to promulgate amendments to the Local Government Council election act[35] arguing that I-voters are in a better position

29 The Estonian Supreme Court case 3-4-1-6-11 [2011] (www.nc.ee/?id=1255 in English).

30 The Estonian Supreme Court case 3-4-1-7-11 [2011] (www.nc.ee/?id=1256 in English).

31 The Estonian Supreme Court cases 3-4-1-10-11 [2011] (http://www.nc.ee/?id=11&tekst=RK/3-4-1-10-11) and 3-4-1-11-11 [2011] (http://www.nc.ee/?id=11&tekst=RK/3-4-1-11-11 in Estonian).

32 The Estonian Supreme Court case 3-4-1-57-13 [2013] (http://www.nc.ee/?id=11&tekst=RK/3-4-1-57-13 in Estonian).

33 The Estonian Supreme Court case 3-4-1-5-15 [2015] (http://www.nc.ee/?id=11&tekst=RK/3-4-1-5-15 in Estonian)

34 For a more detailed view see also Ülle Madise and Priit Vinkel, 'Constitutionality of Remote I-voting: The Estonian Perspective' [2011] *Juridica International*, 18.

35 Draft nr. 607 SE in X *Riigikogu* proceedings. The draft, information regarding parliamentary procedures as well motions to change the draft are available on the parliament's website (http://www.riigikogu.ee/?page=eelnou2&op.=ems2&eid=607&assembly=10&u=20140811113307 in Estonian, accessed 1 August 2014). The I-voting provisions were first adopted as a law in 2002, see drafts nr. 747 SE, 748 SE, 771 SE

when compared to other voters who do not have any right to change the vote once given. The Law sent back to the parliament by the president contained the possibility to replace the I-vote with a paper-ballot not only during advance voting days but also on the Election Day. Therefore, the I-voters were indeed in a favourable position when compared to other advance voters and voters who cast their vote on Election Day. The Estonian parliament *Riigikogu* agreed with the President and restricted the time of I-voting to advance voting days. The option of changing election preference on Sunday, after receiving additional information about candidates in the second half of the week, really put I-voters into better situation. After this change, all voters who use advance poll possibilities are formally in the same position. However, the President did not consider these changes sufficient and he initiated a constitutional review.

The Constitutional Review Chamber of the Supreme Court decided that the right to replace I-vote by another I-vote or by ballot-paper does not unconstitutionally infringe the equality of I-voters and voters who vote in advance by paper ballot. Due to the virtual double envelope scheme, it is guaranteed that only one vote by the I-voter is counted. The right to change the vote does not give any advantages to the I-voters in any way.

The Estonian Supreme Court uses for the analysis of the constitutionality of the infringement of basic rights the so-called proportionality test, best known in the German theory of rational argumentation in legal discourse.[36]

The legal norm limiting a fundamental right is considered to be constitutional, if there is a legitimate aim for a constraining measure; the measure is suitable to achieve the aim; the measure is necessary to achieve the aim; and there is no other, less limiting measure available.

The rational argumentation of the Estonian Supreme Court was the following.

Legitimate aim

The aim declared by the parliament to increase, or at least to stop the decrease in, voter turnout is without any doubt legitimate. The measures the state takes to ensure the possibility to vote for as many voters as possible are justified and advisable. Another aim of allowing I-voting is the modernization of voting practices that coincides with the aims of I-voting listed in the Council of Europe Recommendation Rec(2004)11 on legal, operational and technical standards for e-voting.[37]

---

and 906 SE in IX *Riigikogu* proceedings. Right before the very first use of I-voting in 2005 municipal elections the *Riigikogu* decided to change some I-voting provisions and the President used his suspensive veto mandated in § 107 of the Constitution of Estonia.

36 The proportionality test originated systematically with the jurisprudence of the German Constitutional Court. Its variations are currently used by the European Court of Justice as well.

37 See footnote no. 7.

Suitability and necessity
The court stated that the voter's option to change the vote given by electronic means during the advance polling days constitutes an essential supplementary guarantee to the observance of the principle of free elections and secret voting when voting by electronic means.

A voter who has been illegally influenced or watched in the course of electronic voting can restore his or her freedom of election and the secrecy of voting by voting again, either electronically or by ballot paper, after having been freed from the influences. In addition to the possibility of subsequently rectifying the vote given under influence, the possibility of voting again serves an important preventive function. When the law guarantees a voter, voting electronically, the possibility to change the vote given by electronic means, the motivation to influence him or her illegally decreases.

Lack of alternative measures
There are no other equally effective measures, beside the possibility to change the vote given by electronic means, to guarantee the freedom of election and secrecy of voting when voting electronically in an uncontrolled medium. The infringement of the right to equality and of uniformity, which is what the I-voters' option to change their votes an unlimited number of times can be regarded as amounting to, is not sufficiently intense to outweigh the goals of increasing the participation in elections and introducing new technological solutions.[38]

Norwegian scholars arrived at similar principles independently before obtaining detailed knowledge about the Estonian I-voting system[39] or the work of Estonian scholars.

In short, the fact that the I-voter is in a somewhat different position compared to the traditional voter does not in itself create an infringement of the constitutional values. The Supreme Court thus confirmed the constitutionality of one of the main premises of the remote I-voting project. Without the virtual voting booth (the right to replace the I-vote) it would be impossible to guarantee the freedom of electoral choice, and without guaranteeing this freedom, I-voting would be unconstitutional and could not be used in Estonia.

Another case of general constitutional review did not bring any new important arguments related to the constitutionality of I-voting.[40] This case was initiated

38 The Estonian Supreme Court case 3-4-1-13-05 [2005] (http://www.nc.ee/?id=381 in English).

39 See Gerhard Skagestein, Are Vegard Haug, Einar Nodtvedt and Judith Rossebo, 'How to Create Trust in Electronic Voting over an Untrusted Platform' in Robert Krimmer (ed.), *Electronic Voting 2006: 2nd International Workshop Co-organized by Council of Europe, ESF TED, IFIP WG 8.6 and E-Voting.cc* (Bonn: Gesellschaft für Informatik, 2006).

40 The Estonian Supreme Court case 3-4-1-16-11 [2011] (http://www.nc.ee/?id=11&tekst=RK/3-4-1-16-11 in Estonian).

by the Tallinn Municipal Council six years later, in 2011.[41] Tallinn City Council referred in its petition to the alleged inequality of I-voters and other advance voters and lack of security. The first question was already the subject of constitutional review in 2005. Tallinn did not bring up either new theoretical arguments or new evidence. The municipal council has the right to initiate constitutional review only if there has been an infringement of the constitutional guarantees of local government autonomy. According to the constitution, local government is entitled to manage independently all local issues. The Supreme Court stated that electoral law does not belong to local issues, and therefore the municipal council's petition was declared inadmissible.

As discussed above, the Supreme Court has judged on only some of the constitutional aspects of I-voting. The variety of problems is much broader.

a. The privacy of individual I-voting cannot be supervised by authorities or observed in a traditional way. Therefore, massive buying and selling of votes as well as exercise of other influence or pressure on the voter are possible.
b. The people themselves cannot fully verify I-voting results, and people need to have absolute faith in the accuracy, honesty and security of the whole electoral system (people, procedures, software and hardware). For people who didn't develop the system, only knowing the input and comparing the expected with the actual output can result in verification of the computer operations. Under a secret ballot system, there is no known input, nor is there any expected output with which to compare the electoral results.[42]
c. It is difficult to prove the possible breach of the rights of I-voters and it is difficult to find evidence for arguing the opposite. The electoral administration and courts face new challenges.

The first sub-question should be whether the legal norms comply with the constitutional provisions; and the second, whether the norms are properly implemented using the technical solution. The third question is: how to prove it in court?

---

41 Tallinn is the Estonian capital led by the Centre Party which opposes I-voting and uses any possible methods to compromise or challenge it. Besides its fair concern regarding the security of I-voting, the problem for this party might be that I-voting is not useful to them or any other party whose supporters are ready to turn out on Election Day and use the paper ballot. Behind that calculation could be the knowledge that if I-voting did not exist, some voters could not or would not vote, which would increase such parties' share of the votes in a proportional system. However, as this approach contradicts the principle of universal suffrage, it has never been publicly declared.

42 See also Ülle Madise and Tarvi Martens, 'E-voting in Estonia 2005: The First Practice of Country-wide Binding I-voting in the World' in Robert Krimmer (ed.), *Electronic Voting 2006: 2nd International Workshop Co-organized by Council of Europe, ESF TED, IFIP WG 8.6 and E-Voting.cc* (Bonn: Gesellschaft für Informatik, 2006).

The first sub-question can be answered based on abstract analysis but the second one requires formalized procedures, IT audit results and observation reports. This underlines the importance of qualified certification and auditing of the system as well the need for new approaches in electoral observation.

In the Estonian case the first sub-question could be answered 'Yes', as e-ID enables secure remote identification, e-ID penetration is wide, all advance voters are in the same position, the 'virtual voting booth' (the right to replace an I-vote with another I-vote or a paper ballot) and 'virtual double envelope system' ensure freedom of voting and uniformity of elections. Moreover, it is justified by the aim to guarantee universal suffrage in an information society where e-services (also I-voting) are required by a significant part of the electorate.

According to the teleological interpretation of the principle of secrecy, the privacy of the voting act cannot be seen as an aim but as a measure to guarantee freedom of voting; and the anonymity aspect guarantees the principle of secrecy. An analysis of the compliance of the Estonian I-voting system with the United Nations International Covenant on Civil and Political Rights has given a positive result as well,[43] but emphasizes the importance of special procedures to facilitate the auditing and observation of I-voting.[44]

The answer to the second sub-question is more complicated. The second sub-question could be answered 'Yes' only if there are sufficient measures to check that the IT solutions work properly. This leads to the requirement that auditing, certification and evaluation as required in the Council of Europe guidelines should be foreseen by law or electoral administrative regulation. I-voting in a concrete election is constitutional if the provisions of the law are actually fulfilled: only people entitled to vote can vote, votes given over the Internet are recorded and counted properly, only one vote per voter is counted. Independent IT audit covering all aspects can prove the soundness of the system. The proper performance of the IT system should be certified and audited before, during and after voting.

The personal computer as well as the Internet remain the weak points of the whole system. The scholars are probably right when they say: '[a]lthough perfect real-time knowledge of all cyber threats is an impossible goal, it *is* realistic to do much better at providing a richer, better integrated picture of our cyber security to the technologists, attorneys, and political leaders who will have to collaborate to avert the next cyber-attack'.[45]

---

43 See also: Sutton Meagher, 'When Personal Computers are Transformed into Ballot Boxes: How Internet Elections in Estonia Comply with the United Nations International Covenant on Civil and Political Rights' [2008] *American University International Law Review*, 23.

44 Ibid., pp. 384–6.

45 See Thomas C. Wingfield and Eneken Tikk, 'Frameworks for International Cyber Security: The Cube, the Pyramid, and the Screen' [2010] *International Cyber Security: Legal and Policy Proceedings* (Tallinn: CCD COE Publications).

The answer to the third sub-question is derived from what was said above: all aspects of the I-voting system will be documented, an independent reliable IT audit is required, and in constitutional review cases the results of other sciences will be used.

Constitutional review proceedings put greater weight in rational argumentation, based on well-established theoretical research, opinions presented in the past and to a limited extent the results of other scientific disciplines. The number and the weight of the abstract facts to be proven in these disputes is smaller and lighter. However, it is important to include factors of electoral behaviour analysis and sociological studies – for example, the argument that the possibility of I-voting exists in the information society to ensure the universality (general nature) of elections. In addition to the abstract arguments, 'hard data' studies should be included in the method of research, including studies on voting behaviour.

The impact of I-voting on turnout can evidently be proven only in cases where it is clear that without the I-voting option the voter would not objectively have been able to participate in the elections. For instance, in Estonia postal voting from abroad is allowed only in general and European Parliament elections and referendums. In municipal elections, postal voting is not used and voters staying abroad can only vote via the Internet. Therefore, all the votes received from abroad constitute an increase in turnout.

As for the remainder of the problem, properly devised studies would be in order that explain how many voters would not have voted had I-voting not existed. Of course, these results reflect the reality only to a limited extent, because you can rely only on the testimonies of the people themselves, a matter that is intrinsically impossible to verify.

If the court finds that the disputed act or provision is unconstitutional, it declares the relevant provision invalid.

Complaints against Election Administration

Procedure

Disputes and complaints arising during the preparation and organization of elections are settled according to the procedure for review of complaints provided in the Estonian election acts and the Referendum Act. In Estonia all electoral complaints must be solved before confirmation of the official election result. The only exemption is European Parliament elections as the confirmation of the results is partially regulated by EU law.

The procedures of the Electronic Voting Committee are reviewed on appeal by the National Electoral Committee. Only a person who finds that their (subjective) rights have been violated in the voting process is entitled to file a complaint. A complaint cannot be filed in the public interest.

A complaint must be filed with the electoral committee within three days of the contested resolution or act. The electoral committee reviews the complaint within five working days of the receipt of the complaint.

The electoral committee either satisfies or denies the complaint, or satisfies it partially. If the complaint is satisfied, the electoral committee may decide to revoke the contested resolution of the electoral committee as well as to perform further acts, e.g. initiate supervision of the activities of the electoral committee or issue precepts to electoral committees. Furthermore, the National Electoral Committee has the right to declare (I-)voting results invalid and call for a repeat vote.[46]

If the interested party does not accept the resolution made by the National Electoral Committee after having reviewed the complaint, or finds that the resolution of the National Electoral Committee violates their rights, they may file a complaint with the Supreme Court pursuant to the procedure provided in the Constitutional Review Court Procedure Act. As already stated, the procedure of an electoral complaint in the Supreme Court is different from standard proceedings. The court, in a standard-three-member formation, has only seven working days, with a possibility of an extension, to come to a decision.[47]

Complaints in I-voting cases

The case of H.P. vs National Electoral Committee[48]

I-voting has been offered in a variety of environments and platforms claiming to cover the maximum number of possible voters. In addition, comprehensive information materials and a 24-hour helpline are available.[49] However, a peculiar issue was brought up in the 2011 elections. A few voters used a very rare combination of screen resolution, Windows 7 and font sizes on their computer. Consequently, when using the I-voting application a portion of the interface and control buttons were left behind the Windows taskbar. This would not have been a serious problem unless some of the candidates' names weren't also covered by the taskbar. One of the candidates brought a complaint to the Supreme Court and the judgement stated.[50]

> The Chamber adds that upon organising e-voting, it is the state's responsibility to ensure the compatibility of the software used in elections with the most common

46 See Art 15 and Art 73 of the Riigikogu Election Act, available at https://www.riigiteataja.ee/en/eli/510032014001/consolide (English).

47 The basis of the procedure is stipulated in the main electoral act, Riigikogu Election Act (see Art 72, available at https://www.riigiteataja.ee/en/eli/510032014001/consolide in English) but relies heavily also on the Constitutional Review Court Procedure Act (available at https://www.riigiteataja.ee/en/eli/521012014004/consolide in English).

48 Complaint of H.P for annulment of electronic votes cast in the *Riigikogu* elections 2011. 23.03.2011 Judgement 3-4-1-6-11 (available at www.nc.ee/?id=1255 in English).

49 See also a description of the Internet Voting procedure at https://www.valimised.ee/eng/juhis, accessed 1 August 2014.

50 On page 12 of the judgement of the Estonian Supreme Court case 3-4-1-6-11 [2011] (available at www.nc.ee/?id=1255 in English).

> hardware, operating systems, screen resolutions or fonts. However, achieving such compatibility may be complicated in isolated cases. In case of problems, the voter has the possibility to seek advice from the e-voting technical support. If the technical problems arising during e-voting cannot be eliminated in isolated cases, the voter has the possibility to vote by means of a ballot paper.

Therefore, ensuring the compliance of the computer with the I-voting application is clearly left to the user. Indirectly the court approved the parliament's liberal approach to voting: the voters themselves decide whether to vote, how to vote and which channels to use. The state's responsibility is to offer a possibility, an alternative, but keeping in mind that it is just one of the possible ways.

The same idea of procedural liberty is also found in the first constitutional review case in 2005 and has been accepted not only in matters of elections. Overall, this idea takes note of the general notion of digital solutions in a society where a traditional form of conduct (like the paper based signature) is enhanced by an e-version (like the digital signature). Both forms are equally legally accepted and it is up to the user to find the most suitable method at a given time and place.

The case of P.P vs National Electoral Committee[51] *and the case of T.R. vs National Electoral Committee*[52]

The security analysis of the I-voting concept[53] states clearly that one of the fundamental security problems with e-enabled voting is the necessity to trust the voters' computer. The central system is and can be protected by the state. The spread of malware in private computers on the other hand cannot easily be limited – either by state or by private efforts. The analysis even states that the modern personal computer is a 'black box' that nobody can or is able to control. Therefore, the security of the computer where the voting application is run remains a real issue. The user themselves can of course take actions in protecting their computers, but nevertheless this cannot solve all possible consequences. Consequently the security of the voting application is a topic that requires extra attention.

The issue of security thus stood out prominently during the 2011 elections where a computer enthusiast (P.P) hacked his own vote in his own voting application on his own computer. He was able to modify his own vote in his own computer and create an illusion that the vote was not sent to the central system. He was also keen to go public with his discovery (to national media) and later bring the issue up to the Supreme Court. It is important to say that all the discovered problems and

51 The Estonian Supreme Court case 3-4-1-4-11 [2011] (http://www.nc.ee/?id=1243 in English).

52 The Estonian Supreme Court case 3-4-1-7-11 [2011] (www.nc.ee/?id=1256 in English).

53 The security analysis is available at the NEC website, http://www.vvk.ee/public/dok/E-voting_concept_security_analysis_and_measures_2010.pdf, accessed 1 August 2014.

situations were monitored in the central system by the administrators and were noticed. Moreover, the revealed threats had been discussed already in the 2003 security analysis.

Subsequently, the Supreme Court looked at the issue of the security of the technical solution of I-voting in two separate but similarly motivated judgments.

In the case of P.P (3-4-1-4-11) the court makes a compelling statement[54] that knowingly manipulating his own vote cannot be seen as proof of the overall lack in security of the I-voting system. Looking at an analogy with traditional voting, a voter could easily go to the polling booth and turn in an invalid polling paper (by scrapping or doodling on the paper etc.). That is a conscious decision and is totally legitimate. Here are some excerpts from the decision.[55]

> As it appears from the memorandum, P.P. has conducted an experiment with the full awareness and consent of the test subjects proving, according to P.P., that the electronic voting in Riigikogu elections was unsafe as described above. The Chamber presumes that P.P. participated as a test subject in the experiment organised by himself. As it appears from the circumstances described by P.P., the test subjects had to, in the opinion of the Chamber, be aware that they were casting their vote via a computer infected with a virus.
>
> Pursuant to Art 72 and Art 70 of the Riigikogu Election Act, a complaint can be filed only for the protection of the person's own violated rights. Therefore, the 8 March 2011 complaint of P.P. cannot be filed for the protection of the rights of the other persons who participated in the experiment.
>
> On the basis of the circumstances presented in the memorandum and the 8 March complaint of P.P., the possible participation of P.P. himself in the described experiment cannot violate his right to vote. Namely, a person with the right to choose a voting channel has, by infecting his or her computer with a virus blocking the transmission of 'a vote unsuitable for the virus', put him or herself knowingly in a position where the electronic vote cast by him or her will not be delivered to the National Electoral Committee.

The case presented by T.R (3-4-1-7-11) is based on the same arguments presented by P.P but with more emphasis on the general implication of the security of

54 The Estonian Supreme Court case 3-4-1-4-11 [2011] (http://www.nc.ee/?id=1243 in English).

55 Points 16–18 of the judgement.

I-voting.[56] The general notion of the court is similar to that in the case of P.P, however noting,[57]

> Regarding the argument of T.R. about the non-safety of the e-voting, a hypothetical possibility that someone has monitored, changed or affected in any other way his voting during the election process, as well as a similar hypothetical possibility that the electronic vote cast by him has not been delivered to the specified destination or has not been received, cannot be the reason for satisfaction of the complaint of T.R. even if he himself voted electronically. A prerequisite for declaring the voting results invalid is an established violation of the voter's rights.

The same reasoning was used by the court in a similar case in 2013,[58] where similar arguments were presented.

The problem with evidence

Finding evidence to prove the breach of I-voters' rights is as difficult as in all areas covered by anonymity of the vote. The aspect of verification gives rise to additional case handling problems. On the one hand the electoral administration receives additional information about possible attacks against networks and individual computers; on the other hand it evokes a lot of confusion and may generate questions about the secrecy of the vote.

Consider claims such as: it was not possible for the voter to vote for the desired candidate because of administrative errors; votes were counted incorrectly or not tallied at all; the voting or election result is ascertained incorrectly. These all have to be proven by documents, statements, survey results etc. For those claims the applicant has to be able to credibly demonstrate the violation of his/her rights. On the other hand, the National Electoral Commission and the Supreme Court have to be able to check the election administration activities, including the fact that the I-voting system is operating correctly. Therefore, it has to ensure that the accuracy and stability of the system have been reliably established based on an audit and/or inspection (testing) prior to the start, during and after voting. In the future, the handling of incidents in a more thorough implementation of vote verification[59] has to be able to produce court-approved evidence.

---

56 E.g. the IP address of the voter is at some point tied to the person's vote whereas it could not be ruled out that such information would be used by the organizers; also no specific verification method is available.

57 In point 9 of the judgement.

58 The Estonian Supreme Court case 3-4-1-57-13 [2013] (http://www.nc.ee/?id=11&tekst=RK/3-4-1-57-13 in Estonian).

59 Although first steps with 'cast as intended' and 'accepted as cast' verification as a pilot were introduced in 2013.

We have to agree to the fact, or even the paradox of electoral disputes, that because of the anonymity and secrecy of voting it is often very difficult or even impossible to assess the accuracy of the presented claims. This problem affects not only I-voting, but also paper ballot voting. You can check the correct functioning of the overall system, however not the operation and 'destiny' of a single vote. For example, statements that a vote sent by mail has been lost or somehow altered can only be proven based on information collected under covert surveillance in a criminal investigation or proven by actual witnesses.

A vote shall be annulled only if the infringement found affected or could have affected the election results.

The Supreme Court has emphasized that hypothetical (unproven) suspicions are not enough to declare any results invalid, as this would violate the rights of other voters and candidates. The court has also emphasized the responsibility of the voter: the number of the candidate written on the ballot has to be clearly understandable; the ballot must be equipped with the required information etc. In the case of I-voting, the voter must take care of the computer and the security settings, and, if necessary, ask for technical support in case of problems, or ultimately use the option to vote in the traditional way at a polling station.

Taking into account the tight time-frame between elections, it would be difficult to find a domestic or international public body that would be ready to certify and audit all the elements of the entire I-voting system before, during and after election procedures. In Estonia, the electoral organization performs operational tests in order to check the functionality and accuracy of the system. Furthermore, independent and public testing (demo voting) takes place, and a third party audits the operational procedures that have been carried out.[60]

The Estonian I-voting system was developed following the principle that all components of the system must be transparent for audit purposes. Procedures should be fully documented and critical procedures should be logged, audited, observed and videotaped as they are conducted. A common requirement is that the source code of the voting application should be available for auditing. The source code of the Estonian I-voting system was made public in 2013.[61] It was not universally available before but could have been audited[62] if agreed by the NEC.

As a rule the process audit is carried out by external internationally certified IT auditors. The audit reviews and monitors sensitive aspects of the process, such as updating the voter list, the preparation of hardware and its installation, the loading

60 There has been a computer-science based study on the risks of Estonian I-voting (see Springall, et al, 2014) that was, however, heavily criticised by the Estonian authorities (see e.g. http://www.vvk.ee/valimiste-korraldamine/vvk-uudised/vabariigi-valimiskomisjoni-vastulause-the-guardianis-ilmunud-artiklile/, accessed 1 May 2015 or https://www.ria.ee/e-voting-is-too-secure/ , accessed 1 May 2015)

61 The source code can be found at: https://github.com/vvk-ehk/evalimine, accessed 1 August 2014.

62 Although this possibility was not used before the publication of the source code.

of election data, the maintenance and renewal of election data and the process of counting the votes, etc. At the counting event on Election Day, auditors publicly declare their opinion about the soundness of the procedures used by the electoral administration up to that point. The auditors' report, released after all procedures (including the destruction of all voting equipment including I-votes) have been completed, states if the I-voting procedures followed the rules described in the system's documentation and the integrity and confidentiality of the system was not endangered. To date all reports have been positive.

The I-voting system produces a wealth of system log information that can be used to monitor the work of the system thoroughly. In its different stages, the I-voting system produces different logs on received, cancelled and counted votes, also invalid and valid votes. The Audit Application enables one to determine what happened to an I-vote given by a concrete person without revealing the voter's choice. These logs provide external auditors as well as observers with information they can use to ensure that the system is working correctly.

According to the Estonian electoral laws, all activities related to elections are public. Observers have access to the meetings of all election committees and can follow all electoral activities, including the voting process, counting and tabulation of results. I-voting is no different. All significant documents concerning the I-voting system are public. In order to enhance the observers' knowledge of the system, political parties are invited to take part in a training course before each election in which I-voting is used. Besides political parties, auditors and other persons interested in the I-voting system take part in the training. In addition, observers are invited to follow the test of the whole process and to take part in other preparatory procedures. However, few political parties have so far exercised their opportunity to observe the I-voting procedures.[63] It is important that observers are deployed for a length of time necessary to allow meaningful observation. If some important stages influencing the correctness of final results have not been observed, then conclusions cannot be made about the integrity of the system.

Conclusion

In the case of I-voting almost all principles of democratic elections give rise to several questions in constitutional law and broader questions in social sciences.

In Estonia, as well as in many other countries that have created and allowed postal voting, advance voting and other supplementary voting channels, voting at a polling station has virtually lost its significance as a ritual of transforming people into a nation-state and a carrier of sovereign nationhood.

---

63 See Epp Maaten and Thad Hall, 'Improving the Transparency of Remote I-voting: The Estonian Experience' in Robert Krimmer and Rüdiger Grimm (eds), *Electronic Voting 2008* (Bonn: Gesellschaft für Informatik, 2008).

The Estonian Supreme Court has analysed in its constitutional review process the accordance of Internet voting with the principle of equality. The centre of the argument lies in the question whether the I-voters' ability to change the I-vote by voting again electronically or on paper would give unconstitutional advantages.

Additionally, guaranteeing the freedom and secrecy of vote in an uncontrolled environment was examined. Based on the remote nature, one of the cornerstones of the freedom of vote – mandatory privacy in the voting process – is not applicable in Internet-based remote voting. The two sub-principles of secrecy of voting were analysed – privacy of the voting act and anonymity of the vote. The court explained that to be found constitutional, Internet voting should include a 'virtual voting booth' alternative, the possibility to change the vote in case of infringement of the secrecy of the voting act. It is important to emphasize that the constitutionality of the Internet as a communication channel, together with possible threats on anonymity and secrecy, has not yet been analysed by the Estonian Supreme court.

The second broader category of discussions on Internet voting have taken place in the Constitutional Chamber of the Supreme Court following specific electoral complaints. The principles of equality, secrecy, technical uniformity and security of online voting have been raised in the complaints. One of the main issues that has arisen in these cases is how to obtain applicable and sufficient evidence, which is conceptually difficult due to the anonymity of the vote. New forms of evidence were raised in those cases, like documented test runs of the system, audited processes and verification of the vote.

So far the Supreme Court been quite innovative and liberal in its I-voting electoral complaint judgements, however, granting that the election organizers have done their best in avoiding any malpractice. It remains to be see whether this balance will continue in future cases.

Estonia is one of the (yet) few countries that has had a lot of experience in conducting e-enabled elections, the most important reason being the presence of a working e-ID solution but also the overall support of the general public. The case history in Estonia, both in constitutional review and electoral cases, has after seven successful applications of the concept shown support for the chosen principles. However, although Internet voting has so far been immune to some incremental flaws compared to some otherwise very popular voting channels (e.g. postal voting), the rapid development of the Internet as a communication channel could possibly bring new concerns that could also be held up in court.

Consequently, any new threats and I-voting itself belong both to the information society and it is the task of election organizers and courts to adjust the solutions to netizens' needs.

References

Hubertus Buchstein, 'Online Democracy, Is it Viable? Is it Desirable? I-voting and Normative Democratic Theory' in Norbert Kersting and Harald Baldersheim (eds), *Electronic Voting and Democracy: A Comparative Analysis* (Basingstoke: Macmillan, 2004).

Wolfgang Drechsler and Ülle Madise, 'Electronic Voting in Estonia' in Norbert Kersting. and Harald Baldersheim (eds), *Electronic Voting and Democracy: A Comparative Analysis* (Basingstoke: Macmillan, 2004).

Michael Hauben and Ronda Hauben, *Netizens: On the History and Impact of Usenet and the Internet* (Los Alamitos, CA: IEEE Computer Society Press, 1997).

Sven Heiberg, Peeter Laud and Jan Villemson, 'The Application of I-voting for Estonian Parliamentary Elections of 2011' in Aggelos Kiyaias and Helger Lipmaa (eds), *E-voting and Identity* (Dordrecht: Springer, 2012).

Alo Heinsalu, Arne Koitmäe, Mihkel Pilving and Priit Vinkel, 'Elections in Estonia 1992–2011' [2012] National Electoral Committee and National Library, http://issuu.com/vabariigi_valimiskomisjon/docs/elections_in_estonia_1992-2011_eng/1, accessed 1 August 2014.

Mieke Loncke and Jos Dumortier, 'Online Voting: A Legal Perspective' [2004] *International Review of Law, Computers and Technology*, (18)1.

Epp Maaten and Thad Hall, 'Improving the Transparency of Remote I-voting: The Estonian Experience' in Robert Krimmer and Rüdiger Grimm (eds), *Electronic Voting 2008* (Bonn: Gesellschaft für Informatik, 2008).

Ülle Madise and Epp Maaten, 'I-voting in Estonia' in David Rios Insua and Simon French (eds), *E-Democracy: A Group Decision and Negotiation Perspective* (Dordrecht: Springer, 2010).

Ülle Madise and Tarvi Martens, 'E-voting in Estonia 2005: The First Practice of Country-wide Binding I-voting in the World' in Robert Krimmer (ed.), *Electronic Voting 2006: 2nd International Workshop Co-organized by Council of Europe, ESF TED, IFIP WG 8.6 and E-Voting.cc* (Bonn: Gesellschaft für Informatik, 2006).

Ülle Madise and Priit Vinkel, 'Constitutionality of Remote I-voting: The Estonian Perspective' [2011] *Juridica International*, 18.

Sutton Meagher, 'When Personal Computers are Transformed into Ballot Boxes: How Internet Elections in Estonia Comply with the United Nations International Covenant on Civil and Political Rights' [2008] *American University International Law Review*, 23.

OSCE Office for Democratic Institutions and Human Rights, Estonia Parliamentary Elections; OSCE/ODIHR Election Assessment Mission Report (March 6, 2011).

Gerhard Skagestein, Are Vegard Haug, Einar Nodtvedt and Judith Rossebo, 'How to Create Trust in Electronic Voting over an Untrusted Platform' in Robert Krimmer (ed.), *Electronic Voting 2006: 2nd International Workshop Co-*

organized by Council of Europe, ESF TED, IFIP WG 8.6 and E-Voting.cc (Bonn: Gesellschaft für Informatik, 2006).

Springall, D.; Finkenauer, T.; Durumeric, Z.; Kitcat, J.; Hursti, H.; MacAlpine, M.; Halderman, J. A. (2014) Security Analysis of the Estonian Internet Voting System. In CCS '14 Proceedings of the 2014 ACM SIGSAC Conference on Computer and Communications Security'. 703-715.

Ene-Margit Tiit, 'Estonian Census 2011' [2013] *Papers on Anthropology*, 22.

Alexander Trechsel, *Internet Voting in the March 2007 Parliamentary Elections in Estonia: Report for the Council of Europe* (2007), http://www.vvk.ee/public/dok/CoE_and_NEC_Report_EVoting_2007.pdf, accessed 1 August 2014.

Alexander Trechsel and Kristjan Vassil, *Internet Voting in Estonia: A Comparative Analysis of Five Elections since 2005* (Council of Europe and European University Institute, 2011), http://www.vvk.ee/public/dok/Internet_Voting_Report_20052011_Final.pdf, accessed 1 August 2014.

Kristjan Vassil and Till Weber, 'A Bottleneck Model of E-voting: Why Technology Fails to Boost Turnout' [2011] *New Media and Society*, 13(8).

Priit Vinkel, 'I-voting in Estonia' in Peeter Laud (ed.), *Lecture Notes in Computer Science: NordSec 2011, Tallinn, Estonia 26–28 October 2011* (Berlin: Springer, 2012).

Thomas C. Wingfield and Eneken Tikk, 'Frameworks for International Cyber Security: The Cube, the Pyramid, and the Screen' [2010] *International Cyber Security: Legal and Policy Proceedings* (Tallinn: CCD COE Publications).

PART II
The Regulations

Chapter 7
The French *Conseil Constitutionnel* and Electronic Voting

Jordi Barrat

Electronic Voting in France: *Machines à Voter*[1] (MAV) and Internet Voting

France currently permits two types of e-enabled voting procedures. First, three models of electronic ballot boxes can be used on election day itself in some municipalities and second, French citizens residing abroad may cast their vote remotely via the Internet. While the Electoral Code establishes the main features of the procedure, there are other subordinate legal documents that also have great importance. Voting machines have to meet a long list of requirements set up in 2003 by a technical regulation and a certification procedure exists to evaluate whether they comply with those requirements. Internet voting follows a different legal path. It has to meet the conditions laid out both by the *Commission Nationale de l'Informatique et des Libertés* (CNIL), as a consultative body, and the relevant *arrêté* approved for this voting channel.

The Machines à Voter *(MAV)*

French legislation (Electoral Code art. L57-1) has authorized voting machines since the 1960s, when some mechanical devices were used in order to remedy the chronic electoral fraud observed in particular electoral districts, notably in Corsica and in some areas with a communist majority (cf. Erell, 2007; Descamps, 2010: 4). Devices were purchased that had already been used in other countries, as at least the United States (Smithsonian, 2012) and Mexico (Elizondo, 2005) had also legally admitted these innovations for some time. However, their use in France fell into neglect (Anziani / Lefèvre, 2014), due to their repeated technical faults, among other factors.

For our purposes, the most important feature of those devices, used during the late 1960 and 1970, is the fact that they were mechanical, and not computer-based. They did not under any circumstances require any software to function properly. As recalled by the Senate, they were 'at the beginning simple "pascalines" [calculators], before, without any significant changes in the legal framework, real "electronic ballot boxes" came into use in the 2000s' (Anziani / Lefèvre, 2014: 10).

1 Voting machines.

This distinction is crucial for understanding the real challenges posed by modern electronic voting machines. The challenges obviously lie in their correct technical performance, but also in their transparency, i.e. in their ability to be supervised by any citizen. And unfortunately this second element is often forgotten. While mechanical machines can generally be submitted to external audits that are understandable by the layman, electronic voting machines can only be analysed by experts in computer science, and therefore prevent the grassroots voters from exercising their democratic right to monitor elections.

In any event, the French legislation passed in the 1960s was used decades later with some slight alterations to regulate the use of electronic voting machines. The Ministry of the Interior took advantage of the previous legal authorization to approve a technical regulation in 2003,[2] listing the requirements to be met by these machines, and specifying the procedure for their certification and subsequent accreditation by the State. The companies themselves hire (and pay) one of the certification bodies approved by the Ministry of the Interior (Bureau Veritas, Ceten Apave), and thereby obtain the report which has to be analysed by the Ministry in order to issue the subsequent accreditation of a specific electronic ballot box model (regarding this procedure, cf. Barrat Esteve, 2008). The *Règlement* specifies up to 114 technical requirements that should meet 15 main principles that are mentioned at the beginning of the text (e.g. accuracy, security, transparency, clarity, verifiability, data integrity).

After going through all these phases, in 2004 three voting platforms were accepted, those produced by Indra, Nedap and ES&S. Although there are significant differences between them, all three machines are still being used for recording and tallying votes within supervised environments.

Nedap certified the same devices in France that had for some time been used in the Netherlands (cf. Gonggrijp / Hengeveld, 2007; Loeber, 2008). This is a large machine with a touch-sensitive panel, showing a reproduction of the ballot paper that allows the voter to select a candidate. The main objective of this measure is to cushion the operational change experienced by any voter that uses the computerized device instead of the traditional paper ballot. After the candidate has been selected in the manner described above, the voting machine displays a small screen showing the option chosen, and confirmation is requested.

In view of this layout, that intends to ease the transition to a new method of casting votes, and bearing in mind the French precedents with regard to purely mechanical voting devices, these devices are sometimes described as mere *calculators* of votes (Hertel, 2006: 73).[3] This is a nuance that is by no means innocent, since it conceals the genuinely computerized nature of the devices and the issues which that raises, as noted above. If voting machines are not using any software at all, the oversight of such devices could be conducted by a layman and

---

2 Règlement technique fixant les conditions d'agrément des machines à voter (Annexe à l'arrêté du 17 novembre 2003 / JORF 27 November 2003).

3 See also www.ville-antony.fr/machine-voter.

calculators, or 'pascalines' (Anziani / Lefèvre, 2014: 10), are terms that stress the differences between actual computers and other devices.

Indra and *ES&S* also succeeded in certifying two quite similar models in which the entire voting procedure took place using a touchscreen, therefore removing the need for anything resembling the old mechanical voting slip. Despite these generic similarities, they are two different platforms and the different identification procedures in each one perhaps merit some explanation.

While *ES&S* only requires voters to identify themselves in the traditional manner and to subsequently proceed using a machine activated automatically beforehand, *Indra* introduces a new element consisting of electronic cards. After proving their identity to the authorities in the polling station (i), the voters must personally activate the voting machine with the card (ii). At the end of the session, they must hand the card in again before being added to the electronic count of citizens (iii) who have exercised their right to vote. There are therefore three separate phases, which with the traditional stages, such as the registration of voters who have exercised their right to vote (*emargement*), are risk factors for any possible discrepancy between the final figures in each phase and safeguards that enable possible inconsistencies to be identified.

As in other countries, such as Belgium (art. 1 *Loi* 14 April 1994 / *Arrêté Royal* 30 March 1998), the final decision regarding the use of information technology lies with the municipalities included in a generic list of locations authorized to use those technologies (art. L57-1 Electoral Code). These administrations may decide to use electronic voting machines by selecting one of the accredited models. In 2007 83 municipalities used electronic voting, which means approximately 1.5 million voters or 3 per cent of the electorate (Osce/Odihr, 2007: 9).

The 2007 presidential and parliamentary elections witnessed a significant degree of controversy (Anziani / Lefèvre, 2014: 15–16) surrounding the use of electronic voting machines and, although that debate did not affect the validation of the election results, the Ministry of the Interior significantly changed its policy. Following the findings of an internal discussion group formed in October 2007, the Minister pointed out, in response to a parliamentary question, that 'the number of communes using these machines will remain the same for the 2008 election; for the time being no supplementary authorizations will be given to new municipalities that would like to use voting machines. ... After the 2008 March elections, a global re-evaluation of the system will take place' (Question no. 8131, JO 22 January 2008, p. 587).

Therefore, in 2008 the Ministry halted the increase in the number of municipalities authorized to use electronic voting machines, began a period of evaluation and, five years later, in the 2012 presidential and parliamentary elections, the number of municipalities using electronic devices fell to 64 municipalities representing 1.1 million voters (Anziani / Lefèvre, 2014: 17).

Finally, the role of private certification institutions such as Bureau Veritas and Ceten Apave should be noted. These bodies must also be authorized by the Ministry of the Interior and once this authorization has been obtained, companies selling electronic voting machines may contact them for certification of their products. Interestingly, the reports issued by these companies, which are the documents on which the subsequent accreditation issued by the Ministry of the Interior is based, are confidential as they are only sent to the vendor, who has paid for the certification, and to the Ministry. Neither the political parties nor international observers, nor the French people themselves have access to this document.

Given that the French system provides for a reasoned ruling in the case of a request for public information, it should be noted that, on 3 February 2006, the Ministry of the Interior rejected a request for access to the reports issued by certifying bodies. The governmental decision was guided by the criteria established by the CADA (*Commission d'Accès aux Documents Administratifs*), an advisory body that argued that the documentation requested should not be published, as it could be harmful to 'industrial and commercial secrecy ... [and] hinder the smooth running of the elections'.[4]

Internet Voting for French Living Abroad

As a result of the difficulty to participate effectively in the 2007 elections, which was highlighted by the *Conseil Constitutionnel* (Conseil Constitutionnel, 2012: § III), and taking advantage of the 2008 constitutional amendment that allows French expatriates to elect their own representatives for a total of 11 seats in the National Assembly, the use of the Internet for voting was accepted for the first time in the parliamentary elections of 2012. The electoral code had already been amended in 2009 (art. L330-13) to allow citizens to 'vote by correspondence, either with sealed envelopes, or by electronic means using hardware and software that would ensure the secrecy and the reliability of the vote'. Internet voting was administered by Scytl and was also supervised by the *Agence nationale de la sécurité des systèmes d'information* (Cf. JORF Sénat / 19 October 2012 / pp. 3949–3950) and an independent expert (art. R176-3 II Electoral Code).

Having analysed how electronic voting has been introduced in France, we now provide an overview of the roles that the Constitutional jurisdiction has with respect to electoral matters. This is followed by two sections analysing the *Conseil Constitutionnel*'s findings and positions on electronic voting with regard to first voting machines, then Internet voting.

The Electoral Tasks of the *Conseil Constitutionnel*

Constitutional jurisdiction in France has had a tortuous history, and although the *Conseil Constitutionnel* has succeeded in consolidating this concept in today's Fifth Republic, it is equally true that, compared with neighbouring countries, France, and the *Conseil* in particular, continue to have their own special characteristics

4 www.ordinateurs-de-vote.org/IMG/jpg/cada.jpg.

(Favoreu / Philip, 1995). As we shall see, some of them affect the electoral tasks that French legislation allocates to this body.

In this respect, it is significant that the *Conseil* deliberates on electoral issues with a double and even a triple institutional profile, performing tasks that are advisory, contentious and consultative. The first is the legal profile that we expect, but the other ones can only be understood on the grounds that the *Conseil* is not a standard constitutional court. Such roles emphasize the idea that law and politics cannot be unlinked, that the Constitution cannot be completely reduced to legal terms.

The *advisory role* (i) is due to one of its general tasks as defined by the *Conseil* itself, although it is not explicitly acknowledged in the Constitution,

> the Conseil constitutionnel has always considered that it was within its mandate to suggest to the public authorities all steps that could help to improve this consultation. (Conseil Constitutionnel, 2007: 10247)

Second, the Constitution specifically attributes the task of ensuring the regularity of elections to the *Conseil* and thus it rules, in case of challenges, on the proper conduct of elections or referendums. This is the *contentious* role (ii). At the end, it also proclaims the results

> The Conseil constitutionnel oversees the proper conduct of the elections for President of the Republic. It hears challenges and proclaims the results of the vote. (art. 58CF; also 59 and 60CF)

Finally, the *Conseil Constitutionnel* also plays a *consultative* role (iii) in electoral matters, i.e. the legal texts on the subject are submitted for its consideration prior to their enactment.

Having outlined the electoral competences of the *Conseil*, we analyse the content of the decisions in which it has had to make a comment on the use of electronic voting machines. The following section is therefore devoted to the comments and observations that the *Conseil* has made in its advisory role because they are the most thought-provoking reflections. However, we also comment on some judgements made regarding challenges: in those cases the *Conseil*'s behaviour has been much more conservative. Following a general pattern used both in electoral and other matters, the *Conseil* limits its considerations to those strictly necessary to justify the decision formally. Thus the decisions tend to be very short, as compared to those of other constitutional courts.

The Position of the *Conseil Constitutionnel* on Voting Machines

As mentioned above, the generic observations, issued in its advisory role, refer to matters which, despite being less formal, warrant some attention. The advisory reports also reflect whether there have been judgements linked to the use of voting machines.

Electronic voting machines were used in France for the first time in 2004, but the *Conseil* did not initially pay much attention to them. For example, the advisory report on the referendum on the European Constitution (CONSEIL CONSTITUTIONNEL, 2005) which took place in 2005 devoted a few short paragraphs to what in fact had been a highly significant innovation. The presentation of these voting machines as the successors of the previous mechanical devices, or the general lack of consideration of the challenges associated with these devices, must surely explain the timid position adopted by the *Conseil* in 2005. Moreover, this report does not mention any judgement decision linked to the use of voting machines.

Significantly, the use of electronic voting machines in elections after 2007 also failed to raise greater interest from the *Conseil*, even in 2012 when Internet voting started being used.

Its report in 2005 referred only to the advantages of introducing electronic voting machines to overcome some specific chronic shortcomings in the system, such as difficulties in establishing polling station committees and some irregularities in the completion of forms. Whatever the case, the *Conseil* already warned that some uses of electronic voting machines had revealed the contents of the vote to third parties:

> it would be advisable to ensure that the inputs the voter makes on the voting machine be, in one way or another, always shielded from the view of third parties. That was not always the case on 29 May. (CONSEIL CONSTITUTIONNEL, 2005: 65)

And it warned that there were some sociological challenges that these innovations had to overcome. In anticipation of what would subsequently be one of its main areas of deliberation, it said that electronic voting should provide

> the essential guarantees of technical reliability, confidentiality and, what might be the most difficult, *psychological acceptability* (CONSEIL CONSTITUTIONNEL, 2005: 65, emphasis added)

Having analysed the general approach of the *Conseil* to voting machines, we will focus on four topics, to which the court has paid attention in its different roles. The introduction of new technologies entails a major change for well-known democratic procedures and sometimes the technical performance may not be the main factor to be taken into account. Voters' perceptions are also important. Second, traditional paper-based voting makes a clear distinction between ballot boxes and booths, but voting machines may not provide the same clarity and thus may mix the different roles normally assumed by the two components. Third, the procedure itself becomes a key element. The success of e-voting systems somehow depends on who conducts the controls, what is supervised, when and how. The last of the four subsections that follow analyses some remaining topics.

Psychology: A Hindrance to the Introduction of E-voting

Referring to repeated criticism voiced about electronic voting machines, in 2007 the *Conseil* reiterated the psychological resistance in the electorate to their use:

> Their use, which breaks the symbolic link between the citizen and the act of voting that was made by manual voting and tallying, also faces a psychological resistance which is worth being taken into account. (Conseil Constitutionnel, 2007: 2)

It is unusual for legal bodies to focus their main arguments on socio-political intricacies and this is precisely why the cited paragraph deserves the utmost consideration. While validating the use of electronic voting machines, the *Conseil* considered it appropriate to highlight some possible effects beyond the strictly legal-formal sphere.

Scholarly literature has in fact addressed this point. The symbolic link between the citizen and the electoral act is emphasized. Thus, for example, in reference to voting via the Internet in particular, and less so to voting in supervised environments for obvious reasons, the physical gathering of citizens at polling stations is a link that is difficult to abandon in both the process of political socialization and the articulation of an appropriate democratic consciousness (Reniu Vilamala, 2008: 68).

However, we would play down this factor, noting that the success of political socialization cannot rest on external events that occur on a single day, i.e. on election day. In the same way as the argument runs that abstention will not be eradicated with the use of new electronic devices, since the reasons behind it are much more complex and profound, so democratic consciousness cannot depend solely on the physical gathering of citizens, but instead on many other factors which also occur at different times. Monnoyer-Smith Costech (2006: 67) adopts an intermediate position. While emphasizing the importance of symbolic factors in preventing an implementation of electronic voting which only considers technological issues, her argument notes the emergence of new forms of political participation with a ritualization that should be taken into account.

In any regard, except for the case of votes by foreign residents, the French electronic voting model does not rule out the citizens' physical gathering and does not therefore exclude the so-called democratic liturgy. However, the link between the citizen and the election is not confined to a mere physical presence, but includes his/her active participation in the electoral dynamic itself. According to Mecinas Montiel (2013), there is a dual process in which citizens acquire greater importance within public bodies' structure. They act both as voters and as citizen/public supervisors.

The psychological barriers identified by the *Conseil* primarily relate to the latter point. Its concern lies not so much with the process of political socialization, a matter which remains unchangeable due to it being a face-to-face electronic voting process, but instead a more important factor which the *Conseil* describes particularly emphatically:

> by participating in the work that takes place in a polling station, whether as observer, vote counter, or simple voter, citizens are associated with a kind of democratic liturgy. The intrusion of voting machines deprives the citizens of all that. It makes opaque what had been visible. It confiscates what had been a shared priesthood. It ends the 'communion of citizens'. It deprives the electoral body of its collective supervision of the acts which embody universal suffrage. It breaks the sensory and symbolic link that 'manual' voting and counting had established. (Conseil Constitutionnel, 2007: II-3)

Alluding to the sensory link refers to the necessary transparency that these mechanisms must provide or, in terms of the subsequent German jurisprudence (BVerfG, 2 BvC 3/07, 3 March 2009; cf. Fernández Riveira, 2011), to the public nature which must prevail in any election. Traditional features enable robust and consistent electoral oversight, but the question arises as to whether this is possible in electronic voting, due to its inherent characteristics. In 2012, the Conseil said that the tally should traditionally take place '"under the eyes of the voters" [sous les yeux des électeurs], to use a figure of speech that appears in the minutes' forms that it was able to examine, but that does not appear in the electoral code, where on the other hand it would have its place' (Conseil Constitutionnel, 2012: § IV). This is obviously not a mere visual observation, but instead a real oversight in which voters are able to understand the logic and the content of the activities undertaken.

The *Conseil* reaches these conclusions after finding that

> the use of voting machines is not accepted psychologically, for good or bad reasons, by a significant portion of our fellow citizens. A certain climate of psychosis is involved. (Conseil Constitutionnel, 2007a)

It should be noted, in this regard, that the group *Ordinateurs-de-Vote* undertook an extensive campaign, which, among other points, forced the *Conseil* to publish a significant statement a few days before the 2007 Presidential election, that reads: 'the *Conseil constitutionnel* felt bound to recall, in its session of March 29th 2007, that the use of voting machines for elections, in particular for presidential ones, has been authorized by the legislator since 1969. This use of voting machines under the conditions set forth in article L.57-1 of the Electoral Code has been found by the *Conseil constitutionnel* to be consistent with the Constitution' (*Communiqué du 29 mars 2007 sur les machines à voter* / Link: *ves.cat/bOJ2* [12 December 2012]).

Two factors warrant special consideration. First, it is striking how the *Conseil* establishes a continuity between the reform approved in 1969 and the contemporary use of electronic voting machines. As already noted, the 1969 legislation, which is in fact still in force, is a generic wording authorizing the use of both purely mechanical and fully computerized voting machines. In the 1960s, nobody thought computers would be used to exercise the right to vote, and although it is true that the strictly legislative framework has not changed substantially and there is some legal continuity from that perspective, the lack of any specific reference to the qualitative leap caused by the emergence of information technology is significant.

Second, this statement is evidence of the unusual position occupied by the *Conseil* in electoral procedures. A public statement of the applicable legislation seems more appropriate to the electoral management body than to the judicial authority whose task should strictly consist in the impartial resolution of disputes arising from the election. The truth, however, is that the role of the *Conseil* in this case exceeds its strictly judicial duties and it sees itself as obliged to issue reminders, such as the one that was mentioned here, comments and statements both before and after litigation, which is even more significant given that the citizens have not yet exercised their right to vote. In fact, the *Conseil* provides a very detailed website containing all types of information and guidance for each election, but the statement highlighted here is important because it was issued in isolation after the generic manuals had been published.

In summary, the *Conseil* takes note of an underlying problem in electoral operations and while expressing some surprise at the protests, acknowledges the discomfort of some voters, particularly with respect to touchscreens, and after the first round, took the view that

> in these circumstances, the wisest would be, without doubt, to renounce temporarily to use them [the voting machines], given that serious problems were encountered on 22 April (breakdowns, jamming, controversies), so as to shelter the forthcoming elections, including the second round of the presidential election, from all challenges. (Conseil Constitutionnel, 2007a)

The *Conseil* therefore shifted from an initial disregard for the challenges created by electronic voting machines to a gradual fear that these machines could lead to a loss of legitimacy for the election as a whole. After the incidents in the first round, some municipalities decided not to use computer equipment (cf. Enguehard, 2011). Moreover, in the legislative elections of 2007, which were held two months after the presidential election, the *Conseil* rejected several complaints related to electronic voting, but specifically stated that those decisions were due to the quantitative irrelevance of the possible outcomes and that in any case,

> these incidents may increase the psychological reluctance which confronts the use of a method that breaks the symbolic link between the citizen and the electoral act. The authorities have the duty to ensure, in the future, that these failures, even if minimal, do not contribute to alter citizens' confidence in the reliability of the vote. (Conseil Constitutionnel, 2008: 5)

In fact, many municipalities continued to use these machines afterwards. However, it is also true that since this 2007 electoral period, France appears to have opted for a moratorium on electronic voting so that while the existing system has not been abolished, its use has not been extended.

Voting Booths and Limitations on the Number of Voting Machines in a Polling Station

We have mentioned how in the first round of the 2007 presidential elections the queues that ensued were one of the main disadvantages (Conseil Constitutionnel, 2007a: 2). Although the problem was reduced in the second round, the *Conseil* felt it appropriate to use its advisory role even with *de lege ferenda* solutions, that is to say, suggesting certain changes to the law:

> – under current law, create more polling stations, with only one machine per station and the equivalence 'one voting machine = one ballot box = one voting booth
>
> – through a change in the electoral code, interconnect several machines within the same polling station, but not outside it, and consider this local network as a single electronic ballot box and several voting booths. (Conseil Constitutionnel, 2007: 5-B)

The *Conseil* therefore opens the door to the installation of polling stations in which various voting operations are carried out simultaneously, that is to say, from a legal point of view, there would be a single overall ballot box and several booths. Two points in this proposal are striking. First, if we compare the conclusions of this document with the observations published after the first round (Conseil Constitutionnel, 2007a), it is readily apparent how the *Conseil* has shifted from some degree of indecision and even alarm at the mere possibility of installing polling stations with multiple voting operations to a clear commitment to this model. The document issued after the first round addressed this aspect, but with statements that were to some extent conflicting and with different meanings:

> since a voting machine is assimilable both to a ballot box and a voting booth, in principle there cannot be more than one voting machine per polling station: on the other hand, interconnecting voting machines within a single polling station (which respects the principle of a legally single electronic ballot box) would suffice to prevent queues. (Conseil Constitutionnel: 2007a)

Second, the proliferation of electronic devices in polling stations is no laughing matter as it can jeopardize the electoral process as a whole. Under the provisions of French electoral law (art. L62 of the Electoral Code), there must be one voting booth (*isoloir*) for every 300 voters, i.e. polling stations normally have to have more than one booth. Moreover, each polling station constitutes a single legal unit and besides the number of voting devices in use, there would have to be a unique final poll record for each one. Therefore, different voting machines in a single polling station may generate partial tabulations, but at the end they have to be merged in a common document.

The activities that take place in polling stations are subject to a well-defined pattern, beginning with identification of the voter, the selection of the candidate and the casting of the vote. All variations to this protocol meet this minimum layout and any innovation must be carefully assessed to avoid procedural loopholes that pose a risk to electoral safeguards.

Having several electronic voting machines at one polling station may be allowed depending on the type of devices to be used. While some appliances, such as those used in Belgium (OSCE/ODIHR, 2006: 3–4; 2014: 8), clearly differentiate between selecting the desired candidate and casting the vote in the strictest sense, other models combine the two stages and thereby create major uncertainties. In the Belgian case, there are two types of devices, one to select the candidate in the private booth (*isoloir*) and another to cast the vote. Once the citizen obtains the relevant token from the first device (e.g. a smart card that contains the vote), s/he inserts it into a second device, that assumes the role of a ballot box. This second device reads the content of each token and it will automatically carry out the tallyat the end of the election day. Thus there can be multiple selection devices in the same polling station, i.e. several booths and a single electronic ballot box.

On the other hand, the three French e-voting platforms do not include two different devices, which is why the *Conseil* states that they are simultaneously a ballot box and a voting booth (*isoloir*). In this case, the solution appears to be more complex since, as noted by the *Conseil*, the only solution would be to provide several voting machines for each polling station, but such devices act both as voting booths and as ballot boxes. This innovation would only be accepted if there was, at least from a legal point of view, the guarantee of the existence of a single ballot box and a single global tally. Even if there was a network of voting devices, the required uniqueness of each polling station could not be diminished from a legal perspective, i.e. the results of all the voting machines in a given polling station would have to be tabulated together and create a single final certificate of results. There would therefore be several machines, but legally only one ballot box per polling station.

The implementation of 'their interconnection within a single polling station (which respects the principle of a legally single electronic ballot box)' (CONSEIL CONSTITUTIONNEL: 2007a) would also depend on certain features peculiar to each of the models used in France. The activation of one of the models by a card (*Indra*), another by a wire used by the polling board (*Nedap*) and the third using an auxiliary device to the machine (*ES&S*) adds complexity to the already complicated operation of installing a network of electronic devices in each polling station.

As already stated, art. L62 of the Electoral Code requires one voting booth (*isoloir*) for every 300 voters, but its last paragraph might include an exception stating that 'in polling stations equipped with a voting machine, voters prove their identity or their right to vote under the conditions set forth in paragraph 1 and have their vote recorded by the voting machine'. Does this mean that polling stations equipped with electronic devices must be equipped with multiple voting machines? Or with only one? In short, what should be considered a voting booth in the context of electronic voting in France?

In fact, this doubt led to several legal actions (2007-3418/3450; 2007-3415/3416/3417/3421; 2007-3449; 2007-3606) in the legislative elections of June 2007, but the *Conseil*, acting now as an actual jurisdiction, that is to say, with binding and non-advisory power, rejected them all on the grounds that the aforementioned provision of the Electoral Code does not apply in the case of polling stations equipped with electronic voting machines. This is clearly a compromise to avoid a cancellation of those polling stations as at the same time, as we have already seen, the *Conseil* itself, now acting as a consultative body, theoretically accepted the problem and even proposed solutions *de lege ferenda* consisting of the installation of a telematic network of devices. In the case 2007-3872 relating to the use of multiple voting machines at a polling station in the Marne department, the *Conseil* even accepted a formal irregularity due to an infringement of article 63L of the Electoral Code, but stated that it had no consequences on the result:

> Considering that under the terms of the last paragraph of article L63 of the electoral code: 'In polling stations equipped with a [*une* in French] voting machine, polling officials will publicly ensure before the voting period that the machine works correctly and that all counters are set to zero'; *that it follows from these provisions that only one voting machine can be made available to voters in a polling station*; that the installation of two machines in each of the polling stations in the city of Reims, which was done so as to shorten the waiting time for the voters, must be considered as irregular; however, under the particular circumstances, the facts do not justify any doubts regarding the correctness of the proclaimed results; so that the irregularity does not justify annulling the vote. (*Journal Officiel République Française* (JORF), 9 October 2007, p. 16511, emphasis added)

In fact, the infringement seems less evident here than the infringement of article L62. Article L63 simply states, 'dans les bureaux de vote dotés d'une machine à voter, le bureau de vote s'assure publiquement, avant le commencement du scrutin, que la machine fonctionne normalement et que tous les compteurs sont à la graduation zéro'. Despite using the wording '*une* machine à voter' [a voting machine] (emphasis added), the provision does not really seem to be intended to limit the number of voting machines at each polling station, but merely to ensure they all are checked before they are initialized. It is worth recalling that the French term '*une*' (meaning one) can also be translated as a generic 'a', and in fact this is how we could translate the provision into English: polling stations with 'a voting machine', but not with 'one and only one voting machine'.

In any event, the *Conseil* invoked a hyperliteral reading of article L63 which led it to detect an irregularity in the polling stations with more than one ballot box installed. An earlier judgement, 88_1062, 21 October 1988, which referred to conventional ballot boxes, established that it was impossible to install more than one ballot box, but mentioned both articles together (L62 and L63). Indeed, in cases of conventional ballot boxes, it is more difficult to install several ballot boxes while simultaneously maintaining the legal and operational uniqueness of the polling station, but in the case of electronic voting machines, that goal seems more achievable if an automatic procedure is enabled for the tabulation of the results.

This is therefore a theoretically and legally unresolved issue, about which the *Conseil* prefers not to take determining decisions in its judgements. It was the Ministry that subsequently returned to the issue, deeming the installation of various devices in one polling station to be irregular, in an explicit implementation of the above mentioned decision of the *Conseil* (see Circulaire NOR: /A/08/00023/C, 1 February 2008, issued by the *Bureau des Elections et des Études Politiques / Ministère de l'Interieur*, § 2.1).[5]

Certification of Electronic Voting Machines

Finally, it is worth noting the benevolence with which the *Conseil Constitutionnel* considers the prior certification procedure which electronic voting devices undergo:

> Many countries that are less technically sophisticated than France (for example in Latin America) use voting machines on a larger scale, *consensus* being reached by *pluralistic* audits at the time of certification or by unannounced inspections. (Conseil Constitutionnel, 2007a: § 2, emphasis added)

Although the purpose of this document is not to analyse the auditing mechanisms (cf. Barrat Esteve, 2008), it is worth recalling that the method used in France is not an example of transparency and pluralism. In addition to refusing to publish the resulting report on the certification, as mentioned above, the procedure itself lacks any plurality since there is one inspectorate body for each type of electronic ballot box. The *Conseil* in fact addresses this point in one of the appeals:

> by failing to foresee the public availability of the compliance tests made for each type of voting machine by the certification entities accredited by the Minister, as well as the publication of the 'source code' of the softwares in use, which are protected by industrial and commercial secrecy, the technical statutory regulations establishing the conditions for accreditation of the voting machines … do not violate either the principle of a free vote nor the principle of

5 www.interieur.gouv.fr/content/download/7112/67298/file/INTA0800023C.pdf.

> reliability of the electoral procedures. (no. 3742/3947 AN, 20 December 2007, Hauts-de-Seine, 10ª circ., cons. no. 14)

This is undoubtedly one of the most important findings in the series of actions and opinions analysed here. Certification processes may appear to be purely organizational in nature. It could be argued that they are neutral mechanisms, with the sole purpose of ensuring adequate technical – and only technical – performance of the electoral machinery. Thus, even granting them some degree of relevance, they are tasks that are very remote from the crucial role of elections, in which voters freely deposit a ballot which is then counted in a sincere and honest manner. They would be technical safeguards with no political or democratic consequences.

Nothing could be further from the truth. The previous paragraph highlights some erroneous arguments regarding the complexity concealed within electronic voting mechanisms. In elections of this nature, focusing only on what occurs on election day itself is a serious mistake, because much of what happens then has already been predetermined by previous tasks, which are sometimes carried out well in advance.

The latest trends in election observation methodologies can be used to understand the full scope of what has been noted above. Today, international organizations specialized in observation, such as the OSCE and the European Union, have realized that classic electoral observation, involving a presence in the field which is reduced in the best of cases to two or three months, has become obsolete in the case of electronic voting machines.

In these cases, witnessing the tally is also highly revealing because the participants immediately become aware that, except for minor details, there is really nothing that can be observed and evaluated independently. Except in cases where paper trails are used, the tally is reduced to the automatic printing of a record of results, but nothing is known about the accuracy of the computerized counting conducted by the electronic device itself. The only way to evaluate the procedure properly requires going back to the time when these devices were certified, i.e. it involves returning to the point which sometimes is described as neutral and harmless, as recalled above. There is therefore an inseparable link between the final honesty of the electoral process and these preliminary certification procedures. Any legal analysis should confer the utmost importance on these steps and in this regard, the refusal to publish the resulting documents should not be the subject of an opinion as lenient as the one mentioned in the preceding paragraphs.

It is also surprising that the *Conseil* believes that there is an international consensus in the literature regarding the validity of these voting mechanisms, as it may be said without fear of contradiction that the opposite is true. Although there are many success stories, it is also true that they are often accompanied by intense academic, political and public controversies. Furthermore, there have also been cases in which the implementation of electronic voting has failed.

As Ingo Boltz notes with regard to the United States of America (Boltz 2009: 8), the fact that the electoral administration itself lacks sufficient knowledge about electronic voting strengthens the role of businesses and prevents a fair dialogue between all the interested parties. Something like this may have happened in France in the presidential elections of 2007, and may even occur today, not least because of the erroneous comparison that may perhaps take place between the old mechanical voting devices and the modern computerized mechanisms. While the former had no internal software, the latter are computer-based and therefore pose different challenges.

Additional Opinions

Finally, in addition to the appeals already mentioned in the comments above, the *Conseil* has also analysed various contentious cases related to the use of electronic voting machines, although in all cases it has attempted to contextualize any irregularities which have occurred and concludes that the shortcomings do not affect the validity or reliability of the vote ('la sincérité ou la régularité du scrutin'). For example, this was the case with respect to some technical problems with no subsequent impact on the tally, and with some voters who had to be assisted by third parties, thereby infringing the procedure stipulated by law (Decision 2007-3872).

In some other cases, it has also analysed specific doubts about the accreditation requirements, such as the obligation to include an internal clock in the electronic ballot boxes to enable the calculation of the time spent on the various activities carried out by the device. The *Conseil*, in its judiciary role, understands that the obligation requires the creation of an 'internal clock that the polling station can set when the machine is installed and that enables the timing of the steps of the vote, but did not require that the setting of this clock and the subsequent timings be directly related to the time of day' (cf. CE, ordonnance 2 Mai 2007, no. 305184) (Decision 2007-3449).

Internet Voting

While voting machines already had a legal framework from the late 1960s, Internet voting procedures followed a different legal path, although some of the doubts and challenges remain similar in both cases. This section highlights the main features of this second electronic voting channel focusing our attention on the role of the *Conseil*.

Following a constitutional amendment in 2008, the electoral code was modified in 2009 (art. L330-13 Electoral Code) and in 2012 French citizens living abroad were allowed for the first time directly to select up to 11 members of the *Assemblée Nationale*. Internet voting was one of the ways to cast the vote.

In previous elections, those citizens could express their political will via the so-called *Assemblée des Français à l'Étranger* (AFE), till 2004 *Conseil Superieur des Français de l'Étranger*, an entity which has the right to nominate up to 12 senators. This option is still in use, but in 2008 the French constitutional system intended to broaden the participation of French living abroad by opening the doors of the Lower Chamber. Paradoxically, while Internet voting had already been in use since 2003 (Parliamentary Act 2003-277 / 28 March; Decret 2003-396 / 29 April) for AFE's internal elections, its last elections did not accept Internet votes and simultaneously legislative elections for deputies reintroduced such a voting channel.

In 2006, AFE's Internet voting had already created some controversy as shown by independent reports (see Appel, 2006; Pellegrini, 2006; Lang, 2006), and in 2012 the *Parti Pirate* spread its criticisms to this voting technology. Meanwhile the *Commission Nationale de l'Informatique et des Libertés* (CNIL) had updated its 2003 report on Internet voting. Although this entity was basically focused on internal on-line elections within non-political bodies, the increasing use of Internet voting as well as the constitutional amendment already mentioned led to a new report that, before setting forth a long list of recommendations, highlights the challenges posed by any Internet voting election. The quote is extremely eloquent:

> In light of the extension of internet voting to all types of elections, the Commission wishes to recall that electronic voting presents increased challenges with respect to the above mentioned principles for those who are responsible for organizing the vote and for verifying its course, primarily because of the high technical content of the solutions that are implemented. During the work that the Commission has carried out since 2003, it has, in effect, been able to determine that existing voting systems cannot yet give all the guarantees required by the law. On that basis, taking into account what precedes, the Commission is, in particular, sceptical regarding the use of electronic voting systems for political elections. (JORF, 24 November 2010, texte numero 29)

In June 2012, the *Parti Pirate* filed a complaint[6] highlighting several drawbacks in the Internet voting procedure. They ranged from technical weaknesses, like a potential misuse of personal data in order to create fake voting websites, to chronological contradictions, like approving the legal framework having already sent the personal data to the supplier, or procedural faults, like not inviting party representatives to the meetings of the relevant Electoral Board. The *Conseil* rejected this complaint (Decision 2012-4597/4626AN, 15 February 2013).[7]

Given the variety of topics, our analysis focuses on those issues that the *Conseil* had already considered in previous cases linked to voting machines. While the difference between ballot boxes and booths does not exist in the case of Internet voting, the *Conseil* did not pay much attention to the psychological acceptance of e-enabled methods, which is quite surprising since remote Internet

6 wiki.partipirate.org/images/e/e9/CONSEIL_CONSTITUTIONNEL.pdf.

7 www.conseil-constitutionnel.fr/conseil-constitutionnel/root/bank/download/cc20124597_4626an.pdf.

voting is much more revolutionary than voting machines. If the *Conseil* said that the implementation of voting machines 'breaks the sensory and symbolic link that 'manual' voting and counting had established' (Conseil Constitutionnel, 2007: II-3), Internet voting excludes even any physical gathering of citizens during the voting procedure. Despite such an evident difference, the *Conseil*'s advisory considerations in 2012 did not take this factor into account, probably because we still were at the first stages of the implementation of direct Internet voting. Moreover, neither the judgement 2012-4597/4626AN nor the *Parti Pirate*'s arguments mentioned this issue.

Secondly, the supervision of the e-enabled systems is a main topic both for voting machines and Internet voting, but each case has its own solution. As explained above, suppliers of voting machines choose an entity, which will check the compliance with a previous list of requirements. The certificate can only be issued by a handful of companies previously approved by the government. On the other hand, Internet voting regulations only foresee a report issued by an independent expert:

> The independent audit foreseen in II of article R. 176-3 of the Electoral Code has the purpose of verifying the respect of the secrecy and reliability of the vote and its accessibility. It is carried out by a computer professional specialized in security, who has no financial interest in the company that produces the audited voting system, who has experience in the analysis of voting systems, and who participated in the workshop for experts on electronic voting organized by the *Commission nationale de l'informatique et des libertés*.
>
> The audit covers the full breadth of the system to be used and the operations carried out prior to the vote, the use of the voting system during the elections, the tally and the storage of data after the vote. (Article 2 / *Arrêté* 27 April 2012)

The *Parti Pirate* stressed, 'according to the information given during the training session of May 25th, 10AM (exhibit 16) [sic] that the independent audit of the source code, of the tools, and of the compilation of the electronic ballot box software was performed by 2 people in two phases each of 5 days'.[8] The complaint states that such a timeframe cannot allow covering all the elements to be analysed, but the *Conseil* rejected such criticisms with generic terms that do not provide details refuting the facts alleged by the *Parti Pirate*:

> Considering that the findings of fact do not show that the audit foreseen by paragraph II of article R. 176-3 of the said code has not been carried out under the conditions mentioned in the said article and in article 2 of the *arrêté du 27 avril 2012 relatif au traitement automatisé de données à caractère personnel prévu à l'article R. 176-3 du code electoral*.

8 wiki.partipirate.org/images/e/e9/CONSEIL_CONSTITUTIONNEL.pdf, page 6.

Supervision always is a challenging issue in any e-enabled voting system. Given the generic terms used by the Conseil and the fact that the audit report has not been delivered to some stakeholders (in particular to the Parti Pirate itself),[9] it is difficult to provide an independent and informed opinion and this is why the supervisory system will likely reappear as a pending issue in future implementations of Internet voting in political elections. The assessment report prepared by OSCE/ODIHR underlined the restrictions on openness and suggested 'that the internet voting security requirements, as well as the methodology and results of security assessments, audit protocols, results of all audits performed, the analyzed source code, and minutes of all proceedings be made available to the general public to enhance confidence in the internet voting process' (OSCE/ODIHR, 2012: 11).

While the use of voting machines is limited by a moratorium decision, Internet voting appears as a new voting channel that intends to cover the needs of specific citizens, i.e. French living abroad. Next elections will be a good chance to improve the current procedure taking into account the assessments made by different stakeholders. Otherwise Internet voting might reproduce what happened with voting machines. After a couple of uncontested implementations, presidential elections in 2007 had to deal with several criticisms that finally led to halting the deployment of this voting channel.

References

Anziani, A. / Lefèvre, A., *Rapport d'information fait au nom de la commission des lois constitutionnelles, de legislation, du suffrage universel, du Règlement et d'administration générale sur le vote électronique* (Paris, Sénat, 2014), www.senat.fr/rap/r13-445/r13-4451.pdf (accessed 23 July 2014).

Appel, A.W., *Ceci n'est pas une urne: À propos du vote par Internet pour l'Assemblée des Français de l'Étranger* (Princeton, Princeton University, 2006), www.cs.princeton.edu/~appel/papers/urne.pdf (accessed 4 August 2014).

Barrat Esteve, J., 'Los procesos de certificación de los sistemas electrónicos de votación' in Paloma Biglino Campos (ed.), *Nuevas expectativas democráticas y elecciones* (Madrid, Iustel, 2008) 157–192.

Boltz, I., 'eVote System Certification in the USA. Federal vs. State' in *E-Voting Certification Workshop* (Strasbourg, Council of Europe, 2009), http://ves.cat/l_E8 (accessed 30 November 2014).

Conseil Constitutionnel, [*Bilan General / Référendum des 28 et 29 mai 2005 sur la ratification du traité établissant une Constitution pour l'Europe*] (Paris, Conseil Constitutionnel, 2 June 2005), www.conseil-constitutionnel.fr/conseil-constitutionnel/root/bank_mm/dossiers_thematiques/referendum_2005/bilangeneral.pdf (accessed 30 November 2014).

9 wiki.partipirate.org/images/e/e9/CONSEIL_CONSTITUTIONNEL.pdf, page 6.

——, 'Observations sur l'élection présidentielle des 22 avril et 6 mai 2007' [2007] 134 *Journal Officiel de la République Française* 10247, www.legifrance.gouv.fr/jo_pdf.do?cidTexte=JORFTEXT000000466744 (accessed 30 November 2014).

——, [Élection presidentielle 2007 / Bilan du premier tour] (Paris, Conseil Constitutionnel, 2007a), www.conseil-constitutionnel.fr/conseil-constitutionnel/root/bank/pdf/conseil-constitutionnel-17519.pdf (accessed 28 July 2014).

——, [Élection presidentielle 2007 / Bilan du second tour] (Paris, Conseil Constitutionnel, 2007b), www.conseil-constitutionnel.fr/conseil-constitutionnel/francais/documentation/dossiers-thematiques/2007-election-presidentielle/bilan-du-second-tour-et-decision-de-proclamation.17530.html (accessed 30 November 2014).

——, *Observations relatives aux élections législatives de juin 2007* (Paris, Conseil Constitutionnel, 2008), www.conseil-constitutionnel.fr/conseil-constitutionnel/root/bank_mm/legislatives_2007/obs_legislatives_2007.pdf (accessed 30 November 2014).

——, 'Observations sur l'élection présidentielle des 22 avril et 6 mai 2012' [2012] 145 *Journal Officiel de la République Française* 10354, www.legifrance.gouv.fr/affichTexte.do?cidTexte=JORFTEXT000026052650 (accessed 30 November 2014).

Descamps, C., 'Machines à voter' in *Droit Electoral* ([Paris], portal web, 2010), www.electoral.fr/wp-content/uploads/2010/12/Machines-a-voter-20101204.pdf (accessed 30 November 2014).

Elizondo, M., *Voto electrónico. Antecendentes y despliegue* (León, Votobit, 2005), www.votobit.org/lallave/macarita.html (accessed 30 November 2014).

Enguehard, C., *La controverse des machines à voter en France* (Mémoire de Master 2, Paris, École des Hautes Etudes en Sciences Sociales / Centre Alexandre Koyré, 2011), pagesperso.lina.univ-nantes.fr/info/perso/permanents/enguehard/recherche/Master2_Enguehard_EHESS_2011.pdf (accessed 30 November 2014).

Erell, 'Historique des machines à voter. Petit retour historique sur les machines à voter ou l'art de contrôler les minorités' in *Contre la biométrie. Le Collectif George Orwell* (24 April 2007), 1984.over-blog.com/article-6472845.html (accessed 4 August 2014).

Favoreu, L. / Philip, L., *Le Conseil Constitutionnel* (Col. Que Sais-je?, Paris, PUF, 1995).

Fernández Riveira, R.M., '¿Es inconstitucional el voto electrónico en Alemania?' in Jordi Barrat Esteve / Rosa M. Fernández Riveira (eds), *Derecho de sufragio y participación ciudadana a través de las nuevas tecnologías* (Cizur Menor, Civitas / Aranzadi, 2011) 157–194.

Gonggrijp, R. / Hengeveld, W., 'Studying the Nedap/Groenendaal ES3B Voting Computer: A Computer Security Perspective' in *EVT'07 – Electronic Voting Technology Workshop* (Boston, MA, Usenix / Accurate, 2007), static.usenix.

org/events/evt07/tech/full_papers/gonggrijp/gonggrijp.pdf (accessed 30 November 2014).

HERTEL, O., 'Le bug annoncé des machines à voter' [2006] *Sciences & Avenir* 73, pagesperso.lina.univ-nantes.fr/info/perso/permanents/enguehard/perso/Sciences_et_avenir.pdf (accessed 30 November 2014).

LANG, B., *Rapport sur l'usage du vote électronique par l'Internet pour les élections à l'Assemblée des Français de l'Étranger de juin 2006* ([Paris], Institut national de recherche en informatique et en automatique, 2006), bat8.inria.fr/~lang/ecrits/liste/evote-internet-2006.html (accessed 4 August 2014).

LOEBER, L., 'E-Voting in the Netherlands: From General Acceptance to General Doubt in Two Years' in Robert KRIMMER and Rüdiger GRIMM (eds), *Electronic Voting 2008*, LNI GI Series P-167 (Bonn, Gesellschaft für Informatik (GI), 2008) 21–30.

MECINAS MONTIEL, J.M., *Estudio constitucional del voto por internet* (PhD dissertation, not published, Madrid, Universidad Complutense de Madrid, 2013).

MONNOYER-SMITH COSTECH, L. 'How Technology Challenges Traditional Concepts of Citizenship: An Analysis of French Voting Rituals' in *Electronic Voting 2006* (Bregenz, E-Voting Competence Center, 2006) 61–68, http://www.e-voting.cc/wp-content/uploads/Proceedings%202006/2.3.monnoyer-smith_challenge_citizenship_61-68.pdf (accessed 30 November 2014).

OSCE/ODIHR, *Expert Visit on New Voting Technologies. 8 October 2006 Local Elections. Kingdom of Belgium* (Warsaw, OSCE / ODIHR, 2006), www.osce.org/odihr/elections/22450?download=true (accessed 25 November 2014).

——, *France. Presidential Elections 22 April and 6 May 2007. OSCE/ODIHR Election Assessment Mission Final Report* (Warsaw, OSCE / ODIHR, 2007), www.osce.org/odihr/elections/france/27768 (accessed 28 July 2014).

——, *Republic of France. Parliamentary Elections 10 and 17 June 2012. OSCE/ODIHR Election Assessment Mission Final Report* (Warsaw, OSCE / ODIHR, 2012), www.osce.org/odihr/elections/93621 (accessed 30 November 2014).

——, *Kingdom of Belgium Federal Elections 25 May 2014. OSCE/ODIHR Needs Assessment Report* (Warsaw, OSCE / ODIHR, 2014), www.osce.org/odihr/elections/117281?download=true (accessed 25 November 2014).

PELLEGRINI, F., *Rapport d'observations* (Bègles, ENSEIRB, 2006), www.pellegrini.cc/works/rapport_ADFE-FdM_6anon.pdf (accessed 4 August 2014).

RENIU VILAMALA, J.M., '¿Y dónde está mi voto? Un análisis comparado de los efectos sociopolíticos de la introducción del voto electrónico' [2008] 7(8) *Elecciones* 51–71, www.web.onpe.gob.pe/modEscaparate/downloads/L-0043.pdf (accessed 30 November 2014).

SMITHSONIAN, *Vote: The Machinery of Democracy* (Washington, DC, Smithsonian – National Museum of American History, 2012), americanhistory.si.edu/vote/votingmachine.html (accessed 30 November 2014).

Chapter 8
E-voting Case Law in Argentina

José María Pérez Corti[1]

Introduction

Argentina is organized as a democratic and representative republic under the form of a federal state. This fact determines the electoral system of the national and provincial States.[2] The Argentine electoral system is characterized by provincial autonomy that defines the ability of provinces to enact their own constitutions, regulate their own local institutions and choose their authorities without the intervention of the Federal Government.

This constitutional scheme encompasses the existence of a federal electoral law (Pérez Corti, 2012) which determines the criterion of the distribution of competences in electoral matters among different political levels. The Argentine Nation is organized as a federal state (N.C.; National Constitution, arts. 5 and 129) with four different levels of government (i.e. Nation, 23 provinces, the Autonomous City of Buenos Aires and a great number of municipalities) (Barrera Buteler, 1996; Hernández, 1997; Frías, 1998). The powers assigned to the provinces include that of assessing and defining the mechanisms of voting for provincial and municipal elections,[3] as well as that of designing and organizing their own electoral management bodies and courts. Thus, the federal authority has to establish the norms related to the election of national authorities (deputies, senators, president and vice-president), and also its application and its subsequent judicial control. While the federal states or provinces have the authority to enact their own electoral system by application of articles 5, 121, 122 and 123 of the National Constitution (National Superior Court of Justice [N.S.C.J], Judgements

1 Special acknowledgement is devoted to all who selflessly collaborated with the author to write this chapter. The compilation of administrative and judicial precedents in a federally organized country is not an easy task. That is why I stress the contributions of Guillermo O. Aristía, Ana María Brunello, Marcela Centurión Yedro, Ernesto Torres, Rosana Dalton, Ana Brunello, Teresa Ovejero Cornejo, Horacio Maffei, Marcelo Guzmán, Luis Alfredo Puebla Mauna and Héctor Hernández.

2 In the Argentine Federal System, the provinces conform to local state or sub-state levels, and among all state levels, a connection that we identify as federal relation is established.

3 The degree of autonomy of municipalities depends on the regulations that the provincial constitutions provide, always respecting the minimum level established by the National Constitution in its article 123.

326:2004), the full exercise of the jurisdiction of these issues belongs only to them, without the intervention of the federal government. This includes the right to establish their own electoral system, with a set of political rights derived from their political and institutional autonomy (N.C. article 5), which allows them to enact their electoral norms and those of their political parties, to regulate their electoral system and to incorporate forms of semi-direct democracy.

Addressing the issue of e-voting[4] in a federal country like Argentina involves a great diversity and complexity of legislative and administrative regulations, as well as judicial decisions in this regard. The electoral system corresponds to a multi-level and pluri-legislative State due to the normative and institutional variety that we find in Argentine federalism. It also engenders the harmonious and coordinated co-existence of four government spheres or levels. That is why the tenets of constitutional nature that express the concept of federalist agreement should be the pillars on which this federalism is built, and which has been raised to the level of the constitution itself.

The implementation of a concerted or cooperative federalism (García de Enterría, 1988) reinforces constructively the effective possibilities of autonomy; and the coordination of the attributions must not be sought in generic premises or abstract statements. Instead, special attention must be paid to each situation (N.S.C.J. Judgements 137:212). That is the case for legal provisions that allow the articulation of electoral processes or the rules for political parties between provinces and Nation; or the agreements reached in order to develop national and provincial electoral processes simultaneously, whether internal elections within parties or general elections for which different voting mechanisms are used.[5]

It is important to mention that in Argentina, the principal electoral provisions are in specific laws, while the exercise of governmental normative competences has been restricted, due to the sensitivity of the matter, and placed in the hands of the relevant executive bodies. Nevertheless, this authority is currently more and more frequently and intensely carried out by the electoral management bodies without the existence of a legal or constitutional regulation that determines the limits of its scope and exercise.

---

4 The concept of 'electronic mechanism of casting a vote' is broad and general, and includes all voting and/or tallying mechanisms with computer/ICT assistance, although we may refer to this in general terms as electronic voting.

5 Santa Fe represents a clear example of concerted federalism in electoral matters, since 'the primary, open and compulsory elections P.A.S.O. [Acronym in Spanish] of mid-term in August 2013, in the province of Santa Fe were performed simultaneously with the Nation, but at the same as an unprecedented event in Argentina, two different voting systems being used for the same electoral act: the political party ballot known as 'sábana' (sheet) at a level of national offices and the unique ballot that the Province successfully started using in 2011, for local offices' (cf. Blando, 2014: 3C).

E-voting Experiences in Argentina

E-voting began to appear in Argentina in 1995, when the national government was evaluating the implementation of the Brazilian e-ballot boxes. Twenty years have passed without the enactment of norms related to e-voting or the development of pilot experiences at the national level. That is the reason why there is no case law on the issue in the national electoral justice system.

Instead, many experiences have been carried out at the provincial and municipal levels (Dirección Nacional Electoral, 2004; Pérez Corti, 2005; Tula, 2005; Prince, 2006; Busaniche/Heinz/Rezinovsky, 2008). We will address those related to the provincial elections of Buenos Aires (2009), Chaco (2011), Córdoba (2011) and Salta (2009/2011/2013); and the municipal elections of Ushuaia (2003), capital of the province of Tierra del Fuego; Pinamar (2010) in the province of Buenos Aires; Marcos Juárez (2010) and Las Higueras (2011) in the province of Córdoba; Neuquén (2013), capital of the province of the same name; and San Antonio Oeste (2007) in the province of Río Negro.

Electoral Justice: Characteristics and Special Features

Most electoral institutions in Argentina (Sesin/Pérez Corti, 2006; Pérez Corti, 2012) are of a judicial nature, and they have administrative and jurisdictional powers and competences. This is due to the special administrative nature of the electoral process and to the characteristics of the terms that derive from it (Benalcázar Guerrón, 2014). These institutions can be classified into *uni personal* (i.e. one-member courts) or *colegiados* (i.e. electoral courts, boards or chambers).

Together with the powers and administrative competences by which they carry out the planning, organization, management and direction of the electoral processes, these organisms develop jurisdictional competences. These are materialized through decisions with legally binding effect that relates to controversies of an electoral nature and are manifested as a particular, personal and concrete norm, decided by an impartial and independent organ, constitutionally and legally responsible for performing that function exclusively. It is worth mentioning that, as this is about judicial organs, the political actors tend to rely on their independence and objectivity, but they also bear in mind the antecedents and trends in the matter.

This is not the case for the Electoral Board [Junta] of the Province of Buenos Aires, which has a special situation that makes its constitutional qualification more difficult. The provincial Supreme Court emphasized its non-jurisdictional nature when it was clarified that this Board was not a member of the judiciary nor has this legal nature (Agreement No. 102.434).

It is also important to mention the municipal electoral boards [juntas]. They are usually made up of three members and have electoral competence in the municipal sphere. Their members can be judges and/or judicial officials, teachers and/or local voters, in compliance with the norms established by the municipal systems in each province. Their exclusively electoral competences are determined in these legal regulations and their legal nature, beyond the clear judicial aspect given in some cases, naturally belongs to the administration of municipal issues. Thus, their functions are related to the organization of the local electoral processes and to the resolution in this instance of the challenges that are filed, always with a procedural remedy that allows further judicial control of their decisions.

In order to correctly analyse e-voting case law, we will address the precedents in each case, distinguishing the administrative from the judicial function that these electoral organizations exercise. At the end of this chapter, we present the technical sheet related to the elections and e-voting mechanisms described in each case (see Annex).

E-voting Legislation

E-voting experiences allow us to identify certain typical landmarks. One of these is the legal instrument by which e-voting is enabled. In general, laws,[6] ordinances[7] or decrees[8] are relied upon to provide and regulate the incorporation of these mechanisms in the electoral system, although in some cases, they have

6 Buenos Aires (Law No. 5109, arts. 149/151); Chaco (Law No. 4169, art. 48.d); Córdoba (Law No. 9571, art. 184); Río Negro (Law No. 2431, arts. 135/138, and Law No. 4082); and Salta (Law No. 7730).

7 Marcos Juárez, province of Córdoba, Ordinance No. 2157/10; Ushuaia, province of Tierra del Fuego, Ordinance No. 2578/03.

8 Buenos Aires, Decrees No. 1874/05 (Repealed), No. 1406/07 and No. 755/09 (in reference to statutory regulations approved by Decree No. 1460/07); Ushuaia (Tierra del Fuego), Decree No. 506/2003; and Río Negro, Decree No. 1375/07, developing Law No. 4234/07.

been the result or the cause of agreements,[9] covenants[10] or queries[11] before its implementation. In other cases, even though the creation of this mechanism is recognized by a generic legislative mandate, that generic mandate delegates the function of selection, determination or decision of the area or areas and scopes of the implementation of e-voting.[12]

As a result, the incorporation of e-voting required the electoral management bodies (EMB) to enact diverse resolutions which is considered inadvisable by Rial (2004). These resolutions intended to adapt proceedings and existing norms to the new voting system.

For the purposes of this chapter, and without analysing their legal foundation, such resolutions can be grouped depending on their content and in accordance with their object or goal; distinguishing between governmental statutory regulations –

---

9 In the municipal election of Ushuaia in 2003, the Electoral Court and the parties' representatives signed the *Agreement of implementation and regulation of e-voting in the municipal elections of Ushuaia on the 26th October 2003* (Acta Acuerdo de implementación y reglamentación del Voto Electrónico en las elecciones municipales de Ushuaia del 26 de Octubre del año 2003).

10 In the municipal election of Ushuaia 2003, the mayor agreed on the 21 August 2003 to the *Collaboration Agreement between the Ministry of Interior and the Municipality of Ushuaia for the implementation of new technologies in the electoral processes*, approved by Decree No. 511/13, *ad referendum* of the City Council (Convenio de colaboración entre el Ministerio del Interior y la Municipalidad de Ushuaia para la implementación de nuevas tecnologías en los procesos electorales).

For the implementation of e-voting in the municipal election of 5 September 2010, in the city of Marcos Juárez (Province of Cordoba), the Municipal Executive Department concluded an agreement with the Government of the Province dated 28 July 2010, ratified by the City Council by Ordinance No. 2165/10 on 25 August 2010.

11 This is the case of the municipal election of Neuquén, in 2013, in which, due to the initiative launched by its Mayor (*Intendente*), asking the Electoral Provincial Board [Junta] to consider the possibility of a pilot evoting experience in the municipal elections summoned on 30 July 2013, this electoral organization issued the resolutions No. 239/13 and No. 242/13.

12 Such is the case of the registered antecedent in Ushuaia in 2003, when its Mayor (*Intendente*) decided to put into practice evoting by Decree 06/03, which in its article 2 established to 'request the Provincial Electoral and Registry Judge to regulate all matters related to e-voting, as determined by the Municipal Electoral Rules in Article 124 and next'.

Another similar case takes place in the province of Córdoba, where the Electoral Code regulates evoting and its implementation in its article 184: 'Notwithstanding the provisions of this legislation, the Electoral Court shall – after the first general elections to be performed immediately after the enactment of this Law – proceed to implement progressively and systematically the necessary actions for using an electronic mechanism to cast a ballot. The Electoral Court [competent] in the implementation of an electronic mechanism to cast a ballot in some electoral precincts and of the Unique Ballot Paper in other electoral sections, will *determine the design of the image reproduced on the monitor, which should be similar to the one used by the Unique Ballot Paper used in the electoral act*'.

those devoted to regulating questions that are not considered in the parliamentary acts – and supplementary – those that complement, interpret or adapt the existing legal framework to the new voting system, but do not formally regulate it.

Regulatory Resolutions

When we refer to incomplete normative frameworks, certain details or even the e-voting statutory regulation itself remain under the competence of EMBs. There are normative gaps or laws with inaccurate and vague content that, in some cases, expressly delegate a mandatory action in favour of EMBs. That is the reason why their regulatory functions have the highest importance so as to guarantee a suitable implementation of e-voting.

This is the case of the Electoral Provincial Court of Tierra del Fuego, when as a result of the elections to be held in Ushuaia in October 2003, Resolution No. 90/03 dated 23 September 2003 was issued. Consequently, the Electoral Provincial Court proceeded to modify the Municipal Electoral Regulations (Ordinance No. 2578/03, modified by Ordinance No. 3240/07), specifying the layout and content of the ballots which had to be uploaded in the e-voting software (arts. 1 to 4), and the delivery to political parties of the instructions for polling stations' officials (art. 5), which integrates such resolution as an annex (Maffei, 2005; Tula/Diéguez/Eyherabide, 2005).

Also in Chaco we find, explicitly recognized by the Electoral Court, its own competence to enact and establish practical norms, taking into consideration the role that this court acquires as an executive body in relation to the implementation of evoting (Act No. 777/11, Tula/Diéguez/Eyherabide, 2005). It has performed such functions in all elections for which it was in charge, always in relation to the operative and management issues of the electoral process.

Finally, it is important to point out that in the case of the province of Buenos Aires, the Electoral Board regularly issues technical resolutions through which it develops a regulatory function of varied nature and content. This is a power that this organization fully exercises as administrator of the electoral process. *A fortiori*, the Electoral Board puts this historic competence into practice when implementing evoting (Aristía, 2008).

Supplementary Resolutions

In other cases, e-voting requires certain decisions from electoral organizations, but they are not governmental statutory regulations that develop the electoral law. They rather complement it or adapt it to the requirements imposed by the administration of the electoral process regarding the particularities of the new voting system.

Thus, we find decisions issued by EMBs or courts that, exercising the competences granted to them by the existing legislation, determine the places where evoting will be used. One of these cases was filed in 2010 in the province of Córdoba, where the Electoral Court, in compliance with the legal mandate of article 184 of the Electoral Code, issued Resolution No. 31/10 dated 21 December 2010 by which it decided to start the progressive and systematic implementation of e-voting in provincial elections in the city of La Falda. This decision led the Ad Hoc Provincial Electoral Court, through the General Administration of the Judiciary (Agreement No. 251, Class 'C'), to initiate a public process for selecting the contractor (Agreement No. 123, Class 'C') for a suitable and secure execution of what was specified by the Electoral Court.[13]

Another example is the electoral schedule. This is a timeline with all the acts to be performed by the several political actors involved and by the electoral administration, from the beginning until the end of the electoral process. The electoral schedule includes the deadlines provided by the law for each phase of the electoral procedure, usually expressed in days or hours, and is organized according to three major stages that are part of it, described as pre-electoral, electoral and post-electoral acts (Pérez Corti, 2012: 248). With the implementation of e-voting, it is no longer possible to make a single schedule aimed at specifically electoral acts: it is also necessary to prepare another specific one that provides, includes and reflects all the proceedings and steps necessary for the correct validation of the computer voting system. Its content will illustrate activities of a technical and even expert nature, as well as areas devoted to the controlling and auditing of aspects relative to hardware and software (Hernández, 2011).

The same applies to more specific electoral issues, such as the screen layout, the order of appearance of electoral proposals and candidates, colours, images, sequence or succession of screens in case of numerous electoral candidatures, etc. (Aristía, 2008).

All these issues are covered by EMBs' decisions that are integrated into a timeline forming an implementation schedule for the e-voting system.[14]

A similar situation arises with respect to procedural activities incorporated in the electoral schedule in substitution, or in parallel or as an added feature, for those that would be completed in an ordinary electoral process. Some issues, such as the designation of electoral auditors for electronic equipment, the hearings for

---

13 We highlight the differences in the contracting processes in the provinces of Córdoba and Chaco. In Córdoba, the competent authority to adjudicate the contracting was the provincial Superior Court of Justice (S.C.J), while the implementation was assumed by its administrative unit (provincial S.C.J., Agreement No. 123, Class 'C', § 2). On the other hand, in Chaco the competent authority for the e-voting procurement was the Executive, represented by the Ministry of Government, Justice, Security and Labour whereas the Electoral Court was the implementation authority thereof (Ministry of Government, Justice, Security and Labour, Resolution No. 1123/11, Item 2).

14 Buenos Aires, Electoral Provincial Court, Technical Resolutions dated 8 June 2009; 2 February 2010 and 22 February 2010, among others. In Chaco, we find another example of this (Provincial Electoral Court, Act No. 775/11.) Also, in the case of the municipal elections of Ushuaia in 2003, the Resolution No. 90/03 of the Provincial Electoral Court, when developing the Ordinance No. 2578/03, provided a timeline application schedule of the evoting system.

the presentation of the source program and/or software and the voting machines themselves, the deadlines for formulating comments regarding the source program and/or software, the identification of the required infrastructure in the polling stations, the sealing of the source program and/or software, the loading and/or the insemination of voting machines and their sealing, are among the most frequent.[15]

The IT auditors are technicians and experts in computing who, being legally and professionally certified to act, are formally assigned by the political parties in the electoral administration to protect and represent their interests as regards the implementation of e-voting. They take part in the hearings arranged in order to carry out the relevant procedures, tests and trials for software and hardware verification. For this purpose, deadlines and suitable areas are assigned to develop this audit. They also perform the verification and technical review of the infrastructure provided by the electoral administration for the development of e-voting elections. Based on these reports and considerations, the political organizations that they represent will be able to file comments, challenges and complaints with the EMBs (Boltz/Centeno Lappas, 2005; Hernández, 2011).

Hearings regarding the introduction of definitive evoting systems deserve special attention. These are specific hearings called by EMBs, whose members preside and conduct them as another stage of the electoral process. In these hearings, the electoral organization presents the evoting system to be used in the elections, making it available for critical analysis by the different political entities and their representatives, technicians and consultants, so as to verify its technical characteristics and resolve doubts. Hearings are formalized through documents made by the EMB itself, in order to provide evidence of the activities developed and the comments made during the process. This procedure is intended to protect the interests of the participants in the electoral process since it grants them the opportunity to exercise their rights by recording the observations and filing the appropriate legal complaints (Boltz/Centeno Lappas, 2005; Reniu i Vilamala, 2008; Hernández, 2011; Tula, 2012). Nevertheless, this system has also been subject to criticism, because a democratic control starts to become an elite verification, being provided by a technocratic bastion made up of a select group of technicians and agents (Boltz/Centeno Lappas, 2005; Chaparro, 2004; García Soriano, 2008).

In some cases, there is a confusion of roles between the authorities of the electoral organizations that must always function as unique and unmistakable electoral process commanders and who are responsible for any decision intended to solve the issues that could arise (Tula, 2005), and, on the other hand, the technicians

15 Buenos Aires, Electoral Provincial Court, Resolutions dated 8 June 2009 and 22 February 2010 aforementioned; Río Negro, Decree No. 1375/07 (referenced above), Annex I, art. 1 and 2; Córdoba, Ad Hoc Provincial Electoral Court, decrees dated 19 July 2011, 21 July 2011 and 4 August 2011, and Minute No. 3/11; Salta, Provincial Electoral Court, Minute No. 6297/13; Tierra del Fuego, Ushuaia, Municipal Electoral Board, Minute dated 2 October 2003.

and representatives of the companies that provide IT solutions for e-voting. The latter should limit themselves to answer only technical questions formulated by the interested people who attend the hearing, and only upon authorization by the EMB or the court.

Therefore, the political entities participating in the elections can take part in hearings concerning the introduction of e-voting systems, but the role of judges and election officials as directors of the electoral process is not always clear. Together with political parties' representatives and party technicians, they formulate queries and raise doubts addressed to the representatives of the suppliers about the functioning of the evoting system. Regarding judges and election officials, such a behaviour raises doubts about the certainty or accuracy of their knowledge of the system, even when they have taken part in previous contracting decisions, and are part of the electoral authorities that implement the e-voting systems.[16]

There is also a risk that representatives and experts of the contractors take an active role regarding the technical aspects of the system as well as in questions and answers that determine legal and conceptual notions, even though initially only the EMB or court could be entitled to participate in the second. According to Rial (2004) these situations should never occur. A typical example of this are cases where computer scientists working for the supplier establish the circumstances in which a vote would be null and void, when a vote would be impugned or considered blank. Also, when it would be justified to deliver another ballot paper or re-enable a voter to vote.[17]

It is in these kinds of hearings where the central arguments of the decision of the German Constitutional Court in 2009 become evident. The essential steps of the electoral process and the reliable declaration of the result are to be determined without the need for special technical knowledge.[18] And the same approach applies especially for those arguments related to the democratic principle and the principle of the public nature of elections, that somehow confront the protection of commercial rights of contracting companies. In short, all these pre-electoral acts are not able clearly to overcome the objections raised by the above mentioned European court (Pérez Corti, 2010).

Within this category, we also find decisions that aim at giving responses to the different arguments and comments made regarding evoting. They reflect how

16 Cf. Córdoba, Ad Hoc Provincial Electoral Court, Minute No. 3/2011, sheet 15; for example.

17 Cf. Córdoba, Ad Hoc Provincial Electoral Court, Minute No 3/2011, sheets 16/17.

18 Judgement of the German Federal Constitutional Court, – 2 BvC 3/07, 2 BvC 4/07, §118, §122/125 and §146 – (Spanish version at *Justicia Electoral*, vol. 1, No. 6, 2010, pp. 530/533, 539). For those reasons, the Constitutional Court clearly stated that the democratic legitimation of the election demands the ability to control the electoral process, in order to exclude or correct manipulations and to refute unjustified suspicions (2 BvC 3/07, 2 BvC 4/07, §106 and §108 'aa' and 'bb'), http://portal.te.gob.mx/sites/default/files/publicaciones/doc-relacionado/juel_a6_n2_2.pdf (accessed 2 April 2014).

the process is reshaped bearing in mind the traditional paper voting mechanism.[19] In many cases, once the hearings are concluded and the critical reviews of the e-voting system have been collected, the EMB must face and solve complaints from the political parties and their legal and technical representatives. The EMB uses formal resolutions, whose content include, however, aspects that many times are real instructions, similar to those norms or supplementary rules that make e-voting viable.

E-voting Case Law

In Argentina, there exist some clear judicial decisions concerning the implementation of e-voting specifically, but in general terms, few resolutions are characterized as authentic judicial decisions, and in many cases, they are considered to be merely of an electoral nature. They do not acquire the category of genuine rulings about e-voting or its intrinsic matters. We will address such precedents below.[20]

Ushuaia 2003

In the municipal elections of Ushuaia in 2003,[21] it was alleged that the nature of the great regulatory faculties granted to the Election Judge of the Province of Tierra del Fuego (Municipal electoral system, Ordinance No. 2578, art. 124; and Decree No. 506/2003, art. 2) was unconstitutional, and this in light of the implementation of evoting in Argentina for the first time using the Indra's Point&Vote system (Tula/Diéguez/Eyherabide, 2005).

The appellants initiated this request of unconstitutionality on the principle of normative supremacy, and on the inappropriate nature of the legislative function granted to the Election Judge. They referred to the municipal, provincial and national regulations and argued that, due to these regulations, the possibility for the Election Judge to regulate by ordinances is prohibited, because that competence rests with the City Council exclusively.

As a result of Resolution no. 97/03, the Municipal Electoral Board[22] held that this competence constitutes an executive statutory regulation and is limited by

19 Cf. Tierra del Fuego, Electoral Court, Resolution No. 99/03.

20 Please note that once submitted the final version of this chapter, two new judicial procedures have to be added: (I) Judgement n° 3 / SJC City of Buenos Aires, date 23/01/2015, available at https://www.eleccionesciudad.gob.ar/acordadas.php, accessed 08/05/2015; and (II) a petition of constitutional review in Salta (Petition. n° CJS 37.757/15), the latter with no definitive judgement yet.

21 Decree No. 506/03 dated 25 August 2003, calling for the election of municipal authorities on 26 October 2003.

22 An organism of municipal nature and hierarchy, constituted by an Electoral Judge and a Court of Appeals Judge assigned by raffle, both from the Provincial Judicial

the impossibility to alter or transgress the essence of the parliamentary Act under which such regulation is issued. This Act is the clear limit of constitutional nature which frames the exercise of statutory competences (S.C.J.N.; Supreme Court of Justice of the Nation, Judgements 14:353; 190:301; and 199:442). The Municipal Electoral Board argued that the spirit of the law would not be infringed when the regulations do not go beyond a scope based on the selection of a solution among many equal and possible ones, whether the selection is appropriate or not (S.C.J.N.; Supreme Court of Justice of the Nation, Judgements 259:53). Therefore, they decided that, as established by article 124 of Ordinance No. 2578, the Election Judge had to adapt the procedures to the technological innovations, making sure that the guidelines established in article 217 of the Municipal Charter were implemented.

This issue is of great importance as a result of the lack of specific provisions at both the provincial and municipal level. Due to the absence of norms or the existence of laws that are inaccurate, vague and even delegating the regulatory function to EMBs or courts, this normative function is fully exercised by EMBs so as to guarantee the suitable implementation of evoting.

San Antonio Oeste 2007

After the publication of Law 'O' No. 4082 in Río Negro, a town called San Antonio Oeste was one of the first to adhere to the norm (Decree No. 1236/06) and in the municipal election of 2007 (Decree No. 2505/07), it was decided to implement a pilot test in four polling stations located in Las Grutas (Decree No. 3012/07), using the evoting system from the company Altec S.E.

An appeal against this decision of the provincial and municipal authorities was submitted to the Civil Court No. 3 in the city of Viedma, by a group of citizens of Las Grutas, who challenged being forced to exercise their right and duty to cast a vote through e-voting (Busaniche/Heinz/Rezinovsky, 2008). They requested an optional method of voting for everyone, that is to say, that one would be able to vote using ballot papers or e-voting. They alleged that they were subject to discrimination and that political rights such as universality or equality voting were being restricted, threatened or violated. They considered that some appropriate previous training was necessary in order to be able to adapt to the new voting methodology. Moreover, they felt that they were left aside, since only a given group of citizens was compulsorily included within the e-voting pilot, an unknown mechanism that did not provide them minimum legal security and that they did not consider reliable. They argued that voters would be less reluctant regarding e-voting if its inclusion was foreseen as a supplementary means in addition to the traditional voting system. Finally, they also argued that the feasibility of

Authority; the Highest Prosecutor and two neighbours by raffle. It is not a judicial court and its decisions can be appealed to the provincial Superior Court of Justice (S.C.J.).

the new system should be reviewed in advance (Barrat Esteve, 2008; Reniu i Vilamala, 2011).

The Civil Judge declared himself incompetent and referred the case to the Superior Court of Justice S.C.J.; on the grounds that it was an action of *mandamus* or order of execution (Provincial Constitution, art. 44). The 'acción de ejecución' is the instrumental guarantee designed to request the judge to issue to an official, or public corporation of administrative nature, an order of compliance with an obligation enforced by law, ordinance, decree or resolution. For this purpose, an order of execution is issued (Murcia, 2013).

In relation to the public prosecuting attorney, she argued the incompetence of the provincial Superior Court on the grounds that it was not about an execution mandate and in any case, and only when necessary, the appropriate channel would be the voter's *amparo*, a specific judicial procedure for the protection of the voter (Law O No. 2431, art. 12.); as a result, the lawsuit had to be forwarded to the Electoral Provincial Court.

After that, the provincial Superior Court (Judgement No. 160/07) stated that those issues had to be first brought and treated before the Municipal Electoral Board, under the supervision of the Electoral Jurisdiction. It also considered that, in this issue, none of the *amparo*'s requirements were met, making it clear that the competence for such a procedure rested with the Municipal Electoral Board, and only through the relevant appeal, with the Electoral Provincial Court. In addition, the provincial Superior Court referred to the support provided by the political parties to the implementation of that e-voting pilot experience, as well as to the absence of the discrimination alleged by the appellants, to the extent that the distinction between those who voted through different methods was oriented to a legitimate purpose; that is to say, the court concluded that it did not lead to situations contrary to justice, to reason or to the nature of things.

In short, the provincial Superior Court concluded that none of the stated principles was violated by the procedure adopted by the relevant executive authorities. Furthermore, the principle of non-discrimination was not infringed. Finally, it held that such procedures were reinforced by the political and institutional consensus achieved during their development.

Thus, the pilot experience was carried out as planned from the very beginning. However, despite the outcome of this *amparo*, a year later, it was decided to allow options when implementing the e-voting system from the company Altec S.E. for the 26 October 2008 referendum, in which voters were asked to decide in favour or against the act of municipalizing the town of Dina Huapi (Decree No. 605/08 of the Provincial Executive). This election was conducted with an optional methodology for the voters. Each citizen was able to choose between two methods: using the traditional ballot paper or e-voting. According to the press, about 40 per cent of voters used the latter (CanalAR, 2009).

Pinamar 2010

In 2010, the extraordinary municipal elections[23] of Pinamar took place on 28 March 2010 (Decree No. 2585/09). This time, Indra's e-voting system Point&Vote was used. During its implementation, various issues and questions arose.

First, we note two similar requests, on the part of different political entities. In both cases, requests related to the layout of images, names and numbers of political parties in the voting screens were raised. This layout was not difficult since it was a 'uni-nominal election' (only one position was elected) and there were only four candidates, so it was technically possible to meet the petitions.

The Electoral Board of the Province of Buenos Aires was also requested to foresee that in each polling station, once the result was known, the president, in the presence of the political parties' official auditors, should proceed to the manual count of votes which had been printed and inserted in the ballot box, with the aim to provide more transparency.

The Electoral Board thought (Resolutions on 22 March 2010) that under the provisions of the electoral legislation for the closure of the polling station (Decree No. 1460/07, art. 16), it was impossible to follow a different procedure from that set by the norm. This would mean departing from the valid normative frame and the consequent change in the rules during the electoral process itself. Besides, it would result in a flagrant, illegal act. The Electoral Board stated that the procedure imposed by the norm did not engender less transparency to the system, since the political entities could ask for the opening of ballot boxes during the official tallying, provided there were reasons that made that request relevant (Law No. 5109, art. 102). It finally argued that departing from the provisions contained in the norm would mean that the system would not take into account '... the comparative advantages for this electoral process that e-voting has over the paper voting'. It also considered that it was worth recalling that '... under the current valid regulations, the "vote" is electronic (article 1, Decree 1460/07), not the paper ballot, which could only be used for verifications'.

The facts that have already been reviewed so far allow us to foresee the inappropriateness of incorporating e-voting without an adequate legal framework, since provisions related to traditional paper voting are not always suitable or applicable to e-voting. Moreover, traditional provisions lack other details that are necessary to make the incorporation and operation of such e-voting mechanisms secure, reliable and transparent (Tula, 2005 and 2012; Tullio, 2005).

A clear example can be found in articles 102 and ss. of the Electoral Law No. 5109, which are mentioned by the Electoral Provincial Court when it indicates that the opening of ballot boxes for counting paper receipts may take place during the final tally. However, such procedures are not appropriate for e-enabled frameworks. These provisions refer to the tabulation of official poll records that

23 It was only to choose a Mayor (*Intendente*), due to the destitution of the former (Law No. 5109, art. 123, second paragraph).

always has to be done; whereas manual counting of ballot papers is only authorized exceptionally for those cases where differences exist between data from official poll records and/or the provisional results; or between the number of voters and the number of votes that were cast and recorded in the official poll records. When we refer to e-voting, it is impossible to encounter such situations, since the voting machine would not allow such mathematical inconsistencies at the time of closing the tally. Moreover, the attending political party auditors would not ratify such official poll records (García Soriano, 2008).

Such difficulties highlight the forced interpretations that the electoral management bodies have to make. They have to adhere to an absolute formalism and restrict their decisions to what the unsuitable and non-contextualized norm establishes; or they have to adopt a flexible and broad decision in which the limit of discretionary power is not easy either to determine or to evaluate following applicable and reasoned criteria.

In its arguments, the Board used a reasoning opposite to that of the 2009 ruling of the German Constitutional Court. The Board gave prevalence to the effective validity of the operative advantages of e-voting over paper voting, considering that the paper ballot was useful only in a case where verifications have to be made and holding that '… "the vote" is electronic …'. The principle of the public nature of elections on which the German Court relied to rule out all attempts to limit the public oversight that should govern the electoral events, was left in second place. The German Court's decision holds that public oversight is a fundamental condition for a democratic formation of the political will. Consequently, the German Court understood that evoting can be implemented only if all essential steps of the election as well as the special technical reports can be verified, so as to comply properly with the principle of the public nature of elections (2 BvC 3/07, 2 BvC 4/07, 106, 118 'a'; Pérez Corti, 2010).

It is also worth noting that the impact or effect of such decisions made by the electoral body led the Pinamar City Council to analyse and evaluate the actual context and to completely reject e-voting in upcoming elections (Resolution No. 930/11).

Another issue emerged just three days before the election. A blind elector requested the implementation of a Braille system or an equivalent for visually impaired people, ensuring the secrecy of the suffrage and the principle of equality in its exercise. If that option was technically impossible, the elector requested the election be cancelled in order to avoid infringing the voters' constitutional rights.

The Electoral Board decided that, given the applicable electoral schedule and the preclusion effect of electoral deadlines, the request was time-barred (Resolution on 26 March 2010); nevertheless, it made it clear that the electoral code already foresaw that people with some kind of disability, and those who need help from others, may be assisted by political parties' representatives and by the authority at the polling station (Law No. 5109, art. 73).

It can be observed that this issue was not about the intrinsic aspects of evoting, but it was about any voting device. Such general approach was the one used by the Electoral Board to solve the request.

During the final tally, a new issue was raised in seven polling stations regarding the manual count. The challengers observed irregularities as regards the accuracy of e-voting, such as differences in the starting time, the election date and particularly they mentioned one case where '... there was a bias in counting the votes'.

The Electoral Board explained that the differences noted in some cases had been duly corrected by the relevant supplementary documents that rectified the mistakes and that had been adopted by both the polling board and by the representatives of the different political entities, with no protest or challenge (Law No. 5109, arts. 21 and 85).

Concerning the alleged counting at polling station 14, the Electoral Board said that no evidence in this regard had been provided, and that the appellants had failed to specifically identify the alterations which had been observed. Thus, the re-opening of the ballot box was considered not legally required. But the most important argument, that at the end was definitive for the appellants, hinged on the interpretation that the Electoral Board made of article 1 of the Unique Annex of Decree No. 1460/07. This article specifies that manual counting of votes is not part of the e-voting system. With this decision, ultimately, the Electoral Board denies any possibility of a manual count of the votes cast by e-voting, at least until the end of the final tally (Reniu i Vilamala, 2008).

Marcos Juárez 2010

In addition, another legal case was filed in 2010, in the city of Marcos Juárez, Córdoba. It was related to the fact that the City Council decided to start using e-voting once the electoral procedure had already begun for the elections to be held on Sunday 5 September 2010 (Ordinance No. 2157/10). A series of measures and preventions were taken for this purpose such as the temporary legal freezing of some articles of the Electoral Regulations (Ordinance No. 1096/94) that were in force when calling for the elections. The Indra's Point&Vote system was the one implemented during this process.

The appellants argued that once the methodology had been set up and the electoral schedule was in progress, a modification in the voting mechanism could not legally be introduced. The applicable rules are to be unchangeable once the electoral process has begun.

This claim was rejected by Resolution No. 3 of the Municipal Electoral Board, on the grounds that it was not competent to evaluate the voting methodology established by local government bodies. The political organization which filed the lawsuit did not agree with that decision, since the issue was not about the evaluation of the voting mechanism, but the unexpected alteration of the legal framework, the deadlines and the overall electoral matters that were already in course. The case was appealed to the Provincial Electoral Court and it was rejected by the Judge *in limine* in a decision dated 2 August 2010, that was based on formal issues, namely that the appellant had not filed a notice for reconsideration before the Municipal Electoral body, which is a legal requirement prior to resorting to appeal. This rejection was appealed before the provincial Superior Court of Justice,[24] which after hearing the Public Attorney, decided to declare it inadmissible on formal grounds related to the applicable electoral appeals procedure (Order of Court No. 71/10). Actually the appeal began directly before the Electoral Court, without having first gone through the steps required by the procedural norms, that is, before the organ that enacted the resolution that it attempted to question, the Electoral Board of Marcos Juárez.

This is the only precedent in Argentina that has reached the highest provincial judicial instance concerning e-voting; however, a decision on the issue was not pronounced. The rejection of the appeal in all judicial instances reaffirmed the decision of the Municipal Electoral Board, ratifying the decision of the City Council substituting the traditional voting mechanism by e-voting.

Las Higueras 2011

Finally, in 2011, another issue that reached the judicial instances emerged in Las Higueras, a town in Córdoba province. In this case, it is interesting to mention that the issue arose in connection with the hiring of electoral services, carried out by the Municipal Executive Department, as requested by the Electoral Municipal Board. This is a routine procedure in all the elections and corresponds to the so-called electoral activities of administrative nature that all electoral management bodies and courts in Argentina carry out.

For that purpose, the mayor of the city hired directly the services of a company straight away, considering that '… it offer[ed] the automated system for the printing of ballot papers and the votes casting for each voter, called E-voting ballot, that strictly [met] the goals set up by the electoral reform introduced in the Provincial Code and it is adaptable to the needs of the local election' (Decree No. 1617/11).

This decision was forcefully presented as a discretionary choice between two equally valid options. However, it is clear that there was awareness that the aforementioned choice was not only providing generic electoral services, but also introducing e-voting. Significantly, there was a direct reference to article 184 of the Provincial Electoral Code in the reasons given for the decision.[25]

This situation led to the Electoral Municipal Board adopting an *ex officio* decision (Resolution No. 10/11) which held that, in compliance with the timely

24 Until the enactment of Law No. 9840, which created the Provincial Electoral Jurisdiction, decisions issued by the provincial Electoral Court were appealed directly to the Superior Court of Justice; S.C.J. (Law No. 8643, art. 6).

25 Law No. 9571, of suppletory application due to art. 3 of Decree No. 1608/11.

call for elections decided by the Executive Department[26] and the provisions of the Provincial Electoral Code (arts. 54, 112 and 184), a unique paper ballot had to be used for casting the votes in the municipal elections, so the electoral service to be hired by the Municipality had to comply with such a requirement.

This decision was appealed by a provincial party on the grounds that the characteristics of the election with only two lists of candidates in a district with a small number of electors, simplified election management and constituted the best opportunity for starting to train citizens to use e-voting platforms, while not being an obstacle for the unique ballot paper established by law.

The Provincial Electoral Court rejected the appeal, arguing that '... the Municipal Executive by Decree 1617/2011, extended the system of Unique Ballot with an electronic mechanism that in strict terms, is not the one referred to in Article 184 of Law 9571 ...'. It stated that the call for elections had already set up a procedure from which different acts and stages were put into practice at the pre-electoral stage. Therefore, it rejected the appellant's argument because there was no legislation which foresaw this new method of Unique Ballot voting in which the indelible pen already accepted by the provincial law (Law No. 9571 and amendment., art. 112), was replaced by an evoting mechanism. Moreover, it held that it was neither '... desirable [n]or convenient to change the rules for the groups involved, nor for the whole electorate, especially when the attacked resolution causes no real and concrete harm to the appellant' (Order of the Court No. 275/11).

This decision was not further appealed and thus its content became definitive without having gone through all judicial instances. As the resolution of the Municipal Electoral Board remained valid, the Municipality had to rescind the previous hiring, and limit it to the acquisition and financing of those expenses that were necessary to develop the elections under the Unique Ballot system.

Similarities between this precedent and the city Marcos Juárez (2010) case deserve special attention. In both cases, the negative assessment of the introduction of e-voting was focused on the fact that, around 30 days before the election, a significant change in the voting mechanism was introduced while the electoral process was in progress in compliance with a previously established regulatory system. However, the two situations were treated very differently by the relevant electoral boards and the same happened regarding the requests, due to errors made by the appellants themselves and the different judicial criteria used in each case.

Another aspect that deserves our attention is the clear argumentation on which the Election Judge partially based his judicial resolution in the case of Las Higueras. Despite the fact that the same judge is also one of the members of the Ad Hoc Provincial Electoral Court, those arguments were not considered at the time of approving the procurement of e-voting mechanisms for their first

26 Decree No. 1608/11, calling for an election of municipal authorities on the 26 June 2011.

implementation at the provincial level in La Falda[27] (Law No. 9840, art. 4. a). This highlights the lack of consistency between the guidelines used in judicial decisions related to the use of e-voting in other towns, and the ones that the same EMBs or courts should take into account when developing their own electoral administrative procurement procedures.

Conclusions

From the analysis and study of the different judicial cases regarding the implementation of evoting in Argentina, we can see that they belong to experiences at a sub-state (provincial and/or municipal) level.

In all cases, either the relevant EMB or the court, or both of them, were involved in the form of what we labelled statutory regulations or supplementary resolutions, that entail a highlighted exercise of administrative competences in stages prior to the implementation of the election (queries, covenants and agreements), or directly during the development of the electoral process in which evoting had to take place.

Authentic judicial decisions were adopted in a significantly smaller number of cases. In those cases, problems and issues arose that were not linked to concrete and specific aspects of evoting, but rather to the roles or functions to be developed by EMBs or courts in the absence of specific legislation. They are also related to challenges due to the unexpected replacement of the traditional voting mechanisms by evoting while the electoral process was already in progress; or to general controversies about the casting of votes, such as the exercise of political rights for those with some physical limitation or disability.

In all cases, it is possible to notice a significant normative gap, a framework in which the activities of EMBs and courts have to be developed and enhanced. It is also worth observing the broad and varied regulatory functions assumed by the administrators of the electoral processes, and the multiple roles that they must play, not always with uniform and consistent decisions for each case.

One advantage of federalism is that the incorporation of evoting is subordinated to the gradualness and progressiveness principles. The experiences of each of the entities within the federal structure become important and not negligible precedents in their normative as well as administrative and jurisdictional profiles. These experiences configure useful concrete precedents in order properly to assess the strengths and weaknesses of such computing solutions in the mid and long term.

The risk, however, resides in the atomization of the experiences and in the fact that they would transform the country into a vast testing laboratory for different projects and e-voting models. Different EMBs and courts will have the important

27 Superior Court of Justice S.C.J., Resolution No. 123, Class 'C', especially the first two arguments; and the Unique Annex, Document of General Conditions § 13; Document of Special Conditions, § 5 and § 8; Technical Specifications, Items 2.5, 4.1, very especially 7.1.2, 8, 9 (in particular 9.8.1), 10 and 11; the most important ones.

mission of rationalizing such experiences within their own legal domains, and making them compatible with other jurisdictions as well.

References

Aristía, G., 'Voto electrónico: Experiencia en la provincia de Buenos Aires' in *XII° Seminario del Foro Federal de Organismos Electorales Provinciales* (10 October, Mendoza, 2008), www.joseperezcorti.com.ar/Archivos/Doctrina/Electoral/2008_10_09_Voto_Electronico_en_Pcia_Bs_As_G_O_Aristia.pdf (accessed 2 April 2014).

Barrat Esteve, J., 'Aproximaciones a las urnas electrónicas. Análisis de sus modalidades y evaluación de su utilidad' [2008] 7(8) *Elecciones* 73–85.

Barrera Buteler, G., *Provincias y nación* (Buenos Aires, Ciudad Argentina, 1996).

Benalcázar Guerrón, J.C., 'El acto administrativo en materia electoral' in Santano, Ana C. and Salgado, Eneida D., *Direito eleitoral. Debates Iberoamericanos* (Curitiba, Íthala, 2014).

Blando, O., 'Santa Fe: Boleta Única, simultaneidad y federalismo electoral' [2014] *Comercio & justicia* (Sección Leyes y Comentarios, 1 July).

Boltz, I. and Centeno Lappas, F., 'Riesgos y debilidades del voto electrónico: en busca de transparencia, seguridad y confianza en el proceso electoral' in Tula, María Inés (ed.), *Voto electrónico* (Buenos Aires, Ariel, 2005).

Busaniche, B., Heinz, F. and Rezinovsky, A., *Voto electrónico. Los riesgos de una ilusión* (Cordoba, Fundación Vía Libre, 2008).

CanalAR, 'Crece el voto electrónico en Río Negro' (27 January 2009), www.canal-ar.com.ar/Nota.asp?Id=6956 (accessed 2 April 2014).

Chaparro, E., 'Voto electrónico y software libre' in *Jornada sobre software libre y políticas públicas* (Cámara de Senadores de la provincia de Buenos Aires, 1 June 2004).

Dirección Nacional Electoral, 'Sistemas electrónicos de votación. Fortalezas y debilidades' (Buenos Aires, Dirección Nacional Electoral, 2004).

Frías, Pedro J., *El proceso federal argentino II* (Cordoba, 1998).

García de Enterría, E., *La revisión del sistema de autonomías territoriales: reforma de estatutos, leyes de transferencia y delegación, federalismo* (Madrid, Civitas, 1988).

García Soriano, M.V., 'Aspectos jurídicos del voto electrónico y las garantías de la integridad del proceso electoral' [2008] 7(8) *Elecciones* 87–110.

Hernández, A.M., *Federalismo, autonomía municipal y ciudad de Buenos Aires en la reforma constitucional de 1994* (Buenos Aires, Depalma, 1997).

Hernández, H.T., *Fiscalización informática del voto electrónico* (Cordoba, Tinta Libre, 2011).

Maffei, H.R., 'Ushuaia 2003: El voto electrónico. Más y mejor democracia' in Pérez Corti, José M. (ed.), *Reforma política y voto electrónico* (Ciencia,

Derecho y Sociedad, Cordoba, Facultad de Derecho y Ciencias Sociales / Universidad Nacional de Córdoba, 2005).

Murcia, D., 'Las acciones de ejecución y prohibición en la provincia de Entre Ríos' [2013] 1 *Institutas: Revista de derecho procesal*.

Pérez Corti, J.M. (ed.), *Reforma política y voto electrónico* (Ciencia, Derecho y Sociedad, Cordoba, Facultad de Derecho y Ciencias Sociales / Universidad Nacional de Cordoba, 2005).

——, 'Proceso electoral y nuevas tecnologías en América Latina' (unpublished, Cordoba, 2006).

——, 'Los principios generales del derecho electoral y su gravitación en la inconstitucionalidad del régimen alemán de voto electrónico' [2010] 1(6) *Justicia electoral, Revista del Tribunal Electoral del Poder Judicial de la Federación*, http://portal.te.gob.mx/sites/default/files/publicaciones/doc-relacionado/juel_a6_n2_2.pdf (accessed 2 April 2014).

——, *Derecho electoral argentino. Nociones* (2nd edn, Cordoba, Advocatus, 2012).

Prince, A., *Voto electrónico en Argentina* (Buenos Aires, Dunken, 2006).

Reniu i Vilamala, J.M., '¿Y dónde está mi voto? Un análisis comparado de los efectos sociopolíticos de la introducción del voto electrónico' [2008] 7(8) *Elecciones* 51–71.

——, 'Algunas certezas (pocas) sobre la introducción del voto electrónico' [2011] 46(3) *RAP – Revista de administración pública* 31–52.

Rial, J., 'Posibilidades y límites del voto electrónico' [2004] 3 *Elecciones* 81–108.

Saavedra, H.V. 'Apuntes sobre voto electrónico' (Buenos Aires, ED 192833, 5 June 2001).

Sesin, D.J. and Pérez Corti, J.M., *Organismos electorales* (Cordoba, Advocatus, 2006).

Tula, M.I. (ed.), *Voto electrónico* (Buenos Aires, Ariel, 2005).

——, 'Democracia, elecciones y nuevas tecnologías. El voto electrónico' [2012] 1(2) *Revista mexicana de análisis político y administración pública* 9–21.

Tula, M.I., Diéguez, G. and Eyherabide, Ú., 'Repaso por las experiencias con voto electrónico en la Argentina' in Tula, María Inés (ed.), *Voto electrónico* (Buenos Aires, Ariel, 2005).

Tullio, A., 'Organización, administración y actores electorales frente a las nuevas tecnologías' in Tula, María Inés (ed.), *Voto electrónico* (Buenos Aires, Ariel, 2005).

Annex Table 8.1 Technical details of elections in Argentina

Date	Province	Municipality	Elections	Charges	Voters	Electoral Roll	Voters	Polling Stations	Company	System
26/10/2003	Tierra del Fuego	Ushuaia[1]	Municipal	Mayor (*Intendente*) and Councillors	Natives/ Foreigners	36,158	24,448	105	Indra	Point&Vote
16/12/2007	Río Negro	San Antonio Oeste (Las Grutas)[2]	Municipal	Mayor and Councillors	Natives/ Foreigners	No data	No data	4	Altec S.E.[3]	E-voting System[4]
28/06/2009	Province of Buenos Aires[5]	Almirante Brown	Municipal Provincial	Councillors and School Councillors	Foreigners	No data	No data	No data	Indra[6]	Point&Vote[7]
		Bahía Blanca				No data	No data	No data		
		Berisso				No data	No data	No data		
		La Plata				No data	No data	No data		
28/03/2010		Pinamar[8]	Municipal	Mayor	Natives/ Foreigners	17,493	10,967	No data		
05/08/2010	Córdoba	Marcos Juárez	Municipal	Mayor and Councillors	Natives/ Foreigners	20,278	No data	46		
07/08/2011	Córdoba	La Falda	Provincial	Governor, Deputy Governor, Legislators and National Audit Officers	Natives/ Foreigners	12,791	8,894	37	MSA[9]	Unique Electronic Ballot[10]
18/09/2011	Chaco	Resistencia	Provincial Municipal	Governor, Deputy Governor, MPs, Mayors and Councillors	Natives/ Foreigners[11]	209,032	167,076	706		
		Presidencia Roque Sáenz Peña				64,872	45,854	220		
		Villa Ángela				31,691	23,263	109		
		Charata				21,792	17,296	75		
		Machagai				20,348	13,727	72		

Notes

1 A complete report that allows deeper access to the election features and aspects related to the e-voting mechanism is: www.joseperezcorti.com.ar/Archivos/Voto_Electronico/2004_MinInt_DiNE_VotoElectronico_Fortalezas_y_Debilidades_Fernandez_Marcilesse.pdf .

2 Pilot test at municipal binding election, four polling stations (two female and two male) in Las Grutas, municipality of San Antonio Oeste.

3 Altec S.E., Alta Tecnología Sociedad del Estado, http://www.altec.com.ar/.

4 For more information see: http://www.altec.com.ar/?page_id=789.

5 Data provided by the Electoral Provincial Court, http://www.juntaelectoral.gba.gov.ar.

6 Indra, http://www.indracompany.com/.

7 Information related to the Point&Vote system used in Ushuaia (2003), Almirante Brown, Bahía Blanca, Berisso and La Plata (2009), Pinamar (2010) and Marcos Juárez (2010) is no longer available at Indra's official website: http://www.indracompany.com/soluciones-y-servicios/solucion/procesos-electorales/114/490/proyecto-elecciones-argentinas, although it is possible to retrieve a version at: http://aipo.es/articulos/3/62.pdf. With regard to the municipal elections of Ushuaia (2003), Pinamar (2010) and Marcos Juárez (2010), a brief reference to the experiences, but not to the system is found at: http://www.indracompany.com/soluciones-y-servicios/solucion/procesos-electorales/114/12095/elecciones-municipales-de-argentina-2010.

8 The City Council of Pinamar decided by Resolution No. 930/11 dated 12 May 2011 to reject the implementation of e-voting (art. 1, viewed on 2 April 2014 and available at: http://201.219.79.16:8080/hcd/servlets/Resolucion_0930-11.html.

9 Magic Software Argentina, http://www.msa.com.ar/.

10 For more information, see: http://www.vot-ar.com.ar, and Tula (2005).

11 Data provided by the Provincial Electoral Court, http://www.electoralchaco.gov.ar.

Chapter 9
Internet Voting Case Law in Finland

Jussi Aaltonen

Introduction

In Finland, an electronic voting pilot was implemented in three rather small municipalities – Karkkila, Kauniainen and Vihti – in connection with the municipal elections of 2008.

After the elections, five appeals were lodged in the Helsinki Administrative Court. The appellants requested that the decision of the central municipal electoral committees to confirm the election results be revoked and that new elections be held, because some of the votes cast in the elections had not, against the voters' will, been registered in the electronic ballot box. The Helsinki Administrative Court dismissed the appeals.

The decision was appealed to the Supreme Administrative Court. The Supreme Administrative Court held that, when the Election Act (the governing law on voting) was issued, the characteristics of electronic voting, and the grounds for appeal invoked in the case, could not have been taken into consideration. This had to be taken into account when assessing the actions of the election officials. The court ordered that new elections be held in all the municipalities that took part in the pilot experiment. I will briefly describe the court decision and its reasoning below.

Some Basic Elements

In the pilot municipalities the number of persons entitled to vote was 34 062.[1] In the pilot project e-voting took place only at the polling stations in front of election authorities. Remote internet voting was not an option. The voter had the right to choose between e-voting and the paper ballot.

Election authorities used the election official's application (a special software package) to check the voter's right to vote against the central computerized voting register for the whole country which is automatically compiled for every election from the constantly updated population register. The election official's terminal was a standard PC that had been booted from secured read-only media. The

1 Official Statistics of Finland: *Kunnallisvaalit* [e-publication]. Helsinki 2008. Tilastokeskus [referred: 15.8.2014] http://www.stat.fi/til/kvaa/2008/kvaa_2008_2009-12-03_tie_001_en.html.

terminal included a card reader to manage the e-voting smart cards. The election official identified the voter by the same procedure used when voting with a paper ballot, usually by using the voters identity card or similar official document. After identification the election official registered that voting had started and gave the voter a smart card which allowed her to cast one vote. The election official's application configured the smart card by writing on it the credentials of the voter in question.

In the ballot booth, the voter put the voting smart card into the card reader to identify herself. Using the touch screen interface the voter then entered the candidate's number by using the numeric keys after which the system showed the information of the chosen candidate (name, candidate number, profession, and the party that had nominated the candidate) on the screen. If a voter wanted to cast an empty vote, she had to press a certain button designed for this purpose. The voter had to confirm her choice by pressing the visible OK button on the screen. It was also possible to cancel the choice by pressing a certain button and in this case the system returned to the previous screen and the voter could enter the candidate's number again. After pressing the OK button, the system gave a message that the voting had successfully been finished and asked the voter to remove the voting card from the card reader and to return it to the election official.[2] The voting cards were reused after they had been processed by the election officials.

The voting terminals were connected to a centralized 'electronic ballot box'. The e-vote having been cast, the application encrypted the digital e-vote, provided a digital signature and sent the e-vote to a central server via the internet. The e-vote was saved on the central server in an encrypted format until the vote count. At this stage, the e-vote contained information about both the voter and the vote.

A mixing application was used when decrypting the e-votes to break the connection between the vote and the voter to ensure voter privacy. These processes were executed under the authorities' supervision in an isolated environment with no physical connection to any other computer environment.[3]

A voter-verified paper trail was not used. Instead of a paper receipt, the voter received verification on the screen of the voting terminal when the vote had been cast successfully. For this reason, voters could not ensure whether their vote had been correctly registered in the system. However, in unclear situations the election official could check data in the centralized database mentioned above regarding whether the voter's right to vote had been registered correctly in the system.[4]

2 The Election Act (880/2006) section 83b (in Finnish and in Swedish), http://www.finlex.fi/fi/laki/alkup/2006/20060880.

3 TietoEnator: *Electronic Voting Pilot 2008: Technical Implementation and Security*. Helsinki 2008. [referred 14.8.2014] http://www.vaalit.fi/material/attachments/vaalit/vaalitietoa/kehittamishankkeet/6KveJ3EPH/Maarittelyasiakirjoja_Technical_implementation_and_security.pdf.

4 The Ministry of Justice, memorandum, 30 September 2009 (in Finnish): *Sähköisen äänestyksen pilottihanke vuoden 2008 kunnallisvaaleissa, Kokemuksia ja opittuja asioita,*

Auditing of the Voting System

Under a mandate from the Ministry of Justice, the Department of Mathematics at the University of Turku audited the voting system. The auditors signed a non-disclosure agreement not to publish suppliers' business or trade secrets. The Ministry of Justice also invited a critical NGO, Electronic Frontier Finland, a Member of Parliament, and an experienced IT expert to observe the work of the audit team, but they refused to participate as they were not willing to sign the non-disclosure agreement required by the IT suppliers. The audit report was published on the Ministry of Justice website before the elections.[5]

The Elections

Altogether 12,234 e-votes were cast, representing 58 per cent of all votes cast in the pilot municipalities in the local elections. During the advance voting period from day 11 to day 5 before the Election Day, a total of 4,985 e-votes were cast. The ministry did not receive any immediate feedback from the voters. Neither the electoral officials nor the IT support reported any problems. The only exception was the voting bus (that is a mobile polling station in an bus), where due to inoperative data communications only 44 e-votes were cast and the rest by paper ballot. Media expressed very positive reactions during the whole advance voting period: the voters had regarded the system as user-friendly and easy to use. During Election Day, a total of 7,249 e-votes were cast, and no problems were reported in the use of the e-voting system.

Late in the evening on Election Day, a citizen who had e-voted, sent an e-mail to the chairman of the central electoral committee of one of the pilot municipalities. He argued that the e-voting system seemed to be unreliable. After voting electronically, he had returned to the polling station to check whether his vote had been registered and it seemed that for some reason it had not been. The citizen in question voted electronically again, this time successfully. He suspected that there could have been other similar cases.

The next day, the IT supplier of the entire voting system, TietoEnator PLC, investigated the matter and reported a total of 232 cases in which the e-voting had started but it seemed that there was no registration of actual vote. The Ministry of Justice published a press release about this. According to TietoEnator, it seemed that in these cases the voter, for one reason or another, had removed the voting card from the card reader before confirming the choice by pressing the OK button. The

page 9. [referred 14.8.2014] http://www.vaalit.fi/material/attachments/vaalit/vaalitietoa/kehittamishankkeet/6Ku29QzCB/Muistio_30.9.2009_Sahkoinen_aanestaminen.pdf.

5 *Audit Report on Pilot Electronic Voting in Municipal Elections*, 13 June 2008, http://www.vaalit.fi/uploads/5bq7gb9t01z.pdf.

system did not give the voter an error message in these situations. The interrupted voting was not registered in the electronic ballot box or the voting register.[6]

Consideration of the Matter at the Administrative Court

Appeals concerning the 2008 municipal elections in those municipalities that participated in the pilot experiment of electronic voting were filed with Helsinki Administrative Court. The appellants requested that the decision of the central municipal electoral committee to confirm the election results be revoked and that new elections be held, because the elections had been conducted in an incorrect manner and unlawfully. Some of the votes cast in the elections had not, against the voters' will, been registered in the electronic ballot box. In those three municipalities that took part in the experiment, a total of 232 votes had not been registered in the electronic ballot box. The number of votes not registered showed that there had been a systematic error or errors in the voting system and its planning. The instructions that were appended to the polling card, issued by the Ministry of Justice, had been erroneous. The voting terminal had not informed or instructed the voter if he or she by accident had not completed the voting process. In their appeal, the appellants referred to the election observation report on the Finnish municipal elections drawn up by the Council of Europe in 2008, 'Information report on the electronic voting in the Finnish municipal elections, observed on 26 October 2008'.[7]

The Helsinki Administrative Court dismissed the appeals.[8] The Administrative Court considered that very high quality requirements should have been set for the electronic voting system. From the voters' perspective, it was of utmost importance that the user interface was as clear and easy to use as possible. The feature of the user interface that led to a discontinued voting process if the card was withdrawn from the voting device too early, without notifying the voter of this, could be considered a defect. However, almost 98 per cent of the electronic votes were cast successfully, and the fact that slightly over 2 per cent of the electronic votes failed could not, as such, be considered proof of erroneous conduct on the part of the election authorities.

The appellants had also brought up the fact that the user interface had in some situations reacted to the voter's instructions (given by touching the screen) with a delay and that therefore especially voters with limited ICT skills and older voters ended up in an unequal position. The Administrative Court stated that the

6 Ministry of Justice, press release, 28 October 2008 (in Finnish), http://oikeusministerio.fi/fi/index/ajankohtaista/tiedotteet/2008/10/sahkoisenaanestyksenkokeilusta.html.

7 Council of Europe, Congress of Local and Regional Authorities: *Information Report on the Electronic Voting in the Finnish Municipal Elections Observed on 26 October 2008*, Strasbourg 2008, https://wcd.coe.int/ViewDoc.jsp?id=1380337&Site=Congress.

8 29.1.2009 Nos. 09/0052/2, 09/0053/2, 09/0054/2.

electronic information systems are prone to overload, among other things, and the possibility for problems with data connections cannot completely be ruled out in any system. It is understandable that voters with limited ICT skills and experience may have felt that the electronic voting process was problematic. It must, however, be taken into consideration that the voters had at all times the possibility to ask for assistance from a polling assistant or election official, as well as the possibility to check with an election official whether the voting process had been successful. The voters also were able to choose whether they wished to vote electronically or traditionally by using a paper ballot. Voters cannot be considered to have been put in an unequal position because of the delays in the functioning of the user interface.

Appeal to the Supreme Administrative Court

The decisions of the Administrative Court were appealed in the Supreme Administrative Court. The appellants requested that the decisions of the Administrative Court and the central municipal electoral committee be quashed and that new elections be held.

The Supreme Administrative Court quashed the decisions and ordered that new elections be held in the municipalities that took part in the pilot experiment. In its decision, the Court defined the legal question to be resolved. A decision concerning election results may under section 101(2) of the Election Act be appealed on the grounds that the election has been conducted in an incorrect manner and that this may have had an effect on the election results. It had not been claimed in the case that the election officials in a single participating municipality had acted differently from each other or that any of the participating municipalities had not followed the instructions issued by the Ministry of Justice in its capacity as election authority.

The facts to be established in the case were whether the electronic voting instructions had been in such a manner misleading or inadequate from the voter's perspective that they could have led to erroneous conduct in the voting. In addition, it had to be assessed what the relevance was of the system feature that made it possible for a voter to exit the system without the system informing the voter that the voting process had not yet been completed. By contrast, it was not considered relevant to assess whether a voter who voted in an incorrect manner had done so on purpose.

As a consequence, the first legal question to be resolved was whether the measures taken by the election officials in connection with the electronic voting procedure had been lawful as provided in section 103(1) of the Election Act. Secondly, if the measures were found to be unlawful, it had to be assessed whether this unlawfulness may have clearly affected the election results. After this, it had to be assessed whether the election results could be rectified or whether new elections must be ordered to be held in the municipalities in question.

According to the information the Supreme Administrative Court received from the Ministry of Justice, there was a total of 232 such cases in the three municipalities where the electronic voting process was started but not completed according to the voting register. The votes were not in these cases registered in the electronic ballot box and the votes were thus not cast.

The voters had received the following instructions on electronic voting:

1. A polling card referred to in section 21 of the Election Act was submitted to the eligible voters in the participating municipalities in September 2008. A presentation of electronic voting was appended to the polling card. The presentation contained illustrated instructions and concise written instructions on electronic voting.
2. An introduction to electronic voting was published on the elections website of the Ministry of Justice in February 2008.
3. An electronic voting poster drawn up by the Ministry of Justice was on display at the advance polling stations and in the voting booths. In the poster, the electronic voting process was explained with illustrations.
4. The voting system provided instructions to the voter on the screen.
5. Where necessary, the election officials gave oral instructions to the voters.

When the Ministry of Justice tested the voting system, the testers had brought up as a defect in the operation of the voting terminal that the voter may be left with a misconception that the voting act has been successful even if it has not, because if the card is withdrawn from the device too early, the application returns to the start screen without notifying the voter that the vote had not been registered. However, no measures had been taken in light of this remark. In addition, the supplier of the electronic voting system, TietoEnator, had in its auditing report noted the defect that there is no way for the voter to make sure that his or her vote has been registered in a correct manner, because the voter does not receive any printout or electronic receipt of the voting act.

The Supreme Administrative Court noted that the provisions for appeal in the Election Act had been in force without amendments since 1998 (714/1998). The provisions for the pilot experiment of electronic voting, on the other hand, were issued in 2006 by the Act 880/2006. As a consequence, when section 103 of the Election Act including the formulation 'conduct of the election officials' was issued, the characteristics of electronic voting, and the grounds for appeal invoked in the case, could not have been taken into consideration. This had to be taken into account when assessing the measures of the election officials in connection with the case at hand.

According to the written voting instructions sent to each eligible voter as an appendix to the polling card, the voter was supposed to enter the candidate number by pressing the numbers on the touch screen, after which the corresponding candidate data appeared on the screen. After this, the voter was supposed to approve the vote by pressing the OK button. The instructions advised the voter to press the OK button only once.

In this respect, the instructions were inadequate, because the voter was actually supposed to press the OK button once immediately after entering the candidate number and again when the candidate data had been displayed on the screen. In other words, the voter was supposed to press the OK button twice. The illustrated instructions sent to the voters in advance were correct in this respect.

The illustrated poster drawn up by the Ministry of Justice, displayed at the advance polling stations and in the voting booths, also advised the voter to press the OK button twice during the voting process. Furthermore, the voting system itself guided the voter to do so on the screen.

As noted above, it had come up during the testing of the system that the voter might be left with a misconception that the voting act has been successful even if it has not, because if the card is withdrawn from the device too early, the application returns to the start screen without notifying the voter that the voting act had not been completed.

The Supreme Administrative Court considered that the voting system had been defective in such a way that any notification of a discontinued voting process did not appear on the screen, if the voter withdrew the card from the device before completing the voting process. The voter may therefore have had the misconception that the voting act was completed even if it was not. Because the voter had not been aware of the voting act having failed, he or she had not had any need to turn to an election official for assistance. The presence of election officials was therefore of no help in the situation.

When taking into consideration the above described defects in the instructions on electronic voting included in the appendix to the polling card sent to the voters, as well as the functional error in the electronic voting system, the Supreme Administrative Court held that the measures taken in the preparation of the system had been unlawful when assessed as a whole. As a consequence the elections were conducted in an incorrect order. Moreover, when considering the number of votes not registered, these errors and defects clearly may have affected the election results. The type of errors was such that the election results could not be rectified. Therefore, the Supreme Administrative Court ordered new elections to be held.

The decision of the Supreme Administrative Court was not unanimous. One judge dissented from the majority of four and would not have quashed the decision of the Helsinki Administrative Court. This judge noted that the instructions for use of the electronic voting system had been displayed on the screen of the voting terminal. He held, based on the information available in the case, that the said instructions on the actual voting procedure had been clear and detailed enough. Proof of this was that almost all the voters who used the electronic voting system completed the voting process correctly. The voter could have turned to a polling assistant if he or she had experienced any difficulties or uncertainties in completing the process. The voter also had the possibility to choose between the new electronic voting system and the traditional paper ballot.

Concluding Remarks

In January 2010 the Cabinet decided that in Finland development of e-voting at polling stations will not be continued for the time being, but instead the current election system will be maintained. The Cabinet noted that if it is decided, based on the international experiences, that development of e-voting will be continued, it will most likely concentrate on internet voting (remote i-voting). However, where remote i-voting is concerned, questions relating to the secrecy of the ballot and electoral freedom remain to be solved.[9]

In November 2013 the Ministry of Justice did set up a working group to prepare a proposal on the introduction of a possibility of using internet voting in elections and for electronic consultative municipal referenda. In its interim report of June 2014, the working group considered it to be too early to examine the possibilities to introduce internet voting in general elections, but proposed that internet voting be introduced in consultative municipal referenda along with the other voting channels. The working group proposed that the decision on the introduction of internet voting in general elections be made later separately. In that subsequent decision process, the experiences from the use of internet voting in municipal referenda could be utilized.[10]

In its closing report of April 2015, the working group proposed that an experiment with internet voting is carried out in connection with the advance voting in consultative municipal referenda during a fixed-term of four years. The working group estimated that, if the government decided to implement the pilot, the system could be taken in use, at the earliest, during the years 2016–2017. The internet voting system developed for municipal referenda could also be tested on a smaller scale in connection with, for example, municipal opinion polls or youth parliament elections.[11]

References

Council of Europe, Congress of Local and Regional Authorities: *Information Report on the Electronic Voting in the Finnish Municipal Elections Observed on 26 October 2008*. Strasbourg 2008, https://wcd.coe.int/ViewDoc.jsp?id=1380337&Site=Congress.

---

9 Government Communications Unit, press release, 20 January 2010, http://valtioneuvosto.fi/ajankohtaista/tiedotteet/tiedote/en.jsp?oid=285753.

10 The interim report of the working group, pages 53–4, http://urn.fi/URN:ISBN:978–952–259–384–9.

11 The closing report of the working group, pages 54–7, http://urn.fi/URN:ISBN:978-952-259-458-7.

Finnish Government, press release, 20 January 2010: 'Electronic voting will not be developed further on the current basis', http://valtioneuvosto.fi/ajankohtaista/tiedotteet/tiedote/en.jsp?oid=285753.
Ministry of Justice: *Nettiäänestystyöryhmän väliraportti* [e-publication]. Helsinki 2014, http://urn.fi/URN:ISBN:978-952-259-384-9.
——:Nettiäänestystyöryhmän loppuraportti [e-publication]. Helsinki 2015, http://urn.fi/URN:ISBN:978-952-259-458-7.
——: *Sähköisen äänestyksen pilottihanke vuoden 2008 kunnallisvaaleissa, Kokemuksia ja opittuja asioita*. Helsinki 2009, http://www.vaalit.fi/material/attachments/vaalit/vaalitietoa/kehittamishankkeet/6Ku29QzCB/Muistio_30.9.2009_Sahkoinen_aanestaminen.pdf.
——, press release, 28 October 2008: 'Sähköisen äänestyksen kokeilusta myönteistä palautetta – noin 200 äänestystä kuitenkin keskeytyi erehdyksessä', http://oikeusministerio.fi/fi/index/ajankohtaista/tiedotteet/2008/10/sahkoisenaanestyksenkokeilusta.html.
Statistics Finland, Official Statistics of Finland: *Kunnallisvaalit* [e-publication]. Helsinki 2008, http://www.stat.fi/til/kvaa/2008/kvaa_2008_2009-12-03_tie_001_en.html.
TietoEnator PLC: *Electronic Voting Pilot 2008: Technical Implementation and Security*. Helsinki 2008, http://www.vaalit.fi/material/attachments/vaalit/vaalitietoa/kehittamishankkeet/6KveJ3EPH/Maarittelyasiakirjoja_Technical_implementation_and_security.pdf.
University of Turku, Department of Mathematics: *Audit Report on Pilot Electronic Voting in Municipal Elections*. Turku 2008, http://www.vaalit.fi/uploads/5bq7gb9t01z.pdf.

Chapter 10
The Internet Voting Project in the Mexican Courts

Jordi Barrat

Introduction

Usually courts get involved in legal cases after disputes have gone through several steps. Starting from the adoption of relevant legislation, the effects of its more-or-less successful application cause the dissensions that lead to filing a lawsuit. This sequence has important consequences on the judicial work since it resolves disputes while maintaining a certain temporal distance from what happened. However, some cases follow a different path and that is precisely what happened in the case law that will be presented below. Regarding the introduction of internet voting in the Mexican Federal District, the relevant court was required to rule on the preliminary stages of the process and this is why it addresses some concerns that do not frequently show up.

The chapter provides, first, a quick overview of the emergence and development of electronic voting in Mexico, it then identifies the judicial *iter* of the internet voting project driven by the Electoral Institute of the Federal District (IEDF), and finally it discusses the legal approach adopted by the upper chamber of the highest Mexican electoral court.

Electronic Voting in Mexico: A Chequered History

Electoral procedures are conducted by a wide array of organisms throughout the Mexican Republic, with multiple state and federal administrative and judicial institutions. This diversity is also reflected in the field of electronic voting (Romero Flores / Téllez Valdés, 2010) where, in contrast to what happened in many other areas, progress has been made without a prior federal initiative (Barrat Esteve, 2011). After a first stage devoted to academic seminars and non-binding trials, in 2005 the state of Coahuila used electronic voting machines for the first time with legal binding effect. The Federal District and Jalisco followed such a path and nowadays the second is undoubtedly the most advanced electronic voting jurisdiction in Mexico.

While these three jurisdictions have been developing their respective voting machines with different outcomes, internet voting did not arise until 2011, when the Federal District Electoral Institute (IEDF) proposed its use in the elections to be held in 2012, but only for the capital's citizens who were living abroad.

Internet Voting in the Federal District: An Overview

The vote of Mexicans living abroad led to a lively controversy (Carpizo / Valadés, 1998; Calderón Chelius, 2003) due, among other reasons, to the difficulty in achieving an appropriate vote-casting method that would make voting easier for millions of expatriates. In 2006, during a presidential election, casting a vote from abroad was allowed for the first time, but the procedural requirements (e.g. issuance of electoral IDs only in Mexico, inappropriate voting channels), among other reasons, prevented a high turnout.

Based on these facts and taking into account the previous experience with e-voting machines, the IEDF raised the possibility of using internet voting in the 2012 elections. The previous implementation of similar technologies, though not on-line, and the simplicity of an internet channel emerged as key factors for overcoming the barriers identified in 2006.

After the relevant feasibility studies, IEDF agreed to promote the internet voting project. It did this with decision ACU-69-11, 31 October 2011, by which mechanisms were adopted to obtain the vote of Federal District citizens living abroad, either by post or internet. Internet voting was finally used in July 2012 in order to elect the capital's governor, but prior to that several obstacles had to be overcome, including a couple of court decisions on which we focus our attention in the following paragraphs.

The Decision of the Upper Chamber of the Federal Electoral Court

The Text and Context of the Decision

The main features of the decision of the *Sala Superior del Tribunal Electoral del Poder Judicial de la Federación* (Upper Chamber of the Federal Electoral Court), reference SUP-JRC-306/2011, are discussed below. It is a decision that quashes the previous ones of the Electoral Court of the Federal District, with accumulated references TEDF-JEL-048/2011 and TEDF-JEL-049/2011. Both references belong to the electoral lawsuits filed on 5 November 2011 by the *Partido Revolucionario Institucional* (PRI), the *Verde Ecologista de México* and *Partido del Trabajo* on the one hand, and the *Partido de Acción Nacional* (PAN) on the other.

Some of the discussed features will help us to assess how Mexico took into account already fairly advanced discussions in some other countries, but other features provide inputs on what are to date relatively unknown aspects of electronic voting issues. Both the heterogeneity of electronic voting platforms that are used worldwide and their customization to local legal contexts generate new developments of great interest (e.g. independent bodies such as the Belgian *Collège des Experts*, or the Norwegian return codes, as a way to achieve better verifiability) to solve the Gordian knots that this technology is facing.

Firstly, this section analyses the role of political parties in the democratic oversight of voting procedures. The legal requirements of electronic voting are then discussed, in light of their impact on the hierarchical relationship between parliamentary acts and statutory instruments. Such an issue is often neglected, but it can be, as in this case, of significant importance. Finally, the freedom of the voter as well as the secret of the ballot in internet voting platforms are assessed.

The Role of Political Parties in Electronic Voting

Any electronic voting system implies that the normal and direct supervision conducted by ordinary citizens has to be adapted to a new framework. Electronic voting deprives both voters and official election observers of the right to monitor first-hand the overall electoral operations. One may witness such electoral activities, but as the German Federal Constitutional Court stresses, merely showing up at a polling station and attending some key steps, such as the tally itself, might be not enough. According to this particular approach, which is not, however, followed everywhere, the principles of electoral openness and transparency do require that any citizen conducting the oversight be able to understand what is happening: 'every citizen must be able to understand the key electoral steps without any special technical knowledge' (BVerfG, 2 BVC 3/07, 3 March 2009, § 109; as well as, § 119, 148 and 149) (Barrat Esteve 2009; Fernández Riveira, 2011).

Unfortunately electronic voting is not able to provide this sort of direct democratic control. These systems can generate a consistent and rigorous testing outcome on the correct performance of the voting platform, but these data have such technical complexity that they can only be understood by a select handful of computer experts. Therefore, this inherent limit undermines the traditional openness of any electoral system to public scrutiny.

A compromise might be found by balancing such a loss of citizen power through other measures of procedural control that would generate enough citizen confidence (Barrat Esteve, 2009). Among them, as the Mexican case clearly shows, the tasks assumed by political parties may become very useful. Internet voting opponents denounced the absence of party control over the preliminary activities undertaken by the IEDF and they underlined the

> … violation of the principle of certainty, because the possibility was not given to the political parties to express their views when Internet as the voting mechanism for the expatriate residents of the Federal District was approved, and because the said voting system was approved without prior testing regarding its viability and security. (SUP-JRC-306/2011: 71)

Determining whether sufficient external controls are in place is decisive, since what is really at stake is the public nature of elections. As denounced by Nou, the privatization of democracy is not just a rhetorical game anymore, but a plausible threat in which the public interest is in retreat against legitimate business requirements. In the case of electronic voting, private providers might play an undesirable role if the public authority is not aware of its duties:

> America's existing system of oversight and decision-making in the purchase of voting machines is heterogeneous, partisan, and underfunded. Together, these features result in few levers of accountability and overt incentives to subvert the ones that exist. Not surprisingly, precarious dips in voter confidence threaten to undermine the legitimacy of elections as a whole. (Nou, 2009: 792; Mecinas Montiel, 2013)

As anticipated, the lawsuit submitted to the local court warned about the absence of political parties during the development and implementation of the e-voting system in Mexico's federal district and so was accepted by the capital's court, but the Upper Chamber of the Federal Electoral Court rejected these arguments. The judges describe a process in which political parties had the chance to closely monitor the whole process. For example, they conclude:

> noting that although the participation of political parties in each and every stage of the internet voting process *is not explicitly foreseen*, their participation as observers or auditors must be permitted to the extent that this is reasonable and does not infringe the guiding principles of the electoral functions and the characteristic of voting. (SUP-JRC-306/2011: 82, emphasis mine)

Note that the Court adopts a proactive approach that seems to be satisfied by a generic mention of the presence of political parties. One may wonder, however, if the specificity of electronic voting would not recommend foreseeing explicitly both the presence and active involvement of political parties so as not to give rise to any restrictive interpretations of a generic legal framework.

Reservas de Ley *and* Reservas Reglamentarias

Electronic voting generates multiple legal doubts and most of them have already been identified by the literature, but others remain less noticed, as will be discussed in the following paragraphs. Given that specific rules are required by any electronic voting system, the relationship between a parliamentary act and a statutory regulation may be altered so that the traditional pre-eminence of the former is compromised. Let us start by briefly exposing how Mexico deals with the legal protections of both parliamentary acts and statutory regulations.

The *reserva de ley* (protection of a parliamentary act) is probably the leading element. It consists of identifying certain matters that, as stated by the Constitution itself, must necessarily be regulated by a parliamentary act. The engagement of the Parliament guarantees a public discussion on the subject in which different views, from different political parties, can be expressed. A *reserva de ley* also entails that statutory regulations may only assume a secondary role as governmental developments of what is provided by the parliamentary act. Furthermore, a *reserva de ley* has to be understood and applied as a substantive guarantee, not merely a formal one. That is to say, a blank check, which actually would completely delegate the affected domain to statutory regulations, that is to say, to the government, would not meet the constitutional requirements (see a key example of tax law *reservas* in Torruco Salcedo, 2009: 8–9).

In addition to *reservas de ley*, the Mexican constitution incorporates, as many others, the absence of substantive limits to parliamentary acts; that is to say, the Parliament must regulate at least what is constitutionally mandated (*reservas de ley*), but it can also extend its law-making field without limits (Casarín Leon, 2003). Therefore Mexico does not adopt the French *pouvoir réglementaire autonome* (Barrat Esteve, 1999), that is to say, a domain identified by the Constitution and forbidden to parliament. Despite the democratic composition of the French Parliament, whose members have been directly elected by the citizens, it has limited powers. It cannot act beyond a given sphere. On the other hand, the Mexican Congress' bills have no substantive limits and statutory regulation only develops what has been provided in parliamentary acts.

This approach is consistent with the traditional requirements of liberal democracies, where representative assemblies are given a central institutional position, and this even in presidential systems like Mexico. However, it is also true that both the exorbitant increase of functions assumed by the public administration and the specificities of certain matters put into question the appropriateness of the legislator's unlimited statutory powers. It could be argued that a proper understanding of the role of parliaments should lead to restricting its legislative role and rather focusing its attention on parliamentary control procedures and social mediation (Barrat Esteve, 1999).

In the case of electronic voting, such thoughts acquire some importance. Its particular distinctive features may suggest that a legal framework mostly based on statutory regulations is much more appropriate than a normal schema with parliamentary acts acting as detailed cornerstones. The technical nature of e-voting systems, the constant evolution of technology and the experimental approach of first implementations may lead to reliance upon a sub-legal regulation. Parliamentary acts could even be reduced to a mere formal shell whose only goal consists in justifying the hierarchically inferior statutory regulation. These cases hardly fulfil the ordinary requirements linked to a *reserva de ley*, but they manage to address successfully the peculiarities of electronic voting systems.

The Mexican Electoral Court clearly adopted this view. Once it admitted that

> … everything that corresponds to information and communication technologies is dynamic, … the scope of a legal provision may become out of date or

> anachronistic over time, in such a way that it becomes difficult, through a functional interpretation, to properly follow the tremendous evolution in these areas of human knowledge and technical developments. For this reason it is logical that the electoral legal system of the Federal District allowed ample competences for the IEDF's general assembly to issue directives, norms, deliberations, and resolutions, and to conduct audits, which decisions were supported by the technical areas of the said local electoral management body. (SUP-JRC-306/2011: 46–7)

This is a risky strategy which is linked to a latent controversy in contemporary policy development and even in larger social contexts. Technical advances of all kinds apparently make obsolete (or at least challenge) existing solid structures and require their reformulation. Nobody wants to stop useful innovations, but developments are to be made in such a way that core principles both legal and social, are safeguarded. The same applies with respect to electronic voting. As the Court notes,

> the analysis of its implementation must be consistent with a legal weighing that takes into account the reasonableness of the constraints and characteristics of the system and its ability to ensure the respect of the guiding principles of the electoral function and the characteristics of voting, as well as its relevance in facilitating, respecting, protecting and guaranteeing the active vote of the expatriate residents of the Federal District. (SUP-JRC-306/2011: 46–7)

Thus, the statutory regulation may assume a leading role in this field, but always after a rigorous weighing of advantages and disadvantages. The outcome of this balanced approach should always ensure certain basic aspects, that the Court identifies as the guiding principles of any electoral procedure, the main features being the right to vote and the ability to vote from abroad.

Freedom and Secrecy in Internet Voting

To conclude, we deal with one of the main challenges of any remote e-voting system, that is to say, one in which voters may have the choice to cast their ballots from an unsupervised environment. Both freedom and secrecy of the vote can be seriously compromised in this scenario, as family voting perfectly shows. If a citizen can vote from his/her home without any additional barrier, it seems clear that pressures from relatives might be strong enough to persuade the voter to vote in a certain way.

E-voting platforms may face these challenges by allowing multiple votes, both electronic and paper based, and taking into account only the last electronic or paper ballot. This is what, with some variations, applied in Norway (Smith, 2010) and continues to apply in Estonia (Madise, 2008).

In the Mexican case, the IEDF did not implement such preventive measures and the question arose during the trial based on generic considerations, that is to say, assessing how internet voting manages to protect, without supplementary guarantees, basic electoral principles such as the freedom of the voter and the secrecy of his/her choice.

The electoral Court addressed these doubts by appealing to the necessity and proportionality of the measures undertaken by the electoral management bodies, but it is a bold strategy, since it assumes that, in certain circumstances, neither freedom nor ballot secrecy are sacred principles anymore, as they are often perceived within certain electoral contexts. In relation to the appropriateness and real necessity for internet voting, the Court recalls that it

> helps to extend the coverage of the external electorate, since it would permit a greater number of the expatriate residents of the capital to vote for the elections of the Governor in 2012, without a need to pay postal fees or the voter having to travel to a specific place. (SUP-JRC-306/2011: 91)

Furthermore, internet voting would be a proportionate measure because,

> given the characteristics of the voters, in that they reside abroad and, in general, it is difficult to install polling stations in various parts of the world, the possible risks to voting principles (free, secret, and direct) would be minimal compared to the level of security measures put in place by the electoral management body, and are outweighed by the greater benefits obtained in view of the higher turnout. (SUP-JRC-306/2011: 92)

In general terms, we agree with such an approach. The basic electoral principles always apply with some exceptions, provided the achievement of constitutional and democratic goals advises making exceptions. In fact, in relation to a secret ballot, similar contradictions may arise due to other factors and the Mexican legal system itself already admits some exceptional voting arrangements. For instance, following traditional and ancient customs, Oaxaca's legal framework allows electoral procedures that do not protect the secrecy of the ballot (Recondo, 2013; Barrat Esteve, 2013).

The Court's decision also includes other considerations that deserve careful reading. In relation to ensuring freedom and secrecy, the Court finds an individual right in these guarantees, that is to say, governments would not be obliged to ensure that any ballot is cast secretly. They only have to provide a procedural framework where such an option becomes feasible. Therefore, secret ballot would be not only an official commitment since it would also depend on how each voter uses the means provided by the relevant Electoral Management Body. The Court reveals this when it wonders whether the password used for each voter is correctly handled both by the provider and the citizens themselves. Given that the password is sent by e-mail, 'it is the holder of the right to vote that safeguards the information concerning the said mail box and therefore the same person is responsible for safeguarding the information received through this account' (SUP-JRC-306/2011: 93–4). Once the password is sent to the voter, the election management body assumes no responsibility and thus its oversight does not encompass any further coercion or extortion of the voter. The electoral management body accomplishes its duties by enabling a free and secret vote, but it does not care about the actual use of this option by each vote.

The debate over whether secrecy is merely an official commitment is not new and it has already been addressed in other countries with electronic voting. In Estonia, for example, the Supreme Court itself considered it a mere option available to the voter (Madise, 2008). If it is admitted that secrecy could mean both anonymity of the ballot, that is to say, no links from a given ballot to an ID, and a free casting of the vote, without the scrutiny of other people, then the Estonian approach concludes that the anonymity has to be protected during the whole electoral procedure, but the free casting of a vote may rely upon each citizen; this is in line with the Mexican Court. It is worth recalling, however, that in Estonia multiple voting is allowed and such an important measure mitigates the risks of vote buying in internet voting in uncontrolled environments. Therefore, delegating to each citizen the protection of the secrecy of vote becomes less troublesome because, although there may be cases of coercion, voters will always have a new opportunity to cast their ballots without external hindrances.

Unfortunately this is not the case in Mexico and therefore the Court's approach becomes much more significant. If the secrecy of the ballot is a mere voter's option and multiple voting or other safeguarding measures are not implemented, coercions might undermine the legitimacy of internet voting as a fair and sure voting channel. Surely aware of this fact, the Court backs its decision with other reasons, but the relevant statement is at least very doubtful since it equates the risks that may appear with an internet voting channel and a voting system in controlled environments:

> if the competent court determined that in this step prior to the casting of the ballot there was no infringement of the characteristics of certainty, objectivity, liberty or secrecy of the vote, it, in principle, should not find otherwise regarding the second stage of the internet voting procedure, that is, the casting of the ballot. Therefore one must consider that, usually, it would be certain that whoever votes is the one entitled to, and this because, in principle, only the person who received the password can vote, and that person is nobody other that the one entitled to vote; it must be considered *that the risks that the vote is not cast in secret or that it is cast under duress, are not limited to remote voting: they can be present in all types of voting*, including in-person voting, which can result in annulment of votes that take place at the level of the polling station, the district, etc. (SUP-JRC-306/2011: 98, emphasis mine)

The Court emphasizes the connection, which has been already analysed, between the voting documentation, that includes the password and other relevant information, and the act of voting, but the Court adds that all voting procedures have their own risks in relation to the secrecy of the vote. And certainly such a statement is true, but the comparison is too generic since it also seems clear that the risks, and the subsequent guarantees to be implemented, are not of the same type in one case as in the other.

Furthermore, there is a distinctive element that, in my opinion, seems crucial. One may discover several drawbacks and mistakes with voting procedures that take place in controlled environments, but these procedures are normally designed under conditions (e.g. voting booths, official oversight, sealed ballot boxes) that ensure protection of secrecy of the vote and the freedom of voters, which are assumed to be obligations for the electoral management bodies and not mere options for the voter. Certainly there may be errors, but there are failures in the actual implementation while the theoretical background clearly pursues a full and institutional protection of freedom and secrecy.

On the other hand, internet voting has a different theoretical starting point since secrecy, apart from anonymity of the ballot, and freedom rely upon each citizen. Beyond the appropriate means provided by electoral management bodies, their actual protection is not to be directly assumed by electoral authorities. Therefore the implementation of internet voting might be as challenging as other voting channels, but still internet voting would be based on different premises. It assigns far more responsibility to individual voters to respect the constitutional principles of fair voting. So, any comparison between traditional voting procedures and internet voting channels should take into account such differences.

Conclusions

Internet voting raises numerous questions about its compliance with the democratic principles that are traditionally required in any electoral process. Moreover, it is not a mere cosmetic issue, in which only voting tools are modified. Instead it calls into question key aspects of the whole electoral system. In fact, some countries have failed in its implementation and, not surprisingly, technological factors are not usually the most crucial in these cases. Once one has carefully designed the technical platform, precipitation or ignorance of other variables such as the legal aspects, the social impact or even the training of those involved in the implementation may cause an irreversible failure. This is why the Mexican decision is particularly significant for internet voting developments.

Once a lawsuit is filed, previous controversies are submitted to a neutral procedure that may somehow clarify the factors of dissent. It is not a political debate anymore, but a framed procedure which should achieve a properly motivated solution. In addition, the Mexican case has the advantage that judicial involvement starts at such an early stage that it provides insights into certain aspects usually ignored in other e-voting case law. For instance, the electoral Court had to analyse the role of political parties during the implementation of electronic voting procedures and the hierarchical relationship between the Constitution, parliamentary acts and statutory regulations. The Court also addressed how to protect the secrecy of the ballot and the freedom of the voter when using internet voting in uncontrolled environments.

In my view, the Court adopts a correct approach when dealing with the presence of political parties and with the appropriate weight of statutory regulations, but its way of protecting both secrecy and freedom is much more doubtful. The Court accepts the solution proposed by the IEDF, but that entails an extra cost consisting in transferring to the voter the full responsibility in keeping the passwords safe. It is clearly a compromise so as not to disfranchise expatriates, but it does not take into account the options implemented in other countries, such as the multiple vote already used in Norway and Estonia.

References

Ayala Sánchez, A., (ed.), *Democracia en la era digital* (Mexico DF, IIJ/UNAM 2012), http://biblio.juridicas.unam.mx/libros/libro.htm?l=3191 (11 February 2014).

Barrat Esteve, J., *La reserva reglamentaria* (Leon, Universidad de León 1999).

——, 'Observació electoral i vot electrònic' [2009] 39 *Revista Catalana de Dret Públic* 277–296, http://revistes.eapc.gencat.cat/index.php/rcdp/article/view/2194/2639 (30 November 2014), http://revistes.eapc.gencat.cat/index.php/rcdp/article/download/2194/2640 (30 November 2014, in Spanish).

——, 'El voto electrónico en México: pasado, presente y futuro' in Jordi Barrat Esteve / Rosa M. Fernández Riveira (eds), *Derecho de sufragio y participación ciudadana a través de las nuevas tecnologías* (Madrid, Civitas 2011) 103–130.

——, 'Cultura indígena y procesos electorales. A propósto del secreto del voto' in Antoni Pigrau Solé (ed.), *Pueblos indígenas, diversidad cultural y justicia ambiental* (Valencia, Tirant lo Blanch 2013) 211–228.

Braun, N., *Stimmgeheimnis* (Bern, Stämpfli Verlag 2006).

Calderón Chelius, L. (ed.), *Votar en la distancia. La extensión de derechos políticas a migrantes, experiencias comparadas* (Mexico DF, Instituto Mora 2003).

Carpizo, J. / Valadés, D., *El voto de los mexicanos en el extranjero* (Mexico DF, UNAM 1998).

Casarín León, M.F., *La facultad reglamentaria* (Mexico DF, Porrúa / Universidad Veracruzana 2003).

Fernández Riveira, R.M., '¿Es inconstitutional el voto electrónico en Alemania?' in Jordi Barrat Esteve / Rosa M. Fernández Riveira (eds), *Derecho de sufragio y participación ciudadana a través de las nuevas tecnologías* (Madrid, Civitas 2011) 157–194.

Madise, Ü., 'Legal and Political Aspects of the Internet Voting: The Estonian Case' in Josep Maria Reniu Vilamala (ed.), *E-Voting: The Last Electoral Revolution* (Barcelona, ICPS 2008) 45–60.

Mecinas Montiel, J.M., *Estudio constitucional del voto por internet* (PhD dissertation, not published, Madrid, Universidad Complutense de Madrid 2013).

Nou, J., 'Privatizing Democracy: Promoting Election Integrity Through Procurement Contracts' [2009] 118 *The Yale Law Journal* 744–793, www.yalelawjournal.org/images/pdfs/757.pdf (7 February 2014).

Recondo, D., *La jurisprudencia del TEPJF en elecciones regidas por derecho consutudinario* (Mexico DF, Tribunal Electoral del Poder Judicial de la Federación 2013), http://te.gob.mx/sites/default/files/cuaderno_17_je.pdf (8 March 2014).

Reniu Vilamala, J.M., 'Consideraciones sociopolíticas para los proyectos de voto electrónico' [2013] 13 *Revista General de Derecho Público Comparado* (*El voto electrónico y sus dimensiones jurídicas: entre la ingenua complacencia y el rechazo precipitado*), www.iustel.com/v2/revistas/detalle_revista.asp?id=14&numero=13 (8 March 2014).

Romero Flores, R. / Téllez Valdés, J.A., *Voto electrónico, derecho y otras implicaciones* (Mexico DF, IIJ/UNAM 2010), http://biblio.juridicas.unam.mx/libros/libro.htm?l=2801 (11 February 2014).

Smith, E., 'Hemmelige elektronicke valg?' [2010] 49(6) *Lov og Rett* 307–323.

Torruco Salcedo, S., 'El principio de legalidad en el ordenamiento jurídico mexicano' in Gabriela Ríos Granados (ed.), *Reforma hacendaria en la agenda de reforma del Estado* (Mexico DF, IIJ / UNAM 2009) 5–24, http://biblio.juridicas.unam.mx/libros/6/2724/4.pdf (accessed 8 March 2014).

PART III
Back to Politics

Chapter 11
E-Voting Case Law: A Swiss Perspective

Beat Kuoni[1]

Introduction

Swiss courts have as yet had few opportunities to consider the legal issues arising from e-voting. This contribution looks at the current case law and considers the legal questions that are raised. The first point to note is that Swiss legal precedent is not the driving force behind the development of electronic voting. Nevertheless, litigation raises key issues related to the introduction of electronic voting.

After a short introduction to the Vote électronique project in Switzerland, touching on the importance of federalism in this context, the current judicial practice will be examined. The most important substantive legal questions will then be identified and discussed. Previous and current disputes will then be analysed in the light of the new legal provisions. In conclusion, we look at the case law of the constitutional courts in Germany and Austria.

The Vote électronique Project in Switzerland

For more than 10 years now, Switzerland has been gradually introducing electronic voting through its Vote électronique project. The overarching aim of this project is to enable future generations to participate in democratic processes even as lifestyles change, i.e. in a way that may be compatible with future ways of living.[2] This goal is to be achieved under the motto 'security before speed'.

Federalism and direct democracy lend special character to the way in which electronic voting is being introduced. Vote électronique is a joint project between the Confederation and cantons. The cantons are responsible for conducting elections and referendums and they are therefore developing and operating the electronic

1 Many thanks to Geo Taglioni, Oliver Spycher and Nadja Obreschkow for reviewing the manuscript and providing valuable comments. My thanks also go to Kenneth MacKenzie of the English Translation Service at the Swiss Federal Chancellery for translating the original German version of this chapter to English. Responsibility for the information and views set out in this article lies entirely with the author.

2 BBl 2006 5533.

voting systems.[3] The Confederation coordinates this work and in some cases provides financial and technical support. Switzerland has a highly sophisticated and much used system of direct democracy, with ballots held at regular intervals at all three levels of state. As a result, electronic voting in Switzerland could actually bring gains in efficiency.

An important factor determining the path that Switzerland has chosen is the general use of postal voting, which was introduced in the mid-1990s for elections and votes at the federal level. Introducing postal voting was a bottom-up process. In the late 1970s, federal provisions were introduced that freely permitted the cantons to offer the option of postal voting, even in federal votes. Twenty years later, the Confederation made it mandatory for the cantons to offer the option of postal voting in all federal votes. The introduction of electronic voting is proceeding according to the same principle: it is up to the cantons to decide whether, and if so when, they wish to offer electronic voting. As Switzerland already has a universal system of postal voting, a system in which voters can cast their vote online in an unmonitored environment was considered from the outset.

Since 2004, over 180 trials[4] with electronic voting via the internet, i.e. in an unmonitored environment, have been held. In the current test phase, the option of electronic voting is primarily being offered to expatriate Swiss citizens, who are being prioritised. In the cantons of Geneva and Neuchâtel, voters resident in Switzerland can also cast their votes online in federal ballots.

Federalism and E-voting

Under Article 39 paragraph 1 of the Federal Constitution, the Confederation is granted the power to regulate the exercise of political rights in federal matters, while the cantons are responsible for the regulation of political rights in cantonal and communal matters. However, the Confederation leaves the conduct of all elections and votes to the cantons. To the extent that federal law permits, the cantons may issue additional implementing provisions. The Confederation provides the basic legislative framework, while the cantonal legislation adds the detail.[5] The division of tasks between the Confederation and cantons ensures that the cantons can decide themselves whether, and if so when, they wish to introduce electronic voting.

However, the Confederation lays down requirements that the cantons must meet before they can introduce electronic voting in federal elections and votes. The regulations at the federal level provide that the Federal Council must authorise

3 See Art. 39 para. 1 Federal Constitution of the Swiss Confederation of 18 April 1999 (SR 101; BV) in conjunction with Art. 10 para. 2 Federal Act of 17 December 1976 on Political Rights (SR 161.1: Federal Act on Political Rights).

4 Status as of June 2014.

5 Driza Maurer, 'Internet Voting and Federalism: The Swiss Case' in: *Revista General de Derecho Público Comparado*, No. 13, July 2013.

the use of electronic voting in federal elections and votes.[6] The legal principles envisage a two-tier authorisation procedure. The Federal Council may grant basic authorisation to a canton for a maximum of two years. For each ballot, the Federal Chancellery, which provides administrative support to the Federal Council and is responsible for matters relating to political rights, must check whether the authorisation requirements are still being met.

At present, around half of the cantons offer the option of electronic voting. However, as in most cases they only offer this option to expatriate Swiss citizens, at the national level only some three per cent of the electorate can currently cast their votes electronically.

The principle applies that electronic voting may only be offered if it is an option at all three political levels.[7] This means that voters only need one voter identification card, thereby reducing the risk of double voting.

Case Law

Rights of Appeal in the Field of Political Rights

Procedural aspects

In relation to political rights, federal law requires the cantons to provide a right of appeal to a court *in cantonal and communal matters*.[8] Cantonal rights of recourse must be exhausted before the Federal Supreme Court will consider an appeal.

In *federal matters*, appeal proceedings normally begin at the cantonal level as well. Only in very few cases – in particular appeals against Federal Chancellery rulings – is a direct appeal to the Federal Supreme Court possible.[9] Where an infringement of the right to vote is alleged, or irregularities in votes or in the preparation and conduct of elections to the National Council, the aggrieved parties may appeal to the cantonal government.[10] The decision of the cantonal government may be referred to the Federal Supreme Court.[11]

The requirements that must be met in order to file an appeal in matters of political rights are comparatively low. Any person has the right to appeal, provided

6 Art. 8a para. 1 Federal Act on Political Rights.

7 Art. 27e para. 5 Ordinance of 24 May 1978 on Political Rights (SR 161.11; Political Rights Ordinance).

8 Art. 88 para. 2 Federal Act of 12 June 2005 on the Federal Supreme Court (SR 173.110; Federal Supreme Court Act). See Steinmann, in: Niggli/Übersax/Wiprächtiger (eds), *Bundesgerichtsgesetz*, 2nd edition, Basel 2011, Art. 88 para. 14.

9 Art. 88 para. 1(b) Federal Supreme Court Act in conjunction with Art. 80 para. 2 and 3 Federal Act on Political Rights.

10 Art. 77 para. 1(a–c) Federal Act on Political Rights.

11 Art. 80 para. 1 Federal Act on Political Rights in conjunction with Art. 88 para. 1(a) Federal Supreme Court Act.

he or she has a right to vote on the matter in question.[12] The appellant need not prove a personal interest, as voters, when exercising their political rights, collectively assume the status of a single state institution, the electorate.[13]

The Federal Supreme Court examines the legal issues in the appeal proceedings. It bases its judgment on the facts of the case established by the lower court.[14] The Federal Supreme Court only reviews the findings in fact if these are obviously incorrect or are based on a breach of legal rights.[15]

Substantive aspects

When filing an appeal to the Federal Supreme Court, it may be argued that provisions at various levels have been infringed: grounds for appeal include not only violations of federal law, but in many cases also violations of any cantonal provisions relating to political rights.[16] The Federal Supreme Court's power to review in relation to political rights is broadly based and it can also freely review all matters relevant to a case decided under cantonal law.[17] In relation to federal law, the Federal Supreme Court may refuse to apply provisions contained in ordinances, including numerous regulations on electronic voting, if it takes the view that they that are contrary to the Constitution; however, due to Article 190 of the Federal Constitution, the Federal Supreme Court is bound by provisions contained in acts of parliament.

Generally, in the Swiss legal system inferior courts may also review statutory provisions with regard to their compatibility with the Federal Constitution and need not apply them if they were considered to be unconstitutional (diffuse system).[18]

In the case law, the guarantee of political rights given in Article 34 of the Federal Constitution is crucial. This provision protects not only political rights at the federal level, but also those at the cantonal and communal levels, wherever such rights are conferred. Paragraph 2 of the article protects the freedom to vote and to elect. This gives voters the right to demand that the result of a vote that does not reliably and accurately express the free will of the electorate should not be recognised.[19]

If the Federal Supreme Court establishes a procedural problem, it only annuls the election or vote if the irregularities are substantial and it seems possible that they have influenced the result.[20] The complaint made must relate to a specific irregularity; a mere abstract or theoretical risk is not sufficient for the result

12 Art. 89 para. 3 Federal Supreme Court Act.

13 Federal Supreme Court, Decision of 7 September 2005 – 1P.316/2005, E. 1.; BGE 119 Ia 167, 171f.

14 Art. 105 para. 1 Federal Supreme Court Act.

15 Art. 97 para. 1 and 105 para. 2 Federal Supreme Court Act.

16 Art. 95d Federal Supreme Court Act.

17 Steinmann, in: Niggli/Übersax/Wiprächtiger (eds), *Bundesgerichtsgesetz*, 2nd edition, Basel 2011, Art. 95 para. 61.

18 Haller, *The Swiss Constitution in a Comparative Context*, Zurich 2009, p. 243.

19 See *inter alia* BGE 139 I 195, 201; 138 I 61, 82 f.; 135 I 292, 293 f.

20 Häfelin/Haller/Keller, *Schweizerisches Bundesstaatsrecht*, 8th edition, Zürich 2012, para. 1400.

Table 11.1 Table of cases: 2005–2014

<table>
<tr><th>Vote concerned</th><th>Appellant</th><th>Date of Administrative Court judgment</th><th>Case no.</th><th>Date of Federal Supreme Court judgment</th><th>Case no.</th></tr>
<tr><td>24 April 2005</td><td>Mathias Schmocker</td><td>15 March 2005</td><td>ATA/153/2005</td><td>–</td><td>–</td></tr>
<tr><td>24 April 2005</td><td>Mathias Schmocker</td><td>5 April 2005</td><td>ATA/192/2005</td><td>–</td><td>–</td></tr>
<tr><td>26 September 2004</td><td>Messrs B. and S.</td><td>29 November 2005</td><td>ATA/807/2005</td><td>23 March 2006</td><td>1P.29/2006</td></tr>
<tr><td>17 May 2009</td><td>François von Siebenthal</td><td>–</td><td>–</td><td>1 October 2009</td><td>1C_245/2009</td></tr>
<tr><td>17 May 2009</td><td>Chucri Canaan</td><td>–</td><td>–</td><td>1 October 2009</td><td>1C_257/2009</td></tr>
<tr><td>15 May 2011</td><td>Richard Hill</td><td>17 May 2011</td><td>ATA/303/2011</td><td>–</td><td>–</td></tr>
<tr><td>15 May 2011</td><td>Richard Hill</td><td>28 June 2011</td><td>ATA/414/2011</td><td>22 December 2011 and 19 April 2012</td><td>1C_329/2011 and 1F_5/2012</td></tr>
<tr><td>15 May 2011</td><td>Richard Hill</td><td>30 August 2011</td><td>ATA/536/2011</td><td>–</td><td>–</td></tr>
<tr><td>27 November 2011</td><td>Richard Hill</td><td rowspan="2">21 August 2012 and 25 February 2014</td><td rowspan="2">ATA/533/2012 and ATA/118/2014</td><td rowspan="2">27 March 2013, 29 August 2013 and 22 July 2014</td><td rowspan="2">1C_477/2012, 1C_563/2013 and 1C_136/2014</td></tr>
<tr><td>27 November 2011</td><td>Richard Hill</td></tr>
<tr><td>27 November 2011</td><td>Richard Hill</td><td>19 January 2012</td><td>ATA/42/2012</td><td>–</td><td>–</td></tr>
</table>

of a ballot to be declared invalid. Under the regulations relating to electronic voting, if irregularities are proven, it must be possible to measure the number of defective votes or to assess the extent of their effects on the result of the count.[21] This provision is intended to enable the judicial authorities to reach the correct conclusions in the event of any dispute.

Overview

Litigation relating to the use of electronic voting is rare. To date, it is only in the canton of Geneva that appeals have been filed against cantonal and federal votes in which the option of voting online was offered (see Table 11.1). Several appeals were filed in connection with the cantonal popular votes on 15 May and 27 November 2011 in the canton of Geneva. They were all filed by the same appellant and in certain cases were referred to the Federal Supreme Court.

Case law from 2005 to 2009

In the first decision from 2005, the Administrative Court of the Canton of Geneva rejected the appeal of a voter against the decision to authorise a trial with electronic voting.[22] The appellant essentially claimed that checks on whether the electronic voting system was functioning correctly were inadequate. In addition, the authentication method used would allow proxies to cast votes and voters could sell their votes. The Administrative Court dismissed the appeal on the grounds that the authorisation decision in dispute did not infringe any procedural provisions.

A further decision from 2005 related to documents relating to the electronic voting system being viewed. The appellants requested access to the source code and the contracts between the Canton of Geneva and the system supplier.[23] The Canton of Geneva was in fact prepared to allow the appellants access to the source code. However, the appellants were asked to sign a non-disclosure agreement (NDA), which they refused to do. In order to protect trade secrets, no access was allowed to the contracts with the system supplier. The Administrative Court agreed to consider the appeal. On the question of the disclosure of the source code, it concluded that there was no basis in cantonal law for demanding an NDA from persons who wanted to see the code. However, it affirmed the authorities' decision to refuse access to the contracts with the system supplier. The appellants

21 Art. 27i para. 4 Political Rights Ordinance.

22 CACJ, Decision of 5 April 2005 – ATA/192/2005; previously the court had decided that the appeal did not have the effect of suspending execution of the original decision and that the court did not have to take any interim measures (see CACJ, Decision of 15 March 2005 – ATA/153/2005).

23 CACJ, Decision of 29 November 2005 – ATA/807/2005.

took the appeal to the Federal Supreme Court, which upheld the Administrative Court's decision.[24]

In 2009, an appeal was filed relating to the popular vote on 17 May 2009.[25] The appellant demanded a rerun of the vote and claimed *inter alia* that it was too easy to falsify electronic voting and that voting secrecy was not guaranteed. The Federal Supreme Court took the view that these allegations were unjustified. The appellant had only claimed that there were general risks associated with voting online and had referred to the case law in other countries. The appeal did not raise any issues specifically related to the system used in the canton of Geneva. In addition, the appellant did not demonstrate how the system failed to meet the technical security requirements under federal law.

Appeals relating to the popular vote on 15 May 2011

In connection with the cantonal popular vote on 15 May 2011, a single appellant filed three separate appeals. As no federal proposals were being voted on, authorisation from the Federal Council for the use of electronic voting was not necessary. The limits under federal law relating to the number of authorised voters did not apply. The cantonal authorities decided that all voters in the canton should be able to cast their votes electronically.

The cantonal Administrative Court regarded all three appeals as inadmissible on formal grounds. One of the appeal decisions was referred to the Federal Supreme Court, which affirmed the decision of the lower court.[26] It rejected the contention that both the decision on the findings in fact and the application of the cantonal act on the exercise of political rights had been arbitrary.[27] Subsequently, the Federal Supreme Court also rejected an application for a review of this decision. The appellant claimed under Article 127b of the Federal Supreme Court Act that the Federal Supreme Court had failed to take account of a material fact contained in the files. In particular, the Court did not accept the evidence in the appeal petition that the alleged weakness in the Geneva system had been exploited. According to the appellant, the higher proportion of yes votes cast online for all the proposals when compared with postal voting was clear evidence of manipulation. The Federal Supreme Court denied that this criticism had not been considered

24 Federal Supreme Court, Decision of 23 March 2006 – 1P.29/2006. Since 2010, § 60 para. 8 of the Canton of Geneva Act on the Exercise of Political Rights of 15 October 1982 (LEDP; RSG A 5 05) has prohibited the general disclosure of the source code. The members of the electoral commission have access to the source code at any time (para. 9) and voters are also permitted to see it, provided they have an academic or intellectual interest in doing so and treat the information as confidential (para. 10).

25 Federal Supreme Court, Decision of 1 October 2009 – 1C_257/2009.

26 Federal Supreme Court, Decision of 22 December 2011 – 1C_329/2011.

27 Art. 80 and 76 para. 3 of the Geneva Cantonal Act on the Exercise of Political Rights of 15 October 1982 (LEDP; RSG A 5 05).

in its deliberations. It stated that it had examined all the allegations made by the appellant to determine whether he had made a specific criticism.

Appeals relating to the popular vote on 27 November 2011
At the cantonal popular vote on 27 November 2011, the same appellant who had already taken legal action against the use of electronic voting at the popular vote in May 2011 filed two appeals at the Administrative Court of the Canton of Geneva. As the content of these appeals was practically identical, the two actions were combined.[28] The appellant demanded that the result of the popular vote on 27 November 2011 be annulled. He also asked the Federal Supreme Court to hold that the option of electronic voting should not have been offered to all voters and that the Canton of Geneva should be prohibited from conducting further trials with electronic voting until, in accordance with Article 60 paragraph 1 of the cantonal act on political rights, the implementing provisions have been issued.

In a decree dated 21 August 2012, the Administrative Court of the Canton of Geneva declared the appeals inadmissible.[29] It held that the appellant had failed to make specific allegations, limiting himself to abstract concerns. He could not prove that the alleged deficiencies had in any way been exploited in order to misuse the system. Instead the appellant limited himself to making general accusations.

The appellant appealed successfully against this decision to the Federal Supreme Court, which in a decree dated 27 March 2013 referred the case back to the Administrative Court for a decision on the merits.[30] The Federal Supreme Court criticised the decision of the lower court as being without basis in cantonal procedural law. In regarding the allegations as insufficiently specific, the Administrative Court made a material assessment. The Administrative Court was therefore not entitled to reject the appeal on formal grounds. It could not simply declare the case to be formally inadmissible, but had to consider the substance of the allegations made.

After the Federal Supreme Court reached this decision at the end of March 2013, the appellant requested that the judges who had participated in the decision of the Administrative Court of the Canton of Geneva of 21 August 2012 should recuse themselves. Essentially, he justified his action on the grounds that the judges concerned had heard and decided the appeal already. The judges' committee of the Cantonal Administrative Court rejected the recusal request, to which the appellant appealed again to the Federal Supreme Court, this time unsuccessfully.[31]

---

28 The second appeal of 21 November 2011 differed from the first one of 1 November 2011 in that the appellant had received the voting papers in the intervening period and was therefore able to establish that the same system was to be used for electronic voting as in the popular vote on 15 May 2011.

29 CACJ, Decision of 21 August 2012 – ATA/533/2012.

30 Federal Supreme Court, Decision of 27 March 2013 – 1C_477/2012.

31 Federal Supreme Court, Decision of 29 August 2013 – 1C_563/2013.

On 25 February 2014, the Administrative Court of the Canton of Geneva considered the merits of the original appeal, but again rejected it.[32] The court reiterated that the appellant was unable to provide any evidence of actual wrongdoing. It took the view that it was not the task of an Administrative Court to carry out an abstract review of a legal provision as part of an appeal due to an alleged violation of political rights. The court was only required to examine whether the provisions on political rights had been applied correctly. In his efforts to demonstrate that malware could falsify the result, the appellant failed to see that his criticisms could apply equally to any of the other voting channels. The appellant, however, referred the decision of the Cantonal Administrative Court to the Federal Supreme Court. In a decision dated 22 July 2014, the Federal Supreme Court rejected the appeal.[33] The Supreme Court affirmed the opinion of the lower court that the appellant was simply making general criticism of the electronic voting system used and had failed to provide any credible evidence of specific irregularities.

Selected Legal Issues

Specific allegations or abstract criticism?

No specific irregularities in voting procedures have been established in the appeal cases so far. The allegations have related in each case to the systems used, or more specifically the conditions for their use, such as the requirement that all voters be permitted to vote electronically. Appeals have repeatedly been dismissed on formal grounds. Whereas in earlier appeals specific irregularities in voting procedures were alleged, in the appeal most recently heard by the Federal Supreme Court the only complaint was that there is a high risk of manipulation when using the system employed in the canton of Geneva. The canton of Geneva system is allegedly designed in such a way that it is impossible to identify cases of manipulation.

Contrary to the contention of the appellant, in its decision of 27 March 2013 the Federal Supreme Court did not decide that the allegations were sufficiently specific. It simply made it clear that the question of whether an allegation was sufficiently specific was a substantive legal issue.[34] The cantonal law, it said, does not require that this aspect be examined as one of the admissibility requirements. Accordingly, the Federal Supreme Court referred the appeal back to the lower court for a decision on the merits.

In its decision of 25 February 2014, the Administrative Court of the Canton of Geneva took the view that the appellant's criticism could equally apply to other voting methods. It stated that, as part of an appeal in relation to voting, the court should, however, confine itself to potential infringements of political rights and should not conduct an abstract review of legal provisions. The Federal Supreme

32 CACJ, Decision of 25 February 2014 – ATA/118/2014.

33 Federal Supreme Court, Decision of 22 July 2014 – 1C_136/2014.

34 Federal Supreme Court, Decision of 27 March 2013 – 1C_477/2012, Point 2.2.

Court affirmed this view.[35] It followed the arguments of the lower court that the appellant had made insufficiently specific allegations of procedural irregularities in the popular vote in question. The fact that such irregularities are very difficult, if not impossible to identify was not an issue as far as the Federal Supreme Court was concerned. Instead it took the view that it was not the responsibility of the court to go beyond its assessment of a specific popular vote and become involved in the academic and political debate surrounding the system of electronic voting.[36]

Requirements of legal basis

Article 60 of the Political Rights Act in the Canton of Geneva regulates electronic voting. It provides that the cantonal government should issue regulations on technology, checks and security in relation to electronic voting.[37] In the appellant's view, this duty to regulate not only covers the server-side infrastructure, but also that on the client side.[38] The cantonal government, he argues, has indeed issued regulations in the form of an ordinance,[39] but these regulations only cover the server side.

The Administrative Court takes the view that the ordinance regulates electronic voting in accordance with the statutory requirements. It contains regulations on the process of electronic voting and sets out a variety of security requirements. In addition, system audits have been carried out and the results were positive, according to the court. The Act does not require that all the measures needed to guarantee the security of the electronic voting system be publicised in a form accessible to all; indeed, in some cases it prohibits this. With the exception of this last point, the Federal Supreme Court expressly affirmed the opinion of the Geneva Administrative Court.[40]

Violation of voting freedom?

The complaint has been made that the system currently used in the canton of Geneva breaches Article 34 paragraph 2 of the Federal Constitution. This article

---

35 Federal Supreme Court, Decision of 22 July 2014 – 1C_136/2014.

36 Federal Supreme Court, Decision of 22 July 2014 – 1C_136/2014, Point, 1. In March 2015, seven members of the federal parliament submitted a parliamentary initiative requiring that an e-voting system's compliance with legal provisions can be challenged before an independent cantonal authority and ultimately before the Federal Supreme Court. The initiative also wants such control to be open like an abstract review and not linked to a specific use of e-voting. See parliamentary initiative 15.412 available on www.parliament.ch > Curia Vista Suche.

37 The wording is as follows: 'The Cantonal Council shall issue the provisions on implementing electronic voting, in particular on technical aspects, controls and security. …'.

38 Appeal petition dated 12 March 2014 filed by Richard Hill against the decision of the Administrative Court of the Canton of Geneva dated 25 February 2014, para. 99.

39 These are Art. 14A to 14D of the Implementing Ordinance to the Act on the Exercise of Political Rights (REDP; RSG A 5 05.01).

40 Federal Supreme Court, decision of 22 July 2014 – 1C_136/2014.

guarantees that no result of any vote will be recognised that does not genuinely and reliably express the free will of the voters. One reason why the Geneva system is alleged to violate this principle is because it cannot guarantee that a vote cast online corresponds to that voter's will. It is argued that no mechanisms have been provided to recognise, and, if necessary, remedy such irregularities.

The procedure for elections and votes is regulated by legislation at various state levels. The regulations are designed to protect the freedom to vote and to elect and must be consistent with these freedoms.[41] The cantonal procedural provisions must also be measured against the yardstick provided by Article 34 paragraph 2 of the Federal Constitution. At the same time, however, it must be remembered that neither conventional voting methods nor electronic voting can exclude irregularities entirely. For example, opportunities to manipulate the postal vote exist too, and they are hard to recognise. However, such opportunities are regarded less critically, because voters' trust in the reliability of the postal service is high. In the case of electronic voting, on the other hand, the fear seems to be that systematic manipulation can be carried out with comparative ease.[42]

In relation to electronic voting, risk assessments play an important role.[43] The federal law limits the number of voters permitted to vote online in federal ballots on the basis of a risk assessment.[44] This risk assessment may have a different result when applied to cantonal ballots, which is why a larger electorate at this level should not be ruled out *a priori*. This limitation of the numbers involved does not result from the constitutional requirement of freedom to vote and elect, but is a method of minimising risk. For votes at the federal level, the limitation can also indicate the risks that the Federal Council is prepared to tolerate in fulfilling its implementing tasks in relation to elections and referendums. In doing so, it is exercising its powers under Article 8a paragraph 1bis of the Federal Act on Political Rights and imposing conditions on trials with electronic voting.

Voting by proxy

On various occasions it has been claimed in court cases that anyone can vote more than once online simply by using someone else's voting papers. Although this would also be possible when voting by post, it is argued that the authorities could check on this more easily in the case of postal voting as the voter identification

41 Steinmann, in: Ehrenzeller/Schindler/Schweizer/Vallender (eds), *Die schweizerische Bundesverfassung*, 3nd edition, Zürich / St. Gallen 2014, Art. 34 Federal Constitution, para. 20.

42 See e.g. Federal Constitutional Court, Judgment of 3 March 2009 – 2 BvC 3, 4/07, Federal Constitutional Court 123, 39, 72.

43 See in particular Federal Council Report on the Vote électronique Project of 14 June 2013, BBl 2013 5069, 5145 ff.

44 Art. 27f Political Rights Ordinance. The provision, in conjunction with Art. 4 and 5 Federal Chancellery Ordinance on Electronic Voting (SR 161.116; OEV), sets out the conditions that must be met for trials to be extended to include more voters.

card must be signed by the postal voter and returned in the voting envelope. In a decision from 1995, the Federal Supreme Court held that a postal voting procedure used in the canton of Basel-Stadt in which the ballot paper could be returned with an anonymised voter identification card was unconstitutional. In the opinion of the Federal Supreme Court, this procedure could not adequately prevent persons who were not entitled to vote from obtaining someone else's voting papers and being able to vote without any risk of being discovered.[45] In practice, however, when it comes to checking on these unlawful practices, there are few practical differences between postal voting and electronic voting. It is therefore unfair to claim that multiple voting is a problem specific to electronic voting. It is far more useful to point out that multiple voting by one person is a criminal offence, irrespective of which voting method is used.[46]

Preliminary Conclusion

The case law on electronic voting in Switzerland is in its infancy. Although there have been a number of appeals in recent years, most of these have been dismissed for not meeting procedural requirements. However, the case law so far does allow certain key challenges connected with electronic voting to be pinpointed. These include issues relating to the verifiability of processes and transparency. These challenges have been addressed by the new legal provisions that came into force at the start of 2014. The case law, however, was not the trigger for these changes; the political impetus was more important, along with strategic federal and cantonal considerations.[47]

Legal Provisions on Electronic Voting

The Process of Devising New Legal Provisions

At the start of 2014, new legal provisions on the use of electronic voting elections and votes at the federal level came into force. The new provisions set out the principles for extending electronic voting to a broader electorate. They thus point towards the establishment of electronic voting as a third and complementary voting method. Various factors led to the revision of the regulations, most of which were issued in the initial phase of the trials. The Confederation and cantons decided to introduce electronic voting step by step. In doing so, they agreed that if the system were to be extended to a broader electorate, it would have to be modernised.

45 BGE 121 I 187, 191 ff.

46 In the case BGE 121 I 187, 194 ff. already mentioned, the Federal Supreme Court held that a simple reference to the criminal provision is not sufficient to prevent abuses.

47 See Federal Council Report on the Vote électronique Project of 14 June 2013, BBl 2013 5069.

In order for more voters to benefit from the option of electronic voting, second generation[48] systems will have to be developed. In addition, at both federal and cantonal levels, new legislation was proposed relating to electronic voting.[49]

In formulating the new requirements for the system and operation of electronic voting, a cooperative approach was chosen. The principles underlying the new provisions were devised by a working group comprising representatives of the Confederation, cantons and academia. The working group's findings were incorporated in the Federal Council's third report on the Vote électronique project, dated 14 June 2013. The new legal provisions have their basis in this report. A draft of the provisions was submitted for comment during the consultation of all the cantons and the various organisations involved.[50] The widespread involvement of interested parties in the process increases the likelihood that the provisions will be accepted and aids their implementation.

Structure of the Legislation

The legal provisions on electronic voting at the federal level are set out at three regulatory levels (act of parliament, Federal Council ordinance, Federal Chancellery ordinance). The Federal Act on Political Rights gives the Federal Council the power to conduct trials with electronic voting and contains basic regulations. Before electronic voting can establish itself as the third voting method, these statutory provisions must be amended. The basis for this should be the fourth report on the Vote électronique project, which is expected in 2017/2018.

The new regulations on electronic voting at a subsidiary level to the act of parliament are in some cases very detailed and technical in their nature. Technological advances also mean that it must be possible for the provisions to be adapted in line with new developments. For this reason, the Ordinance on Political Rights has been supplemented by a new Federal Chancellery Ordinance on Electronic Voting (OEV). While the Ordinance on Political Rights primarily defines the requirements for the administrative processes, the OEV sets out detailed requirements for the systems and how they are operated. The new legal provisions thereby lay down the specific requirements for allowing additional voters to participate in electronic voting. Due to the risk involved, electronic voting may only be offered as an option to all voters if all the requirements are met

48 These are systems in which verifiability in accordance with the OEV has been implemented.

49 For a summary, see Federal Council Report on the Vote électronique Project of 14 June 2013 (BBl 2013 5105 f.) and Annex 3 in particular, available at www.bk.admin.ch > Themen > Politische Rechte > Vote électronique > Berichte und Studien > Ergänzende Dokumentation.

50 Procedure under Art. 10 of the Federal Act of 18 March 2005 on the Consultation Procedure (SR 172.061; VlG).

and the risks can be assessed as being sufficiently low.[51] The decision on whether electronic voting can be used remains that of the Federal Council. At any time, it may prohibit trials with electronic voting in a specific location, on a specific matter or on a specific occasion.[52]

Verifiability

The key element in the new requirements is verifiability. It must be possible to verify by independent means that no manipulation has taken place. The specific requirements for verifiability are set out in the OEV. Unless and until the correct procedure and the accuracy of the result using this voting method can be verified, it is not permitted to authorise the entire electorate to vote electronically. The cantons are permitted to meet the requirements step by step.

Verifiability can be implemented in two stages. The first stage involves implementing individual verifiability. This allows voters to recognise whether their votes have been manipulated or intercepted on the user platform or during transmission.[53] Implementation of individual verifiability is a requirement that the cantons must meet in order to authorise more than 30 per cent of the cantonal electorate to take part in the electronic voting trials. Individual verifiability addresses and alleviates various difficulties, including the problem of an 'insecure' platform.[54] The accuracy of the vote may still be verified even if the computer used has been attacked by malware.

Where a canton intends to offer more than 50 per cent of the cantonal electorate the option of electronic voting, it must implement complete verifiability.[55] In this case, the system must ensure that any manipulation that could lead to the falsification of the result is recognised. In particular it must be possible to check whether the vote cast has been registered and counted. This check need not be carried out by every voter but may be done by specially appointed auditors; it is up to the cantons to decide who is responsible for the check.[56]

Audits

The electronic voting system and its operation must be examined by an independent agency before trials may be conducted.[57] Here various criteria and standards apply. The new legal provisions provide for more extensive outsourcing of these audits. In the system checks carried out so far, the Federal Chancellery-

51 See Art. 27f para. 1 Political Rights Ordinance and Art. 4, 5 and 6 OEV.
52 Art. 8a para. 2 Federal Act on Political Rights.
53 Art. 4 OEV and No 4.1 and 4.2 Annex OEV.
54 See BBl 2013 5182, 5186.
55 Art. 5 OEV and No 4.3 and 4.4 Annex OEV.
56 See BBl 2013 5184.
57 Art. 7 para. 1 OEV.

approved agencies responsible for these checks have been appointed according to the peer-to-peer principle (i.e. the system is checked by those responsible for the two other systems). Now if the cantons want to involve more than 30 per cent of their electorates in the trials, they must have the system and its operation audited by an agency accredited by the Swiss Accreditation Service.[58] If the result of the audit is satisfactory, the agency issues a certificate that must be submitted when applying for authorisation for a trial. The certification offices will replace the support groups used so far, which are made up of representatives from various cantons and the Federal Chancellery.

Transparency

Verifiability is an instrument used to demonstrate the integrity of ballot procedures. It encourages transparency and thereby generates trust in electronic voting. In addition to verifiability, the new legal provisions provide that all important official procedures relating to electronic voting and the related documentation must be disclosed to a group of voters' representatives.[59] This provision is general in character and allows the cantons a large degree of latitude. They may decide on their own definition of what the 'voters' representative group' is, while exceptions to the principle are also possible. The inclusion of this regulation in the Ordinance underlines the importance accorded to the integrity of the procedures and thus to voter trust in the new voting method.

Preliminary Conclusion

The appeals filed in 2005 and 2011 alleged that the means for checking on electronic voting procedures were inadequate. Implementation of the new requirements addresses this criticism. The introduction of verifiability is a response to the problem of insecure platforms. It also improves the transparency and integrity of the procedures for electronic voting.

The International Perspective – Foreign Case Law

German Federal Constitutional Court

In 2009, the German Federal Constitutional Court considered in detail the constitutional permissibility of using electronic voting machines. In a judgment dated 3 March 2009, it held that the principle of election transparency required that all the essential stages in an election be subject to public scrutiny, unless other constitutional concerns justify an exception being made. When electronic

58 Art. 7 para. 2 OEV and No 5 Annex OEV.

59 Art. 27m para. 2 Political Rights Ordinance.

voting machines are used, it must be possible for citizens to check reliably and without specialist knowledge the essential steps in the act of voting and the ascertainment of the results.[60] The Federal Constitutional Court further stated that a voting procedure in which voters cannot reliably find out whether their vote has been correctly registered and included in the count and how all the votes cast are allocated and counted fails to meet the constitutional requirements. The Federal Constitutional Court carried out a risk assessment and held that the broad effect of potential errors demanded that special precautions be taken.[61] It proposed a potential solution for upholding the principle of election transparency. In essence, it suggested that a paper receipt be issued for every electronic vote, so that an alternative count could be made (the paper trail solution). In making this proposal, it did not consider whether there are other technical means of establishing integrity that would engender among voters trust in the accuracy of the results procedure.[62]

Austrian Constitutional Court

The Austrian Constitutional Court had to consider the issue of electronic voting in connection with University Board elections.[63] It took the view that the electoral principles must be met in electronic voting as when voting by post. It also called for procedural regulations to be designed to allow voters and the Electoral Commission to reliably find out whether the electoral process was carried out correctly.[64] Thereby, it must be possible for the Electoral Commission to check without specialist knowledge the essential steps in the act of voting and the ascertainment of the results.[65]

Foreign Case Law from a Swiss Perspective

The new Swiss legal provisions take account of the concerns expressed in the decisions of the German Federal Constitutional Court in many respects. They

60 Federal Constitutional Court, Judgment of 3 March 2009 – 2 BvC 3, 4/07, Federal Constitutional Court 123, 39 LS 1 and 2.

61 Federal Constitutional Court, Judgment of 3 March 2009 – 2 BvC 3, 4/07, Federal Constitutional Court 123, 39, 72.

62 Federal Constitutional Court, Judgment of 3 March 2009 – 2 BvC 3, 4/07, Federal Constitutional Court 123, 39, 74.

63 Constitutional Court, Decision of 13 December 2011 – V 85-96/11-15, available at: www.vfgh.gv.at/cms/vfgh-site/attachments/7/6/7/CH0006/CMS1327398738575/e-voting_v85-11.pdf.

64 Constitutional Court, Decision of 13 December 2011 – V 85-96/11-15, para. 21, available at: www.vfgh.gv.at/cms/vfgh-site/attachments/7/6/7/CH0006/CMS1327398738575/e-voting_v85-11.pdf.

65 Constitutional Court, Decision of 13 December 2011 – V 85-96/11-15, para. 22, available at: www.vfgh.gv.at/cms/vfgh-site/attachments/7/6/7/CH0006/CMS1327398738575/e-voting_v85-11.pdf.

combine an improvement in the integrity of procedures with extending the option of electronic voting to additional voters. They go less far in relation to the question of who must be allowed to carry out the checks. In Switzerland, voters should be able to check whether their vote has been cast as intended and has reached the vote server. However, it is sufficient for special auditors to check that the vote has been correctly registered and counted. And in relation to the disclosure of procedures and documents connected with electronic voting, the new legal provisions simply require that information be made available to a group of voters' representatives. The federal regulations allow the latitude required for the voters to be represented in different ways. In addition, in Switzerland there is no requirement that it must be possible for a person without any specialist knowledge to verify all the essential steps in the process, including the result. The integrity of the process can at least in part be verified by experts or by using independent technical aids. In order to guarantee trust in such checks, however, special measures are required, such as appointing the experts in a democratic process.[66]

In Switzerland, a conscious decision has been taken not to address the issue of the integrity of procedures by setting up a paper trail, as the German Federal Constitutional Court has proposed as a possible solution. There is little sense in having a paper-trail procedure for voting from an uncontrolled environment.[67] If electronic votes were to be printed out on the server side, so as to allow for a possible recount, the printing processes would have to satisfy stringent security requirements. But the practical benefits are still limited: in particular, even if a recount reveals a difference between the number of printed votes and the number of electronically recorded votes, it cannot be assumed that the paper votes provide a more reliable result.[68] It could be even more problematic if a printed receipt confirming how a vote has been cast were issued on the client side, i.e. to the voter, as this could facilitate the buying and selling of votes. Under federal law, the electronic voting system must not expressly offer a method of printing out confirmation of the vote cast.[69]

There is no principle of 'election transparency' in Swiss constitutional law. Regulations on election transparency can, however, be found in various provisions of acts and ordinances.

Conclusion

The current case law relating to electronic voting is fairly modest. However there certainly have been interesting legal disputes. In general, the courts grant the political authorities considerable scope in dealing with questions related to

66 Vgl. dazu BBl 2013 5153 und BBl 2006 5514.

67 BBl 2013 5157 und BBl 2006 5513.

68 BBl 2006 5513.

69 See No 2.1.12 Annex OEV.

the systems for electronic voting. Nevertheless, the criticisms made in court have addressed key challenges related to electronic voting. The court decisions have therefore been taken seriously by the authorities and have been monitored with interest. The most recent developments in legislation on the matter and in dealing with electronic voting show that the critics' concerns have been taken into account. The new legal provisions have improved the integrity and transparency of procedures and demonstrated how problems with insecure platforms can be alleviated. In addition, the cantons have already announced that they wish to allow voters access to the source code for the second generation systems.

The case law did not provide the decisive impetus for these processes. Political pressure had a greater influence on developments, along with the evaluation of the test phase made in the second and third reports on the Vote électronique project. However, the case law highlights a variety of issues that have regularly been raised by critics of electronic voting and which the new legal provisions have addressed.

References

Driza Maurer, Ardita, 'Internet Voting and Federalism: The Swiss Case' in: *Revista General de Derecho Público Comparado*, No. 13, July 2013.

Ehrenzeller, Bernhard / Schindler Benjamin / Schweizer, Rainer J. / Vallender, Klaus (eds), *Die schweizerische Bundesverfassung*, 3nd edition, Zürich / St. Gallen 2014.

Häfelin, Ulrich / Haller, Walter / Keller, Helen, *Schweizerisches Bundesstaatsrecht*, 8th edition, Zürich 2012.

Haller, Walter, *The Swiss Constitution in a Comparative Context*, Zurich 2009.

Niggli, Marcel Alexander / Übersax, Peter / Wiprächtiger, Hans (eds), *Bundesgerichtsgesetz*, 2nd edition, Basel 2011.

Chapter 12
Electronic Voting Law in the United States

Daniel P. Tokaji[1]

Introduction

Electronic voting has been a contentious subject in the United States for many years. Interest in the technology used for voting increased dramatically—among election scholars, the media, and the general public—as a result of the contested 2000 presidential election between George W. Bush and Al Gore. That election triggered unprecedented scrutiny of the means by which Americans vote, a topic to which only a small cadre of election officials and experts had previously paid much attention. The most important reform growing out of the 2000 election was a nationwide upgrade of the equipment used for voting, accomplished primarily through implementation of the Help America Vote Act of 2002 (HAVA). The result was that the punch-card and lever machines used in many parts of the U.S. were replaced with optical-scan and direct record electronic (DRE) voting technology.

The replacement of antiquated voting machines was not, however, the end of the story. The introduction of electronic voting technology sparked a fierce backlash, which continues to this day. Although generally favored by disability advocates for their enhanced accessibility, DRE voting machines have come under intense criticism from other voting advocates and computer scientists for their security flaws. These disagreements have sometimes found their way into court. While the U.S. Supreme Court has not decided any voting technology cases since *Bush v. Gore* (2000), there have been a number of important lower court decisions involving electronic voting systems. They include lawsuits by disability advocates demanding their use, as well as cases by electronic voting skeptics challenging the use of systems without a voter-verifiable paper audit trail. Even more serious security concerns have been raised around Internet voting. Another concern—one that has received less judicial attention but is of tremendous significance—is the looming obsolescence of the voting systems purchased after HAVA, which the President's Commission on Election Administration called an "impending crisis" (PCEA 2014, at 62).

This chapter discusses the laws and litigation involving electronic voting in the U.S. It starts by canvassing developments in voting technology from the contested

1 The author thanks Meaghan FitzGerald and Greg Djordjevic for their outstanding research assistance and Juan Gilbert for helpful comments on this chapter. All errors are the author's.

2000 election through HAVA and subsequent controversies over electronic voting. Next, it discusses the laws and institutions relevant to voting technology. Finally, this chapter addresses major judicial decisions affecting electronic voting. An examination of these decisions shows that courts have generally taken a hands-off approach, rejecting most lawsuits seeking to promote electronic voting as well as those seeking to prevent its use.

Before proceeding further, it is important for readers, especially those outside the U.S., to be aware of two distinctive features of American elections. The first is the tremendous decentralization of election administration in the U.S. The national government does not run elections in the U.S.—not even elections for federal office. Rather, elections are administered at the local level by over 10,000 counties and municipalities, pursuant to laws that are made by each of the states and territories. Accordingly, there is not just one election system in the U.S., nor even just 50 systems, but literally thousands, corresponding to all the local government entities that are responsible for running elections. In most states, these local jurisdictions choose their own voting equipment. The multiplicity of relatively autonomous election authorities makes it difficult to generalize about voting equipment (or any other aspect of election administration) in the U.S.

The second feature of which readers should be aware is that there is no single agreed-upon definition of electronic voting (or e-voting) in the U.S., so the term is not always used consistently. This chapter understands electronic voting to mean the *casting* of votes through electronic means (Council of Europe 2004, at 8.). E-voting therefore includes voters' *recording* of their choices and *transmission* of their ballots through electronic means, but not the *counting* or *tabulation* of votes through electronic means. Thus, a DRE machine would fall within the definition of electronic voting. So would a voter marking a paper ballot by hand, using a scanner to generate a PDF ballot image, and then emailing that image to election authorities for counting. But this definition would not include a voter hand-marking a paper ballot that is then fed into an optical scanner for counting. If the counting of ballots through such means were considered electronic voting, then virtually all votes cast in the United States—save for the very small number cast on hand-counted paper ballots—would fall within that definition.

From Florida to HAVA

The modern history of voting technology in the U.S. begins with the 2000 presidential election, including the Supreme Court's decision in *Bush v. Gore* (2000) resolving the dispute over who won Florida. The 2000 election shone a bright and unflattering light on the voting equipment used for U.S. elections, a subject to which very few people had previously paid much attention.

Due to the decentralization of U.S. election administration, many different types of voting equipment are used at any given time. In 2000, five basic types of voting equipment were in use: (1) punch-card voting systems, (2) optical-scan ballots, (3) lever voting machines, (4) direct record electronic (DRE) voting systems, and (5) hand-counted paper ballots.[2] A plurality of U.S. counties (45.3%) used optical-scan voting systems in 2000. The next most commonly used type of system was punch-card voting, employed by 17.8% of counties. These were followed by lever machines (12.8% of counties), DREs (10.7%), and paper ballots (10.6%), with the remaining counties (2.7%) using more than one type of system (Kropf and Kimball 2012, at 29).

The outcome of the 2000 presidential election turned on the result in Florida, where then Vice President Al Gore narrowly trailed Texas Governor George W. Bush by just 1,784 votes out of almost 6 million ballots cast immediately after Election Day (Hasen 2012, at 12). Some Florida counties used punch card voting systems while others used optical-scan systems, but the controversy focused primarily on punch cards—more specifically, on the ballots as to which the perforated "chad" had not been completely punched out. In an effort to close the gap, Gore requested manual recounts in four counties, filing a protest and later a contest action under Florida's election laws. A divided Florida Supreme Court ordered manual recounts in all counties, but that order was stayed and ultimately reversed by the U.S. Supreme Court in *Bush v. Gore*.

The *Bush v. Gore* decision is significant for many reasons, not the least of which is that it partly constitutionalized matters that had formerly been considered to be the province of state law and local practice. The Court held that the manner in which Florida's recount was being conducted violated the Equal Protection Clause of the Fourteenth Amendment to the U.S. Constitution. Long before *Bush v. Gore*, the Court had held voting to be a fundamental right under the Fourteenth Amendment to the Constitution—albeit one that is not specifically enumerated anywhere in the Constitution's text.

The majority opinion in *Bush v. Gore*, signed by five of the nine U.S. Supreme Court justices, relied on the familiar principle that every vote is entitled to "equal weight" and every voter to "equal dignity." The principle of electoral equality was firmly established before 2000. What *Bush v. Gore* added to U.S. constitutional law was its recognition that intrastate inconsistencies in the administration of elections may deny equal protection of laws, required by the Fourteenth Amendment. In

2 It is possible to subdivide these types of equipment further. There were, for example, two different sub-types of punch card equipment in use in 2000: "Votomatic" systems in which a stylus is used to detach the chad from a pre-scored ballot, and "Datavote" systems which utilize a hole-puncher (rather than a stylus) and non-pre-scored ballots. So too, there were and are two sub-types of optical scan systems: central-count optical scan systems in which ballots are counted at a central location, and precinct-count optical scan systems in which ballots are counted at the precinct, allowing voters the opportunity to catch and correct errors. DRE systems may also be divided into two basic types: older full-face DREs in which all contests are listed on a full-face computer screen, and newer scrolling DREs (usually touchscreens) in which the voter scrolls through multiple screens to make choices for different contests. See Kropf and Kimball (2012, at 29).

particular, the Court saw a constitutional problem with Florida's lack of a uniform statewide rule for identifying which punch-card ballots should be treated as valid votes. The lack of a uniform rule led to disparities in which ballots were in fact counted—from county to county and sometimes even within a single county. The Court concluded that such "arbitrary and disparate treatment" of ballots during Florida's recount denied voters equal protection, in violation of the Fourteenth Amendment.

There has been considerable disagreement over the years on what *Bush v. Gore* actually stands for, including the meaning and breadth of the constitutional rule the majority announced. The vagueness of the Court's opinion creates considerable room for argument over the scope of its holding. Subsequent constitutional claims relating to electronic voting are addressed later in this chapter. For now, the critical point is that *Bush v. Gore* furnished a constitutional argument that could be used to challenge disparities in the equipment used for voting, especially in states using more than one type of equipment.

Empirical studies conducted in the wake of the 2000 election revealed serious problems with the equipment used for voting in many parts of the U.S. In fact, even before 2000, there was evidence of a high number of lost votes with pre-scored punch-card voting, the type of voting system that received the most attention in Florida and that was the focus of *Bush v. Gore* (Saltman 1988, at 1188). But this research received little attention before the dispute over Florida's presidential election. After that election, several prominent studies conclusively demonstrated that punch-card ballots resulted in a high rate of "residual votes" (Brady et al. 2001; Alvarez et al. 2001; National Commission on Federal Election Reform 2001). This term refers to the difference between the total number of ballots cast in the election and the number of valid votes cast in a particular race, usually the top-of-the-ticket race. One study by researchers at U.C. Berkeley found that punch-card ballots resulted in a significantly higher residual vote rate than other kinds of equipment (Brady et al. 2001, at 29). Other research found a "racial gap" arising from punch-card ballots, with African Americans more likely to cast invalid votes than whites—a gap that disappeared when other technologies, including DREs, were used (Tomz and Van Houweling 2003, at 51).

The research showing problems with punch-card voting systems triggered lawsuits in several states challenging the use of these systems. The legal claims in these cases are discussed in greater detail below but, in general, there were two issues. The first was whether the use of punch-card voting systems in some but not all counties within a state violated equal protection, by disadvantaging voters living in counties using that type of equipment relative to other voters. The second issue was whether the use of punch-card voting violated Section 2 of the Voting Rights Act (VRA), given the racial disparities that arise from its use. Plaintiffs in these cases achieved some early victories, although none were litigated to final judgment on the merits.

The Help America Vote Act effectively resolved the issue of punch-card voting in the U.S. HAVA did not require the replacement of punch-card voting or any other kind of voting equipment. It did, however, provide money for the replacement of punch-card and lever systems (HAVA, Title I). In addition, it set some modest national standards that all voting systems must meet, including error notification, an audit capacity, and disability access. These requirements are also described in greater detail below.

The replacement of older voting technology, most notably punch-card and lever voting systems, is probably the most important consequence of HAVA. By 2012, punch-card and lever voting equipment was virtually extinct (EAC 2013, at 82–3, Tbl. 42). Most U.S. jurisdictions now employ DREs, optical-scan systems, or some combination of the two. Overall a total of 28 states and territories reported using DREs, while 40 reported using optical-scan systems. Most jurisdictions now use *precinct-count* optical-scan systems—counted at the precinct where the voter votes, rather than at a central location (Kropf and Kimball 2012). Precinct-count optical-scan systems have the advantage of allowing voters to check for inadvertent overvotes before casting their ballots, thus reducing errors. Largely because of the security issues associated with electronic voting, described below, the usage of precinct-count optical-scan systems has increased while the usage of DREs has declined in recent years.

These changes resulted in significant decline in the number of uncounted ballots, as measured in residual votes. One study estimated that the combination of new technology and improved polling places operations saved approximately one million votes (Stewart 2009, at 1). The transition to new voting technology—especially DRE systems without a voter-verifiable paper audit trail—has provoked great consternation in some quarters.

Security and Accuracy Concerns

Even before HAVA was fully implemented, some computer scientists and activists voiced concerns about the security and accuracy of electronic voting technology. While HAVA did not require the use of DREs, many jurisdictions decided to adopt this type of system—in part because it would satisfy both the notification and disability access mandates of HAVA, while also allowing the accommodation of voters in multiple languages (Tokaji 2005, at 1724). But in the years following HAVA's enactment, a movement to oppose paperless voting technology coalesced.

Advocates argued that, without a voter-verifiable paper audit trail, electronic voting machines were subject to error and manipulation, potentially allowing elections to be stolen. A prominent expression of this concern was Bev Harris' book *Black Box Voting* (2004). A number of computer scientists added their voices to the chorus of the concern. Particularly influential was a study by four computer scientists at Johns Hopkins University, finding security flaws in the source code of a voting system manufactured by Diebold (Kohno, et al. 2004). The anxiety surrounding electronic voting reached a crescendo during the 2004 election season, when Diebold President Wally O'Dell wrote in a fundraising letter that he would "deliver" Ohio's votes for President Bush (Hasen 2012, at 173).

State investigations buttressed the security concerns surrounding electronic voting. The State of Maryland commissioned a report that found no malicious code but still concluded that the Diebold DRE system had engineering flaws creating a "high risk of compromise" (SAIC 2003, at 10). California Secretary of State Debra Bowen later commissioned a "Top-to-Bottom Review" of electronic voting systems (California Secretary of State 2007). That study likewise found significant security flaws, causing her to decertify all DRE systems used in the state while allowing for recertification if certain security improvements were adopted. Ohio Secretary of State Jennifer Brunner ordered a similar study, the EVEREST report, which found security flaws with both DRE and optical-scan technology (Ohio Secretary of State 2007, at 4). The shared concern expressed by these reports was that existing electronic voting systems made it too easy to alter election results without detection (Hoke 2012, at 1017). Largely as a result of this controversy, DRE usage peaked in 2006, with around 38 percent of the electorate residing in jurisdictions using this type of technology, dropping to 33 percent in 2010 (Stewart 2011).

Some advocates have urged that a voter-verifiable paper audit trail be required by law. The Carter-Baker Commission, which published a report after the 2004 election, recommended such a requirement (Commission of Federal Election Reform 2005, at 26). DREs can comply with this requirement by having a strip of paper showing the voters' choices print out behind a transparent screen, so that the paper record can be viewed and verified by the voter. Although federal law has never required a voter-verifiable paper trail, most states have adopted such a requirement, either by statute or executive action (Verified Voting 2014). According to the U.S. Election Assistance Commission's 2012 survey, 18 states employ DREs with a voter-verifiable paper audit trail, while 17 employ DREs without one (EAC 2013, at 83, Tbl. 42).[3]

Even more serious security concerns surround Internet voting. There have been scattered experiments with Internet voting in the U.S. over the years, focused primarily on absentee voting (EAC 2011). The first use of the Internet for voting in U.S. elections took place in 2000 (Alvarez and Hall 2004, at 124–37; National Democratic Institute n.d.). Security concerns have stymied efforts to implement fully online voting, although many states allow at least some voters to *transmit* scanned images of their ballots over the Internet (NCSL 2014).

On the whole, there has been less experimentation with Internet voting in the U.S. than in Europe (Alvarez and Hall 2008, at 78–9; Stewart 2011; EAC 2011). U.S. efforts have occurred have mostly focused on military and overseas voters, who have abysmally low rates of participation (Hasen 2012, at 162; Inbody 2013,

3 This total does not equal the total number of states using DREs (28), because some states use both DREs with a voter-verifiable paper audit trail and DREs without a voter-verifiable paper audit trail.

at 2). As the Presidential Commission on Election Administration explained in its 2014 report, "the internet is the election lifeline for many military and overseas voters, in particular" (PCEA 2014, at 59). A 2004 federal pilot project aimed at military and overseas voters, known as SERVE, was scrapped as a result of security concerns raised by computer scientists (Jefferson et al. 2004, Alvarez and Hall 2008, at 77–90; EAC 2011, at 29–32). More recently, the District of Columbia attempted a pilot project aimed at this underserved group of voters. During the pre-election public review period, members of the public were invited to attack the system in a mock election—and a University of Michigan research team succeeded in doing so within 36 hours, commandeering the system so that it played the Michigan fight song after voters submitted their ballots (Hasen 2012; Simons and Jones 2012, at 69). These experiences have persuaded most observers that the security vulnerabilities associated with full-fledged Internet voting make it unsuitable for widespread adoption in the U.S. anytime soon.

Although U.S. voters do not commonly use the Internet to *record* their votes, many states' laws allow for the *transmission* of hand-marked ballots through the Internet. According to the National Council of State Legislatures, 25 states and the District of Columbia allow at least some voters to return voted scanned ballot images through email, and two of those states allow transmission through a web upload as well (NCSL 2014). Most of these states restrict Internet transmission to military and overseas voters. In addition, many overseas and military voters use the Internet to receive a blank ballot (OVF 2013, at 2). Even this limited use of the Internet has prompted security concerns, with some observers warning that it creates an unacceptable risk of tampering (Hoke 2012, at 1019–20).

In sum, the implementation of electronic voting technology in the U.S. has been beset with security controversies. While DREs are still widely used, most states using them require a voter-verifiable paper audit trail. Internet voting poses even greater challenges. There have been just a handful of attempts to experiment with online voting, although half the states now allow the electronic transmission of scanned ballot images.

Legal Framework

For those unfamiliar with the U.S. legal system, the multiple sources of law and institutions responsible for administering them is bound to seem bewildering. A brief summary of laws relating to voting may therefore be helpful, before proceeding to key judicial decisions.

The highest source of law is the U.S. Constitution, two provisions of which are especially relevant to election administration. The first is the Elections Clause, contained in Article I, Section 4 of the Constitution. It authorizes the states to make rules governing the time, place, and manner of congressional elections, while giving the U.S. Congress power to "make or alter" those rules. The Supreme Court has long understood these provisions to confer on Congress broad power to regulate congressional elections. The other relevant provision is the Fourteenth Amendment to the U.S. Constitution, adopted in 1868 after the Civil War. The Fourteenth Amendment requires states to provide all persons with "due process" (the Due Process Clause) and prohibits them from denying "equal protection of the laws" (the Equal Protection Clause). Although the U.S. Constitution does not expressly confer a general right to vote, the U.S. Supreme Court has long declared the right to vote "fundamental" and the Equal Protection Clause is understood as the primary source of this right (*Reynolds v. Sims* (1964)). According to *Bush v. Gore*, the underlying constitutional principle is that all votes must be afforded "equal weight" and all voters "equal dignity."

There are also some federal statutes, laws enacted by the U.S. Congress, germane to electronic voting. The most important is HAVA. As mentioned above, HAVA provided funding for new voting systems while imposing some modest requirements. It required that voting systems notify voters of "overvotes," casting more than the allowed number of choices for a particular contest (52 U.S.C. § 21081(a)(1)). While punch-card voting systems lacked this capacity, HAVA allowed jurisdictions using paper-based systems to satisfy the notification requirement through a voter education program. HAVA also required that all voting systems have an audit capacity—specifically, that they produce a "permanent paper record" for use in manual recounts (52 U.S.C. § 21081(a)(2)). But HAVA did not require that DREs have a "voter-verifiable paper audit trail" or "VVPAT"—a paper record printed at the time of voting that allows voters to review and verify their choices. As described in the next section, the implementation of DREs in many parts of the U.S. resulted in a long-running battle over whether a VVPAT should be required. HAVA also required that people with disabilities be afforded "the same opportunity for access and participation (including privacy and independence) as for other voters" (52 U.S.C. § 21081(a)(3)). This requirement may be satisfied by having "one direct recording electronic voting system or other voting system equipped for individuals with disabilities at each polling place."

HAVA created a new administrative agency, the U.S. Election Assistance Commission (EAC), to distribute federal funds and set voluntary standards for voting systems. While state and local entities are not required to abide by those standards (known as the "Voluntary Voting System Guidelines"), a condition of receiving HAVA money was compliance with the EAC's standards.

The EAC's standard-setting and certification process has proven exceptionally dysfunctional. One peculiarity of HAVA's implementation is that most states had already decided on what new technology to purchase before the EAC promulgated its first set of standards in 2005 (Damschroder 2013, at 197).[4]

4 The authority to set standards for voting systems previously lay with the U.S. Federal Election Commission (FEC), whose primary responsibilities concern campaign finance laws. The FEC promulgated the first set of voting system standards in 1990, updating them in 2002. The 2005 standards promulgated by the EAC were an updated version of the FEC's 2002 voting system standards (Damschroder 2013).

The first certification of equipment pursuant to these standards did not take place until 2008. It is widely acknowledged the standard-setting and certification process for voting systems is broken (GAO 2008, at 8; PCEA 2014, at 62). To make matters worse, the systems purchased with HAVA money are approaching the end of their life cycle, with no more federal money available for new technology.

The lack of a full complement of commissioners on the EAC has exacerbated these difficulties. By statute, the EAC consists of two Democrats and two Republicans, and can only take action with the agreement of at least three members. While the EAC achieved an admirable degree of bipartisan consensus in its early years, that eventually broke down and, due to ongoing partisan bickering. After a long period during which the EAC was without any commissioners, three new commissioners were finally confirmed in late 2014 and updated the 2005 voting system standards in 2015. The EAC is now generally regarded as a failed agency (Tokaji 2009, at 134–6), although there is some hope for improvement now that the agency has a quorum again.

Three other federal statutes, aside from HAVA, are germane to the topic of voting technology. The first is the Voting Rights Act of 1965 (VRA), designed to stop racial discrimination with respect to voting. Section 2 of that statute, as amended in 1982, prohibits practices that "result" in the denial or abridgement of the vote on account of race or color (52 U.S.C. § 10301). Accordingly, Section 2 does not require a showing of intentional race discrimination to establish a violation.

The second federal statute germane to voting technology is the Americans with Disabilities Act of 1990 (ADA). The ADA prohibits discrimination against people with disabilities. Title II of the ADA applies to state and local government entities—including election authorities—prohibiting them from discriminating on the basis of disability with respect to programs, activities, and services (42 U.S.C. § 12132). Title II of the ADA has sometimes been used to challenge the failure to challenge inaccessible polling places and voting equipment, as described in the next section.

The third relevant federal statute is the Uniformed and Overseas Citizens Absentee Voting Act (UOCAVA), enacted in 1986 and amended in 2009 by the Military and Overseas Voter Empowerment Act (MOVE). UOCAVA generally requires that states allow military personnel and civilians residing outside the U.S. to register and to vote by absentee ballot (52 U.S.C. § 20302). Under the MOVE amendments, absentee ballots must be made available to military and overseas voters 45 days in advance of elections. MOVE also requires states to develop procedures for sending blank absentee ballots electronically, although they are not required to accept completed ballots through electronic means.

Beneath this thin layer of federal laws are a multiplicity of laws in the states and the territories. Under both the Elections Clause and the Supremacy Clause of the U.S. Constitution, valid federal laws supersede contrary state laws. But because there are relatively few federal laws regulating election administration, it is state law that mostly governs election administration in the U.S., including the implementation of voting technology.

While it is impossible even to summarize the many state laws relevant to electronic voting in this short chapter, four points are worth highlighting. First, many state constitutions—the highest level of state law—go beyond the U.S. Constitution in offering express protection for the right to vote (Douglas 2014; see, e.g., Pa. Const., Art. VII, § 1). These state constitutional provisions have sometimes given rise to challenges to voting technology. Second, as noted in the preceding section, most states go beyond HAVA by legally requiring voting systems to produce a voter-verifiable paper audit trail (see, e.g., Cal. Elections Code § 19250). Third, the states have their own rules regarding election audits and recounts. Some states make the paper record the official ballot in case of a recount (see, e.g., Ohio Rev. Code § 3506.18). Fourth, about half the states allow some voters to transmit voted absentee ballots through the Internet, although almost all of them limit this right to military and overseas voters (NCSL 2014).

Judicial Decisions

Although U.S. courts have played an active role in policing election administration since 2000 (Hasen 2013), they have shown considerable restraint when it comes to voting technology. Judges have not been the prime movers, either in accelerating the replacement of old systems or in putting the brakes on new systems. The battles over voting technology have, instead, mostly been resolved in political arenas. There have been a number of court decisions regarding electronic voting since 2000, but few successful claims. Broadly speaking, those cases may be grouped into three categories. First are cases challenging punch-card and other older voting systems due to the lost votes associated with those systems, and seeking the adoption of newer voting technology. Second are cases challenging paperless electronic voting systems because of the questions surrounding their security and accuracy. The third are disability access cases seeking the adoption of accessible voting technology. With few exceptions, federal and state courts have been reluctant to intervene in all three categories.

Punch Cards

The first generation of lawsuits following *Bush v. Gore* sought to eliminate the voting equipment that had proved so troublesome in that election. Litigation in Florida, Georgia, Illinois, California, and Ohio alleged that punch-card voting systems resulted in more lost votes than other systems.[5] Some of these cases also challenged the use of central-count optical-scan systems that, like punch cards, did not provide voters with notice of and the opportunity to correct errors. Relying

5 The author was one of the plaintiffs' attorneys in the California and Ohio cases.

in part on *Bush v. Gore*, plaintiffs challenged these systems under the Fourteenth Amendment, arguing that they denied equal protection to voters using non-notice systems. They also made race discrimination claims under Section 2 of the VRA, arguing that they sought the implementation of either electronic voting or precinct-count optical-scan systems, both of which do provide voters with notice.

Plaintiffs achieved early victories in these cases, including favorable district court decisions in Ohio and Illinois (*Common Cause v. Jones* (2002), *Black v. McGuffage* (2002)). There were two important decisions from federal courts of appeals accepting the equal protection argument—although both of them were ultimately vacated on procedural grounds. The first case was *Southwest Voter Registration Education Project v. Shelley* (2003), in which plaintiffs sought to delay California's 2003 recall election until the following year, when the state's punch-card voting systems were scheduled to be replaced. A three-judge panel of the Ninth Circuit Court of Appeals accepted plaintiffs' equal protection argument, concluding that "the weight of a citizen's vote cannot be made to depend on where he lives." That decision was ultimately vacated by the same court, sitting *en banc*,[6] citing the general rule against enjoining an election that (by that time) had already begun.

The other important punch-card case was *Stewart v. Blackwell* (2004). In that case, a three-judge panel of the Sixth Circuit Court of Appeals held that Ohio's voting systems violated equal protection, due to the disparate treatment accorded to people using punch cards and other non-notice systems, as compared with those in counties using more accurate technology. That court also allowed plaintiffs race discrimination claim under Section 2 of the Voting Rights Act. That decision too was vacated *en banc*, with the full Sixth Circuit concluding that the case was moot.

Paperless Electronic Voting

The next generation of voting technology litigation involved challenges to electronic voting systems lacking a voter-verifiable paper audit trail. Plaintiffs in these cases argued that, without such a paper trail, DRE voting systems were unreliable and accordingly that plaintiffs using this equipment were less likely to have their votes counted accurately than voters using paper-based systems. Challenges to paperless electronic voting systems have been brought under the U.S. Constitution, HAVA, and state laws. With two limited exceptions, the legal claims against electronic voting have failed.

The most significant challenges to paperless DRE systems raised claims under the Equal Protection Clause of the U.S. Constitution. In cases arising from

6 Federal appellate courts usually hear cases before three-judge panels as an initial matter. Appellate courts may rehear cases *en banc*, which generally means that they are decided by all active judges of the court. The exception is the Ninth Circuit Court of Appeals which, because of its large number of judges, decides *en banc* cases with 11 judges rather than all active judges.

California, Florida, and Texas, federal appellate courts rejected these claims. The basic structure of the equal protection argument in these cases parallels the one made in the punch-card cases. In both lines of cases, plaintiffs argue that some voting systems are less reliable than others used in the same state, denying equal protection to voters in jurisdictions that use the inferior equipment. The main difference is that plaintiffs in the punch-card cases presented statistical evidence that this type of equipment was more prone to error than systems that provide notice of and the opportunity to correct errors. Comparable statistical evidence was not present in the constitutional challenges to paperless DREs.

Citing the lack of evidence, federal courts have uniformly rejected constitutional challenges to electronic voting. The first significant case was *Weber v. Shelley* (2003). In turning aside the challenge to California's use of paperless DREs, the Ninth Circuit noted that every electoral regulation has some impact on the right to vote. But only those imposing "severe" restrictions are subject to strict scrutiny under the Constitution. By contrast, those imposing only "reasonable, nondiscriminatory" restrictions on voting may generally be justified by the state's important regulatory interests.

The Ninth Circuit drew its test from two Supreme Court decisions that have become very important in constitutional litigation over election practices: *Anderson v. Celebrezze* (1983) involving candidates' access to the ballot, and *Burdick v. Takushi* (1992) involving a prohibition on write-in voting. Although neither case concerned voting equipment, courts have applied the *Anderson-Burdick* test in equal protection challenges to various electoral practices, including voter ID, absentee voting, and provisional voting rules as well as voting equipment. Because the California plaintiffs failed to show that voters using electronic voting were less likely to have their votes counted, the Ninth Circuit affirmed the denial of the constitutional claim in *Weber*.

The Eleventh Circuit applied a similar analysis in rejecting a constitutional challenge to Florida's electronic voting machines. Brought by a Florida Congressman and other voters in the state, *Wexler v. Anderson* (2006) alleged that touchscreen DREs violated the Fourteenth Amendment. In contrast to the optical-scan ballots used in other parts of Florida, the state's DREs did not generate a contemporaneous paper record at the time of voting that could be used in the event of a recount. The Eleventh Circuit defined the central constitutional issue as whether "voters in touchscreen counties are less likely to cast an effective vote than voters in optical scan counties." Plaintiffs failed to allege that DREs had this result. Accordingly, the Eleventh Circuit found no severe burden on voting. It went on to conclude that the use of touchscreen DREs was justified by the state's important regulatory interests in avoiding ambiguously marked ballots and other voters errors, as well as providing access for people with disabilities. For similar reasons, the Eleventh Circuit affirmed the dismissal of plaintiffs' claim that Florida's use of DRE's was fundamentally unfair in violation of due process.

The third federal appellate court to decide a constitutional challenge to DREs arose from Texas. The Fifth Circuit issued a one-paragraph, unpublished decision in *Texas Democratic Party v. Williams* (2008), rejecting the constitutional challenge to that state's use of DREs. The Fifth Circuit cited the *Anderson-Burdick* balancing test, as well as the U.S. Supreme Court then-recent decision in *Crawford v. Marion County Election Board* (2008), which applied that test to reject a challenge to a state voter identification requirement. The implication is that, as in *Weber* and *Wexler*, plaintiffs had failed to show that paperless DREs imposed a severe burden on voting and that the state's use of electronic voting was justified by its important regulatory interests. Although the issue has not reached the U.S. Supreme Court, the three federal appellate courts to have addressed the issue have all upheld electronic voting against constitutional challenges.

Claims under HAVA have fared no better. As noted above, HAVA requires that voting systems have an audit capacity, but does not expressly require a voter-verifiable paper audit trail. In *Crowley v. Nevada* (2012), the Ninth Circuit considered a HAVA-based challenge to paperless DREs. It did not reach the merits, instead concluding that voters had no private right of action to enforce HAVA's voting system requirements with respect to *local* elections. This decision thus leaves the door open to a subsequent claim challenging the use of paperless DREs in *federal* elections. A federal district court, however, concluded that plaintiffs seeking to challenging electronic voting in Pennsylvania had no right to sue under HAVA (*Taylor v. Onorato* (2006)).[7]

The result has mostly been the same in challenges to paperless DREs under *state* law. While the particulars of the state claims vary, they all involve the certification or use of electronic voting systems, raising security and reliability arguments similar to those made in the federal constitutional cases described above. A state appellate court decision from Maryland, *Schade v. Maryland State Board of Elections* (2007), is typical. The trial court heard extensive expert evidence from both sides regarding the claimed problems with the security and accuracy of electronic voting machines, concluding that the state acted reasonably in deploying paperless DREs. The state court of appeals affirmed the lower court's weighing of the evidence as well as its legal conclusion. State courts in Georgia, New Jersey, and Texas have adopted a similar line of reasoning in upholding the use of DREs under those states' laws (*Favorito v. Handel* (Ga. 2009), *Gusciora v. Corzine* (N.J. Super Ct. Law Div. 2010), *Andrade v. NAACP* (Tex. 2011)).[8]

---

7 A court in the U.S. territory of Virgin Islands followed a similar line of reasoning in rejecting a HAVA-based challenge to paperless electronic voting systems used there (*Bryan v. Abramson* (2010)). On the other hand, an Arizona court found that there was a right of action under state law to assert claims under HAVA, given that state law incorporated federal legal requirements (*Chavez v. Brewer* (2009)). That decision, however, did not rule on whether the challenged equipment actually violated state law.

8 In addition, a state court in Pennsylvania rejected a procedural challenge to electronic voting. Plaintiffs in *Kuznik v. Westmoreland County Board of Commissioners* (Pa. 2006) claimed that the replacement of lever voting machines with electronic voting machines had to be submitted to voters through a referendum. The *Kuznik* court disagreed,

There are two narrow counterexamples to the general pattern of rejecting state-law challenges to electronic voting systems. An Arizona court declined to dismiss claims under that state's constitution, thus allowing plaintiffs to produce evidence while stressing that they "may have a difficult time establishing their entitlement to relief" (*Chavez v. Brewer* (2009)). A Pennsylvania court likewise allowed claims challenging the certification of DREs under that state's constitution and statutes to proceed, without deciding whether those claims were ultimately likely to succeed (*Banfield v. Cortes* (Pa. Commw. Ct. 2007)). In general, however, both federal and state courts have demonstrated a strong disinclination to second-guess decisions to certify and use electronic voting systems.[9]

Disability Access

The final category of electronic voting cases involves access for people with disabilities. These cases have mostly arisen under two federal statutes. One is the Americans with Disabilities Act, which forbids public entities from discriminating on the basis of disability with respect to their programs, services, and facilities. The other is HAVA, which requires election authorities to provide accessible voting technology, with at least one DRE or other accessible voting machine at each polling place. Disability advocates in the U.S. have generally favored the DREs, arguing they are necessary to ensure that people with disabilities—including those with visual impairments—are able to vote privately and independently.

A handful of cases have sought to force state or local election authorities to comply with the ADA's and HAVA's access mandates by adopting or expanding the use of DREs. As in the cases challenging paperless systems, courts have generally been reluctant to intervene. Two cases brought by the American Association for People with Disabilities, a leading advocacy group, are exemplary. In *AAPD v. Harris* (2012), the Eleventh Circuit rejected the group's ADA claim, on the ground that voting is not a program, service, or activity and therefore falls outside the scope of Title II. In the other case, *AAPD v. Shelley* (2004), plaintiffs sought a court order stopping the California Secretary of State's decision to decertify electronic voting systems. A federal district court rejected the plaintiffs' claim under the ADA on the ground that this statute does not require "secret, independent voting" for people with disabilities.

Some courts have been reluctant even to entertain disability access claims under HAVA. The court in *AAPD v. Shelley* rejected such a claim as unripe, given that HAVA's mandate had not yet taken effect. In a later case, also arising from California, another federal district court rejected a HAVA claim on procedural grounds, finding that plaintiffs had no right to sue for violations of that statute's

concluding that HAVA's requirements preempted any state law that might be understood to require voter approval of new equipment.

9 For further discussion and analysis of the cases challenging electronic voting systems, see Hoke (2012, at 1024–30).

disability access requirement (*Paralyzed Veterans of America v. McPherson* (2006); Tokaji 2013, at 206).

On the other hand, a more recent federal district court decision from California exhibits greater receptivity to disability access claims. The plaintiffs in *California Council for the Blind v. County of Alameda* (2013) argued that the failure to provide accessible voting systems violated the ADA. The district court expressly disagreed with the decisions in both *AAPD v. Harris* and *AAPD v. Shelley*. It concluded that voting is a service protected under Title II, and that this statute requires that people with disabilities be afforded the opportunity to vote privately and independently. While not deciding whether the ADA had been violated, the district court allowed this claim to proceed.[10] This case thus stands as another qualified exception to the general rule that courts are loath to intervene, either to stop electronic voting or to compel its implementation.

Conclusion

Electronic voting has been a prominent subject of academic, legislative, and public debate in the U.S. since the contested 2000 presidential election and Congress' enactment of the Help America Vote Act in 2002. In addition to battles in legislative bodies over whether to adopt a voter-verifiable paper audit trail, there have been several significant cases involving electronic voting systems, including some seeking to rely on the equal protection logic of *Bush v. Gore*. The voting technology lawsuits fall into three categories: (1) cases seeking to compel the replacement of punch-card systems with more modern technology, (2) cases seeking to stop the implementation of electronic voting due to concerns about their security and accuracy, and (3) cases seeking to promote electronic voting in order to allow independent and private voting by people with disabilities. With rare exceptions, litigation in all three of these categories has been unsuccessful. Although U.S. courts have generally taken an active role in policing election administration since 2000, they have—for better or for worse—mostly left the resolution of questions involving electronic voting to the political branches of local, state, and federal government.

References

Books

R. Michael Alvarez and Thad E. Hall, *Point, Click, and Vote: The Future of Internet Voting* (Brookings Institution Press, 2004).

---

10 The district court in *California Council for the Blind* also allowed a disability discrimination claim under California state law to proceed.

——, *Electronic Elections: The Perils and Promises of Digital Democracy* (Princeton University Press, 2008).
Bev Harris, *Black Box Voting Ballot Tampering in the 21st Century* (Talion Publishing 2004).
Richard L. Hasen, *The Voting Wars from Florida 2000 to the Next Election Meltdown* (Yale University Press 2012).
Martha Kropf and David C. Kimball, *Helping America Vote: The Limits of Election Reform (Controversies in Electoral Democracy and Representation)* (Routledge 2012).

Articles

Matthew M. Damschroder, "Of Money, Machines and Management: Election Administration from an Administrator's Perspective" (2013) 12 *Election Law Journal* 195.
Joshua Douglas, "The Right to Vote Under State Constitutions" (2014) 67 *Vand. L. Rev.* 89.
Richard L. Hasen, "The 2012 Voting Wars, Judicial Backstops, and the Resurrection of *Bush v. Gore*" (2013) 81 *Geo. Wash. L. Rev.* 1865.
Candice Hoke, "Judicial Protection of Popular Sovereignty: Redressing Voting Technology" (2012) 62 *Case Western Reserve Law Review* 997.
David Jefferson, Aviel D. Rubin, Barbara Simons, David Wagner, "Voting Security: An Extensive Assessment of a Proposed Internet-Based Voting System" (2004) 47 (10) *Communications of the ACM* 59–64.
Roy G. Saltman, "Accuracy, Integrity and Security in Computerized Vote-Tallying" (1988) 31 *Communications of the ACM* 1184.
Barbara Simons and Douglas W. Jones, "Internet Voting in the U.S." (2012) 55 *Communications of the ACM* 68.
Charles Stewart III, "Election Technology and the Voting Experience in 2008" (2009) Prepared for Midwest Political Science Association Presentation, http://web.mit.edu/cstewart/www/papers/stewart_midwest2009.pdf.
——, "Voting Technologies" (2011) 14 *Ann. Rev. Pol. Sci.* 353.
Daniel P. Tokaji, "The Paperless Chase: Electronic Voting and Democratic Values" (2005) 73 *Fordham Law Review* 1711.
——, "The New Vote Denial: Where Election Reform Meets the Voting Rights Act" (2006) 57 *S. C. L. Rev.* 689.
——, "The Future of Election Reform: From Rules to Institutions" (2009) 28 *Yale L. & Pol'y Rev.* 125.
——, "HAVA in Court: A Summary and Analysis of Litigation" (2013) 12 *Election L.J.* 203.
Michael Tomz and Robert P. Van Houweling, "How Does Voting Equipment Affect the Racial Gap in Voided Ballots?" (2003) 47 *American Journal of Political Science* 46.

U.S. Vote Foundation and Overseas Vote Foundation (OVF), "Voting Research Newsletter" (2013) 4 *Voting Research Newsletter* 1.

Reports

Michael Alvarez, Stephen Ansolabehere, Erik Antonsson, Jehoshua Bruck, Steven Graves, Nicholas Negroponte, Thomas Palfrey, Ron Rivest, Ted Selker, Alex Solcum. Charles Stewart, "Residual Votes Attributable to Technology An Assessment of Reliability of Existing Voting Equipment" (The Caltech/MIT Voting Technology Project 2001).
Henry E. Brady, Justin Buchler, Matt Jarvis, John McNulty, "Counting All the Votes: The Performance of Voting Technology in the United States" (University of California, Berkeley, CA, 2001), http://ucdata.berkeley.edu/pubs/countingallthevotes.pdf.
California Secretary of State Debra Bowen, "Top to Bottom Review" (2007), http://www.sos.ca.gov/voting-systems/oversight/top-to-bottom-review.htm.
Commission on Federal Election Reform, *Building Confidence in U.S. Elections* (2005).
Council of Europe, "Legal, Operational and Technical Standards for E-Voting," Rec(2004)11, Council of Europe Publishing (2004).
Donald S. Inbody, "Voting by Overseas Citizens and Deployed Military Personnel" (2013), https://www.supportthevoter.gov/files/2013/08/UOCAVA-Analysis-June-2013-Inbody.pdf.
Tadayoshi Kohno, Adam Stubblefield, Aviel D. Rubin, Dan S. Wallach, "Analysis of an Electronic Voting System" (2004).
National Commission on Federal Election Reform, "To Assure Pride and Confidence in the Electoral Process" (2001).
National Conference of State Legislatures (NCSL), "Electronic Transmission of Ballots" (2014), http://www.ncsl.org/research/elections-and-campaigns/internet-voting.aspx.
National Democratic Institute (NDI), "Internet Voting" (n.d.), https://www.ndi.org/e-voting-guide/internet-voting.
Ohio Secretary of State, "EVEREST: Evaluation and Validation of Election-Related Equipment, Standards and Testing" (2007), http://www.patrickmcdaniel.org/pubs/everest.pdf.
Presidential Commission on Election Administration (PCEA), "The American Voting Experience: Report and Recommendations of the Presidential Commission on Election Administration" (2014).
Science Applications International Corporation (SAIC), "Risk Assessment Report Diebold AccuVote-TS Voting System and Processes" (State of Maryland, 2003).
U.S. Election Assistance Commission (EAC), "A Survey of Internet Voting" (September 2011), http://www.eac.gov/assets/1/Documents/SIV-FINAL.pdf.

——, "2012 Election Administration and Voting Survey: A Summary of Key Findings" (September 2013), http://www.eac.gov/assets/1/Page/990-050%20 EAC%20VoterSurvey_508Compliant.pdf.

United States Government Accountability Office (GAO), "Elections Federal Program for Certifying Voting Systems Needs to Be Further Defined, Fully Implemented, and Expanded," Report to the Chairman, Committee on House Administration, House of Representatives (2008), http://www.gao.gov/assets/290/280935.pdf.

Verified Voting, "Voter Verified Paper Record Legislation" (2014), https://www.verifiedvoting.org/resources/vvpr-legislation.

Chapter 13
Electronic Voting in Australia

Greg Taylor*

Limited Trials Only

Overview

The famous Anglo-American commentator Alistair Cooke pointed out in 1979, just after the epoch-making British election of that year:

> Americans who don't like to see Britain going American in anything – if only because of the uncanny British gift for picking up the worst of America instead of the best – were greatly relieved to hear that nobody has yet thought of introducing the voting machine: the system whereby a million voters walk in turn into a curtained cubicle, tap little levers of their choice, then pull a big lever which locks their preferences and rattles up the cumulative vote, so that a couple of hours later the city count is in, and the Irish Democrats on Third Avenue are already steeped in sorrow or reeling in ecstasy. It was good to hear, and was in keeping with the American fondness for Old England, that men and women of matchless honesty, dexterity and patience would, on the contrary, be separating out bits of paper, some white, some off-white, and making two piles of votes, one for local councillors and one for Members of Parliament, and then dividing these piles into other piles till their lips grew tired in the dawn.[1]

Australia also has remained true to this heritage. This chapter will show that – with one outstanding exception, namely elections to the legislature of the Australian Capital Territory – electronic voting has been used in Australia mainly for the handicapped or absent and has not been seen as an option for mass voting, and will explore the reasons for this state of affairs.

Thus, 35 years later, despite vast progress in technology in the meantime, Australia – which famously led much of the world in the adoption of the secret

---

* The author wishes to thank Professor Graeme Orr, Dr Vanessa Teague and the editors of this book for their comments on a draft of this chapter, but all arguments and conclusions are the author's own.

1 Cooke, *The Americans: Fifty Letters from America on Our Life and Times* (Bodley Head, London 1979), pp. 320f.

ballot for legislative elections,[2] and was also an early adopter of postal voting[3] – has largely retained the services of the 'men and women of matchless honesty, dexterity and patience' and eschewed electronic voting technology. The only extensive use of computers in the electoral system does not directly involve the voter at all: in tallying the votes cast in the more complicated systems of election prevalent for most Australian upper Houses, e-counting may be employed and the contents of paper ballots transferred to a computer programme.[4] But only a small minority of voters actually cast their ballots using e-voting technology. That small minority of voters may use, depending on the election they are voting in, either remote internet-based voting options or the stand-alone off-line voting kiosk located in the controlled environment of a polling place which does not involve communication over the internet; there is also a very small amount of voting by e-mail. But the vast majority of Australian voters still use the traditional pencil and paper and will never see a voting machine of any type. Those who cannot attend at the traditional polling station to use pencil and paper will, as a rule, use postal voting or a secret telephone voting process to be described later and which does not involve computerised voting.

Given the comparative lack of use of electronic voting in Australia, there is at present no case law resulting from its use in Australia, although there is a small amount of case law under anti-discrimination statutes about whether electronic voting methods must be provided to handicapped people to allow them to vote in complete secrecy. It is also possible to extrapolate from existing case law on traditional voting methods in order to have some idea of the manner in which electoral law will be applicable to electronic voting when legal issues arising from its use arise – as they inevitably will.

---

2 See, for example, Brent, 'The Rise of the Returning Officer: How Colonial Australia Developed Advanced Electoral Institutions' (PhD thesis, Australian National University 2008), ch. 6; McKenna, 'Building a "Closet of Prayer" in the New World: The Story of the "Australian Ballot"' in Sawer (ed.), *Elections: Full, Free and Fair* (Federation, Leichhardt 2001).

3 The system may be traced back to the *Electoral Act* 1889 (W.A.) s 52 and the *Absent Voters Electoral Act* 1890 (S.A.), although it was, from the perspective of the present day, a composite system, involving the use of the post to communicate the vote but also the postmaster as a government official at the place of voting. See further Brent, *Rise of the Returning Officer*, ch. 8.

4 E.g. *Commonwealth Electoral Act* 1918 (Clth) s 273A; *Electoral Act* 1985 (S.A.) Part 10 Division 3A; Hughes, 'Institutionalising Electoral Integrity' in Sawer (ed.), *Elections*, pp. 152f; below, fn 14. It may also be mentioned that electronic enrolment initially met with unsuccessful resistance on the part of the electoral authorities: *Get Up* v. *Electoral Commission (Clth)* (2010) 189 FCR 165. This resistance has ceased and enrolment is now available on line for most, if not all jurisdictions.

Background

The most frequently encountered structure of Australian parliamentary elections involves the election of two Houses on the one date by the same electorate: the lower House to determine the make-up of the government and the upper House for monitoring the government's actions and as a second forum for considering proposed legislation. In five of the nine Australian jurisdictions – federally and in the States of New South Wales, Victoria, Western Australia and South Australia – the lower House is elected by means of the alternative or preferential vote in single-member constituencies,[5] and the upper House uses proportional representation in multi-member constituencies.[6] While there might be between six and 10 candidates at the average lower House single-seat election, and any more than 12 is very unusual, the complicated and lengthy process of distributing preferences in the elections for the multi-member upper House constituencies – in the larger States the number of candidates at an average election can exceed 100 – is the reason for the widespread adoption of e-counting for those elections.

In tiny Tasmania, the usual bicameral pattern is reversed, with the upper House being elected on the single-member system and the lower by means of proportional representation in multi-member constituencies. The bicameral pattern of Australian parliaments is broken by Queensland, which in 1922 abolished its upper House, then consisting of unelected nominees of the Crown in a quixotic and doomed attempt to create a colonial House of Lords; its sole remaining House is elected by the same method as that used for other State lower Houses, the alternative vote in single-member constituencies. The legislatures of the two mainland territories,[7] the Northern Territory and the Australian Capital Territory (which contains Canberra), reflect the small size of those jurisdictions by also containing one House only. In the Northern Territory the usual pattern of single-member constituencies and the

5 The expression of preferences by the voter (beyond first preference) is optional in New South Wales and Queensland, and compulsory in the other jurisdictions.

6 The constituency is the whole State in New South Wales and South Australia, and subdivisions of the whole in the other three jurisdictions. There is again variation about the extent to which a voter must indicate preferences (in some jurisdictions it is wholly compulsory; in others, it is optional to some extent). In May 2014, a federal parliamentary committee recommended that in the federal Senate elections compulsory preferential voting should be abandoned, and a system of optional preferential voting similar to that in force in New South Wales should apply: Joint Standing Committee on Electoral Matters, *Interim Report on the Inquiry into the Conduct of the 2013 Federal Election – Senate Voting Practices* (The Committee, Canberra 2014).

7 No account is taken here of the external Territories outside the Australian mainland, of which only one – Norfolk Island – has its own Legislative Assembly, which the federal government is currently proposing to demote to the status of a mere local council. Christmas Island and the Cocos (Keeling) Islands have local councils; the others are uninhabited or too sparsely inhabited for any form of elected representation.

alternative vote is followed, while the Australian Capital Territory uses a system of multi-member electorates and proportional representation.

There is, finally, provision for referenda on specific questions: at the federal level, these almost always involve proposals to amend the federal Constitution, which cannot be changed except by referendum; at the State level, constitutional proposals are occasionally made the subject of referenda, but the more frequent case concerns some specific issue of policy such as whether summer time should be introduced or longer trading hours for shops permitted in the jurisdiction concerned. There is no provision for citizen-initiated referenda in Australia, and such occasions are accordingly infrequent, but sometimes a deadlock in Parliament can be broken only by such a device or it is otherwise thought desirable to refer a question to the public at large. Some provision is made for electronic voting for the blind at such referenda,[8] but as no federal referendum has been held in Australia since November 1999 – when Australians voted to retain the Queen as head of state and against a proposal to establish a republic – and there appears to have been no use of electronic voting at the most recent State referenda, in Western Australia, no further mention will be made of the possibility of electronic voting at referenda. When the next referendum occurs, consideration will have to be given to whether electronic voting should be used at it. It is conceivable that the simple binary choice that is generally involved – 'Yes' or 'No' – may militate against the elaborate and expensive use of e-voting technology and in favour of the aforesaid men and women of matchless honesty, etc.

One further election should be mentioned at this point, because it so vividly highlights the lack of presence of electronic voting in Australia: in 2013, the Australian Labor Party[9] announced that (like its sister party in the United Kingdom) it would henceforth elect its federal parliamentary leader, who is the Prime Minister of Australia when the Party has a majority in the federal lower House, by means of a vote involving not merely, as theretofore, the members of its federal parliamentary caucus, but also the ordinary members of the Party. Each of these two groups now has 50 per cent of the weighting in determining the successful candidate. (Unlike in the United Kingdom, no votes were given to trades union members or other affiliated organisations.) The number of members of the Party is not officially published, but 30,426 Party members participated in the inaugural election of the parliamentary leader.[10] Accordingly the electorate for the purposes of determining the federal Labor leadership increased at a stroke from around a hundred people (being the number of members of the parliamentary caucus) to over 30,000. Nevertheless there was no thought, at least in public, given to the

8 E.g. *Referendum (Machinery Provisions) Act* 1984 (Clth) Part IVB.

9 Its name is spelt without the 'u', partly because the British spelling did not come to include the 'u' consistently until after it was founded; partly because an early luminary was American; and partly to enable differentiation between collocations such as 'labour movement' (trades unions) and 'labor lawyers' (those involved with the political party).

10 Bramston, *Rudd, Gillard and Beyond* (Penguin, Melbourne, 2014), p. 143.

possibility of conducting the ballot of the rank-and-file members by electronic means; a postal vote was used.

In completing this introductory survey, it should be mentioned that, at common law, jurisdiction to decide questions of disputed election returns was vested in the House of Parliament itself to which they related, a position which still finds an echo in s 47 of the federal Constitution. However, both federally and in all the States and Territories legislation has been passed reflecting the English reform of 1868 confiding the determination of disputed elections to the Courts.[11]

Existing Provision for Electronic Voting

Australian electoral authorities have made different, and sometimes very divergent use of electronic voting, but in no jurisdiction has it become the usual method of casting one's vote.

By far the most widespread use of electronic voting may be found in elections for the legislature of the Australian Capital Territory (Canberra, the national capital, and a small surrounding area). This is not surprising given that its small population (under 400,000 people) and small area (about the same as Luxemburg's, and one-thousandth the area of the largest State) make it easy to transport computer terminals as necessary and to supervise their use adequately. The above-average educational level of the populace in question (which is weighted towards federal public servants) also contributes to the demand for and success of electronic voting. Electronic voting has been available to voters since 2001. It was introduced in the wake of a discovery that a mistake had been made in counting traditional paper ballots in the election of 1998, albeit a mistake that was corrected on a re-count.[12]

At the last election in the Australian Capital Territory, in 2012, approximately one in four voters voted by means of computer terminals in controlled environments – namely, selected polling stations also used for traditional pencil-and-paper voting. There was no provision for internet voting; the terminals were off-line. Voters received a barcode on a card which was swiped through a reader in the polling station and which permitted the process of voting to commence. The barcode was given to the voter without recording the voter's identity, thus securing secrecy.[13]

---

11 Orr/Williams, 'Electoral Challenges: Judicial Review of Parliamentary Elections in Australia' (2001) 23 *Syd LR* 53, 61.

12 Kelly, 'Australian Electoral Administration and Electoral Integrity' in Tham/Costar/Orr (eds), *Electoral Democracy: Australian Prospects* (Melbourne University Press, Melbourne, 2011), pp. 114f.

13 Descriptions and analysis of the system may be found at: http://www.elections.act.gov.au/elections_and_voting/electronic_voting_and_counting/the_electronic_voting_process and in Elections A.C.T., *Report on the A.C.T. Legislative Assembly Election 2012* (Elections A.C.T., Canberra 2013), pp. 33–6, 51.

Section 118A (2) of the *Electoral Act* 1992 (A.C.T.) provides the legal framework for this procedure: it states that the computer programme used must:

> (a) allow an elector to show consecutive preferences starting at '1'; and
> (b) give an elector an opportunity to correct any mistakes before processing the elector's vote; and
> (c) allow an elector to make an informal vote showing no preference for any candidate; and
> (d) not allow a person to find out how a particular elector cast his or her vote.

Under s 182 (8) of the Act, paper ballots may also be entered into the computer programme for the purpose of counting them, and this is in fact done by means of a scanner the results of which are checked for accuracy manually.[14]

The Territory's Electoral Commission reports that the system of electronic voting has been very successful and reduced the number of informal votes significantly (the reason for the provision in paragraph (c) above that an informal vote must still be possible will be explored later; for now it should be noted that Australia makes no formal distinction among ballots that do not comply with the rules and accordingly cannot be counted, and in this chapter 'informal' is used in accordance with Australian practice to describe non-valid votes of all types). The Electoral Commission has recommended the extension of the system of electronic voting to as many voters as possible,[15] which could easily happen if more voting locations were equipped with the necessary technology.

The Australian Capital Territory is the only Australian jurisdiction in which electronic voting is available to voters who are not confronted with a special hindrance in recording their votes in the traditional manner. The next most prevalent use of electronic voting may be found in the most populous State, New South Wales, where internet voting is available to the disabled, to those in remote locations within the State and to those outside the State on election day (who would traditionally have been able to vote, if at all, only in another State capital, at some embassies or, if time sufficed, by post). The legislation limits the availability of electronic voting, however, by specifically providing that it may be available only to the categories of electors just mentioned[16] and that the procedures adopted for electronic voting must benefit the voters in question.[17] Unlike in the Australian Capital Territory, therefore, it is not a system for all comers.

---

14 Elections A.C.T., *Report on the A.C.T. Legislative Assembly Election 2012*, pp. 52f.

15 Elections A.C.T., *Report on the A.C.T. Legislative Assembly Election 2012*, p. 75.

16 *Parliamentary Electorates and Elections Act* 1912 (N.S.W.) ss 120AB (1), 120AC (1).

17 *Parliamentary Electorates and Elections Act* 1912 (N.S.W.) s 120AC (4); s 120AJ requires those procedures to be published on the Internet – see http://www.elections.nsw.gov.au/publications/policies/ivote_approved_procedures.

The origins of electronic voting in New South Wales may be found in a complaint under anti-discrimination law brought before the State's Administrative Decisions Tribunal in 2008 by a blind elector who complained of the lack of a Braille ballot paper, making it necessary for him to compromise (however slightly) the secrecy of his vote by stating his choices to an electoral officer who could fill in the paper-based ballot for him. The complaint was upheld.[18] The State government disdained half-measures, and instead of creating a Braille-based system developed 'iVote', a system for remote voting, in State elections.

Using 'iVote', voters may vote either by telephone or over the internet and are provided with a personal number and a security code which is required in order to use the service. The votes are stored and printed out in order to be counted with traditional ballot papers. At the first State election conducted under this system, 44,605 votes were cast via the internet using 'iVote', of which only about 2,000 were cast by the handicapped and the rest by remotely located voters within the State and above all (92 per cent) by voters outside the State on election day. The system was pronounced a success by an independent audit,[19] but another audit mentioned bugs in the system which had resulted in 43 votes being incorrectly recorded (using meaningless letters instead of the required numbers) – at least, that was the extent of the known and obvious error perpetrated by the computer programme. In addition, the report noted that a number of unspecified security vulnerabilities had persisted throughout the election period.[20] It is somewhat unsettling to learn that there are security vulnerabilities but not to be told even what they are, let alone how they are to be fixed.

As this book went to press the State general election of 2015 had just occurred. There was a much stronger usage of 'iVote' at that election – although official figures were unavailable, media reports indicated that perhaps a quarter of a million voters had used it. The system was however 'hacked' by University-based computer experts, who, as a demonstration of its vulnerability, showed that votes could be read and changed while being transmitted, and it also malfunctioned without any input from outsiders, failing to show for a number of days one of the two options available for voting for two minor parties in the upper House. Fortunately one of those parties, the Animal Justice Party, won a seat in the upper

18 *Fittler* v. *New South Wales Electoral Commission* [2008] NSWADT 116. The complaint actually concerned an election for a local council, not the State government. I do not deal with local elections in this chapter. In New South Wales, responsibility for elections to local government bodies was shortly after *Fittler* wholly transferred to those bodies under the *Local Government Amendment (Elections) Act* 2011 (N.S.W.). See further below, fn 83.

19 Allen Consulting Group, *Evaluation of Technology-assisted Voting Provided at the New South Wales State General Election, March 2011* (Allen Consulting Group, Melbourne 2011), p. 19.

20 Price Waterhouse Coopers, *Technology Assisted Voting Audit*, p. 5, available at http://www.elections.nsw.gov.au/__data/assets/pdf_file/0007/93481/iVote_Audit_report_PIR_Final.pdf.

House anyway, and thus, in the absence of a wronged potential plaintiff, a challenge to the result is not likely. It is nevertheless still disturbing to find such errors.

In a recent submission to the Electoral Matters Committee of the Parliament of Victoria, the Electoral Commission of New South Wales stated that it planned to introduce a system for allowing voters to verify the inclusion of their own ballots in the count and rejected criticism expressed by a computing expert that the system did not sufficiently provide for transparency and verifiability.[21] However, legislation in New South Wales enables the computer programme to be kept secret,[22] and it also contains no specific requirement to act upon the defects in the system identified in the audit mentioned above – although it can confidently be expected that the annual report of the Electoral Commission of New South Wales will deal with the incidents that occurred in the election of 2015 when it is next tabled[23] and thus becomes publicly available, and considerable trust is warranted in the likelihood that the electoral authorities would act, and that politicians and the general public would demand action, on defects that are drawn to their attention.

Reference should also be made to s 120AC (2) (c) of the legislation,[24] which requires procedures to be adopted by the Electoral Commission 'for the authentication of the eligible elector's vote'. It is unclear what this means, and the debates on the legislation as it passed through Parliament leave one no wiser. Paragraph 4.8 of the approved procedures have interpreted this phrase to mean the provision of a voting receipt to the voter,[25] but this does not constitute complete authentication or verification of the inclusion of the vote as it was intended by the voter, because it takes no account of what may happen during transmission over the internet – which is exactly the point at which the University 'hackers' exposed a vulnerability. There is potential for a challenge to the procedures to arise here and for case law to be created on what exactly the phrase quoted means.

Of the remaining Australian jurisdictions in which legislation allows for the casting of votes electronically – federally and in Victoria, Queensland, Tasmania and the Northern Territory[26] – no use has been made of the possibility in the Northern Territory, where electronic voting 'would be challenging ...

21 Electoral Commission of New South Wales, submission to Electoral Matters Committee, Victoria, 30 January 2013, available at: http://www.parliament.vic.gov.au/images/stories/committees/emc/ifvea/Submissions/Submissions_2013/No_6_Electoral_Commission_New_South_Wales.pdf.

22 *Parliamentary Electorates and Elections Act* 1912 (N.S.W.) s 120AG (2).

23 Under the *Parliamentary Electorates and Elections Act* 1912 (N.S.W.) s 120AM, a report was also made on the topic of electronic voting specifically after the 2011 election; it was mentioned above, fn 19.

24 *Parliamentary Electorates and Elections Act* 1912 (N.S.W.).

25 https://www.elections.nsw.gov.au/publications/policies/ivote_approved_procedures/4._approved_procedures/4.8_authentication_of_vote.

26 Electoral Council of Australia and New Zealand, *Internet Voting in Australian Election Systems* (2013), p. 45, available at http://www.eca.gov.au/research/files/internet-voting-australian-election-systems.pdf.

due to its demographic make-up and difficult geography, which leads to limited connectivity'.[27] In Queensland the *Electoral Reform Amendment Act* 2014 had just been passed as this chapter was completed. It allows for computer-assisted or telephonic voting in that State. The Attorney-General said on introducing the Bill:

> The government supports offering electronically assisted voting to all Queenslanders, if associated security and integrity arrangements can be assured. In the short term, the priority is to make electronically assisted voting available on a targeted basis for blind and vision impaired voters and voters who require assistance voting because of a disability, motor impairment or insufficient literacy. Electronically assisted voting will, for the first time in Queensland, enable these voters to cast their votes independently and in secret.[28]

But details are clearly lacking at present,[29] and there has been an election and change of government since anyway.

In Victoria legislation provides for off-line voting at voting booths by those absent from the State and the blind, those insufficiently literate in English or their native language and the disabled.[30] In the election of 2010 it was available both to such electors within Victoria and, for the general public with or without a handicap who were absent from the State, at eight inter-State venues and in London and Manchester. The system involved off-line voting kiosks with touch screens. The take-up rate was disappointing: only 961 electronic votes were recorded.[31] The Victorian Electoral Commission states on its website that present legislation

> says that electronic voting can only be made available at voting centres, which is why the [Victorian Electoral Commission, unlike that of New South Wales] cannot currently offer remote or online voting. However, Victoria's electronic voting system is designed to be 'future ready' should there be any changes to legislation. This includes the potential to offer a completely online service.[32]

This is excessively optimistic. Internet-based voting was not permitted at the State election in November 2014 and does not appear to be on the agenda at present. The Chairman of the Electoral Matters Committee said in Parliament on 27 March

27 Electoral Council of Australia and New Zealand, *Internet Voting*, p. 81.

28 Queensland Parliamentary Debates, Legislative Assembly, 21 November 2013, p. 4227.

29 Legal Affairs and Community Safety Committee, *Electoral Reform Amendment Bill 2013: Report No. 56* (The Committee, Brisbane 2014), pp. 28–32.

30 *Electoral Act* 2002 (Vic.) s 100, Part 6A.

31 Electoral Matters Committee (Victoria), *Inquiry into the Conduct of the 2010 Victorian State Election and Matters Related Thereto* (Parliamentary Paper No. 114/2010-2014), pp. 103f, 106f.

32 https://www.vec.vic.gov.au/Vote/vote-eav.html.

2014 that 'at this stage the committee cannot recommend the wholesale use of internet or electronic voting at Victorian elections'.[33] Rather, a system similar to that of 2010 in the sense that it does not involve any remote voting capability, but will include a capacity for individual voters to verify that their votes have been included as cast, was used at the election of November 2014; it also allowed for electronic counting of the votes cast electronically.[34] Indeed, having examined and received submissions on New South Wales' internet-based 'iVote' system, the Committee recorded pointedly that '[w]hile the Committee appreciates the efforts of inquiry participants to examine and discuss iVote, the Committee has no comment on iVote as a courtesy to'[35] the electoral authorities in New South Wales. Clearly, considerable credence was given to the wariness about its security expressed in some of the submissions to the Committee.

A Tasmanian innovation which might usefully be considered elsewhere in Australia[36] is supported by the very general permission of ss 131 (1) (c) and 132 (c) of the *Electoral Act* 2004 (Tas.) for the adoption of alternative means of transmitting votes to the returning officer: Tasmanian voters may both receive their ballot papers and transmit them to the returning officer after voting by fax or e-mail. As the Tasmanian Electoral Commission's website states, this form of voting, which the Commission has named '[e]xpress voting, is only available to voters in remote areas or overseas. While express voting is significantly faster than postal voting, the secrecy of the ballot cannot be guaranteed'.[37] Obviously the person in receipt of an e-mail will know who it is from, but most voters are not

33 Victorian Parliamentary Debates, Legislative Council, 27 March 2014, p. 950.

34 Electoral Matters Committee (Victoria), *Inquiry into the Future of Victoria's Electoral Administration* (Parliamentary Paper No. 307/2010-2014), p. 125; see the detailed description of the process in Appendix 1 to the Victorian Electoral Commission's submission to that enquiry, available at http://www.parliament.vic.gov.au/images/stories/committees/emc/ifvea/Submissions/Submissions_2013/No_5_Victorian_Electoral_Commission.pdf. Further background may be found in Burton et al., 'A Supervised Verifiable Voting Protocol for the Victorian Electoral Commission', available at http://epubs.surrey.ac.uk/723026/; Burton et al., 'Using Prêt à Voter in Victorian State Elections', available at http://epubs.surrey.ac.uk/726039/1/EVT.pdf; Holmes, *E-Voting: The Promise and the Practice* (Parliamentary Library, Canberra 2012), pp. 12f; Teague, Submission to the Electoral Matters Committee, Parliament of Victoria, available at http://www.parliament.vic.gov.au/images/stories/committees/No_14_Vanessa_Teague.pdf.

35 Electoral Matters Committee (Victoria), Parliamentary Paper No. 307/2010-2014, p. 129.

36 Although it is outside the scope of this chapter, our friends and cousins in New Zealand enjoyed a similar system at the election there in September 2014: *Electoral Amendment Regulations* 2013 (N.Z.). A website created to provide information to voters in that election (http://www.elections.org.nz/voters/get-ready-enrol-and-vote/enrol-and-vote-overseas) indicated that voting papers could be downloaded from, and after completion uploaded to, the website of the Electoral Commission.

37 http://www.tec.tas.gov.au/StateElection/Ways%20to%20Vote.html.

unduly concerned about the secrecy of their votes as far as the electoral officials are concerned. Furthermore, relatively simple measures could be adopted to confirm that the vote, if received by e-mail, was received in the form in which the voter sent it and has not been altered by hacking, although here there is also the danger that the vote may be revealed by the means of verification to others at the voter's home, workplace, etc.[38] Equally significant is the threat of influence by others at the point of voting, in the workplace or home, but these dangers exist also with traditional postal voting. Nevertheless, in an electorate of about 350,000, this service also has had a remarkably low take-up rate: in the 2010 election, 754 'express' votes were issued (representing about one-quarter of 1 per cent of voters), of which 576 were returned – 58 per cent by email, 21 per cent by fax and 21 per cent by post.[39] In the 2014 election, 1058 'express' votes were received (there appears to be no information about how they were transmitted back to the electoral authorities).[40]

Computer-assisted voting is also available in Tasmania for the blind, but it involves nothing more elaborate than the dictation of the voter's choice to the computer, which then prints out a paper ballot reflecting those choices which can be deposited in a traditional ballot box. A similar system exists in Western Australia and has 'proved to be very popular with the targeted electors'.[41]

Finally, there is the federal sphere – the best resourced and most important of all Australian jurisdictions. In conjunction with the 2007 election, a trial was conducted of remote electronic voting for defence force personnel serving overseas and of electronically assisted voting for the blind. (Other voters overseas were not included because of concerns about the security of internet-based voting.)[42] Both trials were not deemed by the parliamentary Joint Standing Committee on Electoral Matters to have been a success. The high cost of providing electronic

38 An example of such a verification method that attempts to meet the danger in question is given and discussed in Barrat et al., 'Internet Voting and Individual Verifiability: The Norwegian Return Codes', available at: http://www.e-voting.cc/wp-content/uploads/downloads/2012/07/35-45_Barrat_et-al_Norway-Verifiability.pdf. This would be difficult to adapt to voting by e-mail in the manner practised in Tasmania as multiple submissions of the vote make far less sense in such a setting. It is not for me to design electoral systems, but given the small numbers involved one could think of low-technology means of verification such as written records of votes as received sent by post to the voter and to be delivered only on personal signature by the addressee at a post office, or the ability to verify the vote at the electoral office on return to Tasmania on presentation of satisfactory evidence of identity.

39 Tasmanian Electoral Commission, *Fifth Annual Report 2009–2010* (Tasmanian Electoral Commission 2010), pp. 12, 32f.

40 Tasmanian Electoral Commission, *Report on Parliamentary Elections 2011–2014* (Tasmanian Electoral Commission 2014), p. 22.

41 Western Australian Electoral Commission, *Annual Report 2012–2013* (The Commission, Perth 2013), p. 26.

42 Joint Standing Committee on Electoral Matters, *The 2004 Federal Election: Report of the Inquiry into the Conduct of the 2004 Federal Election and Matters Related Thereto* (Commonwealth of Australia, Canberra 2005), p. 271.

voting facilities to each defence force member – it worked out at about 140 times the cost for the standard voter – combined with the need for a paper-based back-up had made the system too great a burden; the cost of providing electronically assisted voting to the blind was even more astronomical, being over double that for the defence forces personnel. As the participation rate was also disappointing, the trial was terminated.[43] At present, therefore, there is no electronic voting of any sort in federal elections, and provisions in the legislation permitting remote voting for the blind are used to authorise a system of call centres so that voting can take place by telephone. Voting over the telephone takes place according to a statutory framework[44] that is designed to enable the blind to cast their vote with the same privacy as others enjoy: the voter must first register in advance by telephone and then receives a letter, S.M.S., telephone call or e-mail which contains a secret personal number that is then used to cast a vote over the telephone without the need to mention one's name.

Electronic Voting in Australia – Why Not?

A number of unrelated reasons ensure that the widespread adoption of electronic voting remains on the back burner in Australia.

Perhaps the most important is the Australian system of compulsory voting, which applies in all jurisdictions. The widely accepted, obeyed and enforced obligation to vote minimises the need for any system of off-site electronic voting in order simply to raise the turn-out. Rather, voters appear, in recent years, to have made increasing use of the facility for voting in advance of the election at designated early-voting centres, originally designed for those unable to attend at the polling booths on election day for some serious reason, so as to avoid the queues and disruption of the weekend involved in attending on the Saturday – it is always a Saturday – which is chosen as the official date of the election.[45]

Compulsory voting has a further impact on electronic voting options which was hinted at above. One reason why the obligation to vote remains widely accepted is that most voters know that they retain the option of deliberately casting an informal vote in order to deny all candidates their approval. The system, given the secrecy of the ballot, is thus really not a system of compulsory voting at all, but of compulsory attendance at the polling booth. This is why requirements were encountered above to the effect that deliberate informal voting must continue to remain possible even under a system of electronic voting. There is therefore only

43 Joint Standing Committee on Electoral Matters, *Report on the 2007 Federal Election Electronic Voting Trials* (Parliament House, Canberra 2009), pp. 36, 63.

44 *Commonwealth Electoral Act* 1918 (Clth) Part XVB; *Electoral and Referendum Regulations* 1940 (Clth) Part III, Division 2.

45 See Electoral Matters Committee (Victoria), Parliamentary Paper No. 307/2010-2014, pp. 15–33.

a limited extent to which computer-based voting can be used to eliminate informal voting: some of it is mistaken, but some of it is also deliberate and a means of satisfying the legal obligation to cast a ballot while avoiding voting for anyone.[46]

One further reason why there is greater difficulty in designing a system for universal electronic voting, particularly if it is web-hosted, is that, in accordance with British tradition, there is no national identity number or card in Australia to provide a single source of identity-related information about voters.

Low-technology voting methods such as those adopted in the United States of America were shown to have their problems by the events in the presidential election of 2000. The observation of this experience from a distance impressed the perils of technology vividly on Australians, as, perhaps, does many people's daily experience of bizarre behaviour by computers in their everyday work – to say nothing of the dangers of deliberate action such as hacking. In Victoria, in particular, it is abundantly clear that scepticism about security, privacy and verifiability of electronic voting, particularly over the internet, have contributed to reluctance to adopt electronic voting in a widespread way.

In 2013, it was, however, the perils of traditional paper-based voting that were emphasised when a federal half-Senate election for the entire State of Western Australia had to be repeated owing to the loss of 1,370 ballot papers by the Australian Electoral Commission which might have affected the result.[47] The supplementary election involved great cost both to political parties and to the public purse, some deviation from the usual course of federal elections and a consequent privileging of West Australians, who were enabled to vote for six members of the Senate not (as is usually the case) in ignorance, but in full knowledge of the election result in the other House and in the other States' half-Senate elections. This reminder that traditional pencil-and-paper ballots can also be flawed did lead to some calls for electronic voting to be introduced, although the main advocate was the fringe member of Parliament Mr C.F. Palmer.[48] The federal Parliament's Joint Standing Committee on Electoral Matters was not persuaded, and reported, as this chapter went to press, that

> [T]he argument that the lost W.A. ballot papers are a reason to move to electronic voting does not appear to be supported by evidence that the inherent

46 Hill, 'Informal Voting under a System of Compulsory Voting' in Tham/Costar/Orr (eds), *Electoral Democracy*, pp. 48f; Orr, 'The Choice not to Choose: Commonwealth Electoral Law and the Withholding of Preferences' (1997) 23 *Mon ULR* 285, 310f.

47 *Australian Electoral Commission* v. *Johnston* (2014) 251 CLR 463, 475f.

48 E.g. in a speech at the National Press Club, Canberra, on 13 February 2014, reported at http://www.abc.net.au/news/2014-02-13/national-press-club-clive-palmer/5258990. It should be said, however, that the Hon. M.B. Turnbull MP, Minister for Communications, had also advocated electronic voting shortly after the federal election of 2013: http://www.abc.net.au/news/2013-09-10/turnbull-advocates-electronic-voting/4949408. See also Orr, 'The Ritual and Aesthetic in Electoral Law' (2004) 32 *Fed LR* 425, 440f.

> vulnerabilities of a paper-based voting system are any greater than those of an electronic system.
>
> Indeed, evidence to the inquiry indicates a similar 'lost votes' error rate with an electronic system without the advantage of a verifiable paper trail for remaining votes.[49]

Another significant reason for the lack of enthusiasm for electronic voting, particularly if it dispenses with the need for attendance at the polling booth, involves the advantages of the public performance of citizens' electoral duties. On the one hand, many polling stations in Australia are, at election time, not merely places for just recording one's vote, but also sites where a community gathers and celebrates its political freedom and egalitarianism.[50] A barbecue, for example, is often put on by a community group at the polling station, and the very act of attending with one's fellow citizens, discarding all differences attaching to one's station in life, speaks a powerful language which should not be weakened by a widespread abandonment of polling booths in favour of one's home computer or mobile telephone. Furthermore, if it were generally possible, outside cases of necessity, to perform electoral duties in one's home or workplace via the internet, an unacceptable risk of coercion, real or imagined, by other family members or colleagues at work would exist.[51] These dangers are much reduced in a public environment. 'Therefore, even if it is technologically possible, [federal Parliament's Joint Standing Committee on Electoral Matters] has no desire to see widespread remote electronic voting introduced at any time in the future'.[52] This reservation does not, however, apply to on-site kiosk-style voting machines, nor to those who are unable to come to the traditional polling booth anyway, whether because they are overseas or handicapped.[53]

Finally, it may be thought, as internet-based voting for everything from one's favourite brand of ice cream to the contestants who should be expelled from the cast of the television show is now commonplace, that there is no little advantage in having a unique, and even deliberately cumbersome procedure for voting in

49 Joint Standing Committee on Electoral Matters, *Second Interim Report on the Inquiry into the Conduct of the 2013 Federal Election: An Assessment of Electronic Voting Options* (The Committee, Canberra 2014), p. 52.

50 Heeney, 'The False Promise of Elections on the Internet' (2014) 58:4 *Quadrant* 34, 35f; Mercurio, 'Discrimination in Electoral Law: Using Technology to Extend the Secret Ballot to Disabled and Illiterate Voters' (2003) 28 *Alt LJ* 272, 273; Mercurio, 'Overhauling Australian Democracy: The Benefits and Burdens of Internet Voting' (2002) 21 *U Tas LR* 23, 40–43. For a similar discussion and conclusions in relation to the United Kingdom, see Lardy, 'Modernising Elections: The Silent Premises of the Electoral Pilot Schemes' [2003] *PL* 6.

51 Electoral Council of Australia and New Zealand, *Internet Voting*, p. 53.

52 Joint Standing Committee on Electoral Matters, *2004 Election*, p. 271.

53 Electoral Council of Australia and New Zealand, *Internet Voting*, p. 66.

governmental elections in order to emphasise the solemnity and uniqueness of the choice to be made.[54]

Case Law and Electronic Voting

Introduction

There has been little serious[55] litigation on electoral law in Australia,[56] partly because problems are not very frequently encountered. In addition, in the interests of ensuring that questions of parliamentary representation are settled finally and as quickly as possible, time limits on challenging elections are strictly enforced[57] and there are strong statutory restrictions, upheld as constitutionally valid by case law,[58] on the bringing of appeals through the usual appellate channels – an important matter in a common-law precedential system, in which the decisions of the higher Courts create stronger precedents. Needless to say, the fact that electronic voting is not widely used in Australia also reduces the opportunity for case law on it to develop. In fact, all that can be done in discussing case law and electronic voting in Australia is to extrapolate from existing case-law principles on traditional forms of voting, with which I shall now deal.

Constitutionally Based Case Law

Sections 7 and 24 of the federal Constitution provide that the federal Senate and House of Representatives, respectively, shall be 'directly chosen' by the people, and some State Constitutions use a comparable phrase;[59] all require lower and (in those jurisdictions that have one) upper Houses to be popularly elected using some form of words.

---

54 Cf. Mercurio, 'Overhauling Australian Democracy', 41f.

55 Much of the litigation that is carried on involves plaintiffs who are somewhat eccentric or have a broader hobby-horse to ride: Gageler, 'The Practice of Disputed Returns for Commonwealth Elections' in Orr/Mercurio/Williams (eds), *Realising Democracy: Electoral Law in Australia* (Federation, Leichhardt 2003), pp. 186f.

56 Orr, *The Law of Politics: Elections, Parties and Money in Australia* (Federation, Leichhardt 2010), p. 207.

57 E.g. *Rudolphy* v. *Lightfoot* (1999) 197 CLR 500, 508; Gageler, 'The Practice of Disputed Returns for Commonwealth Elections', pp. 190–92; Orr/Williams, 'Electoral Challenges', 74–8.

58 *Sue* v. *Hill* (1999) 199 CLR 462, 485; 521; *Smith* v. *Australian Electoral Commission* (2009) 175 FCR 523, 526–8, 531; Orr/Williams, 'Electoral Challenges', 79–82 (who go on to point out that there are exceptions in certain circumstances which permit electoral law to come before an appeals Court).

59 E.g. *Constitution Act* 1975 (Vic.) ss 26 (2), 34 (both Houses to be 'elected'); *Constitution of Queensland* 2001 (Qld) s 10 (sole House to be 'directly elected').

While case law holds that such wording does not protect voters taken, so to speak, in the aggregate against distortion of electoral results caused by gerrymandering or malapportionment of constituencies[60] – an evil that now largely belongs to the past in Australia – in recent years several cases have dealt with the individual right to vote in terms which are also applicable to those who vote electronically. It can therefore be said that, while there is little to no constitutional protection of the use that is made of one's vote – whether the rules of the electoral system render its worth the same, greater or lesser than that of any other voter – there is some constitutional protection of the right to cast a valid vote – to engage, as an individual citizen of age, in the procedure which constitutes contributing to the overall democratic choice. As the Chief Justice, Sir Gerard Brennan, put it in *Langer* v. *Commonwealth* in 1996, 'What the Constitution requires is that the law prescribe a method of voting which leaves the voter free to make a choice, not that the law leave the voter free to choose the method of voting by which a voter's choice is to be made'.[61]

More recently, in *Roach* v. *Electoral Commissioner (Commonwealth)*[62] the highest Court in the land, the High Court of Australia, recognised that the constitutional term 'directly chosen' by the people placed constitutional limits, enforceable by the Courts, on federal Parliament's capacity to disenfranchise otherwise eligible citizens (in the case at hand, persons in prison). In *Rowe* v. *Electoral Commissioner (Commonwealth)*,[63] the same Court even more recently held that a federal provision prohibiting enrolment to vote in an election after the official setting of the election date was invalid because it could not be justified as a law for regulating the franchise as it was not required to protect any essential interest in running elections efficiently or fairly, and that therefore the previous rule, under which there was a seven-day grace period for enrolment after the calling of an election, remained in force.

In the case of 2014 involving the loss of 1,370 ballot papers for the Senate in Western Australia, Hayne J., a Judge of the High Court of Australia sitting as the Court of Disputed Returns,[64] even went so far as to refer to the constitutional requirement of direct choice by the people and to add that '[d]irect choice by the people requires that the lawful expression of every voter's choice is taken into account in determining who has been chosen'.[65] At first blush this might appear to amount to proposing a supererogatory constitutional requirement that every vote

60 *Attorney-General (Clth) (*ex rel. *McKinlay)* v. *Commonwealth* (1975) 135 CLR 1 (federal); *McGinty* v. *Western Australia* (1996) 186 CLR 140 (State).

61 (1996) 186 CLR 302, 316 (referring to methods of voting in the sense of proportional representation, first-past-the-post, etc., but also applicable to methods of recording the vote such as electronic or pencil-and-paper voting).

62 (2007) 233 CLR 162.

63 (2010) 243 CLR 1.

64 This is the Court that decides questions relating to electoral results; see above, fn 11.

65 *Johnston*, (2014) 251 CLR 463, 490; emphasis in original.

should be counted, with invalidity of the election as the constitutional consequence if even one were missed, but the context makes it clear that his Honour was, rather, attempting to interpret the ordinary legislation governing elections, the *Commonwealth Electoral Act* 1918 (Clth), by reference to 'the constitutional purposes pursued by the Act' rather than interpreting the Constitution as such directly. As we shall shortly see, the legislation contains a provision about what to do in cases of error resulting in the failure to reach that ideal.

Rowe dealt with a purported complete denial of the right to cast a valid vote in a particular election (on the basis that a citizen had failed to enrol for it as required by law – enrolment to vote as well as voting itself is compulsory in all Australian jurisdictions). Although it is notable that one – dissenting – judge in *Rowe* made extensive reference to German case law on the topic of proportionality,[66] there is no sign of any support in the Australian Constitution, and accordingly none also in the case law, for any broader principle based on German law such as that all aspects of elections must be conducted openly in all respects, including the counting. It was such considerations that led the German Federal Constitutional Court to cast doubt on whether computerised systems of voting without an independent means of paper-based verification can be used at all there.[67] Thus, in Australia scrutineers for the candidates have a statutory right to be present at the counting,[68] but there is no general right for citizens to be present, and when computerised methods of tallying votes are used neither the scrutineers nor any other representatives of candidates or political parties, let alone the general public, have any right, either constitutional, common-law or statutory, to have access to the computer programming, for example.[69]

Partly for that reason, it is unlikely that any statutory provision for electronic voting would run afoul of the constitutional protection of the right to vote. It is

66 (2010) 243 CLR 1, 139–42.

67 See Taylor, 'Constitutional Restrictions on Touch-Screen Voting Computers in Germany' (2010) 9 *Election LJ* 443; and see Mercurio, 'Beyond the Paper Ballot: Exploring Computerised Voting' in Orr/Mercurio/Williams (eds), *Realising Democracy*, p. 236.

68 E.g. *Electoral Act* 1985 (S.A.) s 90 (1).

69 Green, 'Transparency and Elections in Australia: The Role of Scrutineers in the Australian Electoral Process' in Orr/Mercurio/Williams (eds), *Realising Democracy*, pp. 226–8. Section 273A (6) of the *Commonwealth Electoral Act* 1918 (Clth) provides, to take an example from the federal arena, that the scrutineers need have access only to:

(a) a record of the preferences on the ballot papers that have been received by the Australian Electoral Officer and whose details have been stored in the computer (including informal ballot papers, and formal ballot papers that are not sequentially numbered); and

(b) a record of the ballot papers that are notionally transferred, or exhausted, at each count; and

(c) a record of the progress of the count of the votes, at each count.

This knowledge will go a long way towards ensuring confidence in the system, but further openness, e.g. access to the computer system's programming on the part of qualified people, could be provided for.

unlikely in the extreme that any statutory provision would openly state that a voter's democratic choice is to be wholly disregarded or to count for nothing, as long as it is expressed according to the usual rules that apply to all votes about the number of preferences that must be indicated and so on.

The conclusion that constitutional protection of voting rights would cover only extreme and unlikely cases should not cause alarm. There is a very strong democratic culture in Australia, protected not, in the main, by words on constitutional paper but by a strong feeling for fairness in elections, egalitarianism, watchful media and a belief in democratic institutions. There is room for legitimate disagreement in borderline cases, such as prisoners and those who fail to enrol when required to do so, but the core of the principle is soon reached, easily understood and not subject to debate or doubt. It is inconceivable that any electronic, or any other system of voting would be adopted which deliberately and frankly ran counter to these beliefs and permitted the legal disenfranchisement of citizens who have taken the trouble to record a valid vote.

The Common Law

Originally much electoral law was derived from the common law inherited by the Australian colonies on the commencement of settlement from Great Britain, along with ancient English statutes such as the *Statute of Westminster I* 3 Edw. I c. 5 (1275). That thirteenth-century statute is still in force in some, at least, of the Australian jurisdictions,[70] and provides, in full: 'And because elections ought to be free, the King commandeth upon great forfeiture, that no man by force of arms, nor by malice, or menacing, shall disturb any to make free election'. Also famous is the early modern English case of *Ashby* v. *White*,[71] in which it was held that a voter whose right to vote was improperly denied was able to obtain damages at common law as if a property right had been denied to him.

In modern Australia, these ancient cases and statutes play little practical role, however much they may remind us of the great age of the political institutions we are co-heirs to. Each jurisdiction has its own very detailed and modern electoral legislation, constituting – if not a code – then something very close to it; thus,

70 It is preserved, for example, in the law of Victoria expressly by the *Imperial Acts Application Act* 1980 (Vic.) Part II Division 1. The translation of the statute from Norman French that follows immediately in the text is taken from that Victorian Act also (there being a few variant readings). In *Kean* v. *Kerby* (1920) 27 CLR 449, 459, Mr Justice Isaacs, not a stranger to the *ipse dixit*, speaks as if the statute reflected a prior common-law principle, but his Honour quotes no authority for that statement, nor have I been able to find what its basis, if any, might have been. See further Orr/Williams, 'Electoral Challenges', 55f.

71 (1703) 2 Ld Raym 938; 92 ER 126. For a modern analysis of this case, see *Watkins* v. *Home Secretary* [2006] 2 AC 395, 404f, 408.

legislation largely eliminates the free-standing common law.[72] Case law applying to elections in Australia arises exclusively under a statutory umbrella.

Statute

As we have seen, Australia has, on the whole, not embraced electronic voting, but the pattern is not even across the country – in the Australian Capital Territory electronic voting is of considerable significance, being available in essence to all voters who encounter it or make a small effort to seek out a polling booth with the necessary facilities; and in New South Wales, Australia's most populous State, voting over the internet is allowed, although not generally but only for those who really need it. Despite these two local concentrations of significant potential for problems to arise with electronic voting, no case law has yet arisen recording any such difficulties or in any other way directly involving electronic voting. As was mentioned above, at the 2015 State election in New South Wales the internet voting system 'iVote' malfunctioned, but luckily the party that was disadvantaged as a result won a seat anyway and, as a result, no challenge to the result is expected and another opportunity to develop case law seems to have been missed.

Should some problem occur with electronic voting and a challenge to the result ensue, the federal legislation governing elections may be taken as representative of the provisions that would be applicable. After providing that breaches of the Act may, if it is just to do so, lead to an election's being declared void,[73] it goes on to provide:

> 365. Immaterial errors not to vitiate election
>
> No election shall be avoided on account of any delay in the declaration of nominations, the provision of certified lists of voters to candidates, the polling, or the return of the writ, or on account of the absence or error of or omission by any [electoral] officer which did not affect the result of the election:
>
> Provided that where any elector was, on account of the absence or error of, or omission by, any officer, prevented from voting in any election, the Court shall not, for the purpose of determining whether the absence or error of, or omission by, the officer did or did not affect the result of the election, admit any evidence of the way in which the elector intended to vote in the election.

72 *Cameron* v. *Fysh* (1904) 1 CLR 314, 317; Re *Berrill's Petition* (1976) 134 CLR 470, 474 (qualifying *Ashby* in effect, although – tellingly – the case is not mentioned); *Hudson* v. *Lee* (1993) 177 CLR 627, 631; *Sue* v. *Hill* (1999) 199 CLR 462, 553; Orr/Williams, 'Electoral Challenges', 72.

73 *Commonwealth Electoral Act* 1918 (Clth) ss 352 (1), 360 (3), 362 (3).

Case law, most recently the case of the missing West Australian Senate ballot papers,[74] establishes that the reference to 'voting in any election' means voting with effect – that is, not merely going through the mechanics required to vote, but the successful communication of the choice. Accordingly, the election in which 1,370 ballot papers had been lost was declared void: the voters had done their part to state their choice, but official error (namely, the loss of the ballot papers) prevented it from being an effective act, and, as far as the requirements of the first paragraph of s 365 were concerned, the result was certainly close enough that the ballot papers in question might have affected who was finally elected. The potential for application of this statute and the case law under it to a sabotaged or malfunctioning computer system needs no elaboration.

The proviso to s 365 prevented any effort at identifying the voters in question, which would, under the secret ballot, have been impossible anyway, and also prohibited – more to the point – using computer records of their ballots made during electronic counting in order to discover what votes were recorded on the 1,370 ballot papers in question. Consideration should be given to removing that legislative prohibition on consulting electronic records in cases where ballot papers are lost. The proviso containing the prohibition was inserted into the Act in 1922[75] following a case of 1920[76] in which the Court of Disputed Returns actually questioned electors who had been prevented from casting a ballot at all in order to have them say how they would have voted. It took this step in the 1920 case in order to determine whether the denial of the electors' right to vote had actually affected the final result, which would not have been the case if they had intended to vote for the candidate who obtained the majority of votes cast. This procedure was out of line with English law and – although the Court was at pains to emphasise that it did not require answers to the questions it posed – obviously could compromise a citizen's desire to keep his political opinions to himself, or even lead to pressure on or bribery of citizens prevented from voting by official error to give 'helpful' evidence at the Court proceedings.

In the present author's view, this statutory reaction of 1922 to the case law of 1920 attacks evils that do not exist when it prohibits reference to an electronic record made of a ballot paper which had already been rendered anonymous on its deposit into the ballot box, let alone during the entry of its contents into a computerised counting system. It prevents advantage being taken of even the limited degree of computerisation of elections that has occurred at federal level, and should be amended to permit reference to electronic, anonymous records.

---

74 *Johnston*, (2014) 251 CLR 463, 489–94; *Bridge* v. *Bowen* (1916) 21 CLR 582, 618.

75 *Commonwealth Electoral Act* 1922 (Clth) s 25 (c); Commonwealth Parliamentary Debates, Senate, 26 July 1922, p. 752.

76 *Kean* v. *Kerby* (1920) 27 CLR 449.

Anti-discrimination Case Law – Voting for the Blind

As we saw above,[77] the genesis of internet-based voting in New South Wales lay in a successful complaint by a blind man to that State's Administrative Decisions Tribunal under the *Anti-Discrimination Act* 1977 (N.S.W.), the claim of the applicant, one Darren Fittler, being that, if a blind voter could vote only by communicating his choice to an amanuensis, the secrecy of his ballot was compromised in a manner that did not affect persons without his disability – clearly correct assertions of fact. The case – *Fittler* v. *New South Wales Electoral Commission*[78] – leads us into another area of case law, also arising, as can be seen, under statute. Although the case law in question has intruded into our topic from outside the narrow field of electoral law, the statute is one of more than usual importance. Indeed, given that Australia has no constitutional charter of rights, it is no exaggeration to refer to anti-discrimination legislation enacted by Parliaments as 'quasi-constitutional'.[79]

The Equal Opportunity Tribunal of South Australia, much to its regret, was compelled to disagree with *Fittler* in an equivalent case two years later (*Rankin* v. *State Electoral Commissioner*),[80] in which the applicable legislation, both of the electoral and anti-discrimination varieties, was relevantly indistinguishable. The South Australian Tribunal disagreed largely on the ground that it had no power to override the prescriptions of form in the electoral legislation, which, while making elaborate specifications for the form of the ballot papers, did not authorise a Braille ballot paper. Furthermore, the Electoral Commissioner was not legally able to modify the methods of voting prescribed by the legislation in order to suit the interests of the blind, however legitimate they were. Nevertheless, the Tribunal stated that it was:

> surprised that the Electoral Commissioner has not yet raised with the relevant Minister of the Crown the need to implement appropriate voting options, such as computer assisted or electronic voting, for blind and vision-impaired electors.
>
> It is most unsatisfactory, particularly in light of the innovations in other States and countries and the technological advances made in the past decade, that the *Electoral Act* in this State does not allow for more satisfactory options for electors with a disability, such as computer-assisted or electronic voting. The voting system needs to be modernised in the interests of enabling electors with

---

77 Fn 18.

78 [2008] NSWADT 116.

79 Saunders, 'Concepts of Equality in the Australian Constitution' in Lindell (ed.), *Future Directions in Australian Constitutional Law: Essays in Honour of Professor Leslie Zines* (Federation, Leichhardt 1994), p. 210.

80 [2010] SAEOT 3.

> a disability to cast their vote themselves, and in secret, as can persons without a disability.
>
> It is not for us to recommend that computer-assisted or electronic voting be adopted in South Australia. We note that there are a variety of forms of voting that would enable blind and vision-impaired voters to cast a secret vote. We note with approval the work being done by the Blind and Vision-Impaired Reference Group of the Electoral Council of Australia, under the chairmanship of the Australian Electoral Commissioner. We note that at the April 2010 meeting the chairman concluded with comment about working towards an Australian standard for voting for the disabled, which would be of benefit to all.[81]

With all due respect to the Tribunal in New South Wales, it has to be said that the South Australian decision must be preferred: although the electoral regulations in question in New South Wales provided quite clearly that the ballot papers must be in the English alphabet and none other,[82] and the *Anti-Discrimination Act* 1977 s 54 (1) (b) excepted from the Act's purview things done in accordance with such legal requirements, the Tribunal felt able to conclude, nevertheless, that the regulations also were compatible with the printing of the ballot papers in Braille, as Mr Fittler had demanded. (In preference to that, as we have seen, the New South Wales government instead created the internet-based voting option for State elections.) But Australian electoral statutes cannot and should not be subjected to such liberties, given the clear terms of s 54 (1) (b) and the fact that our electoral legislation is distinguished by its relentless detail and the prescriptiveness of the provisions regulating official performance of electoral procedures in aid of ensuring that, as far as possible, electoral law is certain and has an answer to every question that may conceivably arise. While this is not a goal that can ever be perfectly achieved, a statute that had achieved it so far as it clearly required ballot papers to be in the English alphabet was undermined by the Tribunal's decision.

Furthermore, the *Anti-Discrimination Act* 1977 ss 49C, 49M (2) also contains an exception allowing discrimination on the basis of disability when 'unjustifiable hardship' would be imposed on the other party to the transaction by eliminating discrimination; to get around this obstacle the Tribunal employed the ridiculous argument that no-one other than Mr Fittler had asked for a Braille ballot paper on the election day and the consequences of extending such a facility to all other blind people in New South Wales could therefore be entirely disregarded in its decision.[83]

81 At [80] – [82].

82 Then the *Local Government (Elections) Regulation* 1998, r. 38 (5) and (8) and Schedule 8, Forms 4, 5 and 6; now the *Local Government (General) Regulation* 2005, r. 305 (5), (8) and Schedule 11, Forms 4, 5 and 6. However, r. 388A of the latter Regulations now allows for Braille ballot papers in local government elections; 'iVote' is available only in State elections.

83 At [97].

Later cases establish the common-sense proposition that, in considering what counts as 'unjustifiable hardship', the defendant is of course permitted to point out the consequences for it not just in relation to the person currently seeking redress, but in making the rule that would accommodate that one person apply to all others in a comparable position.[84] But the New South Wales Tribunal's decision was not appealed against; it may be speculated that, despite the ruling's obvious deficiencies, the government decided to acquiesce in it by creating 'iVote' rather than appeal and thereby appear to be hostile to disabled voting rights.

It is not unknown – indeed, it is only natural and human – for tribunals that are set up to right the genuine disadvantages suffered by identified groups to become partial to fulfilling the task for which they were set up, rather than declaring, even when the law – properly interpreted – requires them to do so, that nothing can be done under the law as it stands. To this may sometimes be added a certain level of disregard for the broader cost of taking action compared to the various other priorities for governmental action. It is also, finally, unsurprising that an anti-discrimination tribunal might pay insufficient regard to the need for certainty in applying the electoral legislation, with which it does not frequently deal.

As far as can be determined, no comparable case has been brought in any other Australian jurisdiction. In all of them except South Australia and the Northern Territory some provision for secret voting by the blind now exists.[85] Victoria's off-line, but fully computerised system caters for the desire of blind voters for complete privacy. As noted above, Western Australia and Tasmania have developed simple computer-assisted voting options involving the printing out of the ballot paper by a computer to which the elector conveys his vote via a keypad, followed by its deposit in a traditional ballot box. They have thus also obviated the need for the blind to commence litigation seeking the same level of privacy as everyone else. At federal level, action has been taken to deal with the problem without using computers. As we have already seen, telephone voting is used there and the process is set up so as to assure secrecy. It is therefore not necessarily the case that, despite the views of the South Australian Equal Opportunity Tribunal quoted earlier, electronic voting is the only possible solution to the difficulties in this area. Australian hesitancy about electronic voting has led some jurisdictions to accommodate the special needs of the handicapped, if at all, by other means, and others to adopt the simplest form of computer-assisted voting that can be imagined.

84 *King* v. *Jetstar Airways* (2012) 286 ALR 149, 189–92; (2012) 293 ALR 613, 624f.

85 The Electoral Commission of South Australia has set itself the goal of conducting a trial of electronic voting in the State election of 2018: see its 'Disability Access and Inclusion Plan', available at: http://www.ecsa.sa.gov.au/component/edocman/?task=document.download&id=25&Itemid=0.

Conclusion

Almost two-and-a-half millennia ago, Socrates is said to have recalled being ridiculed when he was unable to conduct a simple vote:

> οὐκ εἰμὶ τῶν πολιτικῶν, καὶ πέρυσι βουλεύειν λαχών, ἐπειδὴ ἡ φυλὴ ἐπρυτάνευε καὶ ἔδει με ἐπιψηφίζειν, γέλωτα παρεῖχον καὶ οὐκ ἠπιστάμην ἐπιψηφίζειν. (I am not one of the politicians, and indeed they laughed at me for not knowing the electoral procedure when I was elected to the council last year and my tribe presided so that I had to take the vote.)[86]

Electronic voting is considerably more complicated than the voting system that tripped up Socrates – it involves difficult challenges which Australia has so far, and largely by refusing to participate, managed to avoid, being wary not so much of ridicule but of novelty in tried and tested democratic processes which had their origins in the grant of full self-government to all but one of the Australian colonies in the mid-1850s. As we have seen, there are some exceptions, most notably in New South Wales and the Australian Capital Territory, for Australians are, of course, aware that their traditional electoral processes are neither perfectly suitable for all people in all situations nor free of all vulnerabilities to error and fraud – as was most recently shown with the loss of 1,370 ballot papers in Western Australia, referred to earlier, and the consequent need to repeat a State-wide election. But overall, in this field, Australia has been distinguished largely by its caution, which is well-founded given the surpassing importance of the topic and the fact that technology has by no means reached a stage at which it could be said that it was clearly superior, on any measure, to traditional methods in dealing with the great majority of voters who are not handicapped nor outside the country.

In the consequent absence of any direct experience with case law and electronic voting, it is difficult to speculate about what factual circumstances might give rise to possible challenges in the future. Experience shows that problems often arise where they are least expected to do so – indeed, many would not have dared to hope that the limited operation of electronic voting in Australia so far could have been as smooth as it has been. To some extent, solving problems as they arise and not beforehand is the point of a system of case law: answers can be postponed to questions until the precise shape and circumstances of those questions are known.

Should something go awry, then case law developed with traditional voting methods in mind presents us with a number of general principles which were conveniently summarised in *Mitchell* v. *Bailey (No. 2)*[87] and could be easily adapted, with the change of a few words (such as 'ballot paper'), to a case involving electronic voting:

86 Socrates in Plato, *Gorgias*, secs. 473e – 474a.

87 (2008) 169 FCR 529, 549.

> [T]he two cardinal principles are those identified by Gummow J. in *Langer v. Commonwealth*[88] namely 'that the ballot, being a means of protecting the franchise, should not be made an instrument to defeat it and that, in particular, doubtful questions of form should be resolved in favour of the franchise where there is no doubt as to the real intention of the voter'. ... Other, subordinate, principles may be identified which assist in giving effect to the two cardinal principles. These are:
>
> - When seeking to determine the voter's intention resort must be had, exclusively, to what the voter has written on the ballot-paper.
>
> - The ballot-paper should be read and construed as whole.
>
> - A voter's intention will not be expressed with the necessary clarity unless the intention is unmistakeable and can be ascertained with certainty. A Court of Disputed Returns must not resort to conjecture or the drawing of inferences in order to ascertain a voter's intention.

How precisely these principles would 'cash out' in a case involving electronic voting, and what they would reveal, for example, about the concepts of verifiability and integrity that lie in the background of such case law, cannot be said unless and until such a case arises.

References

Allen Consulting Group, *Evaluation of Technology-assisted Voting Provided at the New South Wales State General Election, March 2011* (Allen Consulting Group, Melbourne 2011).

Barrat et al., 'Internet Voting and Individual Verifiability: The Norwegian Return Codes', available at: http://www.e-voting.cc/wp-content/uploads/downloads/2012/07/35-45_Barrat_et-al_Norway-Verifiability.pdf.

Brent, 'The Rise of the Returning Officer: How Colonial Australia Developed Advanced Electoral Institutions' (PhD thesis, Australian National University 2008).

Burton et al., 'A Supervised Verifiable Voting Protocol for the Victorian Electoral Commission', available at: http://epubs.surrey.ac.uk/723026/.

——, 'Using Prêt à Voter in Victorian State Elections', available at: http://epubs.surrey.ac.uk/726039/1/EVT.pdf.

Cooke, *The Americans: Fifty Letters from America on Our Life and Times* (Bodley Head, London 1979).

88 (1996) 186 CLR 302, 347f.

Elections A.C.T., *Report on the A.C.T. Legislative Assembly Election 2012* (Elections A.C.T., Canberra 2013).
Electoral Commission of New South Wales, submission to Electoral Matters Committee, Victoria, 30 January 2013, available at: http://www.parliament.vic.gov.au/images/stories/committees/emc/ifvea/Submissions/Submissions_2013/No_6_Electoral_Commission_New_South_Wales.pdf.
Electoral Council of Australia and New Zealand, *Internet Voting in Australian Election Systems* (2013), available at: http://www.eca.gov.au/research/files/internet-voting-australian-election-systems.pdf.
Electoral Matters Committee (Victoria), *Inquiry into the Conduct of the 2010 Victorian State Election and Matters Related Thereto* (Parliamentary Paper No. 114/2010-2014).
——, *Inquiry into the Future of Victoria's Electoral Administration* (Parliamentary Paper No. 307/2010-2014), available at http://www.parliament.vic.gov.au/images/stories/committees/emc/ifvea/Submissions/Submissions_2013/No_5_Victorian_Electoral_Commission.pdf.
Gageler, 'The Practice of Disputed Returns for Commonwealth Elections' in Orr/Mercurio/Williams (eds), *Realising Democracy: Electoral Law in Australia* (Federation, Leichhardt 2003).
Green, 'Transparency and Elections in Australia: The Role of Scrutineers in the Australian Electoral Process' in Orr/Mercurio/Williams (eds), *Realising Democracy: Electoral Law in Australia* (Federation, Leichhardt 2003).
Heeney, 'The False Promise of Elections on the Internet' (2014) 58:4 *Quadrant* 34.
Hill, 'Informal Voting under a System of Compulsory Voting' in Tham/Costar/Orr (eds), *Electoral Democracy: Australian Prospects* (Melbourne University Press, Melbourne 2011).
Holmes, *E-Voting: The Promise and the Practice* (Parliamentary Library, Canberra 2012).
Hughes, 'Institutionalising Electoral Integrity' in Sawer (ed.), *Elections: Full, Free and Fair* (Federation, Leichhardt 2001).
Joint Standing Committee on Electoral Matters, *The 2004 Federal Election: Report of the Inquiry into the Conduct of the 2004 Federal Election and Matters Related Thereto* (Commonwealth of Australia, Canberra 2005).
——, *Report on the 2007 Federal Election Electronic Voting Trials* (Parliament House, Canberra 2009).
——, *Interim Report on the Inquiry into the Conduct of the 2013 Federal Election – Senate Voting Practices* (The Committee, Canberra 2014).
——, *Second Interim Report on the Inquiry into the Conduct of the 2013 Federal Election: An Assessment of Electronic Voting Options* (The Committee, Canberra 2014).
Kelly, 'Australian Electoral Administration and Electoral Integrity' in Tham/Costar/Orr (eds), *Electoral Democracy: Australian Prospects* (Melbourne University Press, Melbourne 2011).

Lardy, 'Modernising Elections: The Silent Premises of the Electoral Pilot Schemes' [2003] *PL* 6.

Legal Affairs and Community Safety Committee, *Electoral Reform Amendment Bill 2013: Report No. 56* (The Committee, Brisbane 2014).

McKenna, 'Building a "Closet of Prayer" in the New World: The Story of the "Australian Ballot"' in Sawer (ed.), *Elections: Full, Free and Fair* (Federation, Leichhardt 2001).

Mercurio, 'Overhauling Australian Democracy: The Benefits and Burdens of Internet Voting' (2002) 21 *U Tas LR* 23.

——, 'Beyond the Paper Ballot: Exploring Computerised Voting' in Orr/Mercurio/Williams (eds), *Realising Democracy: Electoral Law in Australia* (Federation, Leichhardt 2003).

——, 'Discrimination in Electoral Law: Using Technology to Extend the Secret Ballot to Disabled and Illiterate Voters' (2003) 28 *Alt LJ* 272.

Orr, 'The Choice not to Choose: Commonwealth Electoral Law and the Withholding of Preferences' (1997) 23 *Mon ULR* 285.

——, 'The Ritual and Aesthetic in Electoral Law' (2004) 32 *Fed LR* 425.

——, *The Law of Politics: Elections, Parties and Money in Australia* (Federation, Leichhardt 2010).

Orr/Williams, 'Electoral Challenges: Judicial Review of Parliamentary Elections in Australia' (2001) 23 *Syd LR* 53.

Price Waterhouse Coopers, *Technology Assisted Voting Audit*, p. 5, available at: http://www.elections.nsw.gov.au/__data/assets/pdf_file/0007/93481/iVote_Audit_report_PIR_Final.pdf.

Saunders, 'Concepts of Equality in the Australian Constitution' in Lindell (ed.), *Future Directions in Australian Constitutional Law: Essays in Honour of Professor Leslie Zines* (Federation, Leichhardt 1994).

Tasmanian Electoral Commission, *Fifth Annual Report 2009–2010* (Tasmanian Electoral Commission 2010).

Taylor, 'Constitutional Restrictions on Touch-Screen Voting Computers in Germany' (2010) 9 *Election LJ* 443.

Teague, Submission to the Electoral Matters Committee, Parliament of Victoria, available at: http://www.parliament.vic.gov.au/images/stories/committees/No_14_Vanessa_Teague.pdf.

Western Australian Electoral Commission, *Annual Report 2012–2013* (The Commission, Perth 2013).

Chapter 14

Venezuela: Finding the Relationship between E-Voting and Democracy

Rubén Martínez Dalmau

Introduction

Electronic voting has a central role in the consolidation of the guarantees in the electoral process. Venezuela was a pioneer country in the implementation of electronic voting not only in Latin America but also in the world. Prior to the 1999 Constitution, the electronic ballot box was used in major elections, including the election in December 1999 that resulted in the end of four decades of agreement between parties (*puntofijismo*), which agreement has started to fray in the middle of the 1990s (Álvarez Díaz, 1996:43). During the 2000s, the electronic voting system progressed technically and politically. Somehow, the objective of Venezuelans has been to define the relationship between e-voting and democracy; it is a relationship that has taken place in a context of high political polarization, in which electronic voting has served both to legitimize the transparency of the elections and, at the same time as an element of suspicion by some sectors of the opposition (Martínez Dalmau, 2013).

Despite the importance of electronic voting, the Venezuelan case law on the subject is not extensive. The laws that have developed the implementation of electronic voting have largely been based on international recommendations, but have been adapted to local needs. The controversies regarding of the results of the elections have been more political than legal. The judges, therefore, have not made many decisions on electronic voting. Furthermore, the Venezuelan Constitution of 1999 did not progress towards a concentrated control of constitutionality, and the Constitutional Chamber of the Superior Court of Justice does not have all the tools needed to make a *strong* interpretation of the Constitution.

Despite the small number of juridical decisions on electronic voting to date, we do have some exemplars. There are two important decisions of the Supreme Court: *Militantes por la Libertad & Co. v CNE* (2005) Electoral Chamber TSJ,[1] regarding the 2004 recall, and the most recent *Mesa de la Unidad Democrática v CNE* (2013) Constitutional Chamber TSJ,[2] which concerned the presidential elections of 2013. It should be added that the Constitutional Court is responsible

1 http://www.tsj.gov.ve/decisiones/selec/julio/86-140705-000082.htm.

2 http://www.tsj.gov.ve/decisiones/scon/agosto/1115-7813-2013-13-0565.html.

for exercising constitutional jurisdiction under Article 266 of the Constitution of the Bolivarian Republic of Venezuela; its decisions are binding on the other chambers of the Supreme Court and other judges of the Republic.

The Supreme Court of Justice was created by the Venezuelan Constitution of 1999 and consists of six specialized chambers. The Electoral Chamber has jurisdiction over claims against the acts of the Electoral Power; but the Constitutional Chamber, as has been said, is competent to declare the total or partial nullity of public acts contrary to the Constitution. The statute of the Tribunal is set forth in Articles 253 and following of the Constitution and the Organic Law of the Supreme Court of Justice of May 19, 2004.

It is necessary to note that the Venezuelan cases occurred in a polarized political context between supporters of Hugo Chávez and his followers, on the one hand, and their opponents, on the other. There is not a general climate of acceptance and trust of electronic voting. The suspicion of electoral fraud, or the use of new technologies to control the vote, remains widespread in the country. This situation is, however, related to the particular political tension arising from the attempted coup of Hugo Chávez (2002) and the recall referendum that Chávez finally won in 2004. The constancy of this tension does not diminish the importance of e-voting: on the contrary, continuing the use of a manual system in which fraud was part of Venezuela's electoral history and made it difficult to interpret the behavior of voters (Bunimov-Parra, 1968; Jiménez, 1987), would possibly have led to even more violent conflict.

This chapter aims to analyze the main decisions of the Venezuelan Supreme Court on electronic voting, considering the disputes raised by the applicants and the solutions given by the judges. In that sense, it will start with a short overview of the history and operation of electronic voting in Venezuela; subsequently reviewing the decision on *Militantes por la Libertad & Co. v CNE* (2005) Electoral Chamber TSJ, followed by the arguments of *Mesa de la Unidad Democrática v CNE* (2013) Constitutional Chamber TSJ, which consolidates the previous decision discussed. The work will end with brief conclusions on the above.

Electronic Voting in Venezuela: Between Political Difficulties and Electoral Advances

Venezuela has been one of the first countries in the world to incorporate new technologies in the electoral process, and is currently one of the most experienced countries in the world in the use of electronic voting (Carey, 2003). With the approval of the Law of Suffrage and Political Participation (*Ley Orgánica del Sufragio y Participación Política*) of 1997, the Venezuelan electoral process was reformed and it was decided to automate it. Between 1999 and 2003 the electronic ballot box was used. This technology, based on an Optical Character Recognition (OCR) system, was provided by the Spanish company Indra. The vote, in this system, did not take place directly on the machine: it was manually marked on a ballot. Thus the system was a counting machine that used scanning technologies to read the marked ballots at the time of placing them in the box. Its purpose was to count votes quickly, but it still was mainly paper-based. During the elections held between 1999 and 2000 these OCR scanners were present in all polling stations; because of their introduction, the design of the ballot had to be modified, so that its width was compatible with the input requirement of the machines. Because of the electoral regulations that were current at that time in the country, in some cases ballots were more than a meter long and 24 centimeters wide. The introduction of these machines also involved a strong civic campaign to teach people how to mark the ovals drawn on the ballots, so that they could be read by the OCR scanner (RIAL, 2004:88). No relevant case law has come before Venezuelan judges since the introduction of the OCR counting of paper ballots.

Widespread electoral fraud had been the tradition during the *puntofijismo* period. A semblance of representative democracy – limited to a two-party electoral competition (Democratic Action [*Acción Democrática*] and COPEI) – was built despite the presence of vice in manual voting procedures, with political representatives being the sole presence during the counting of ballots ("The record kills the vote"—*Acta mata voto*). The situation was inflamed by the country's oil affluence, which imploded during the crisis of the 1980s and 1990s (VICIANO PASTOR and MARTÍNEZ DALMAU, 2001). The electronic ballot box helped in eradicating electoral fraud and it improved transparency in elections, facilitating the emergence of new political landscape in the late twentieth century, particularly after the elections of December 1998.

The recall referendum of August 15, 2004 was important from the point of view of electronic voting because the electronic ballot box (OCR) was replaced by the direct-recording electronic voting machine (DRE). It is this system, with some changes, which has since been used in all elections in the country. For the implementation of the new electoral technology the National Electoral Council decided to use equipment provided by the consortium of Smartmatic, Bizta and CANTV (SBC). The system consists of a touch-screen terminal where the voter chooses an option by tapping directly on the choices that appear on the screen. Before that, the elector has been identified at the polling station by use of a fingerprint machine. Following the act of voting, the electronic voting machine issues a receipt for the vote (technology known as voter-verified paper trail or VVPT), which is deposited by the voter into a box for subsequent physical audit of the electronic results. Once the voting is closed, the aggregation system totals the votes and decides who is the winner in each case. It stores the scrutiny records of the voting machines. It also issues a final paper proof of the results (GONZÁLEZ, 2012:308–10), and the system transmits the results to the tabulation center. Voting machines do not have internet access; data are encrypted and transmitted through a private network, and there is no connection between the voting machines and the data network before transmission.

Venezuela's electronic voting process can be seen to be in accordance with international standards. The voting machine's interface is easy for the elector to see and use, and voting requires no previous computer knowledge. Nonetheless an information campaign regarding the system is carried out by the National Electoral Council prior to the vote. The National Electoral Council has also been legally mandated to resolve specific issues related to use of the machine by people with disabilities, and to provide contingency for any specific problems, such as technical questions, that could occur with the use of machines during the election process. The system therefore falls in line with the principles of universal suffrage as determined by the Council of Europe,[3] although that is only one reference point among the international standards on electronic voting.

Strictly speaking the Venezuelan voting process is a mixed system because it retains some manual elements, essentially the paper trail necessary for subsequent audits. In comparative electoral systems, in some countries the paper trail is not considered necessary to provide confidence in electronic voting (Thompson Jiménez, 2009:21). In Venezuela, where the electronic voting system had to help solve important problems of electoral and political polarization but still faced major suspicions, this paper trail was decisive because it enabled audit results based on physical evidence; thus it has diminished the specter of election fraud (Martínez Dalmau, 2013:15). Indeed, incorporation of the paper trail in voting machines was a political demand made by the Venezuelan opposition; they demanded that the Government perform, after the elections, a physical audit on a random sample and thus directly compare the results of the paper trail of votes and the results stored in the computer system (Thompson Jiménez, 2009:20–21).[4]

3 "I. Universal suffrage. 1. The voter interface of an e-voting system shall be understandable and easily usable. 2. Possible registration requirements for e-voting shall not pose an impediment to the voter participating in e-voting. 3. E-voting systems shall be designed, as far as it is practicable, to maximise the opportunities that such systems can provide for persons with disabilities. 4. Unless channels of remote e-voting are universally accessible, they shall be only an additional and optional means of voting." Council of Europe, *Recommendation Rec(2004)11 of the Committee of Ministers to member states on legal, operational and technical standards for e-voting*, September 30, 2004. We should note that the adoption of the recommendation of the Council of Europe subsequent to the adoption of the rules for the recall referendum of August 15, 2004; therefore, it is not possible to conclude that the recommendation had a direct effect on the Venezuelan regulation.

4 In line with the mentioned Rec(2004)11 of the Council of Europe: "24. The components of the e-voting system shall be disclosed, at least to the competent electoral authorities, as required for verification and certification purposes. 25. Before any e-voting system is introduced, and at appropriate intervals thereafter, and in particular after any changes are made to the system, an independent body, appointed by the electoral authorities, shall verify that the e-voting system is working correctly and that all the necessary security measures have been taken. 26. There shall be the possibility for a recount. Other features of the e-voting system that may influence the correctness of the results shall be verifiable. 27. The e-voting system shall not prevent the partial or complete re-run of an election or a referendum." Ibid.

The finger print machine was another element of the Venezuelan electronic voting system that was incorporated in the recall of 2004. The Authentication System of Voting (*Sistema de Autenticación de Votantes*), as it is officially known, is a biometric recognition system that identifies the voter through the fingerprint scanner. The Authentication System of Voting stores the voter identification data and checks the polling station database to verify that the voter belongs to the station, and has not already voted (González, 2012:307–8). These machines, which record the fingerprints of voters who access the polling station, are used to update the electoral register.[5] More recently a connection was established between the fingerprint machine and the electoral roll; now it is the fingerprint machine that allows access to the voting system, so duplication or voter impersonation is avoided.[6]

The use of fingerprint machines has not been uncontroversial; their introduction initially delayed the voting process, and aroused some fears about the demise of the secret ballot due to suspicions regarding a possible connection between the fingerprint machine and the voting terminal. This technological tool, designed to improve the electoral system, was seen by many people, especially those close to the opposition, as a means of intimidation. Some government supporters hinted that the authorities were able to track the vote of each elector, this provoked the opposition to denounce the reliability of the mechanism and to allege election fraud (Álvarez Díaz, 2009:67). These complaints led to the *Decision Militantes por la Libertad & Co. v CNE* (2005) Electoral Chamber TSJ, to which we refer below. Ultimately, the fingerprint machines have been shown to be a useful mechanism to improve the electronic voting process, but the controversy is not yet over, as demonstrated in the last presidential election, which led to *Mesa de la Unidad Democrática v CNE* (2013) Constitutional Chamber TSJ.

Indeed, despite the features of electronic voting in Venezuela, the issue of its reliability is still raised. The test of transparency and the auditing of electronic

5 As recognized by International IDEA, new technologies including scanners and biometrics for voter registration can help to improve the quality of electoral processes, especially where large amounts of data have to be processed quickly, as they do in the delimitation of electoral districts, voter registration, the voting and vote-counting process. Opinions are therefore divided on the question of the sustainability of this electoral development. (International IDEA 2006:261).

6 The Integral Authentication System (*Sistema de Autenticación Integral*) was used completely for the first time in the presidential elections of October 7, 2012. Previously, the fingerprint scanners had been used to obtain information about the voters, and were not connected with the voting machine; so voter identification was mainly through traditional means.

voting made both by the Venezuelan authorities[7] and international organizations[8] should have increased reliability. But the political polarization of the country, a difficult to remove tradition of electoral fraud, and the communication difficulties of the National Electoral Council have not helped to raise confidence in electronic voting as much as would have been desirable. The main example of the manifestation of this lack of confidence, as we shall see, was the 2004 presidential recall, which electoral process was repeated in the presidential elections of 2013.

Militantes por la Libertad & Co. v CNE (2005): The Security of Voting Machines

The political context of *Militantes por la Libertad & Co. v CNE* (2005) Electoral Chamber TSJ is well known. On August 15, 2004, the first presidential recall in Latin America took place in Venezuela; it was made possible by the incorporation of the recall referendum in Article 72 of the Venezuelan Constitution:

> All magistrates and other offices filled by popular vote are subject to revocation.
>
> Once half of the term of office to which an official has been elected has elapsed, a number of voters constituting at least 20% of the voters registered in the pertinent circumscription may call for a referendum to revoke such official's mandate.
>
> When a number of voters equal to or greater than the number of those who elected the official vote in favor of revocation, provided that a number of voters equal to or greater than 25% of the total number of registered voters have voted in the revocation election, the official's mandate shall be deemed revoked, and immediate action shall be taken to fill the permanent vacancy as provided for in this Constitution and by law.

---

7 The Venezuelan ordinary procedure provides 14 different audits: voting software, production of voting machines, voting machines predispatching, infrastructure, Biometric Identification System, production Biometric Identification System, network data transmission, aggregation, close, reports, posterior, electronic ballots, printed notebooks and indelible ink. In each election the National Electoral Council establishes the audit process in accordance with Articles 156–63 of the Electoral Law of July 31, 2009, and Articles 442–5 of the General Rules of Law Process Election of January 18, 2013.

8 As in the well-known case, in the recall referendum, of the Carter Center and the OAS (Carter Center 2005). Subsequently, civil organizations such as CAPEL (*Centro de Asesoría y Promoción Electoral*—Center for Electoral Promotion and Assistance) participated in the audit, and reported favorably on the correct operation of the system. Some reports claim Venezuelan observer organizations were critical of the referendum, but barely made mention of the electronic voting process. See, for example, Súmate (2004).

> The revocation of the mandate for collegiate bodies shall be performed in accordance with the law. During the term to which the official was elected, only one recall petition may be filed.

In 2004 the political situation in Venezuela was characterized by a division between two positions. On the one side stood the government of Hugo Chávez and his allies, who had won the presidential election in 1998 with the purpose of a democratic regeneration of the country. In this sense, they called a referendum on the need for a Constituent Assembly, and boosted the constituent process. Venezuela's most democratic Constitution to date entered into force on December 1999, and replaced the Constitution of 1961, which was the product of the coalition of the two major political parties (*puntofijismo*); previous constitutions, including the 1961 Constitution, were not approved by popular referendum and most of them were not the result of a democratic Constituent Assembly (Viciano Pastor and Martínez Dalmau: 2001). On the other side stood the Chávez opponents, a heterogeneous political, social and economic group who had participated in the Constituent Assembly only timidly. Part of this group supported the coup attempt against the Chávez government that took place in 2002, and the subsequent economic strangulation of the State (*paro petrolero*, oil strike). With the participation of almost 70 percent, victory in the recall by Hugo Chávez with 59.1 percent of the votes offered a democratic solution to the crisis and reduced the chances of a coup, but it did not improve the lack of political dialogue or the extreme polarization of political positions.[9]

The voting process in the recall referendum of August 15, 2004 was electronic in 4,766 polling stations (57 percent), covering 89 percent of the voting population. In 3,628 polling stations, mostly rural areas with small populations, the vote was manual (Martínez Dalmau 2009:103). As has been mentioned, according to negotiations with the opposition and the recommendations of IDEA, the machines approved by the National Electoral Council (CNE) incorporated paper support to perform an audit of electronic voting with a physical trace. For IDEA (2006:243), if a fault occurs or challenges are presented, DRE systems without a paper trail cannot verify the result. Introduction of traditional paper support was an additional guarantee to convince skeptics, who were especially sensitive in such a polarized climate (Barrat i Esteve 2007:122).

Militantes por la Libertad & Co. v CNE (2005) Electoral Chamber TSJ was a result of the accumulation of several cases that were presented to the Court during the months following the publication of the official results of the referendum. The appellants acted in the electoral process as participants in the recall and, therefore, as representatives of collective interests. Some of the appellants were part of civil

9 For some authors, the discrepancies between the exit polls before the election and the final results offered by the National Electoral Council indicate that the official results should be suspected of fraud. Cf. Prado and Sansó (2011:517–27); Grima and Ríos Insua (2010:224).

society groups who had prompted the recall, such as "Militantes por la Libertad" (Militants for Freedom) and "Democracia Siglo XXI" (Twenty-first Century Democracy). Senior Venezuelan opposition figures such as Timoteo Zambrano also appeared in the proceedings. The main common denominator of all the appellants was a request that the elections carried out through electronic voting systems be canceled, and that the voting process be repeated manually.

One of the major complaints of the appellants concerned deficiencies regarding decisions on manual counts (or rather, the lack of manual counts). Article 74.8 of the Law of Suffrage and Political Participation and Article 44 of the Rules Regulating the Referendum Process (*Normas para Regular los Procesos de Referendos Revocatorios de Mandatos de Cargos de Elección Popular*) establishes scrutiny, defined as the recognition and counting of votes in elections. Therefore, the votes, and ballot papers deposited in the ballot boxes, had to be scrutinized in a public act once the polling station had closed. But this was impossible because the votes had already been cast using the electronic voting system, and did not exist physically. Therefore, the law could not be applied.

According to the judges[10] of the Electoral Chamber of the Supreme Court, the core of the complaint is that once the act of voting had ended the National Electoral Council should proceed to a manual count of ballots, and only after completing the manual count can it proceed with data transmission. One of the main arguments mentioned by the complainants was the unconstitutionality of electronic voting because the 1999 Venezuelan Constitution expressly mentions transparency in elections.[11] For this reason, some articles of the decisions of the National Electoral Council on how votes were processed would be invalid.

But the Court states that, in accordance with Articles 293[12] and 294[13] *in fine* of the Constitution of the Bolivarian Republic of Venezuela, the Electoral Power is governed by the principles of electoral process efficiency and speed of the acts of voting and counting. These requirements are developed in Article 3[14] of the

10 *Militantes por la Libertad & Co. v CNE* (2005) Electoral Chamber TSJ, para. IX.2.

11 Article 294: "The organs comprising the Electoral Power are governed by the principles of organic independence, functional and budgetary autonomy, separation of the electoral organs from the political parties, impartiality and citizen participation, as well as decentralization of electoral administration, transparency and expeditiousness of the voting process and tallying of votes."

12 Article 293: "The following are the functions of the Electoral Power: 1. To regulate election law and resolve any doubts and unregulated areas raised by or contained in such law .... 5. Organization, administration, direction and vigilance of all acts relating to elections to fill public offices by popular vote, as well as referenda ... Electoral Power organs shall guarantee the equality, reliability, impartiality, transparency and efficiency of electoral processes, as well as the implementation of the personal suffrage and proportional representation."

13 *Supra* fn 11.

14 Article 3: "The Electoral Power is governed by the principles of organizational independence, functional and budgetary autonomy, partisanship representation in electoral

Electoral Law of November 19, 2002 (*Ley Orgánica del Poder Electoral*), which enshrines the principle of speed in all actions and decisions of the Electoral Power, and Article 4[15] of the same Act, which establishes the duty of the National Electoral Council to ensure the effectiveness of the electoral process. Moreover, Article 154[16] of the Law of Suffrage and Political Participation clearly requires that the processes of voting, counting and aggregation should be entirely automated; thus, even if that law is a pre-constitutional instrument, it is in perfect harmony with the spirit of those constitutional requirements. Speed and effectiveness must be combined rationally with citizen and audit control, and the law does not require that the vote count should be manual. "In other words, it is obvious that the appellants confuse the process that corresponds to the count of votes in automated elections with the count in the manual voting system."[17]

It is not true, therefore, that the votes are not counted in accordance with the law. The judges held that the Law of Suffrage and Political Participation provides that the counting process is electronic (Articles 154[18] and 168[19]), and that manual counting can take place only exceptionally when the electronic count cannot be performed. In the automated process, therefore, the counting is done by the voting machine, and manual counting of the votes is not required. The printing of the report of the overall results provides support for the exercise of control mechanisms and also for a possible appeal. The Supreme Court noted that the Decision of the Electoral Chamber of the Supreme Court No. 114 of October 2, 2000 stated that "the thesis of manual recount would be contrary to the principles contained in the law; we could just imagine the time it would require to count

---

bodies, impartiality and citizen participation, decentralization and electoral administration, cooperation, transparency and speed in all their actions and decisions."

15 Article 4: "The Electoral Power must ensure equality, reliability, impartiality, transparency and effectiveness of electoral processes and the implementation of personal suffrage and proportional representation."

16 Article 154: "The process of voting, counting, calculating totals and determining final results will be fully automated. In cases in which this system is unable to be implemented for reasons of transport, security, infrastructure services, which are expressly determined well in advance, the National Electoral Council, by special resolution, will allow the manual system of voting, counting aggregating and determining final results, strictly subject to the provisions of this Act and the related Regulations."

17 *Militantes por la Libertad & Co. v CNE* (2005) Electoral Chamber TSJ, para. IX.2.

18 *Supra* fn 16.

19 Article 168: "The counting process will be automated.

The National Electoral Council shall establish the specifications at least six (6) months prior to the date of the election. The ballots are counted manually only in those cases where the conditions of transport, infrastructure and security services do not permit automation.

Whatever automated system (machine-based voting systems) is adopted, it must be auditable.

When these systems transmit results to aggregation centres, these transmissions may be made only to sites and under the conditions specified in the General Election Regulations."

again the votes in an election for Governor or President, during which the country would be marked by political instability." The Court, for these reasons, did not consider repeating the voting process to be appropriate.

Another reason for repeating the vote given by the applicants was related to the fingerprint scanners. In their opinion, the use of fingerprint readers during the act of voting in the recall referendum as a condition to exercise the vote contradicted the rules contained in Articles 63[20] and 64[21] of the Constitution, and Articles 161[22] and 254.3[23] of the Law of Suffrage and Political Participation. The constitutional articles mention the right to vote, and the characteristics of the elections—free, universal, direct and secret—as well as the conditions for voting: being Venezuelan, being 18 years of age, and not being subject to disqualification.

In this regard the Chamber notes that the National Electoral Council had issued the Rules on Procedure and Fingerprint Capture (*Normas sobre el Procedimiento de Captación de Huellas Dactilares y Garantía del Principio un Elector-Un Voto*), published in the Gazette electoral number 207 of August 12, 2004. From the Rules as well as the relevant constitutional and legal provisions, it follows that this requirement does not result in a distortion of the right to vote. Such an assertion is justified by the following reasons: (1) the use of fingerprint readers is an ancillary guarantee of the vote; (2) electoral matters are governed by the principle of *one person, one vote*, which has been expressly recognized by the jurisprudence of the Court (Decision No. 163 of December 18, 2000), and the fingerprint capture is a mechanism for implementing the principle; (3) this procedure is in line with the duty of the National Electoral Council to ensure the principles of reliability, transparency and equality in the electoral process, under Articles 293 and 294 of the Constitution, and Articles 3 and 4 of the Law of the Electoral Power; and (4) it should be noted that the use of fingerprint readers also helps prevent the commission of the offense under Article 256.8 of the Law of Suffrage and Political Participation: vote twice or more, impersonate someone else, or assume the identity of a deceased in voting.

The claim of the appellants was, therefore, denied. In conclusion, the reasoning of the Court that emerges from *Militantes por la Libertad & Co. v CNE* (2005) Electoral Chamber TSJ shows the importance of electronic voting for the Venezuelan electoral system and its relationship to a higher quality of democracy. The legal vote is solely the electronic vote, which replaces the previous ballot

---

20 Article 63: "Suffrage is a right. It shall be exercised through free, universal, direct and secret elections. The law shall guarantee the principle of personal suffrage and proportional representation."

21 Article 64: "All Venezuelans who have reached the age of 18 and are not subject to political disablement or civil interdiction are qualified to vote."

22 Article 161: "Any elector who appears in the Voting Notebook and can be identified with their identity card shall not be denied the right to vote."

23 Article 254: "[The following] Shall be punished by a fine …: 3. The Elections Officer who refuses to accept the vote of an elector entitled to vote."

papers; the paper trail, therefore, is not legally the vote, but physical evidence; the paper trail will only be used for the corresponding audit or in cases where it is impossible to use the electronic machines.

The presence of the paper trace serves, according to the Venezuelan electoral legislation, to detect and correct possible errors of automatic counting. If a comparison between the automatic results and those generated by manual counting result in numerical inconsistencies that cannot be remedied, in accordance with Article 174 of the Electoral Law the results of the official count must be nullified. Thus, the audit involves legal implications in the event of a discrepancy between the two records, even though the discrepancy margin is usually zero or negligible (PRINCE 2006:120).

Mesa de la Unidad Democrática v CNE (2013): Consolidation of the Jurisprudence

On August 7, 2013 the Venezuelan Supreme Court ruled again on electronic voting. This time, however, the case came before the Constitutional Chamber of the Court, not the Electoral Chamber. It is important to remember that the Constitutional Court is responsible for the concentrated control of constitutionality in the Venezuelan judicial system. Its decisions are, therefore, binding on the other chambers of the Supreme Court, as well as on other judges of the Republic. Although this decision is less detailed than the one discussed above, it follows its reasoning and provides very strong constitutional arguments.

As in the previously analyzed decision, this time the court decision took place in a particularly polarized political climate. The death of Hugo Chávez during the course of his mandate as President led to new presidential elections, which took place on April 14, 2013. Chávez supporters presented as their candidate Nicolás Maduro, who had been vice president and inherited the legacy of the deceased. Most of the opposition, grouped around the Coalition for Democratic Unity (*Mesa de la Unidad Democrática*), rallied around Henrique Capriles. The difference between the votes for the two candidates in the elections of April 14, 2013 was very small: 1.49 percent. Maduro was proclaimed winner by the National Electoral Council. The conditions for conflict were ripe.

The claim of the appellant, the Coalition for Democratic Unity, was the annulment of the elections for several reasons. One of the main reasons referred to the electronic vote.[24] The appellants understood that a comprehensive count of the paper trails should take place, because they had detected inconsistencies between vote count records and the results issued by the voting machine. The appellants understood that only the manual recount could resolve these inconsistencies, so they called on the National Electoral Council to undertake this recount.

24 *Mesa de la Unidad Democrática v CNE* (2013) Constitutional Chamber TSJ, para. IV.2.

The Constitutional Chamber of the Supreme Court dismissed the petition. According to *Mesa de la Unidad Democrática v CNE* (2013) Constitutional Chamber TSJ, it was not appropriate to demand the National Electoral Council perform a manual count of the ballots. As a main argument, the Court reiterated the jurisprudence of the *Militantes por la Libertad & Co. v CNE* (2005) Electoral Chamber TSJ case: by law, the count is automatic, not manual. Manual counting can be performed only in cases prescribed by law, for audit during a challenge process or for exceptional reasons. The paper trail is, therefore, incidental (the legal vote is the electronic vote), and must be considered in the usual audit processes and in particular cases in which examination is requested, but not as a general procedure. This decision will therefore be the binding decision for the judges of the Republic.

Recognizing the importance of the paper trail (VVPT) for the Venezuelan e-voting system is necessary as the counting of the paper trail is just one of the many steps involved in the audit of the electoral process, but politically is the most important one, as has been revealed in the analyzed sentences. According to Article 437 of the General Rules of Law Process Election of January 18, 2013, citizen verification involves the comparison of the paper trail with the data reflected in the electronic record. It is, therefore, a highly important element in the verification process. Article 439 provides the National Electoral Council the ability to determine the number of polling stations that will be verified in every election. The selection of polling stations will be by lot, but the law does not set a minimum number of polling stations to be audited; the National Electoral Council determines the scope of the audit. This is, in fact, a loophole with important political consequences for transparency in elections. In summary, the two analyzed judgments of the Supreme Court show that the paper trail is important to enable the audit of elections and provide more transparency to the act of voting, but in no case should it replace the count made by the electronic machines.

Conclusions

The problem faced by electronic voting in Venezuela is not a technical problem; not even a legal problem, because the Supreme Court decisions have been clear in supporting the constitutionality of electronic voting. It is a matter of trust. Or rather, distrust. Distrust of the use made by technology in cases such as that brought by the people who signed the recall referendum in 2004 (*Tascón list*[25]); mistrust that the internet connection can be used to control the vote; distrust of the possible connection between the fingerprint machine and the voting terminal, or that the sequential order of the operation could end the right to a secret vote. The

25 List of names posted on the Internet by Luis Tascón, deputy of Hugo Chávez's political movement, where the names of people who had signed the petition for the recall referendum could be found. Cf. Spanakos (2011:14.27).

Venezuelan case reveals the relationship between reality and perception in the use of technology in the electoral processes, given that sometimes even the most reliable technological tool might prove useless if citizen perception points to the opposite (Gutiérrez 2012:65), although, as discussed above, suspicions are usually based on unfounded fears; on the other hand, the Venezuelan authorities have decided to make a total migration to e-voting, besides implementing additional technological elements to—allegedly—enhance the integrity and quality of the democratic process and its results (Reniu, 2011:139)

Militantes por la Libertad & Co. v CNE (2005) Electoral Chamber TSJ and *Mesa de la Unidad Democrática v CNE* (2013) Constitutional Chamber TSJ reveal the confidence of the Supreme Court in electronic voting. The arguments of the appellants are based on interpretations of constitutional and legal norms; in no case was there a disagreement regarding the results of the manual recounts to which the opposition had access. But there may be an alternative interpretation of the relationship between e-voting and constitutional objectives (especially the democratic principle), which is made by the Supreme Court. It is true, as we have seen, that the Venezuelan system of electronic voting is more auditable than others thanks to the presence of the paper trail that, while not replacing the automated count, makes the system more transparent and reliable. Without this physical evidence, the Supreme Court decisions could have been different. In Venezuela, the judges understand confidence is a decisive element in electoral voting systems, in the same manner that the German Federal Constitutional Court did in 2009 (Barrat i Esteve, 2009:3–11).

As Montoya said, the Venezuelan case makes it clear that the struggle for transparency lies beyond the establishment of the numerical or procedural constructions on which it is based—it must be grounded on respect for autonomous institutions, the integrity and rights of citizens, and the implementation of the nation's laws and agreements, as well as on a will to reach compromise with adversaries. In such an atmosphere, it is possible to reach consensus through political negotiation. Transparency is not possible without the trust that evolves from such respect, as well as deference to the principles of democracy. Transparency is a socially embedded process that is always in the making, built on historical experience, consultations and willingness by all (Montoya 2008:278).

References

Ángel Eduardo Álvarez Díaz, *El sistema político venezolano: crisis y transformaciones* (Universidad Central de Venezuela, Caracas, 1996).

——, "El Consejo Nacional Electoral y los dilemas de la competencia electoral en Venezuela" (2009) *América Latina Hoy* 51, 61–76.

Jordi Barrat i Esteve, "El voto electrónico en Latinoamérica: radiografía de un proceso en vías de consolidación," in Josep Maria Reniu et al., *Voto electrónico. Estudio comparado en una aproximación jurídico-política (Desafíos y posibilidades)* (Fundación Universitaria de Derecho, Administración y Política, Santiago de Querétaro, 2007).

——, "Observación electoral y voto electrónico" (2009) *Revista Catalana de Dret Públic* 39, 1–12.

Boris Bunimov-Parra, *Introducción a la Sociología Electoral Venezolana* (Arte, Caracas, 1968).

John M. Carey, "Discipline, Accountability, and Legislative Voting in Latin America" (2003) *Comparative Politics* 35.2, 191–211.

Carter Center, *Observación del Referendo Revocatorio Presidencial en Venezuela. Informe integral* (Carter Center, Atlanta, GA, 2005).

José Daniel González, "Venezuela: voto electrónico. Auditorías y legitimidad del sistema automatizado de votación" (2012) *Espacio Abierto* 21.2, 305–21.

Carlos Grima and David Ríos Insua, "A Generic System for Remote e-Voting Management," in David Ríos Insua and Simon French (eds), *E-Democracy: A Group Decision and Negotiation Perspective* (Springer, London, 2010).

Pablo Gutiérrez, "Different Views about the Use of Mobile Technology and the Internet in an Election Process from the Perspective of the OAS Observation Missions," in Ravneet Singh et al., *Technology and Citizen Participation in the Construction of Democracy* (Instituto Electoral y de Participación Ciudadana, México, 2012).

International IDEA, *Electoral Management Design: The International IDEA Handbook* (International Institute for Democracy and Electoral Assistance, Stockholm, 2006).

Rafael Jiménez, *Continuismo y reeleccionismo en la Venezuela contemporánea: un tema para la reflexión política de hoy* (Artística, Caracas, 1987).

Rubén Martínez Dalmau, "Observación electoral internacional y voto electrónico: el caso de Venezuela," in Fabiola Meco and Àngela Muñoz (eds), *Observación electoral internacional. Sentido, actores y retos* (Ediciones del CEPS, Valencia, 2009).

——, "Polarización política, administración electoral y voto electrónico en Venezuela" (2013) *Revista General de Derecho Público Comparado* 13, 1–26.

Miguel Montoya, "Transparency as Tool and Weapon: The Case of the Venezuelan Presidential Recall Referendum," in Christina Garsten and Monica Lindh de Montoya (eds), *Transparency in a New Global Order: Unveiling Organizational Visions* (Edward Elgar, Cheltenham, 2008).

Raquel Prado and Bruno Sansó, "The 2004 Venezuelan Presidential Recall Referendum: Discrepancies Between Two Exit Polls and Official Results" (2011) *Statistical Science* 26.4, 517–27.

Alejandro Prince, *Consideraciones, aportes y experiencias para el voto electrónico en Argentina* (Dunken, Buenos Aires, 2006).

Josep Maria Reniu, "(Very) Few Certainties Concerning the Establishment of E-voting" (2011) *Revista de Administración Pública* 46.

Juan Rial, "Posibilidades y límites del voto electrónico" (2004) *Elecciones* 3, 81–108.

Anthony Peter Spanakos, "Citizen Chávez: The State, Social Movements, and Publics" (2011) *Latin American Perspectives* 38.1, 14–27.

Súmate, *Informe White Paper. Protegiendo la integridad del voto* (Súmate, Caracas, 2004).

José Thompson Jiménez, "La experiencia reciente del voto electrónico en América Latina: avances y perspectivas" (2009) *Revista de Derecho Electoral* 7, 1–35.

Roberto Viciano Pastor and Rubén Martínez Dalmau, *Cambio político y proceso constituyente en Venezuela (1998–2000)* (Tirant, Valencia, 2001; *Venezuelan edition*, Vadell Hermanos, Caracas, 2001).

Chapter 15
Conclusions

Ardita Driza Maurer and Jordi Barrat

E-voting has evolved quickly in the past two and a half decades. From an acceptance point of view, it has gone from euphoric introduction (in the hope of increasing participation and other electoral improvements), to total rejection (because of security and transparency concerns), to a more balanced approach (giving priority to specific groups of voters) which tries to exploit the advantages that come with technology while acknowledging and mitigating the associated risks. The challenge for all actors involved lies in the fact that the use of high-tech in votes and elections is a disruptive development that raises new questions. Below we list some of them. Ultimately the challenge is to define a clear, systematic approach in treating digitalized information and the paperless environment in the electoral field. Further we propose a few ideas on how to negotiate the turn.

Legislators are faced with the issue of 'parallelism' between traditional and electronically-backed voting methods. What is similar and what is different? Is existing legislation sufficient to regulate electronically-backed voting or should it be completed by an e-voting specific regulation? What should such regulation contain and at what level of detail? Judges face questions related to the division of competences and responsibilities in this area as well as issues such as the legal conformity of technical solutions and the impossibility of proving alleged defects. Implementation authorities on their side need to clarify their room for manoeuvre in introducing e-voting. Issues such as legal conformity of design, operation and control of an e-voting system are at the centre of their preoccupations. Ensuring such conformity constantly over time and finding ways to make e-voting transparent are others.

The introduction of e-voting cannot be assimilated to a simple extension of existing rules to cover the use of electronically-backed solutions. A rethinking of the requirements and procedures is needed, as is possibly also process re-engineering. E-voting, or more generally computers, have so far been used in a very pedestrian way[1] based on the assumption that, if we use a machine to replace the existing process, the machine must mimic the existing process. But one can do better. It is possible to use the power of ICT systems to come up with better electoral processes. Individual verification as introduced by the so-called second generation e-voting systems is an example of that. The authorities should probably start by recognizing that an automated process is very different from a

1 The authors thank Richard Hill in Geneva for bringing forward this argument.

manual process. Indeed, important improvements in business processes have been achieved precisely by recognizing such differences.

Beyond the challenge of integrating ICTs, the discussion around e-voting can also become an opportunity to review, clarify and formalize current electoral legislation and procedures more generally. The quest for transparency is a good example. Lessons learned through the practical use of e-voting in the past years led to the introduction of verifiable e-voting systems. Legislators, however, may take the opportunity (and in some cases have) to analyse and formalize transparency requirements more broadly, for example by ensuring meaningful observation in the context of traditional voting channels as well.

Below we present a few measures that may help the different players to organize work on e-voting.

The Role of Parliaments

The Constitution and formal laws introduced by parliament enunciate constitutional principles, such as voting freedom, secrecy and equality. Examining the compliance of highly technical secondary regulations to such principles has proven difficult for judges. In this context one should remember that parliaments ensure a democratic oversight, not just through normative initiatives, but also by other means, for example parliamentary control activities such as parliamentary questions, hearings, ad hoc committees. Such an approach allows parliaments to achieve their mission of monitoring electoral management issues. The same happens with other fields where the legal implications of technical developments overwhelm the capacity of traditional parliaments. This type of parliamentary control will be useful to courts when assessing acts and regulations introduced by the executive.

Recommendation 1: Enhance specific parliamentary procedures linked to the oversight of e-voting.

The Election Cycle Approach

E-voting cannot be considered on a short-term basis since it includes several actions that must be performed before and after the so-called election period, which may only encompass a few weeks. E-voting procedures impact the whole electoral cycle:[2] pre-elections, election day, and post-elections. It is therefore more realistic to consider e-voting as a longer-term project intended to improve elections.

2 For an example of the electoral cycle see http://ecycle.idea.int.

Such an approach may require an overall modification of the internal structure of Electoral Management Bodies (EMBs). Timelines, roles, reporting procedures and so on will have to be adapted accordingly.

Recommendation 2: Promote institutional understanding of e-voting's place in the election cycle. EMBs and courts recognize that e-voting is not something to decide shortly before upcoming elections.

The In-house Expertise of Electoral Management Bodies and Courts

If neither EMBs nor courts have developed an internal awareness about the challenges faced with e-voting projects, this will be reflected in their work and decisions. An electoral cycle approach to e-voting becomes difficult if institutional players ignore the real implications of an e-voting initiative. A fair dialogue between vendors and public institutions is impossible if neither EMBs nor courts realize the real consequences that a given commercial proposal entails.

Once the necessity of such a previous institutional capacity building is admitted, it is important to define who provides such expertise. Vendors should not act as the unique information source to provide expertise. Independent experts may be solicited and contradictory opinions should be considered, while recognizing that the final decision rests with the competent authority in line with democratic legitimacy. A plurality of opinions will hopefully inform nuanced and balanced decisions.

Recommendation 3: Foresee specific institutional initiatives to enhance the general awareness of EMBs and courts on e-voting challenges.

The Role of Vendors and Non-Disclosure Agreements

Democratic preoccupations and legitimate commercial interests that underlie the behaviour of vendors, differ. E-voting needs balanced relationships between suppliers and public institutions. Non-Disclosure Agreements (NDA) may constitute barriers when trying to assess such relationships.

As happens in the commercial field, an agreement between two or more parties, when challenged in court, may be found to contain unfair conditions which may be declared void. This approach is intended to protect consumers (e.g. when they take a loan or a mortgage and sign highly technical documents). EMBs are not private players and thus they are subject to different rules, but the agreements that they accept can also contain an inappropriate balance between contradictory interests. Please note that suppliers may encompass e-voting companies as well as other private stakeholders, such as the private firms that carry out certification and audits.

The Finnish experience as well as e-voting implementation in France and the United States, three countries whose approaches are analysed in the book, show that vendors may play a crucial role in disclosing information or, on the contrary, protecting sensitive data on the grounds that their disclosure could endanger other legal goods, such as intellectual property. Norway (not discussed in this book) represents another interesting point of reference on disclosure.

Recommendation 4: Assess the legal implications of Non-Disclosure Agreements, taking into account the different interests at stake.

The Evidentiary Value of Individual and Universal Verifiability

Verifiability appears to be the appropriate way to create a climate of trust between voters, political parties and public institutions. If the e-voting mechanisms themselves allow a broad verification that encompasses both individual and universal verifiability,[3] then the amount of information on the e-voting system that the vendor discloses becomes secondary. The sounder the verifiability introduced in e-voting, the lower the importance of the disclosure arguments discussed above.

Moreover, verifiability could address one of the main problems that we have seen in the case law comparison. Courts regularly require evidence of the alleged problems and that is sometimes difficult to obtain. Sound verification might overcome such a barrier. Given that there are different e-voting platforms and different verifiability systems in use, it is important to clarify the role that proofs obtained through verifiable systems can later play in court.

Verifiability needs to take into account legal and judicial requirements. Again, e-voting is not merely a technical development. It is rather a procedure that should achieve a correct technical performance as well as a proper legal oversight. Furthermore, a perfect technical verification scheme that does not generate legal evidence admissible to be used in court may be more difficult to accept.

Recommendation 5: Review verification systems from a legal point of view so that their outcome is useful also in judicial procedures.

A Multidisciplinary Approach

Finally, it is important to stress the necessity of a multidisciplinary approach to e-voting. A couple of decades ago e-voting began its path as an academic

3 Individual verifiability refers to the ability of an individual voter to verify that his or her vote was received and counted correctly by the electoral authority. Universal verifiability refers to the ability of any voter to verify that all votes were received and counted correctly.

project based on computer science research and most initiatives had (and still have) a technical bias. Less focus was put on legal and social challenges. However, a multidisciplinary approach remains crucial. Social research linked to e-voting for example would be very useful to nuance and balance technical and legal conclusions.

The dialogue between technical, legal and social perspectives still needs major improvements. For sure it is a difficult task because each party has to understand the specific language of the others, but a common meeting point would be very useful for the consistent development of future e-voting platforms. Many inter-disciplinary meetings have occurred where representatives of these three perspectives were able to present their views, but a more systematic approach where each issue is reviewed from the three points of view is still needed.

Recommendation 6: Always adopt a multidisciplinary approach to e-voting.

Outlook

Ultimately, e-voting case law cannot be analysed as an isolated field limited and based only on judicial parameters. As happens in any legal domain, case law is the last legal reaction to a given dispute where many factors are to be taken into account. Case law is not built in a pure sphere. Judges have to solve real problems with legal means, that is to say, with impartial and fair reasoning, but the solution will usually not depend only on abstract approaches. This is why a case law comparison may be extremely useful for future e-voting developments. While specific cases deal with concrete and real problems and the relevant judicial solution obviously takes into account such particularities, comparing different cases provides a broader overview. Local problems receive a new analytical approach that puts them in relation with other similar cases and the overall result helps develop an understanding of how e-voting is deployed in real cases and how the problems are solved by judicial bodies. The six recommendations listed above refer to the influence of different factors on e-voting – political (role of parliaments), administrative (in-house expertise, electoral cycle, NDA), technical (evidence) and social (multidisciplinarity, trust) factors. These factors illustrate the mutual interaction between judicial considerations and extra-judicial inputs.

In the future, e-voting case law will likely have to address new challenges due to the on-going evolution of electoral technology. If the so-called second generation of e-voting solutions incorporate verifiability as a key element and such solutions become generally accepted, further developments will depend on the actual maturity of both e-voting channels and electoral systems as a whole to address new trends in political representation and individual participation. Nobody knows yet the form that this may take. In this case, e-voting will be closely linked to e-democracy, that is to say, a new way to understand the political landscape. E-voting would not be a collateral experiment anymore. It would enrich the set of ICTs that are reshaping the relationship between citizens and public institutions. Social networks, new participatory processes linked to global threats, the actual absence of national boundaries or similar issues that are already present in contemporary democracies, will also influence e-voting development and thus judicial decisions.

If internet voting is going to be used by a majority of voters in a given country, which is not the case nowadays, new legal issues may arise as e-voting becomes the main voting channel. As for today, the transition from partial pilots to a generalized use is still pending in most countries. When (and if) this happens, case law may have to address new legal questions on risk assessment, the effective use of verifiability tools, the impact of possible negative results (such as proof of manipulation of individual votes) obtained through verifiability methods on the overall voting results, and so on.

In any case, the path is still very long. As recalled in this book, the first stages of e-voting development have shown much more complexity than expected. Dialogue between computer and social sciences such as law and political science must be intensified and challenges faced by both legislation and case law resolved. This book provides a first collection of e-voting case law and a comparative analysis that highlights some of the main lessons that can be drawn from different local and national situations.

Index

Note: The main legal instruments and cases discussed in this book are listed in the tables at pp. vii–xx.

For Product Safety Concerns and Information please contact our EU
representative GPSR@taylorandfrancis.com
Taylor & Francis Verlag GmbH, Kaufingerstraße 24, 80331 München, Germany

www.ingramcontent.com/pod-product-compliance
Ingram Content Group UK Ltd.
Pitfield, Milton Keynes, MK11 3LW, UK
UKHW020018200926
475702UK00014B/1954
* 9 7 8 1 1 3 8 0 9 0 2 0 0 *